1 MONTH OF FREE READING

at
www.ForgottenBooks.com

By purchasing this book you are eligible for one month membership to ForgottenBooks.com, giving you unlimited access to our entire collection of over 1,000,000 titles via our web site and mobile apps.

To claim your free month visit: www.forgottenbooks.com/free40425

* Offer is valid for 45 days from date of purchase. Terms and conditions apply.

ISBN 978-0-365-37750-4
PIBN 10040425

This book is a reproduction of an important historical work. Forgotten Books uses state-of-the-art technology to digitally reconstruct the work, preserving the original format whilst repairing imperfections present in the aged copy. In rare cases, an imperfection in the original, such as a blemish or missing page, may be replicated in our edition. We do, however, repair the vast majority of imperfections successfully; any imperfections that remain are intentionally left to preserve the state of such historical works.

Forgotten Books is a registered trademark of FB &c Ltd.
Copyright © 2018 FB &c Ltd.
FB &c Ltd, Dalton House, 60 Windsor Avenue, London, SW19 2RR.
Company number 08720141. Registered in England and Wales.

For support please visit www.forgottenbooks.com

DAINTY DISHES

FOR

INDIAN TABLES.

We may live without poetry, music, and art;
We may live without conscience, and live without heart;
We may live without friends, we may live without books;
But civilised man cannot live without cooks.

He may live without books,—what is knowledge but grieving?
He may live without hope,—what is hope but deceiving?
He may live without love,—what is passion but pining?
But where is the man that can live without dining?

(Lucile.) Owen Meredith.

SECOND EDITION

Calcutta:
W. NEWMAN & CO., 4, DALHOUSIE SQUARE.
1881.

CALCUTTA,
PRINTED BY W. NEWMAN & CO., AT THE CAXTON PRESS,
1, MISSION ROW.

THE cordial reception with which "Dainty Dishes" has been received may be taken as a proof that such a work was needed by English residents in India. In preparing a second edition for the press, the Author has, at the suggestion of numerous friends, added two new chapters on *Curries* and *Pelaus*, giving a few simple recipes. The subject, however, is a large one to deal with, and scarcely comes within the scope of the present work. A few other recipes have been added, and some errors which had crept into the first edition have been corrected.

June, 1881.

PREFACE TO THE FIRST EDITION.

IT is with some diffidence we add another to the long list of existing Cookery Books, in the face of the fact that the amount of teaching would already seem to be out of all proportion to the progress made in the art. Where Francatelli, Soyer, Miss Acton, and a host of others have spoken in vain, what hope is there for a new teacher, unless indeed he be the pioneer of a new path up the hill of difficulty? And this is in truth our claim to be heard, that the present work contains an element of success in which its predecessors have been wanting. The principal stumbling block in the way of teachers has hitherto been the impossibility of relying on the memory of their cooks to retain the numerous ingredients and often complicated processes of a variety of dishes of which they have no record. It seemed to us that this obstacle would be removed by the possession of a Cookery Book which our cooks could read, in which they could find a simple clear account of the dishes they have to make, instead of being as heretofore dependent on a garbled, inaccurate, vague *vivâ voce* translation.

It was at first suggested to us to translate one of the many existing Cookery Books instead of compiling a new one, but we found they contained much that was useless for India, and that moreover, as a rule, the recipes were so carelessly written, and pre-supposed so complete a mastery of his art in the learner, as to be practically useless. Both these defects we have striven to avoid, and while confining ourselves almost entirely to the preparation of European dishes, (in making which our cooks seem to us peculiarly unskilful) we have endeavoured to provide a great variety, all of them within the means at the disposal of an ordinary Anglo-Indian establishment.

A good deal of attention has been devoted to the preparation of vegetables, eggs, macaroni, &c., as dishes composed of these ingredients do not, we think, occupy the place they deserve on our dinner tables. People, as a rule, scarcely realise how agreeably a diet in which meat now plays too important a part may be varied by the introduction of vegetable and farinacious food, especially during the hot weather.

It may be objected that as many cooks cannot read, the Urdú copy of this work will avail them nothing, but in all households some member will be found possessing the necessary accomplishment who will be glad to display it for the benefit of his brethren.

One other difficulty which lies in the way of reform in our *cuisine* is the painful fact that, with most cooks, lining their own pockets is to them a matter of far greater importance than the excellence of the dishes they are called on to make. One means of doing this, which finds special favour in their eyes, is to use half the ingredients named in the recipes, and to write down the full amount in the bill.

The only way to meet this difficulty is to face the fact that a certain percentage of his master's money will surely find its way into the cook's pocket, and therefore it will

PREFACE.

be wise to allow him a certain latitude in the matter of prices, which will leave him at liberty to do justice to the recipe, and deliver him from the temptation to ruin our entrées by a fatal curtailment of eggs and butter.

It will be found a good plan to practise new dishes at your daily dinners till they are perfected. It flurries the cook to task him with experiments when you have a dinner party, and he will be likely to fail even in the dishes which he understands if he is anxious about the results of first efforts.

Good dinners are not achieved by lavishing money, but by bestowing care on their preparation, and the result will be proportioned to the attention given to each particular dish, and the careful working out of every detail.

Good, wholesome food, daintily prepared, is one of the minor luxuries which oil the wheels of life, and we shall be well pleased if this book brings it within the means of those who, while appreciating its value, have, from various causes, been unable to procure it till now.

1879.

CONTENTS.

Page.

GENERAL DIRECTIONS AND REMARKS.

IN order that the dishes prepared should be good, it is absolutely necessary that all the ingredients should be good and fresh, otherwise the result will not be satisfactory.

All the cooking utensils should be scrupulously clean, and the degchees should be tinned at least once a month, or if possible every fortnight.

The minutest directions have been given and often repeated several times, and all the quantities most carefully apportioned, in order that even an inexperienced cook need feel no doubts as to the result of an experiment.

In many instances when cream is not attainable, such as in sauces, soups, &c., fresh goat's milk, with the yolk of an egg beaten up in it, will be found to answer equally well.

When herbs cannot be procured fresh, they can always be purchased dried in bottles at the English store-shops.

The following is a list of stores, which should always be kept in readiness as they are required for all dishes.

Loaf sugar, moist sugar, sifted loaf sugar, whole pepper, ground pepper, black and white, cayenne, mustard, fine salt, soy, anchovy sauce, Harvey sauce, tomato sauce, chutney, mushroom ketchup, capers, pickles, vinegar, Lucca oil, Tarragon vinegar, Chilli vinegar, all kinds of herbs in bottles, and Parmesan cheese.

We would also strongly recommend our readers to procure Cre-fydd's sauces, sold by Crosse and Blackwell, one of which, Casureep, supplies the place of all other seasoning.

Moulds.—Moulds must be dipped into cold water before putting either jelly or cream into them; and when about to turn out the contents they must be quickly dipped into hot water and wiped dry.

Vanilla Sugar is made by keeping six sticks of vanilla in a glass jar with a stopper filled with sifted loaf sugar. Thus it will always be ready for use, and is better for flavouring than either the sticks themselves or the essence.

Tea to be good, requires three teaspoonsful to a breakfast cup. *Coffee* one ounce (½ chittack) to a coffee cup. To make them good the water must be perfectly boiling.

In *Soups* where ham is not available, the root of a salted boiled tongue may be substituted, and in forcemeats, &c., some slices of tongue may be used instead.

Garlic, though indispensable to good cookery, has a most disagreeable flavour when too much is used, therefore the directions about rubbing the bottom of the cooking pot with it must be strictly adhered to.

Baked Flour.—Put one pound (two chittacks) of fine flour into a soup plate and bake in a cool oven until it is quite dry, but not colored; when cold, pound it and put it into a glass jar; tie it over with paper, and keep for use when directed.

Dried or prepared Crumbs.—Put some bread on a sheet of paper, place it in a cool oven, and let it remain until perfectly dried through. Divide the crust from the crumb and pound them separately till in a very fine powder. Put them into jars, and keep them in a dry place.

The white crumbs are used for sweetbreads, cutlets, fried fish, puddings, &c. The brown crumbs are to be used for hams, bacon, coloring broth, &c. Any pieces of bread then left should be baked daily as the bread should not be stale, and should be pounded twice or thrice a week.

Burnt Sugar for coloring Soups, &c.—Put ⅛ of a ℔. (two chittacks) of sifted loaf sugar into a small iron saucepan (untinned), and place it over the fire to bake until it becomes black, but not crisp like a cinder; add a pint (ten chittacks) of water, and simmer till the sugar dissolves and the water is reduced to half a pint (four chittacks), strain through a cloth, and when cold bottle and keep for use. Great care is required in flavoring not to put too much, and it must be used by drops until the desired result is attained.

Black Onions for Soups, &c.—Peel six large onions and put them on a tin dish. Knead together ¼ of a ℔. (four chittacks) of salt butter and ⅛ of a ℔. (two chittacks) of moist sugar; divide it into six equal parts and place one on each onion. Put them in a slow oven and bake until they are black *through*, but not burnt crisp. Baste them frequently with the liquor; when done, put them in a pie dish and keep for use. These onions give a finer color to soup and gravy than anything else; they also impart a good flavor.

Spinach greening for Sauces.—Take two handsful of spinach, wash it, and put it *wet* into a mortar; pound it to a pulp, and then pour all the contents of the mortar into a strong cloth, which two people, one at each end, must twist opposite ways to wring out all the juice. Pour the extract into a small stewpan and set it over the fire;

when it curdles scrape it out with a spoon and lay it on a sieve that the water may drip off. Place it in a covered basin and keep in a cool place till wanted.

Quenelle forcemeat of Veal.—Take 1 ℔. of lean white veal cut from the leg or chump end; scrape it with a knife; pound and rub it through a wire sieve upon a plate. Take 12 oz. of this, and put it in a mortar. Steep 8 oz. of the crumb of a new loaf in tepid water and wring it in a cloth to extract the water; place it in a degchee with ¾ of an ounce of butter and a saltspoonful of salt, stir it over the fire with a wooden spoon until it ceases to stick to the stewpan and becomes a smooth paste; then put it beween two plates to cool. When it is cold put it into the mortar with the veal and 6 oz. of butter, and pound well together; then add the yolks of five eggs and the whites of three, two tablespoonsful of good white sauce, (*see* Sauces No. 2), one teaspoonful of salt, and one saltspoonful of white pepper. When these ingredients have all been well mixed by pounding, take the whole out of the mortar, put it into a basin, and keep it on ice or in a cool place until required for use.

The Liquor in which beef or mutton are boiled should be reserved in uncovered earthen pans for soups. (*See* Economical Soup.) The milk in which fowls, rabbits, &c., are boiled should be reserved for white sauces.

Curry Rice.—Take ½ lb. of Patna rice; wash it in three changes of cold water; let it stand in the last for half an hour. Pour off the water, and put the rice into a

Note.—All varieties of quenelle forcemeat are to be prepared in the same way using for the different varieties the fillets of fowls, pheasants, pea-fowl, partridges, snipe, hares, rabbits, &c., using exactly the same proportions.

degchee and cover it to the depth of two or three inches with cold water, add a teaspoonful of salt and boil quickly for twenty minutes. Then dash in a cup of cold water, take it off the fire instantly and put it on a sieve before the fire or in the oven with a dry cloth or a sheet of brown paper over it. Leave it for seven minutes and then serve as directed.

Recipe for preserving Vegetables.—The vegetables which preserve best are French beans, carrots, and broad beans; green peas, asparagus and cauliflower are more difficult to preserve, and require more careful dressing when opened to conceal a certain tinned flavour which is almost always noticeable, though this can be got rid of by rinsing them for a second in *scalding* water before preparing them for the table. The process of preserving, then, is as follows: In the first place, the tins in which the vegetables are to be preserved must be most carefully cleaned, being boiled in soda and water the day before they are used, and *perfectly* dried. The vegetables are prepared just as they would be if they were going to be cooked for the table; they are then thrown into *boiling* water, slightly salted, and are boiled till they are *almost* but not *quite* as tender as they would be if they were to be eaten at once. They are then lifted out of the saucepan with a cullender (or sieve-spoon) and laid in the tins, which are filled within an inch of the top. The tins are then filled to the top with some of the water in which the vegetables were boiled. The same tin can be used over and over again, but a new cover must always be provided. The cover must be soldered on; and, as each tin is ready, it is placed in a large pan of *boiling* water, so that the tins are quite immersed. They must be left in the pans for 10 minutes, and this will test whether they are quite air-tight or not. If they are not wholly air-tight, small bubbles of air will rise to the surface; and when this is the case, the tin must be taken out and carefully examined and the weak spot soldered: then the tin must be tested again, and must be examined and repaired until no more air bubbles rise and it is quite air-tight. The tins are then set aside to cool down gadually; and when they are quite cold, they may be packed in cases and deposited in a cool, dry place till wanted. Every now and then, as may be expected in spite of all precautions, it will be seen within the first fortnight that on one or two of the tins the covers bulge and rise. This shows that the covers were not air-tight, and the vegetables contained in them are useless and can be thrown away. If, however, this process does not take place after a few weeks, the tins are perfect and may be kept for two years or even longer. It is quite easy to grow mushrooms in any quantity, and they can be preserved in the same way. They form a most palatable and wholesome dish, and it is difficult to understand why they should be imported year after year at great cost, when the means of growing them is so simple and so inexpensive.

We should strongly advise every one to have a little iron stove with an oven, such as can be procured at Roorkee or from England, as it is very difficult to regulate the heat of the common ovens found in an Indian Kitchen, and it is almost impossible to make light pastry except in a good oven.

KITCHEN UTENSILS.

1 Large Iron Fish Kettle or Ham Boiler.
6 Copper Stewpans with covers, of various sizes.
2 Copper Saucepans or Sautè-pans.
3 Iron Saucepans
3 Frying pans, (1 enamelled for Omelets).
2 Iron Spits for roasting.
1 Brass Pestle and Mortar.
1 Marble „ „
1 Tin Dripping Pan.
1 Basting Ladle.
1 Meat saw.
1 Chopper.
6 Wooden Skewers.
6 Plated „
2 Cook's Knives.
6 Forks.
1 Roasting Fork.
1 Fluted Gridiron.
1 Fish Slice,
1 Egg „
1 Iron Tea Kettle.
1 Small Block-Tin Kettle.
1 Wire-frying Basket.
1 Box of plain round Cutters.
1 Grater.

1 Small Grater.
6 Iron Spoons.
6 Wooden „
1 Flour Dredger.
2 Block-Tin Gravy-strainers.
1 Dozen Tartlet Pans.
2 Block-Tin Jelly Moulds.
1 „ „ Cake Mould.
1 Egg Whisk.
2 Hair Sieves.
1 Wire „
1 Cullender.
1 Tannery Cloth.
1 Jellybag and Stand.
1 Weighing Machine with Weights.
1 Steak Tongs.
1 Biscuit Forcer.
1 Wire Drainer.
Some Larding Pins.
„ Coarse Earthen-ware Bowls.
„ Enamelled Cups, Plates, and Bowls.
2 Boards, one for chopping on, one for pastry.
2 Rolling Pins.
1 Camp Oven.
1 Dùtch „

We would in addition strongly recommended to every household Captain Warren's Cooking Pot for making Soup, cooking Vegetables, and steaming Puddings.

WEIGHTS AND MEASURES.

We append a table of the Weights and Measures used in this volume:—

2½ tolahs	equal to	1 oz.
2 oz. or 5 tolahs	,, ,,	1 chittack.
16 oz. or 8 chittacks	,, ,,	1 pound.
2 pounds	,, ,,	1 seer.
40 seers	,, ,,	1 maund.
1 quart	,, ,,	2 pints = 1 sr.
20 oz. or 4 soup ladles	,, ,,	1 pint.
8 tablespoonsful	,, ,,	1 ladle.
1 ,, ,,	,, ,,	½ oz.
1 dessert ,,	,, ,,	¼ oz.
1 tea ,,	,, ,,	⅛ oz.
1 cayenne ,,	,, ,,	1 grn. (the 60th part of a drachm.)

An ordinary tumbler holds about ½ pint.

When the term "gill" is used, it may be understood to mean a quarter of a pint.

SAUCES, CONDIMENTS, AND PICKLES.

1.—White Bechamel Sauce.

Ingredients.
4 oz. flour
2 oz. butter
1 onion, 1 bunch of parsley
1 small carrot
½ head of celery
1 leaf of bay and thyme
1 teaspoonful of salt
1 saltspoonful of white pepper
1½ pint of milk

Put the flour and butter into a degchee, and knead together with a wooden spoon; add the vegetables cut into slices, the pepper and salt, and moisten with the milk. Stir over a clear fire while it boils sharply for twenty minutes, taking great care to stir all round the edges and the bottom so that it does not burn, then strain through a hair-sieve or coarse cloth and place in a basin for use.

2.—White Sauce.

(Two ways.)

Ingredients, No. 1.
¼ pint of new milk
½ inch of mace
2 inches of thin lemon peel
The yolks of 2 eggs
1 gill of good cream

Ingredients, No. 2.
3 oz. of fresh butter
1 tablespoonful of baked flour
½ pint of milk
2 tablespoonsful of cream

Boil the milk with the mace and lemon peel; beat the eggs with the cream. Strain the milk and pour it by degrees into the eggs and cream, beating all the time; then pour into a small saucepan and stir until it thickens. Serve immediately.

Boil the milk; knead the butter with the flour and stir into the milk; boil ten minutes, add the cream and serve at once.

B

3.—Bread Sauce.

Ingredients.

3 oz. of bread crumbs
1 good sized onion
3 peppercorns
2 cloves
½ saltspoonful of salt
¾ of a pint of new milk
1 oz of fresh butter, or
2 tablespoonsful of cream

Put into a small saucepan the bread crumbs, onion, pepper corns, cloves, salt, and milk; boil gently for twenty minutes stiring constantly, then rub through a fine sieve or cloth; cover and let it stand for an hour, put it back into the saucepan, stir in the butter or cream and serve at once in a tureen.

4.—Onion Sauce.

Ingredients.

6 large onions
2 oz. of flour
2 oz. of butter
1 pint of milk
1 saltspoonful of salt
1 saltspoonful of pepper
1 tablespoonful of cream

Peel and slice the onions and boil for ten minutes, drain and put them into a small degchee with the butter and flour; mix well, add the milk, pepper, and salt, stir over the fire for ten minutes, add the cream and serve at once.

5.—Soubise Sauce.

Ingredients.

8 large onions
2 oz. of butter
1 teaspoonful of salt
1 saltspoonful of pepper
4 oz. of flour
2 fresh boiled mealy potatoes
1 pint of milk

Peel and slice the onions, and put them into a degchee with the butter, pepper, and salt; cover and stew very slowly until the onions are dissolved, but they must not be allowed to color. Add the flour, the potatoes, and the milk, stir over the fire for fifteen minutes, rub through a seive or coarse cloth and keep hot in a covered degchee until used according to directions.

6—Maitre d'Hotel Sauce.

Ingredients.

1 gill of Bechamel. (No. 1)
2 oz. of fresh butter
1 tablespoonful of chopped parsley
1 teaspoonful of salt
1 saltspoonful of pepper
1 teaspoonful of lemon juice

Put the Bechamel sauce in a small degchee, and when it is hot stir in the butter, parsley, pepper, salt, and lemon juice; boil five minutes and serve.

Note.—If no Bechamal Sauce is prepared, use instead the same quantity of milk in which the bones of a fowl have been boiled for half an hour, and knead 2 oz. of butter and 1 oz. of flour into it. Boil ten minutes until quite thick, and then proceed as with the Bechamel.

7.—Melted Butter.

Ingredients.

2 oz. butter
1 oz. flour,
1 gill of water
1 saltspoonful of salt
½ ,, ,, ,, pepper

Knead the butter and flour in a small saucepan, add the water, pepper, and salt, and stir over the fire till it thickens, but do not let it boil. Then stir in a bit of butter the size of a walnut, or the yolk of an egg.

Note.—A gill of milk may be substituted for the water.

8.—Melted Butter.

(Another way.)

Ingredients.

¼ lb of fresh butter
4 tablespoonsful of Arrowroot, or Oswego flour
About a gill of milk or water
¼ saltspoonful of pepper
1 ,, ,, salt

Mix the flour into the butter with a knife until it is perfectly incorporated with it; put it into a small saucepan with the salt and pepper, and milk or water, and stir it *always one way* until it presents the appearance of thick cream; but be careful not to let it boil.

9.—Melted Butter for Vegetables.

Prepare as No. 8, but at the moment of serving add the yolks of two eggs and two teaspoonsful of lemon juice.

10.—Mayonnaise Sauce.

Ingredients.
9 fresh eggs boiled hard
2 raw yolks
3 teaspoonsful of salt
1 ,,   ,, of dry mustard
1 grain of cayenne
12 tablespoonsful of Lucca oil
2   ,,   Tarragon vinegar
4   ,,   French vinegar

When the eggs have been boiled quite hard and are cold, pound the yolks in a mortar, and add whilst pounding the salt, mustard, and cayenne, and the beaten yolks. When well mixed stir in *drop by drop*, first all the oil, and then the vinegar. Care must be taken to stir all the time and always the same way. Cover the mortar and let it stand in a cool place for three hours, or on ice for one. The excellence of this sauce depends on the making, and it should look like rich smooth cream.

The quantities given are sufficient for a Mayonnaise for eight or ten people.

11.—Mayonnaise Sauce.

(Another way.)

Ingredients.
3 yolks of eggs
6 teaspoonsful of fresh oil
3   ,,   of white vinegar
A little parsley
Some chopped eschalots
A pinch of pepper (white)
1 saltspoonful of salt

Beat the yolks of the eggs; then stir in the oil (always one way) drop by drop, then the vinegar, and continue stirring until the sauce looks like thick cream; add the eschalots and parsley (chopped as fine as possible) and the pepper and salt.

12.—Tartar Sauce.

This is made in the same way as Mayonnaise Sauce, only the proportions of the eggs are eight boiled to four raw ones, and when about to serve add a teaspoonful of finely chopped chives, green onions, or shalot, and a teaspoonful of chopped gherkin.

13.—Horse Radish Sauce.

Ingredients.
2 tablespoonsful of grated horse radish
4 tablespoonsful of cream
3 dessertspoonsful of vinegar
1 teaspoonful of salt
1 dessertspoonful of made mustard

Grate the horse radish, put it into a basin, and blend it with the cream, add the vinegar, salt, and mustard, and hold it over the fire till it thickens, stirring it all the time, but on no account let it boil. Then serve in a sauceboat.

14.—Dutch Sauce.

Ingredients.
4 yolks of eggs
2 oz. of butter
½ gill of cream
1 saltspoonful of salt
1 ,, of pepper
1 teaspoonful of elder vinegar

Put the raw yolks, the butter, cream, pepper, salt and vinegar into a small saucepan, and place this within a degchee containing one pint of hot water. Put it on the fire and whisk it briskly either with a wire whisk or a small wooden spoon till it thickens and looks like rich yellow cream. Great care must be taken that the sauce does not curdle, and therefore the fire must not be too fierce. If however it should curdle, add the yolks of two more eggs, or a desertspoonful of white sauce.

15.—Celery Sauce.

Ingredients.
4 heads of celery
1 saltspoonful of pepper
1 teaspoonful of salt
4 oz. of butter
1 onion, sliced
4 oz. of flour
1 pint of milk

Thoroughly cleanse the celery and slice it very thin; put it into a degchee with the salt, pepper, butter, and the sliced onion; cover the degchee and set it on a slow fire to stew until the celery is dissolved, but not colored. Then add the flour and milk; stir over the fire and let it boil for twenty minutes, then rub through a sieve or coarse cloth, and keep in a small degchee ready for use as directed.

16.—Oyster Sauce.

Ingredients.
1 tin of oysters
2 oz. of butter
1 oz. of flour
1 gill of cream (or milk)
1 teaspoonful of lemon-juice
1 grain of cayenne

Take off the beards and put the oysters into a basin of cold water with the lemon-juice. Boil the beards in the liquor with a grain of cayenne for ten minutes, knead the butter with the flour and mix into the liquor, stir in the cream, drain the oysters, put them into the same, boil five minutes, and serve at once.

17.—Apple Sauce.

Ingredients.
6 apples
1 oz. of moist sugar
The rind of half lemon
A piece of butter (the size of a walnut)
1 gill of water

Peel, core, and slice the apples, and put them into a small saucepan with the sugar, lemon, butter, and water; stew over a slow fire till quite in a pulp, rub through a sieve of coarse cloth, and serve very hot.

Note.—This Sauce can be made with preserved apples.

18.—Green Sauce.

(For boiled Chicken or boiled Mutton.)

Ingredients.
1 cupful of spinach greening
1 teaspoonful of lemon-juice
½ ,, of sugar
½ pint of the milk in which the first has been boiled
1 saltspoonful of salt
1 ,, of pepper
2 oz. of butter
1 oz of flour.

Put the milk into a saucepan; knead the flour with the butter and stir into the milk; then add the lemon-juice, sugar, salt, and pepper, boil for ten minutes, carefully stirring until it thickens; then add the greening and serve, poured over the fowl or mutton.

This is a most excellent sauce, and may also be eaten with boiled lamb.

19.—Ketchup Sauce.

(For Steaks and Mutton Chops.)

Ingredients.
1 claret glass of red wine
1 ,, ,, of ketchup
1 piece of butter (the size of a walnut)
1 saltspoonful of pepper
1 teaspoonful of vinegar

Stir all the ingredients together over the fire for 5 minutes, and serve, poured over the steak or chops.

20.—Sauce Appetissante.

Work the sugar into the mustard, then add all the other ingredients one by one, stirring all the time. When they are well blended put the sauce into a degchee; put in any slices of cold meat and let it cook till hot, but not boil. Then serve.

Ingredients.
1 dessertspoonful of mustard
1 ,, ,, of sugar
2 ,, ,, of Harvey's sauce
1 teaspoonful of shalot vinegar
1 tablespoonful of claret

21.—Butter Sauce.

(For kidneys and broiled meat.)

Ingredients.
4 oz. of butter
1 saltspoonful of salt
1 ,, ,, of pepper
2 teaspoonsful of chopped parsley
1 ,, ,, of lemon juice
1 grain of cayenne

Mix all the ingredients well together, and keep an hour in a cool place. Then serve in a sauceboat.

22.—Sauce for cold Pheasant.

Ingredients.
1 small shalot
1 teaspoonful of mustard
1 ,, of oil
1 ,, of vinegar
1 ,, of ketchup
1 saltspoonful of salt

Chop the shalot as fine as possible, add all the other ingredients, one by one, mix thoroughly, and serve in a sauceboat.

23.—Cream Sauce.

Ingredients.
½ pint of milk
¼ inch of mace
Yolks of two eggs
3 tablespoonsful of cream

Boil the milk with the mace; beat the yolks and add them to the milk while it is hot but not boiling; stir over the fire till it is as thick as cream, then strain into a basin. Add three tablespoonsful of cream, stir in quickly. Serve as directed.

Note.—Small mushrooms added to this sauce are a great improvement. In this case fry them in butter for five minutes.

24.—German Sauce.
(For Asparagus or Seakale.)

Ingredients.
1 tablespoonful of baked flour
½ pint of cream
1 yolk
½ oz. of butter
1 pinch of white pepper
1 ,, ,, salt
1 teaspoonful of white vinegar

Mix the baked flour and the cream; stir it over the fire until it begins to thicken; then add the yolk of the egg beaten, the butter, pepper, salt, and vinegar; stir until well mixed, and serve.

25.—Maitre D'Hotel Butter.

Ingredients.
4 oz. fresh water
1 teaspoonful of finely chopped parsley
½ teaspoonful of finely chopped onions
½ saltspoonful of salt
¼ ,, ,, of pepper
The juice of one lemon

Put all the ingredients into a small basin, stir them well together with a spoon, and keep in a cool place until required for use as directed.

26.—Anchovy Butter.

Ingredients.
6 anchovies
2 oz. butter
1 grain cayenne
1 dessertspoonful of anchovy sauce

Clean the anchovies; split them and take out the bones, pound them in a mortar with all the other ingredients, rub through a sieve, and use as directed.

27.—Epicurean Butter.

Ingredients.

Tarragon
Parsley
Chervils
Chives
6 anchovies
1 tablespoonful of capers
1   „   of Oude sauce
4 oz. butter

Take a large handful of tarragon, parsley, chervil, and chives in equal proportions; parboil and squeeze in a cloth; add the anchovies, (cleaned), the capers, sauce and butter; put all the ingredients into a mortar, pound thoroughly, rub through a sieve and use as directed.

28.—Tomato Sauce.

Ingredients.

1 teacupful of tomato sauce
1 dessertspoonful of vinegar
1 teaspoonful of bake flour
½ oz. of fresh butter. d

Put the sauce and vinegar into a small degchee; knead the butter with the flour, and stir it into the sauce for five minutes. Serve as directed.

29.—Parsley Sauce.

Chop one handful of parsley fine, and boil three minutes; drain and put it into melted butter or any other white sauce. (See Nos. 1, 2, 7, 8.)

30.—Tapp Sauce.

Ingredients.

Green mangoes,   8 oz
Salt,   8 oz
Red chillies,   4 oz
Chilli vinegar,   1 gill
Moist sugar,   8 oz
Raisins,   8 oz
Green ginger,   6 oz
3 bottles of vinegar
1 pint of lime juice

Pound the first seven articles until they are well mixed, then stir in the vinegar and lime-juice. Put it into jars, cover them and put them in the sun every day, after which stir them well and cover again. Do this for a month, then strain through coarse muslin and bottle for use.

The remainder makes excellent chutnee.

31.—Ne-plus-ultra Chutnee.

Wash and dry the mustard seed in the sun; then gently bruise to remove the husks. Slice the ginger, garlic, and chillies very thin. Boil the sugar to a syrup, peel and cut the mangoes into small pieces and boil them in the vinegar of three bottles; then stand till cold. Mix all the ingredients together and add the remaining bottle of vinegar. Then bottle for use.

Ingredients.

Moist sugar,	2 seers
Salt,	1 seer
Garlic,	1 ,,
Green ginger,	1 ,,
Mustard seed,	1 ,,
Raisins,	1 ,,
Dried chillies with the seeds extracted	1 ,,
Good vinegar,	4 bottles
Unripe mangoes	55

Note—Should the Chutnee become dry at any time, add a little vinegar to moisten it.

32.—Mushroom Ketchup.

Put the mushrooms and salt into an earthen pan, stir together and let them stand twelve hours. Then drain off the liquor by pressing it through a sieve. Add all the ingredients, except the claret, put the whole into a degchee and boil slowly, skimming frequently for two hours. Then boil *fast* for twenty minutes, skimming constantly. Pour the ketchup into a earthen pan, and when quite cold strain it, add the claret, and bottle it. Cork it closely, and keep two months before using it.

Ingredients.

28 lbs. of mushrooms,
1½ lb. of salt
To every quart of liquor, put:
¾ of an oz., bruised ginger
¾ of a nutmeg bruised,
10 cloves
1 saltspoonful of allspice
1 teaspoonful of whole pepper
6 corns of long pepper
1 blade of mace
1 small onion
1 piece of garlic, the size of a pea
2 inches of horse radish, chopped
2 glasses of claret

33.—Pickled Walnuts.

Boil three pounds of salt in two gallons of water for ten minutes, pour it into an earthen pan, and when cold put in the nuts and let them remain twelve

Ingredients.

14 lbs. of young walnuts
6 lb. of salt
1 gallon of the best vinegar
1 oz. of bruised ginger

SAUCES, CONDIMENTS, AND PICKLES. 19

Ingredients of Pickled Walnuts.
5 blades of mace (bruised)
20 cloves
¼ oz. of peppercorns
½ oz. of mustard seed
1 clove of garlic
6 shalots

hours; then pour off the brine, add some fresh made in the same manner and proportions, and let it stand twelve hours longer. Drain off the brine and lay the walnuts in the sun until they turn black; turn them frequently. Boil the vinegar with all the other ingredients; place the walnuts in large jars; pour the vinegar over, boiling hot; put an equal quantity of the spice into each jar, and when cold tie them down and keep for three months before using.

34.—Tomato Sauce.

Ingredients.
14 lbs. of tomatoes
4 Spanish onions
2 ounces of shalot
¾ of an oz. of garlic
1 ,, ,, of mace
3 ,, ,, of bruised ginger
3 drachms of cayenne
1 quart of good vinegar
1 ,, of strong old ale

The tomatoes must be ripe, and gathered in dry weather. Wipe them with a soft cloth and slice them; peel and slice the onions, the shalot and garlic; put them into a degchee with the spices and vinegar; skim and stir frequently and simmer for two hours. Add the ale and boil moderately fast for half an hour, or till the sauce thickens. Rub the whole through a coarse hair sieve, or cloth, and then through a fine one; put it into *dry* wide-mouthed bottles, and when *cold* cork tightly and seal over the top.

35.—Sauce for cold Fish.

Ingredients.
1 teaspoonful of made mustard
1 ,, of salt
1 ,, of black pepper
1 ,, of red ,,
2 tablespoonsful of oil
1 ,, of vinegar
1 dessertspoonful of sherry

All these put in the order in which they are enumerated and well mixed. Serve in a sauceboat.

36.—Another Sauce for cold Fish.

Ingredients.

2 yolks of eggs (boiled hard)
½ teaspoonful of black pepper
½   ,,   ,, salt
½   ,,   ,, red pepper
½   ,,   ,, made mustard
1   ,,   ,, chopped parsley and chives
½   ,,   ,, anchovy sauce
3 tablespoonsful of oil
1 dessertspoonful of vinegar
1   ,,   of Tarragon vinegar

All the ingredients to be well mixed, always stirring one way, and poured over the cold fish as directed.

37.—Oxford Brawn Sauce.

Ingredients.

1 tablespoonful of brown sugar
1 teaspoonful of made mustard
1 saltspoonful of salt
½   ,,   of pepper
2 tablespoonsful of *very* good oil
2   ,,   of vinegar

Mix well and serve with brawn, calf's-feet, or any cold meat.

38.—Christopher North's Own Sauce.

Ingredients.

1 saltspoonful of cayenne (powdered)
½   ,,   of salt
1 small desertspoonful of pounded sugar
1 tablespoonful of strained lemon-juice
2 oz. of Harvey's sauce
1 teaspoonful of mushroom ketchup
3 tablespoonsful of port wine
A few drops of garlic, or eschalot vinegar may be added if liked

Put all these ingredients into a small basin; mix them well. Put the basin into a saucepan of boiling water to heat it; mix it for some hours before it is served, and then use as directed.

39—Chutney Sauce.

Ingredients.

1 lb. of new raisins, stoned
1 lb. of tamarind,   ,,
3 oz. of garlic, peeled
3 lbs. of sour apples peeled, cored, and sliced
1 lb. of coarse brown sugar
2 quarts of vinegar
¼ lb. of salt

Mince the raisins, tamarinds and garlic quite fine. Boil the apples in half of the vinegar till they are a soft pulp. Boil the sugar in the rest of the vinegar till in a clear syrup. When these are *quite* cold, mix the

Ingredients of Chutney Sauce.
¼ of an oz. cayenne
2 oz. of ground ginger
3 oz. of yellow mustard-seed, pounded

whole of the ingredients together and stir well with a wooden spoon. Put the mixture into wide-mouthed bottles, cork them closely, tie bladder over the corks, and place the bottles in a warm closet near the fire for three weeks; turn the bottles every day. Keep for six months before using, and serve with curries.

CURRY POWDERS.

Calcutta Curry Powder.

1 teaspoonful of turmeric.
1 tablespoonful of coriander-seed.
1 ,, ,, poppy-seed.
½ teaspoonful of ginger.
¼ ,, ,, red chilli.
½ ,, ,, cummin-seed.

The seeds should be of the finest quality, well dried, pounded, and mixed.

Madras Curry Powder.

2 drachms of turmeric.
4 chillies.
2 grains of mustard-seed.
2 drachms of coriander-seed.
2 grains of cummin-seed.
2 drachms of poppy-seed.
Pound and mix.

Mr. Arnott's Curry Powder.

8 oz. of turmeric.
4 ,, ,, coriander-seed.
2 ,, ,, cummin-seed.
2 ,, ,, Fœnugreek-seed.
½ ,, ,, cayenne.

SOUPS, BROTHS, &c.

1.—Stock No. 1.

Four Quarts.

Ingredients.
Garlic
10 lbs. fresh-killed shin of beef
1 pint of water
¾ of a lb. lean ham
3 onions, 3 carrots
A small head of celery
4 cloves, 6 allspice
10 peppercorns
A large black onion, (*see* page 3)
A tablespoonful of brown sugar
A teaspoonful of mustard
A teaspoonful of salt

Rub your degchee six times across the bottom with garlic. Put in the beef and a pint of water; let it stand by the fire an hour, then add all the ingredients. Simmer and skim frequently for six hours. Strain through a fine hair sieve (or a coarse cloth) which has been dipped in cold water into an *earthen* pan (uncovered), and when cold remove the fat.

Note.—In India the stock should be made every day, therefore judgment must be used as to the quantity required.

2.—Stock No. 2.

Four Quarts.

Ingredients.
1 knuckle of veal (7 lbs.)
A cow heel
A fresh-killed old fowl
A turnip, 2 onions
A lettuce, 1 blade of mace
¼ of a nutmeg
½ lb. (4 chittacks) lean ham
1 teaspoonful of salt
A *small* bunch of sweet herbs
6 quarts of water

Put all the ingredients into a degchee, simmer gently and skim frequently for six hours. Strain through a fine hair sieve (or a coarse cloth) that has been dipped in cold water into an earthen pan (uncovered), and when cold remove the fat.

Note.—Two fresh truffles will be found a great improvement to both stocks.

3.—Calf's Foot Stock.

Ingredients.
2 calves feet
Five pints of water

Split the two feet, put them into a degchee with the water, and simmer for five hours very gently; skim frequently. Strain through a fine hair sieve (or a coarse cloth) that has been dipped in cold water into an uncovered earthen pan, and the next morning take off every particle of fat.

4.—Glaze.

Glaze is made by boiling any kind of stock till it is reduced to the consistency of cream.

5.—Stock Fat.

Have a saucepan of boiling water by the side of the stock-pot; when the scum has all been removed and fat only rises, skim it off the stock, and throw it into the water in the saucepan. Pour it all together into a basin, and next day well wash the fat and boil it in a degchee until it becomes quite clear. It will then be fit for any use, and will supply the place of ghee, butter, and oil.

6.—Stock Meat.

Ingredients.
For every pound of stock meat put:
2 saltspoonsful of salt
1 ,, ,, black pepper
1 grain of cayenne
The 6th part of a nutmeg grated
The peel of ½ lemon grated
1 teaspoonful of chopped parsley

Stock meat may be made into a very savoury dish as follows:—for every pound ($\frac{1}{2}$ seer) of meat mix all the ingredients, leaving out the yolk of the egg. When well mixed form into cakes half inch thick; dip them into the beaten yolks of the egg,

Ingredients for Stock Meat.
1 small onion finely chopped
½ saltspoonful of mixed herbs
2 oz. of good dripping or butter
1 egg

dredge them with *baked* flour, and fry in the dripping for eight or ten minutes.

Note.—Stock meat is also very good chopped and mixed with salad.

7.—Jelly Stock Meat.

Remove the bones, cut the meat into small pieces, season with salt and pepper, and add all the ingredients. Make a tablespoonful hot, rub it with fresh cut garlic, stir the meat well with it, and press it into a plain mould. This is good for breakfast or supper, and is improved by being garnished with aspic jelly and hard boiled eggs neatly cut.

Ingredients.
For 2 calf's-feet:
1 saltspoonful of salt
1 ,, ,, pepper
⅛ teaspoonful of Tarragon vinegar
The strained juice of ½ lemon

8.—Economical Stock.

This is prepared in the same way as No. 1 Stock, only instead of the fresh-killed beef, use any bones, old joints, carcasses of fowls or ducks or game, the bones being well broken up. It may be improved by the addition of one pound of lean beef chopped fine, pounded and mixed with one quart of cold water and two whites of eggs.

9.—Clear Gravy Soup.

(Two Quarts.)

Peel, scrape, wash, drain and slice the onion, carrot, turnip, celery, and fry them to a pale brown color in the butter. Boil the stock and put in the

Ingredients.
2 oz. butter
1 onion, 1 carrot
½ turnip, ½ head of celery

Ingredients for Clear Gravy Soup.
1 saltspoonful of salt
1 " " loaf-sugar
½ grain of cayenne
½ grain saffron
5 pints (4 seers) of stock, No. 1
1 small wine glass of Marsala

vegetables, salt, sugar, cayenne, and saffron. Boil gently for ¾ of an hour, skimming frequently. Strain; put the soup into a clean degchee, and boil fast (uncovered) for ten or fifteen minutes. Then set it aside to settle. Put the wine into the soup-tureen, pour in the soup, and serve.

Note.—Eggs carefully poached and floating in the soup are an improvement.

10.—Thick Gravy Soup.

This is made in the same way as the clear soup, with three tablespoonsful of baked flour mixed with a gill of cold water, and a teaspoonful of mushroom ketchup added.

11.—Julien Soup.

Clean and cut the vegetables into small slices, and put them into a degchee with the salt, sugar, vinegar, and the cold water. Boil till tender, about twenty minutes, then drain. Boil the stock, put in the vegetables, and boil moderately fast (uncovered) for half an hour. Add the cayenne and the sherry, and serve at once.

Ingredients.
2 carrots, 1 turnip
The white part of a leek (or spring onions)
½ head of celery, (or a small endive)
1 teaspoonful of salt
1 " " sugar
1 " " vinegar
1 quart of cold water
½ grain cayenne
2 tablespoonsful of sherry
2 quarts and ½ pint of stock (No 1)

Note.—Green peas and asparagus, a teacupful of each, are an improvement.

12.—Almond Soup.

This may be considered the very best of white soups.

Ingredients of Almond Soup.
A good fowl
4 oz. blanched and pounded almonds
1 tablespoonful of cream
2 tablespoonsful of baked flour
5 pints of stock, (No. 2)
The white heart of a lettuce
1 dessertspoonful of loaf sugar
1 teaspoonful of salt
2 fresh eggs
2 oz. of butter

Put the fowl and the lettuce into the stock, boil up slowly, and then simmer for eighteen minutes. Take out the fowl, cut off all the white meat, and put back the bones and trimmings into the pot with the sugar and salt. Simmer for 1½ hours, and then rub through a cloth. Pound the white meat of the fowl with the almonds, and blend with the eggs beaten with the cream, then pass through a coarse cloth. Put the soup into a degchee, rubbed twice across the bottom with garlic. Mix the paste, work the flour and butter together, and mix them with the fowl paste, stir it into the soup, simmer the whole for half an hour, and serve.

13.—Green Pea Soup.

(Two Quarts.)

Ingredients.
2 handsful of young spinach
2 sprigs of mint
1 large lettuce
12 spring onions
3 tablespoonsful of moist sugar
1 quart of old peas
¾ pint of young peas
1 teaspoonful of salt
1 " of loaf sugar
3 pints of stock
2 tablespoonsful of baked flour
2 oz. of butter
1 quart of water

Wash the spinach, mint, lettuce and onions; leave them in cold water with the sugar for two hours. Shell the old peas, and put them with the soaked vegetables into a degchee containing one quart of boiling water; add the salt and loaf sugar, and boil fast (uncovered) for an hour. Then add the stock; stir frequently, knead the flour with the butter, and stir in for 10 minutes.

Rub the whole through a fine hair sieve, (or coarse cloth) put it back into the stew-pan and boil up; shell the young peas, put them into the soup, stir frequently, and boil fast (uncovered) for 20 minutes, and serve.

Note.—The soup should be pale green in color and of the consistency of cream; if it is not green enough, add a little spinach greening (*see* recipe) until the right color is attained.

14.—Oyster Soup.

Ingredients.
2 quarts of stock, (No. 2).
1 tin of oysters.
1 teaspoonful of lemon juice
3 tablespoonsful of baked flour
1 gill of cream (or of milk with 2 yolks of eggs beaten in it.)

Take the beards off the oysters, and throw them into a pint of cold water with the strained lemon juice, and let them stand till wanted. Put the beards into the stock, and let them boil up. Mix the baked flour with half a pint of the oyster liquor taken out of the degchee and then stir it into the soup and boil fast for a quarter of an hour. Strain through a fine sieve or cloth; take the oysters out of the water, put them into a degchee and pour the soup over. Boil fast for eight minutes, stir in the cream, and serve.

15.—Macaroni Soup.

Ingredients.
¼ lb. Naples macaroni
3 pints stock, (No. 1)
2 tablespoonsful grated parmesan
1 teaspoonful fresh-made mustard
1 saltspoonful of salt
1 saltspoonful of loaf sugar
1 wineglass of marsala.

Break the macaroni into inch lengths and soak it in cold water for an hour; drain. Put into the degchee three pints of the stock (boiling hot), the cheese, mustard, salt and sugar, and simmer gently for an hour, stirring frequently. Add the rest of the stock (two pints) and the marsala. Boil slowly for 10 minutes longer, and serve with a separate dish of grated Parmesan cheese.

16.—Vermicelli Soup.

Follow the preceding receipt exactly, substituting vermicelli for macaroni, and boiling 10 minutes less.

17.—Mock Turtle Soup.

Ingredients.

A small calf's head
2 lbs. of lean veal
2 lbs. of fresh lean beef
½ lb. of lean ham (or tongue)
3 onions
1 large head of celery
2 large carrots
1 turnip
1 small bunch of mixed sweet herbs
1 bunch of parsley
3 sage leaves
6 peppercorns
4 cloves
1 blade of mace
1 piece of garlic, the size of a pea
1 teaspoonful of salt
1 tablespoonful of loaf sugar
1 gill of marsala
5 tablespoonsful of baked flour slightly browned
½ lb. of butter
2 grains of cayenne
1 teaspoonful of flour of mustard
1 saltspoonful of white pepper
1 saltspoonful of salt
1 dessertspoonful of soy
1 teaspoonful of anchovy sauce
1   ,,   ,, lemon juice
1 wineglass of good sherry

Peel, scrape, wash and slice the vegetables, and fry them in quarter of a pound of the butter till of a pale brown color. Put the veal and beef into a degchee with one pint of cold water and let it stand by the side of the fire for an hour to draw out the gravy; then add the vegetables, ham, herbs, peppercorns, cloves, mace, garlic, salt, and sugar, the head (with the skin on) uppermost and four quarts of cold water. Boil up quickly and skim. Put in the marsala and simmer gently for two hours, skimming frequently. Take out the head, pull out the bones, and trim off all the rough pieces; put the meat between two dishes, with a heavy weight on the upper one, and let it get cold. Put the bones and trimmings into the pot and simmer constantly. Knead quarter ℔. of the butter with the flour, mustard, cayenne, pepper and salt, and stir this with the soup. Add the soy and anchovy sauce. Boil for quarter of an hour, and strain through a fine sieve or cloth. Cut the meat of the head into inch-square pieces; put it into the soup with the lemon juice, simmer 20 minutes, pour in the sherry, and serve immediately with cut lemons handed round.

18.—Pea Fowl Mulligatawny Soup.

Ingredients.
A Pea Fowl
6 peppercorns
4 cloves
1 blade of mace
1 piece of garlic, (the size of a pea)
3 onions sliced
6 oz. of butter
5 tablespoonsful of baked flour
2 dessertspoonsful of curry powder
1 teaspoonful of salt

Clean and cut up the bird, separate all the joints and put it into a degchee with three quarts of water, and the spices; when it boils, skim it and let it simmer for two hours; then strain. Take some of the bits of meat and the sliced onions, and fry until brown in the butter. Add them to the broth and simmer half an hour. Then mix the baked flour, curry powder, and salt, and stir into the soup; let it simmer for half an hour, and serve with rice (dressed as for curry,) handed round in a separate dish, and cut lemons on a plate.

19.—Mulligatawny Soup

Ingredients.
A good fowl
6 oz. of butter
1 large apple
3 large onions
The heart of a lettuce
2 oz. of cocoanut
1 dessertspoonful of tamarind
2 tablespoonsful of curry powder
2 ,,   ,,   of flour
1 teaspoonful of salt
4 leaves of mint
1 teaspoonful of loaf sugar
1 quart of water
1 quart and ½ pint of stock (No. 2)
1 teaspoonful of lemon juice
1 gill of cream

Roast the fowl before a quick fire for half an hour, and baste with the butter; put it aside till cold. Peel and slice the apple, onions, and the lettuce, and fry until colored, in the butter with which the fowl was basted. Cut the white meat off the fowl into pieces one inch square, break the bones and put them into a degchee with the trimmings, vegetables, cocoanut, tamarind, curry powder, flour, salt, mint, loaf sugar and water. Boil 1½ hours, and strain through a fine sieve or cloth. Add to this the stock and the pieces of simmer very gently for half an hour. Stir in the lemon, fowl, and juice and cream, and serve immediately with a dish of boiled rice, and some cut lemons on a plate.

20.—Partridge Soup.

Ingredients.

2 Partridges
2 small carrots
1 head of celery
2 onions
2 oz. of raw ham
bunch of parsley
A little thyme
6 cloves
1 blade of mace
4 shalots
2 o. of butter
2 quarts of stock, (No. 1)
1 glass of sherry
1 grain of cayenne

Roast the partridges, and while they are roasting cut up the vegetables and put them with the ham and spices into a stewpan to fry with the butter until they are brown. Cut the fillets out of the birds, and put them aside in a plate; pound the carcasses, bones and all, in a mortar, and put them into a degchee with the fried vegetables and one quart of water. Boil 1½ hours, and strain through a fine sieve or cloth. Cut the fillets of the birds into small strips, and put them into the strained soup with the stock; simmer *very* gently for half an hour, pour in the sherry, add the grain of cayenne and serve.

Note.—Pheasants, snipe, rabbits, and hares, may be prepared in the same way.

21.—Potato Soup.

Ingredients.

1 dozen good potatoes
6 onions
4 oz. of butter
1 saltspoonful of pepper
1   „   „   salt

Peel and slice the potatoes, slice the onions, and put them in a degchee with the butter, pepper, salt, and stock, and boil gently for one hour. Then rub through a sieve or cloth, put it

E

Ingredients of Potato Soup.
½ pint of cream (or ½ pint of milk with 2 yolks of eggs beaten in it)
2 quarts of stock (No. 2)

back into a degchee, simmer for half an hour, add the cream, and serve immediately with fried sippets on a separate dish.

22.—Knuckle of Veal and Rice Soup.

Ingredients.
A knuckle of veal
2 quarts of water
4 onions
2 turnips
2 carrots
1 head of celery
6 peppercorns
1 teaspoonful of salt
¾ of a lb. of rice

Cut the veal into six pieces, sawing the bone through neatly. Put the pieces into a degchee, and stew until all the meat is off the bones. Set the good pieces of meat aside, strain the broth, and skim off the fat. Add all the vegetables, the peppercorns, and the salt to the broth, and boil for half an hour. Put the best pieces of the veal into the soup. Half boil the rice separately, add it to the soup, boil half an hour, and serve hot.

23.—Celery Soup.

Ingredients.
6 heads of celery
4 onions
1½ quarts stock, (No. 2)
½ lb. of flour
½ pint of cream (or milk with 2 yolks of eggs beaten in)

Slice the celery and the ham, and put them into a degchee with the butter and one pint of the stock. Simmer very gently until the celery is quite soft; then add the flour, mixing it well in; pour in the remainder of the stock, and stir the soup over the fire for 20 minutes. Rub it through a sieve or cloth, put into a degchee, boil for five minutes, pour in the cream, and serve with fried sippets handed round separately.

24.—Italian Soup.

(This soup may be made either with duck, fowl, pheasant, partridge, or rabbit.)

Ingredients.
1 duck
4 oz. of raw ham
2 onions
6 ripe tomatoes
1 head of celery
1 carrot
4 shalots
1 small bunch of sweet herbs
1 blade of mace
4 cloves
12 peppercorns
1 pint of stock
1 glass of Marsala
3 anchovies
1 teaspoonful of capers
1 grain of cayenne

Half roast the bird and put it into a degchee with all the vegetables sliced, and the spices. Moisten with the stock and the wine, boil slowly for two hours. Add two quarts of water and simmer for one hour. Skim and strain the liquor into a pan; reserve the bird on a plate; pound all the vegetables in a mortar, and put this pulp into a degchee; pour the liquor out of the pan into the degchee and stir it over the fire till it boils; skim it well; make a paste of the capers, anchovies, and cayenne, and stir it into the soup; cut the fowl into neat slices about an inch long, put it into the tureen, and pour the soup over it.

25.—Scotch Hotch-Potch.

Ingredients.
3 scrags of mutton
2 quarts of water
3 carrots
1 turnip
1 lettuce
The heart of a young cabbage
6 cutlets of mutton
1 pint of green peas
1 dessertspoonful of chopped parsley
1 dessertspoonful of salt
1 small cauliflower
1 teaspoonful of pepper

Put the scrags of the mutton and water into a degchee and stew them till all the meat is off the bones; strain the broth and skim off the fat. Slice one of the carrots, the turnip, lettuce and cabbage, and grate the *red* part of the other two carrots. Add all these to the broth, and boil for half an hour; then put in the cutlets neatly trimmed, with the remainder of the ingredients; simmer very gently for 1¼ hours, and serve all together, very hot.

26.—Carrot Soup.

Ingredients.

9 carrots
2 onions
½ head of celery
1½ quarts of cold water
1 tablespoonful of vinegar
1 teaspoonful of salt
1 dessertspoonful of sugar
1 grain of cayenne
2 oz. of butter
1 quart and ½ pint of stock, (No. 1)

Scrape, peel, and wash the carrots, onions, and celery, and put them into a degchee with the water, vinegar, salt, sugar and cayenne. Boil for 2¼ hours; break up the vegetables in the water, and when they are quite in a pulp, rub the whole through a fine hair-sieve or cloth; then stir in the butter. Add the stock, and put the whole into a degchee; stir over the fire for 25 minutes, and serve.

Note.—The soup should be the color of carrots and of the consistency of cream.

27.—Palestine Soup.

Ingredients.

3 ℔s. of Jerusalem artichokes
1 large onion
1 small head of celery
2 oz. of lean ham
1 small blade of mace
1 dessertspoonful of loaf sugar
2 quarts of stock, (No. 2)
2 oz. of butter
3 tablespoonsful of baked flour
½ pint of cream

Peel and wash the artichokes, onions and celery, put them into a degchee with the ham, mace, sugar and stock, and boil (uncovered) for an hour. Knead the butter into the flour, and stir it into the soup for 20 minutes. Rub the soup through a sieve or cloth with a wooden spoon. Put it back into the degchee, boil up; skim if necessary, then stir in the cream and serve immediately.

28.—White Onion Soup.

Peel and slice the onions and potatoes; put them into a degchee with the water, the sugar, salt, pepper, and the

Ingredients of White Onion Soup.
6 large onions
4 large potatoes
2 quarts of water
1 tablespoonful of loaf sugar
1 teaspoonful of salt
1 saltspoonful of white pepper
The crumb of a small loaf
3 eggs (the yolks only)
2 tablespoonsful of grated Parmesan cheese
½ pint of cream

crumb of the loaf. Boil fast for two hours, rub the soup through a fine sieve ; put it back into the degchee, and boil up. Beat the yolks with the Parmesan cheese, and stir in for two minutes. Add the cream, and serve at once.

29.—Brown Onion Soup.

Follow the preceding receipt, using two quarts of stock (No. 1) instead of water, and substituting a wineglassful of white wine for the eggs and cream. Stir in the cheese just before serving.

30.—Pea Soup.

Soak the peas in water for two hours and take out all that are black ; put them into a degchee with one quart of water, and let them simmer by the side of the fire till quite soft. Boil the beef in two quarts of water with the onions, carrots, celery, turnip, peppercorns, mint, moist sugar and salt. Boil gently for two hours, strain the liquor, and put in the peas. Boil and skim until the peas are quite mixed with the soup. Knead the butter with the flour and the remaining ingredients, stir it into the soup, boil 20 minutes, rub through a sieve or cloth, and serve very hot, with fried sippets and powdered mint handed round on a separate plate.

Ingredients.
1 pint of split peas (or dhåll)
3 quarts of water
2 lbs. of beef or pork
3 onions
2 carrots
1 head of celery
1 turnip
8 peppercorns
1 saltspoonful of dried mint
1 tablespoonful of moist sugar
1 saltspoonful of salt
3 oz. of butter
2 tablespoonsful of flour
1 teaspoonful of salt
1 grain of white pepper
1 saltspoonful of flour of mustard

31.—Mutton Broth.

Ingredients.
3 lbs. of fresh sciag of mutton
2 onions
2 turnips
½ head of celery
1 sprig of thyme
1 sprig of majoram
4 ,, of parsley
2 quarts of water
1 teaspoonful of loaf sugar
2 saltspoonsful of salt
1 dessertspoonful of chopped parsley

Cut the mutton into small pieces and put it into a degchee with the onions, turnips, and celery, (all sliced) the thyme, majoram and parsley (all tied together); two quarts of water, the loaf sugar and salt. Boil up quickly, skim carefully and simmer for 3½ hours. Skim off all the fat. Put the dessertspoonful of chopped parsley into the tureen, strain the broth into it, and serve.

Note.—Barley or rice may be added: the barley will require two hours, the rice one hour boiling in ¾ of a pint of the broth before adding to the rest.

32.—Raviuoli Soup.

Ingredients for the Soup.
1 fowl or pheasant
2 patridges
3 lbs. of veal
3 lbs. of lean beef
½ lb. of lean ham
2 carrots
4 onions
1 head of celery
4 mushrooms
1 small bunch of mixed herbs
4 sprigs of parsley
½ clove of garlic (the size of a pea)
2 hard-boiled eggs
1 tablespoonful of soy
1 dessertspoonful of loaf sugar
1 teaspoonful of salt
1 ,, ,, flour of mustard
1 grain of cayenne
1 saltspoonful of pepper
1 blade of mace
4 allspice
3 cloves
6 peppercorns

Peel and cut up the vegetables and the half clove of garlic: put them into a degchee with 6 oz. of butter, the beef, ham and veal, and stand one hour by the fire to extract the gravy. Then put in one quart of warm water, and the birds, breast uppermost; simmer for one hour. Take out the birds, cut off the meat from the breast without the skin. Put the carcasses back into the pot with four quarts of warm water, the herbs (tied together), the soy, sugar, salt, mustard, cayenne, pepper, and the spices. Simmer gently and skim

Ingredients of the Raviuoli.
3½ oz. of butter
2 oz. of flour
2 beaten yolks
1 oz. of lean ham
1 oz. Neufchâtel cheese
2 yolks of hard-boiled eggs
1 oz. of cooked spinach
1 shalot
½ of a nutmeg grated
¼ saltspoonful of white pepper
¼ of a saltspoonful of flour of mustard
½ teaspoonful of thick anchovy sauce
½ saltspoonful of loaf sugar
2 tablespoonsful of grated Parmesan cheese
1 wineglassful of sherry
1   „   „ port wine

frequently for five hours. Meanwhile make the Raviuoli as follows :—Rub two oz. of the butter into the flour, moisten with the two beaten yolks of egg, and one gill of cold water ; knead and roll out the paste a quater of an inch thick, and let it stand in a cool dry place for three or four hours ; pound the breasts of the birds with the ham, Neufchâtel cheese, the yolks of the hardboiled eggs, the spinach, and the shalot. Season with the nutmeg, the pepper, sugar, mustard, anchovy sauce, add ½ oz. of butter and one tablespoonful of grated Parmesan cheese. Pound to a smooth paste, and add one wineglass of marsala or sherry. Roll the paste as thin as possible; cut it into 2½ inch squares, (about 16) ; brush them over with water ; divide the forcemeat into the same number of parts; put one into each square ; turn over one corner so as to make small three cornered puffs ; press the edges well round with the thumb to make them adhere; drop them one by one into a saucepan of boiling water with a teaspoonful of salt in it, and boil slowly for seven minutes. Take them up carefully, drain them on a sieve in the oven for 10 minutes. Stir into the soup the 4½ tablespoonsful of baked flour, and one tablespoonful of grated Parmesan cheese, then strain. Put the soup into a degchee, boil up ; throw in the Raviuoli ; boil slowly for twenty minutes ; add the port wine, and serve immediately with a dish of grated Parmesan cheese separate.

Note.—Leveret or pigeons may be substituted when partridges cannot be had.

33.—Economical Soup, (No. 1.)

Ingredients.
3 onions
1 head of celery
1 quart of split peas, or dhall
4 tablespoonsful of dried flour
1 teaspoonful of flour of mustard
1 saltspoonful of black pepper
½ grain of cayenne
1 tablespoonful of moist sugar
1 teaspoonful of dried mint
1 desertspoonful of vinegar
¼ of a pint of cold water

Skim the fat off the liquor in which a brisket of beef has been boiled, put it into a cloth and squeeze out the moisture. Slice the onions and celery, and fry them in this fat until they are of a nice brown color. Boil the peas in one quart of water till tender; beat them with a wooden spoon, pour over the beef liquor, add the vegetables, and boil six hours, keeping it well stirred. Mix the dried flour and all the remaining ingredients with the cold water; pour it into the soup, and stir until it thickens. Boil an hour longer. Cut some slices of bread a quarter of an inch thick into dice, and fry in plenty of good dripping or butter until brown. Drain before the fire on a sieve; pour the soup into a tureen, throw in the fried bread, and serve immediately with some fine powdered mint on a plate.

34.—Economical Soup, (No. 2.)

Ingredients.
The liquor in which a leg of mutton has been boiled
1 lb. of pieces of stale bread
3 large onions (sliced)
Any cold vegetables
1 tablespoonful of salt
1 teaspoonful of pepper
1 bunch of parsley
1 sprig of marjoram
1 " thyme
½ clove of garlic
1 pint of new milk

Skim the fat off the mutton liquor. Put all the ingredients, except the milk into a degchee; pour over the liquor; boil for two hours; rub through a sieve or cloth; put it back into the degchee, pour in the pint of milk, boil up, and serve at once.

35.—Golden Quenelle Soup.

Prepare two quarts of clear soup (No. 1). Prepare the

SOUPS, BROTHS, &C.

Ingredients of Golden Quenelle Soup.
6 eggs
½ pint of cream
1 gill of strong stock
1 saltspoonful of salt
1 ,, ,, pepper

custard quenelles as follows:— Break the egg into a basin and add the stock, (game if possible) pepper and salt, and beat with a fork until well mixed; strain into a plain well buttered mould; put the mould into a degchee containing about three inches depth of water, cover the degchee, and steam gently for about half an hour, or until the custard has become firm to the touch; then take out the mould and stand it in a cool place. When it is quite cold turn the custard out on a plate and cut it up into neat square dice. Place these gently in the soup-tureen, pour in the soup, and serve.

Note.—A few asparagus heads or green peas may be added.

36.—Asparagus Soup.

Ingredients.
60 stalks of asparagus
8 spring onions
1 saltspoonful of salt
1 dessertspoonful of sifted sugar
1½ pints of cold water
3½ pints of stock (No. 1)
1 wineglassful of brown sherry

Scrape and wash the asparagus, (if in tins this is unnecessary); cut off the heads and throw them into cold water; put the stems into a degchee with the onions, salt, sugar, and cold water. Boil fast for an hour, then strain off the water and add it to the stock. Boil rapidly (uncovered) for half an hour; add the asparagus heads and the sherry; continue to boil for fifteen or twenty minutes, and then serve.

37.—Giblet Soup.

Ingredients.
Goose or duck giblets
1½ pints of cold water
1 teaspoonful of salt

Clean the giblets nicely and cut them into pieces two inches long. Put them in a degchee with the cold water, salt,

Ingredients of Giblet Soup.
1 saltspoonful of white pepper
1 „   „ flour of mustard
½ grain of cayenne
½ „ „ grated nutmeg
2 quarts of stock (No. 1)
3 tablespoonsful of baked flour
½ gill of cold stock
1 teaspoonful of soy
1 dessertspoonful of mushroom ketchup
1 small wineglassful of sherry

pepper, mustard, cayenne, and nutmeg. Boil up slowly; skim, then simmer one hour. Take out the giblets, strain the liquor and skim off every particle of fat. Add the liquor and the giblets to the two quarts of stock, and simmer gently 1½ hours. Mix the baked flour with the soy and ketchup, stir this into the soup; boil for twelve minutes; add the sherry, and serve.

38.—Aspic or Savoury Jelly.

Ingredients
1 ox foot
2 large pigs feet
1 small knuckle of veal
1 „   „   „ ham
2 onions
1 clove of garlic
2 carrots
2 apples
2 truffles
4 cloves
4 allspices
½ teaspoonful of mustard seed
1 blade of mace
2 bay leaves
1 laurel leaf
2 sprigs of thyme
The thin rind of a lemon
8 leaves of tarragon
1 teaspoonsful of salt
1 tablespoonful of moist sugar slightly burnt
6 quarts of cold water
The thin rind of a lemon
The strained juice of 2 lemons
The whites of 8 eggs
1 gill of cold water
½ pint of marsala

Put the ox foot, (unboiled) pigs feet, veal and ham (all well cleaned and chopped into pieces) into a large degchee, with the onions, garlic, carrots, apples and truffles (all scraped, washed and cut up); add all the other ingredients down to the six quarts of cold water, inclusive. Boil up quickly; then skim and simmer seven hours or longer. Strain into an earthen (uncovered) pan, and let it stand in a cool place until next day. Take off every particle of fat, and wipe the surface of the jelly with a soft cloth wrung out of hot water. Turn the jelly out and cut off the sediment. Put the jelly into a bright degchee with the rind of one and the juice of two lemons. When nearly boiling, whisk in the whites of eggs beaten with the cold water. Boil fast and whisk rapidly for 10 minutes, then let it simmer gently for twenty minutes more. Strain through a jelly bag; add the marsala. If not perfectly bright strain it a second or third time. Pour it into earthen moulds or pie dishes, and when firmly set it is ready for use.

39.—Aspic Jelly.

(An economical way for small quantities.)

Ingredients.
2 tablespoonsful of any aromatic herbs you may have
½ pint of white vinegar stock jelly
½ saltspoonful of salt
½ „ white pepper
1 teaspoonful of moist sugar
The whites of four eggs
1 sherry glass of water
1 sherry glass of marsala

Have ready the quantity of stock jelly given in the receipt (*see* stock jelly). Boil the herbs in the vinegar for half an hour; put the jelly, seasoned with the salt, pepper, and sugar into a degchee; when it is nearly boiling take it off the fire, add the whites of eggs whipped with the water, whisk well; pour the vinegar on, put the degchee back on the fire; beat and stir constantly until the jelly gets white but *does not boil;* put it where it will simmer gently, with a little fire on the top, for half an hour; strain through a jelly bag, add the marsala, and when it is firmly set, it is ready for use.

FISH.

1.—Boiled Salmon.

Take the salmon out of the tins and put it into plenty of water that is nearly boiling, with a dessertspoonful of salt; boil up quickly, skim, and simmer very gently for six minutes. Two pounds will require 12 minutes, four pounds 18 minutes, aud so on. Serve the salmon on a neatly-folded napkin, with either shrimp or cream sauce, (No. 20).

2.—Shrimp Sauce.

Boil the shrimps four minutes; put half of them in a mortar and pound to a smooth paste; add the cream, knead the butter with the baked flour, and stir into the boiling water. Boil eight minutes, put in the whole shrimps, simmer three minutes, then stir in the shrimp cream, and serve immediately.

Ingredients.
1 small tin of shrimps
3 tablespoonsful of cream
3 oz. fresh butter
1 tablespoonful of baked flour
½ pint of boiling water

3.—Salmon in Potato Paste.

(Second dressing.)

Mash the potatoes with a wooden spoon until quite smooth; add two spoonsful of the salt, the butter, and the yolk; beat till very light. Divide the

Ingredients.
6 mealey potatoes
3 saltspoonsful of salt
2 oz of oiled butter
1 yolk

FISH. 45

Ingredients for Salmon in Potato Paste.
½ lb. of cold salmon
½ saltspoonful of white pepper
3 tablespoonsful of shrimp sauce (or melted butter if there is none)

salmon into neat pieces an inch long, free from skin and bones. Mix with it one saltspoonful of salt, the pepper and shrimp sauce. Put a layer of the potato into a flat dish, lay in the fish, cover it with the rest of the potato. Smooth over the top with a knife, and bake in a quick oven for 20 minutes. Serve in the same dish.

4.—Salmon Cutlets with Milanese Sauce.

Cut each cutlet in half; take off the skin and remove the bone. Have six pieces of thin white paper; rub them three times across with fresh cut garlic, and spread them with the butter (½ oz. for each).

Ingredients.
3 salmon cutlets
3 oz. butter
1 wineglass of marsala

Put the wine into a soup-plate; dip each cutlet in the wine, then fold it in the buttered paper and boil over a slow fire, or fry in plenty of boiling fat for one hour; drain on a sieve before the fire. Take off the paper or serve them in it according to taste, with the following sauce on a sauce-boat.

Note.—Pieces of Plantain-leaf may be used instead of the paper; they are fastened with a clove stuck in like a pin and look very nice.

5.—Milanese Sauce.

Wash and bone the anchovies, peel the mushroom and shalots; chop these small and put them into a small degchee with the butter; fry till nicely browned, stirring; dredge in the

Ingredients.
2 anchovies
1 large mushroom
4 shalots
2 oz. butter
1 tablespoonful of baked flour
1 ,, ,, caper vinegar
½ half grain of cayenne

Ingredients for Milanese Sauce.
1 tablespoonful of marsala
1 saltspoonful of salt
1 tablespoonful of fresh made mustard
¾ of a pint of stock (No. 2)
2 tablespoonsful of capers

flour. When well mixed add the vinegar, cayenne, marsala, salt, mustard and stock. Boil slowly for twenty minutes, stirring and skimming, occasionally strain; add the capers, boil fast for five minutes, and serve as directed.

6.—Fried Salmon with Tartar Sauce.

Wipe the salmon in a clean dry cloth. Season the bread-

Ingredients.
2 salmon cutlets
1 oz. of fine bread crumbs
½ saltspoonful of white pepper
1 teaspoonful of chopped parsley
2 oz. of butter
½ lb. of butter or ghee

crumbs with the pepper and parsley, dissolve the 2 oz. of butter, dip in the fish, and strew it over with crumbs. Fry in the butter or ghee (which must be boiling) over a gentle fire for eighteen or twenty minutes. Drain and serve on a napkin with the Tartar sauce (No. 9) in a sauce-boat.

Note.—The sauce should be made half an hour before the fish is commenced.

7.—Salmon Cutlets with Indian Sauce.

Strip the skin off the cutlets, take out the bones, and

Ingredients.
3 cutlets
1 tablespoonful of flour
1 saltspoonful of salt
1 teaspoonful of curry powder
2 oz. of butter
¾ lb. ghee or butter

cut each slice in two. Wash and well dry each piece. Mix the flour with the salt and curry-powder. Dissolve the butter in a soup-plate rubbed three times across with garlic. Dip in the cutlets, dredge them with the seasoned flour, and fry in the ¾ lb. boiling ghee or butter for twelve minutes. Serve with the following sauce in the dish.

8.—Indian Sauce.

Peel and chop the shalots and put them into a saucepan

Ingredients for Indian Sauce.
4 shalots
2 tablespoonsful of vinegar
1 teaspoonful of moist sugar
1 gill of good stock
1 teaspoonful of mixed Indian pickles
1 teaspoonful of curry-powder
1 tablespoonful of pickle vinegar

with the vinegar and sugar; stir over the fire till the shalot is tender, and then add the stock. Boil up; skim; add the pickles (cut into half inch pieces) the curry-powder and pickle vinegar, and simmer for fifteen minutes. Serve the sauce in the centre, and the cutlets neatly round it.

9.—Mayonnaise of Salmon.

Wash and chop the tarragon, chervil, and onions. Free

Ingredients.
10 tarragon leaves
1 sprig of chervil
4 small sprig onions
½ lb. cold salmon
1 saltspoonful of salt
2 large fresh lettuces
Some beetroot and cucumber

the salmon (cooked either in the ordinary way or as in the following recipe No. 10) from skin and bones and divide it into pieces 1½ inches square, season it with the chopped herbs, onions and salt. Skim and wash the lettuces; let them remain half an hour in very cold water, dry them in a clean cloth, and cut them into small pieces (it is best to break them with the fingers). Put a layer of salad into a bowl, on that two tablespoonsful of the sauce, (*see* No. 8) and half the salmon; cover with some more sauce, add the remainder of the salmon, cover that with sauce; then a layer of salad and the rest of the sauce; finish with the remainder of the salad.

Note.—Some persons object to onions and herbs; either or both may be omitted. The receipt will in all respects do for Turbot, Lobster, Mahaseer and Hilsa.

10.—To dress Salmon for Mayonnaise.

If you have any salmon ready dressed you can use it, but

if not, the following will be found preferable:—

Put into a degchee the shalots, carrots, parsley, thyme, salt, and butter. Boil for five minutes. Put in the salmon with the wine and water, boil up quickly, then simmer very gently twelve minutes, and drain.

Ingredients.
2 shalots
½ carrot
2 sprigs of parsley
1 sprig of thyme
½ teaspoonful of salt
3 oz. of butter
1 tumbler of marsala
1   "   of water
2 lbs. of salmon

When quite cold take off the skins, pull out the bones and divide the pieces into flakes two inches square, and finish the receipt according to the Mayonnaise.

Note.—The quantities given will be sufficient for six or seven persons.

11.—Turbot.

Take the turbot out of the tin, rub in some lemon juice, and put it into a degchee with plenty of cold water, the salt and white vinegar. Boil for five minutes, simmer for five, and skim and serve on a fine napkin with lobster sauce (*see* No. 12) in a tureen.

Ingredients.
2 tins of turbot
1 dessertspoonful of salt
1 wineglassful of white vinegar
A little lemon juice

12.—Lobster Sauce.

Take the pieces of lobster out of the liquor; dry them in a soft cloth. Put the liquor into a saucepan with a blade of mace, boil five minutes; take out the mace; knead the flour with the butter and stir it into the liquor; add the pieces of lobster and the lemon juice, and boil for five minutes. Stir in the cream and serve.

Ingredients.
1 tin of lobster
1 blade of mace
6 oz. of butter
2 tablespoonsful of dried flour
1 teaspoonful of lemon juice
1 wineglassful of thick cream

13.—Fillets of Turbot fried in Butter.
(Second dressing.)

Ingredients.
1 egg
1 teaspoonful of flour
1 gill of milk

Make a batter with the egg, flour, and milk; beat it till quite smooth; cut up the cold turbot into neat fillets three inches long and 1½ inches broad; dip each fillet into the batter, and fry it in boiling ghee or butter until of a pale brown color.

14.—Turbot with Cream Sauce.
(Second dressing.)

Ingredients.
1 ℔. of fish
2 saltspoonsful of salt
A tenth part of a nutmeg
1 teaspoonful of lemon juice
1 pint of new milk
1 small piece of lemon peel
3 yolks
½ pint of cream

Turn the fish into neat fillets 3 inches long and 1½ inches broad. Season with the salt, nutmeg, and lemon juice, and let it stand one hour. Boil the milk with the lemon peel. Beat the yolks with the cream, strain the milk over the fish, boil up for five minutes; stir in the cream carefully; let it come nearly to the boil, then serve.

15.—Scolloped Fish.

Ingredients.
¾ of a ℔. of any cold fish (except mackerel)
4 oz. of bread crumbs
1 saltspoonful of salt
¼ ,, ,, ,, white pepper
½ grain of cayenne
2 tablespoonsful of white sauce (or butter)
2 oz. of dissolved butter

Season the bread-crumbs with the salt, pepper, and cayenne. Divide the cold fish into pieces three-quarter of an inch square, and mix with it the sauce or butter. Put a layer of crumbs into a dish or into scollop shells; lay in the fish; cover it thickly with crumbs; pour the dissolved butter over the top, and bake in a quick oven or before the fire for quarter of an hour. Serve in the same dish on a folded napkin.

16.—Ling Pie.

Ingredients.
½ lb. of ling (for any salt fish)
4 hard-boiled eggs
4 onions
8 mealy potatoes
3 oz. of butter, some pepper
1 teaspoonful of made mustard
1 ,, ,, anchovy sauce
1 ,, ,, mushroom ketchup
1 gill of water

Put the fish to soak in cold water the previous night; then boil it for half an hour, and remove the bones and skin. Divide it into flakes three inches long, and set it on a sieve or cloth to get cold. Peel and slice the hard-boiled eggs, slice the onions; boil the potatoes, and mash them with 2 oz. of the butter. Put a layer in the bottom of the dish, then a layer of onions, and season with half a saltspoonful of pepper, then the fish, then the eggs, and so on, until the dish is full.

Mix the mustard, anchovy sauce, ketchup and water, and pour over the top. Cover the whole with a layer of potato, and bake for one hour.

(Another way.)

Ingredients.
½ lb. of ling
8 mealy potatoes
1 oz. of butter
2 teaspoonful of pepper

Boil the potatoes and mash them with the butter and season with the pepper. Break up the fish (prepared as in the above recipe) into tiny strips, and mix them with the potato and bake in a quick oven for half an hour. Turn out and serve with egg sauce in a sauce-boat.

17.—Soles fried in oil.

Rub the soles with lemon-juice and salt, let it remain for one hour; roll it in a cloth to dry; dredge it with baked

Ingredients of Soles fried in oil.
A little lemon juice
A saltspoontul of salt
Some baked flour
Some olive oil

flour, and fry in plenty of boiling olive oil till of a plain brown color. Drain for two minutes on a sieve before the fire, anb serve on a neatly-folded napkin, with either melted butter (No. 7), or tartar sauce (No. 12) in a sauce-boat.

18.—Buttered Soles.

Ingredients.
A piece of garlic
Some baked flour
6 oz. of butter
1 teaspoonful of finely chopped chives or parsley

Rub a tin dish four times across the bottom with a piece of fresh cut garlic; wipe the sole, (two) dry and dredge them with flour. Lay them in the dish with the butter, and bake in a moderately heated oven for half an hour. Serve on a very hot dish with the butter poured over, and the chives or parsley sprinkled over the top.

19.—Fillets of Sole.

Ingredients.
Lemon juice
2 yolks beaten
Dried bread-crumbs

One sole will make eight small fillets. Saturate them for half an hour in lemon-juice, dry, and dip each fillet into beaten egg and then into bread-crumbs. Fry them in boiling olive oil or fat for ten minutes, (till of a pale yellow color) drain and serve upon neatly-folded white paper, placing them in a circle resting one on another. Serve with melted butter (No. 7), or tartar sauce (No. 12), or anchovy sauce (No. 26), in a turteen.

20.—Curried Fish.

Mix the butter and the curry-powder; peel and slice thin

Ingredients of Curried Fish.
¼ lb. of butter
1 tablespoonful of curry-powder
1 large onion
1 lb. of cold fish
1 teaspoonful of lemon juice
1   ,,   ,, salt
1   ,,   ,, baked
2 tablespoonful of cream

the onion, and fry in the butter until quite tender. Remove the skin and bones from any cold fish and divide it into pieces one inch square, and put it into the frying pan; add the strained lemon-juice, the salt and baked flour. Stir constantly over a slow fire for three-quarters of an hour. Add the cream, mix it well with the curry, and serve at once with a wall of rice placed round the dish.

Note.—Chutney should be served with curried fish.

21.—Whitebait, fried.

Ingredients.
1 tin of whitebait
Some flour
Fried parsley

Drain it on a sieve. Strew a cloth thickly with flour and sprinkle the fish lightly over it with your hand; turn it about quickly and deftly with the cloth in your hand until all the whitebait are well covered, then put them by handfuls into a wire-frying-basket, shake off all the superfluous flour, and dip the basket containing the whitebait into a frying-pan full of boiling butter or oil. A few minutes will suffice to give them a silvery tinge and will make them perfectly crisp; lift out the frying-basket, and turn the whitebait on to a neatly-folded napkin. Garnish with fried parsley, and serve at once with slices of brown bread and butter, cayenne, and quarters of lemons handed round separately.

Note.—It is impossible to prepare whitebait unless you have a frying-basket, as the whitebait always break when prepared in any other way.

22.—Oysters.

When eaten uncooked, they must be accompanied by cut lemons, cayenne, and thin cut brown bread and butter.

23.—Scolloped Oysters.

Ingredients.
1 tin of oysters
2 oz. of butter
2 oz. of flour
1 gill of cream
½ saltspoonful of salt
½ „ „ pepper
¼ grain of cayenne
½ teaspoonful of lemon-juice
Bread-crumbs
½ teaspoonful of chopped parsley
2 yolks of eggs

Beard the oysters, and put the beards and liquor into a small stew-pan with a few drops of lemon-juice. Boil five minutes, then strain into a degchee; knead the butter with the flour, the cream, salt, pepper and cayenne; pour it into the sauce, and boil for ten minutes; then add the two yolks, the remainder of the lemon-juice and the parsley; add the oysters, boil two minutes, and then pour the mixtures into scollop-shells (or a small tin dish.) Cover with a thick coating of bread-crumbs and bake about fifteen or eighteen minutes till of a pale brown color.

24.—Fried Oysters.

Ingredients.
½ tin of oysters
3 tablespoonsful of flour
1 teaspoonful of lemon-juice
2 eggs

Boil the liquor, pour it over the oysters, and let them remain till cold. Mix the flour with ⅓ of a pint of the oyster-liquor and the lemon-juice till in a smooth batter; add the yolks of the eggs well beaten; beat the batter for twenty minutes. Dry and beard the oysters. Beat the whites of the eggs to a stiff froth; mix well with the batter, throw in the oysters. Put them into a frying-pan with plenty of boiling ghee or butter, and fry till of a pale brown color—about eight minutes. Drain on a sieve before the fire one minute, and serve very hot, placed in a circle upon a neatly-folded napkin or paper.

25.—Oyster Vol-au-vent.

Prepare the Vol-au-vent as directed, (*see* recipe) and fill

Ingredients for Oyster Vol-au-vent.
- 3 dozen oysters
- 1 blade of mace
- 1 grain of cayenne
- 1 teaspoonful of lemon-juice
- The thin peel of one lemon
- 1 grain of pepper
- 3 oz. of butter
- 1 dessertspoonful of baked flour
- 1 gill of fresh cream

the vacancy with oysters prepared as follows:—Beard the oysters; put their liquor into a saucepan with the beards, the mace, lemon-juice and peel, and pepper; boil up. Knead the butter with the flour and stir in; boil till it is quite thick, fifteen or twenty minutes; strain; add the oysters, simmer six minutes; stir in the cream, and use as directed. Serve the vol-au-vent on a neatly-folded napkin.

26.—Oyster Patties.

Make the puff paste as directed *(see* recipes—*Chapter on Pastry &c.)* roll it out ⅓ of an inch thick; have ready two circular patty cutters, dip them into flour and cut out eight of the larger size;

Ingredients.
- 2 dozen oysters
- ½ inch of mace
- The *thin* rind of half lemon
- 1 grain of white pepper
- ¼ grain of cayenne
- 1 tablespoonful of Oswego flour
- 1 gill of cream
- 1 tablespoonful of lemon-juice

press the smaller size on the centre of each piece of paste and cut it *half-way through*. Roll out the remainder of the paste, and cut out eight of the smaller pieces; place them all on a baking tin, and bake in a quick oven till of a pale brown color,—about twenty minutes. Take them out, and with a sharp penknife remove the centre paste from the larger pieces. Fill the vacancies with oysters prepared as follows:—Take the beards off the oysters; throw the oysters into boiling water; put the beards and liquor with the mace, lemon-peel, pepper and cayenne into a small saucepan, and boil *fast*, ten minutes; strain. Cut the oysters into six pieces; stir the Oswego flour into the cream; put the oysters into the sauce, add the lemon-juice, simmer two minutes, stir in the thickened cream, boil for a few minutes till quite thick, fill the oyster patties, cover over with the small lids and serve on a neatly-folded napkin.

27.—Mahaseer, boiled.

Fill a good sized degchee with cold water and add salt to it until it will float a fresh egg. Then set the water on to boil. When it is boiling furiously put in the fish and boil from fifteen to twenty minutes. (A ten pound fish is the best size.) When done take it out and serve *at once*, or it will be utterly spoiled. Serve with anchovy, egg, or Dutch sauce.

28.—Mahaseer, cold.

Ingredients.
1 lb. cold fish
Green chillies
Green ginger
8 peppercorns
4 cloves
½ tumbler of the water in which the fish was boiled
Vinegar

The night before you require it, put the cold fish (divided with two silver forks into pieces two inches square) into a soup tureen; sprinkle the chillies and green ginger cut up over it, then the cloves and peppercorns. Add the liquor in which the fish was boiled. Boil sufficient vinegar, about half bottle, and pour it over boiling till it *just* covers the fish. Leave it till the morning when it will have formed into a compact jelly. Serve on a dish with the following sauce poured over:

29.—Sauce for cold Mahaseer.

Ingredients.
1 teaspoonful of fresh made mustard
1 teaspoonful of salt
1 ,, ,, ,, black pepper
1 ,, ,, ,, red pepper
2 tablespoonsful of oil
1 ,, ,, of vinegar
1 dessertspoonful of sherry

Stir all these ingredients well together in the order in which they are given and use as directed, or in a separate tureen.

BEEF.

1.—Roast Beef—Ribs or Sirloin.

Wipe the beef dry with a clean cloth and envelope it in thin paper thickly spread with sweet beef dripping, hang it before the fire, and let it roast there, basting frequently for a quarter of an hour. Then withdraw it to a distance of 18 inches from the grate, and let it roast there slowly till done. Half an hour before it is ready, take off the paper, dredge it with baked flour, and baste with 2 oz. of dissolved butter; place the beef on a *hot* dish; pour off the dripping; add one teaspoonful of boiling water and half a saltspoonful of salt, to the gravy dripped from the beef. Serve at once with a garnish of grated horse-radish, and horse-radish sauce (No. 10) and Yorkshire pudding on separate dishes. (Allow 11 minutes to the ℔. for roasting *underdone*.)

2.—Boiled Salt Round of Beef.

Choose a round of beef well covered with rich delicate-looking fat; take out the kernels; rub in and all over it about 4 ℔s. of salt, and rub it well with the salt every morning for ten days; roll it round, fasten it with skewers and bind it round with tape. Put it in a good sized degchee with plenty of cold water, and boil it very gently, skimming frequently until done. Allow half an hour to the pound *after it boils*. Take the beef out, trim off any soiled pieces of fat, cut off the first slice, garnish it with boiled carrots or greens, pour over a teacupful of the liquor, and serve with a sweet pudding handed round.

Silver-side and ribs of beef are prepared in the same manner.

3.—Stewed Brisket of Beef with French Beans.

Have a neatly cut square piece of brisket of beef; hang it before a quick fire for half an hour to brown; baste it well; put it into a degchee with the chopped onions fried brown, and sufficient water to reach the top, but not cover it; boil up and skim; then add the pepper, mustard, soy, sauce, sugar, ketchup, and vinegar; simmer gently for 4½ hours, skimming frequently; add the French beans (uncut), the wineglassful of vinegar mixed with the flour, and simmer for another hour. Then serve—the beef in the centre, and the beans round the dish.

Ingredients.
7 lbs. of beef
3 onions (chopped)
1 teaspoonful of pepper
1   ,,   fresh made mustard
1 dessertspoonful of soy
1 tablespoonful of anchovy sauce
1 teaspoonful of moist sugar
2 tablespoonsful of mushroom ketchup
1 dessertspoonful of vinegar
1 lb. of French beans
1 wineglassful of white vinegar
1 tablespoonful of baked flour

4.—Stewed Beef with Maccaroni and Tomato Sauce.

Take 6 lbs. of silver-side of beef with a skin on one side nicely shaped, and make some very deep cuts in it, nearly through to the skin; make a forcemeat of the ham, herbs and garlic, and fill the cuts with this; then bind so that the stuffing may not escape. Put

Ingredients.
6 lbs. of beef
1 slice of ham
bunch of savoury herbs
1 pea of garlic
4 lbs. suet fat
½ lb. of maccaroni
4 tablespoonsful of tomato sauce

the fat into a degchee which will just hold it and the beef, and when the fat quite *boils* lay in the beef, and let it simmer six hours, turning it once in every hour. Boil the maccaroni and drain it. Make a gravy for the beef, and put in the maccaroni and the tomato sauce. Boil five minutes. Take out the beef; dish it, pour the maccaroni and sauce round, and serve at once.

5.—Spiced and pressed Beef.

Ingredients.
2 lbs. of salt
1½ lbs. of saltpetre
½ oz. of salt of prunella
¼ lb. of moist sugar
½ cayenne spoonful of powdered cloves
½ ,, ,, powdered mace
½ ,, ,, ,, allspice
¼ of an oz. of black pepper
¼ ,, ,, ,, bruised mustard seed
1 cayenne spoonful of bruised coriander seed
1 clove of garlic, chopped fine

Have a piece of brisket of beef twelve inches long and seven wide. Mix all the ingredients, and rub well into the beef on both sides. Let the beef remain in this pickle five days, turning and rubbing daily. Dress it as follows :—Put the beef into plenty of cold water; boil up ısowly; skim; then simmer as gently as possible for four hours; take it out, remove the bones, roll it up, skin outwards, as tightly as possible; sew it up in a strong cloth and simmer for two hours longer; put it between two boards with a heavy weight on the upper one. When cold, take off the cloth, and serve cold or glazed as perferred.

6.—Fillet of Beef, larded.

Ingredients.
The juice of a lemon
1 teaspoonful of salt
1 saltspoonful of pepper
1 ,, ,, ,, sugar
1 onion, finely chopped
} Pickle.

Have a piece of the under side of a sirloin of beef about three pounds. Mix the lemon-juice, salt, pepper, sugar and onion; rub this well into the beef and let it remain all night. Take

BEEF. 59

Ingredients of Fillet of Beef larded.
Bacon
1 carrot
1 onion
½ head of celery
1 piece of garlic
4 sprigs of parsley
1 spring of thyme
2 cloves
2 allspice
4 peppercorns
1 saltspoonful of salt
¼ ,, ,, pepper
Some stock (No. 1)
1 dessertspoonful of flour
1 tablespoonful of ketchup
1 ,, ,, brandy

off the skin and fat, and lard the round side nicely with fat bacon, deep and thick; cover the larding with writing-paper thickly buttered; put round the beef the carrot, onion and celery (all sliced), the garlic, the trimmings of the beef, the parsley, thyme, cloves, allspice, peppercorn, salt, pepper, and just sufficient stock to reach up to the larding; put the stewpan over a brisk fire for quarter of an hour; then place it where it will simmer *very* gently for two hours. Take out the beef, place it in a slow oven; rub the gravy through a fine sieve; take off all the fat. Mix the flour, ketchup and brandy, and stir them into the gravy; boil quickly for eight minutes. Place the beef on a dish; take off the paper, pour the sauce round, and serve immediately.

7.—Rump Steak, broiled.

Have the steak cut half an inch thick and in one piece.

Ingredients.
1 oz. of butter
½ saltspoonful of salt
¼ ,, ,, pepper

Put it on the gridiron over a quick bright fire till done, turning it with steak-tongs, or a fork placed *in the fat.* Eight minutes *underdone;* ten minutes *with the gravy in.* Put it on a hot dish, rub the butter quickly over both sides, sprinkle with the salt and pepper, and serve immediately.

8.—Rump Steak, with Fried Potatoes.

Prepare the steak as in the preceding receipt; when it

Ingredients for Rump Steak broiled. is done pour over the lemon-
2 shalots chopped, fine
1 teaspoonful of lemon juice juice and sprinkle with the chopped shalots. Serve at once with fried potatoes round he dish.

9.—Beefsteaks à la Francaise.

These are cut from the fillet, or undercut from a sirloin. Procure about 1½ lbs., trim off all the skin and fat; cut the fillet into slices about half inch thick; lay them on a plate and season them with a little oil, pepper and salt; boil on both sides, a little underdone; serve them on a dish with fried potatoes round and Maître d'Hotel butter (No. 25) under them. Serve at once.

10.—Beefsteaks with Anchovy Butter.

Prepare them as in the preceding receipt, substituting Anchovy butter (No. 26) for the Maitre d'Hotel butter.

11.—Epicurean Beefsteak.

Prepare as in à la Francaise, but dish up with Epicurean butter (No. 27.)

Beefsteaks prepared as above may be also served with oyster, tomato, tartar, or white mushroom sauces.

12.—Stewed Rumpsteak with Oysters.

Have a rump steak ¾ of an inch thick to weigh 1¼ lbs.

Ingredients.
2 doz. oysters
1 onion
½ carrot
2 oz. of butter
1 saltspoonful of pepper

Put the onion and carrot, sliced, into a degchee with the butter; when it is dissolved, lay in the steak, and slightly brown both

BEEF.

Ingredients for Stewed Rumpsteak with Oysters.
1 mustardspoonful of fresh made mustard
1 clove
4 sprigs of parsley
1 tablespoonful of flour

sides; strain the liquor of the oysters and put in sufficient to reach to the top of the steak, but not to cover it; add the pepper, mustard, clove and parsley, and simmer gently for 1½ hours; take out the steak, strain the gravy, mix with it the flour and boil up; put back the steak; beard the oysters and put them in; simmer six minutes, and serve.

13.—Rumpsteak Pie.

Ingredients.
1½ lbs. rump steak
2 saltspoonsful of salt
1½ ,, ,, pepper
1 gill of gravy
1 teaspoonful of Oude or Harvey sauce
½ lb. of flour
1 gill of cold water
The juice of ½ lemon
7 oz. of butter

Cut the steak ⅓ of an inch thick and divide it into two inch pieces; season it with the salt and pepper. Grease the edge of the pie-dish and lay in the steak with the gravy and the sauce. Make a paste as follows:—
Moisten the flour with the water and lemon juice; knead to a fine paste; lay it flat on the board, put in the butter, and roll it out seven times; each time dredge it slightly with flour; let it stand two hours in a cold place. Take a sixth part of the paste, roll it out, and line the edge of the dish; moisten with water, roll out the remainder to the size of the dish, put it over, press round the edge with the thumb; trim with a sharp knife, notch at inch distances; make a hole in the centre, ornament it to fancy, and bake in moderate oven for 2¼ hours.

Pigeons, hard-boiled eggs, and oysters can be added.

14.—Beefsteak and Oyster Pie.

Prepare the steak as in the foregoing receipt; fry the

Ingredients for Beefsteak and Oyster Pie.

1½ lbs. of rumpsteak
2 saltspoonsful of salt
1½   ,,   of pepper
1½ oz. of butter
1 teaspoonful of Harvey sauce
2 tablespoonful of flour
2 doz. oysters
1 gill of thin liquor
1 chopped onion
6 new potatoes (boiled)

pieces in the butter, shake in the flour; add the oysters and one gill of thin liquor, the Harvey and the onion; shake round over the fire, simmering for five minutes. Put the whole into a pie-dish, cover with a paste prepared as above, bake one hour, and serve.

15.—Rumpsteak, Kidney and Oyster Pudding.

Prepare and season the steak as in the preceding receipt; make a paste with the flour and suet chopped fine. Grease a pint pudding basin, lay in the paste; press it to an equal thickness all round; put in the steak with the kidneys, oysters and liquor, and cover with a circular piece of paste; press it to make it adhere; tie a cloth over; put into boiling water and boil four hours. Turn out carefully, and serve immediately.

Ingredients.

1½ lbs. of beefsteak
2 kidneys
2 doz. oysters
1 gill of oyster liquor
½ lb. of flour
7 oz. of beef suet

16.—Ox Palates, Stewed.

Put the palates into hot water for one hour; wash them in three waters, take off the black skin and cut each palate into six pieces. Put into a degchee the bacon, onion, carrot, garlic, herbs, cloves, sugar, pepper and curry-powder, and stand it over the fire to brown the vegetables;

Ingredients.

2 palates
4 slices of fat bacon
1 onion } sliced
1 carrot }
1 piece of garlic, (the size of a pea)
3 cloves
1 saltspoonful of mixed herbs
1   ,,   ,, sugar
1   ,,   ,, curry powder
1 pint of good stock
1 tablespoonful of brandy

BEEF. 63

Ingredients for Ox Palates Stewed.
1 tablespoonful of vinegar
1 ,, ,, rice-flour
1 ,, ,, mushroom ketchup
1 desertspoonful of soy
1 wineglassful of port wine

add the stock, brandy and vinegar, and put in the palates; simmer gently for four hours and skim frequently. Take out the palates, skim off every particle of fat, and strain the gravy. Mix the rice-flour with the ketchup and soy, and stir it in to thicken the gravy; put in the palates, simmer another hour; add the port wine, and serve immediately.

17.—Ox-Kidney, Grilled.

Cut the kidney in slices about half inch thick; season with pepper and salt on both sides; place them on a gridiron over a clear fire and broil them until done on both sides; dish up on a hot dish with Maitre d' Hotel butter (No. 25,) and serve immediately.

18.—Stewed Ox-Kidney.

Cut the kidney in thin slices, take off the skin and pith, and fry them in the butter for two minutes, season with all the other ingredients, and stir over the fire until the whole has simmered together for five minutes, and dish up with sippets of fried bread round the dish.

Ingredients.
10 oz. of butter
1 saltspoonful of pepper
1 ,, ,, salt
¼ grain of cayenne
1 tablespoonful of flour
1 mushroom chopped
1 teaspoonful of Harvey sauce
1 gill of stock

18.—Broiled Oxtail.
(An excellent entree.)

It should be sent from the butcher ready jointed; soak and wash well; throw it into plenty of boiling water slightly salted and simmer for fifteen minutes

Ingredients.
½ pint of gravy
Some salt, cayenne and pepper
Some bread crumbs
Some clarified butter

take it out and put it into fresh water to cool, wipe it and lay it in a small round stewpan; just cover with the beef gravy and stew very gently until it is tender. Drain it; sprinkle it with salt, pepper and cayenne; dip the pieces into clarified butter and then into bread-crumbs, (with which it should be thickly covered) lay on a gridiron, (or fry in a pan with 1 oz. of butter) then put into the oven for twenty minutes until colored of a light golden brown. Serve with gravy or tomato or Tartar sauce. (*See* recipes.)

SECOND DRESSINGS OF BEEF.

1.—Beef with Acid Sauce.

Ingredients.
2 onions
1 mushroom
2 oz. of butter
1 teaspoonful of salt
1 saltspoonful of pepper
1 teaspoonful of flour of mustard
1 "   " grated horse-radish
¼ of a grain of cayenne
1 dessertspoonful of flour
½ wineglassful of vinegar
½ pint of beef gravy
2 lbs of cold beef
1 tablespoonful of any wine

Chop the onions and mushroom, and put them in a degchee with the butter, salt, pepper, mustard, horse-radish and cayenne; fry till the onions are a bright brown color; dredge in the flour, and add the vinegar and gravy. Cut some neat slices of cold beef free from skin and gristle, lay them in the degchee, and simmer as gently as possible for quarter of an hour. Stir in a tablespoonful of any wine, and serve at once.

2.—Beef with Savoury Rice.

Ingredients.
1¼ lbs. of cold beef
Some salad oil
Some lemon juice
Some baked flour
1 teaspoonful of salt
1 saltspoonful of pepper
1 "   "   " flour of mustard
1 "   "   " loaf sugar
1 pinch of cayenne
2 shalots (finely chopped)
Some garlic
2 oz. of butter
½ pint of gravy
½ teacupful of pickled mushrooms
2 tablespoonsful of marsala

Cut the slices of beef off the sirloin a quarter of an inch thick, and trim off the fat and gristle; dip each piece into fine salad oil and then into lemon-juice and let them remain four hours; then dredge both sides with flour, and season with the salt, pepper, mustard, sugar, cayenne and shalots. Heat a degchee, rub it twice across the bottom with garlic, put in the butter, and when it is dissolved, put in the beef; add the gravy and the mushrooms (but none of the vinegar); shake the pan and simmer very gently for half an hour; skim frequently; add the marsala, and serve immediately with savoury rice round it.

3.—Savoury Rice.

Wash the rice and boil it in one quart of water for ten minutes; drain; put it in a degchee with all the ingredients. Stir and simmer until the gravy is entirely absorbed, about quarter of an hour. Serve immediately as directed.

Ingredients.
½ lb. of rice
2 oz. of butter
1 teaspoonful of salt
1 " " loaf sugar
½ saltspoonful of white pepper
The rind of ½ lemon (grated)
The strained juice of ½ lemon
¼ pint of good gravy
1 teaspoonful of chutney sauce

4.—Beef Pie with Potato Crust.

Boil the potatoes, mash them quite smooth, add the salt, the butter, and the beaten yolk, and beat with a wooden spoon until perfectly light. Cut the beef into thin slices; take off the fat and gristle, season with the salt and pepper; spread a layer of potatoes in a shallow piedish, lay in the beef, pour over the gravy and the sauce; cover with potato, smooth over with a knife, bake in a moderate oven for half an hour, and serve.

Ingredients.
5 large potatoes
1 saltspoonful of salt
3 oz. of dissolved butter
One beaten yolk
¾ lb. cold roast beef
1 *small* saltspoonful of salt
1 saltspoonful of pepper
1 teacupful of beef gravy
1 tablespoonful of Harvey sauce

5.—Beef Cutlets in paper.

Mince the meat and bacon as fine as possible, also the mushroom and shalot; add the salt, pepper, cayenne and mustard; beat the yolk of an egg

Ingredients.
¾ lb. of cold roast beef
2 oz. of fat bacon
1 mushroom

Ingredients of Beef Cutlets in paper.
½ shalot
1 saltspoonful of salt
1   ,,   ,, pepper
1 pinch of cayenne
1 mustardspoonful of mustard
1 yolk of an egg
1 teaspoonful of beef gravy
1 dessertspoonful of sherry
2 oz. dissolved butter
Some dried flour
2 oz. of fine bread-crumbs
1 saltspoonful of mixed salt
Herbs in powder
½ saltspoonful of salt
1 egg

with the gravy and sherry, mix it well, and form the whole into six cutlets; dip them into the dissolved butter and dredge them lightly with the flour; stand them in a cold place for an hour. Season the bread-crumbs with the herbs and salt; beat the egg; dip each cutlet into the egg, and then into the bread-crumbs. Butter thickly 6 half-sheets of foolscap; put each cutlet into one, and fold over the edges neatly; place them on a tin dish, and bake in a moderate oven for 25 minutes. Serve in the paper.

6.—Beef with Sauce Appetissante.

Cut ¾ lb. of cold roast beef into slices, trim off the fat and gristle, and lay them in the sauce appetissante (No. 20) on a silver dish over a spirit lamp. Let it get boiling hot, and serve at once.

7.—Vinageret of Beef.

Cut the beef in *very* thin slices, and lay them in a salad

Ingredients.
¾ lb. cold braised or boiled beef
Some beetroot sliced
2 eggs
Some boiled potatoes
1 saltspoonful of salt
1   ,,   ,, pepper
3 tablespoonsful of salad oil
2   ,,   of white wine vinegar
1   ,,   of Taragon vinegar
1 teaspoonful of chopped parsley and shalot

bowl with the beetroot, the eggs hard boiled and cut in quarters, and the potatoes cold and sliced; season with pepper, salt, salad-oil and vinegar, and chopped parsley and shalot. Mix well, serve as a luncheon dish.

Note.—Cold roast hare minced fine or grouse, teal, or quail, can be served in the same way, and celery or any sort of salad may be added.

LAMB.

1.—Fore-quarter of Lamb.

Cover the joint with white paper thickly spread with sweet dripping or butter, hang it before a clear fire, and roast for an hour and a half constantly basting. Half an hour before serving take off the paper, dredge the lamb slightly with flour and a little salt, and continue to baste until every part is of a delicate brown color; just before taking it up. baste it with one ounce of dissolved butter. Place the joint on the dish, and with a sharp knife divide the shoulder from the ribs; rub the ribs over with an ounce of butter, and drop equally over it the strained juice of a small lemon; then replace the shoulder. Pour off the fat; add a teacupful of boiling water and a saltspoonful of salt to the gravy dripped from the lamb; pour the gravy into the dish (not over the meat), and serve at once, with mint sauce separately, and a hot dish to receive the shoulder.

2.—Mint Sauce.

Chop some fresh well-washed mint quite fine, and put two tablespoonsful in a sauce tureen with two tablespoonsful of good vinegar and the same quantity of moist sugar.

3.—Ribs or Target of Lamb.

This consists of the breast and neck-joints left in their natural position, and the ribs are partially sawn through.

Follow the preceding receipt, allowing half an hour less time; serve as directed with mint sauce, but omit the butter and lemon-juice.

4 —Saddle of Lamb.

Cover it with white paper thickly spread with dripping, or butter and roast, basting constantly before a clear fire for 1½ hours. Half an hour before serving, remove the paper; dredge the lamb with baked flour and baste till nicely browned. Place the saddle on a hot dish, the fat side uppermost; pour off the fat, add a teacupful of boiling water and saltspoonful of salt to the gravy dripped from the lamb; pour it into the dish (not over the lamb), and serve at once with mint-sauce in a tureen.

5.—Haunch of Lamb.

Follow the preceding receipt, but roast *at a distance* from the fire, and allow 17 minutes to the pound. Serve with mint-sauce.

6.—Shoulder of Lamb.

Follow the receipt for the saddle, but allow 18 minutes to the pound, and just before you take it from the fire baste it with 10 oz. of dissolved butter. Serve with mint-sauce.

7.—Roast Leg of Lamb.

Follow the receipt for the saddle, allowing 22 minutes to the pound.

8.—Boiled Leg of Lamb.

Put the lamb in sufficient cold water just to cover it; boil up quickly; skim; add a dessertspoonful of salt, then simmer as gently as possible until done; allow 19 minutes to the pound *after it boils.* Serve with either Caper sauce, (*see* page 76) or Maitre d'Hotel sauce poured over it, or with Spinach sauce which is excellent and preferable to either. Garnish with turnips or carrots.

9.—Spinach Sauce.

Take half pint of the liquor the lamb was boiled in; stir into it 3 oz of butter, knead into it a tablespoonful of baked flour; add a teaspoonful of Spinach greening (*see* page 3), then stir in a tablespoonful of cream (or some fresh goat's milk with one yolk beaten up in it,) boil for three minutes, and serve poured over the lamb.

10.—Lamb Chops.

Cut the chops the width of the bones. Season the breadcrumbs with the salt, pepper and parsley finely chopped; dip each cutlet into beaten egg and then into crumbs, and fry in boiling lamb's dripping, at a distance from the fire for eighteen or twenty minutes; when done they should be of a golden-brown color. Serve on a hot dish with fried parsley in the centre. Wash and pick a large bunch of parsley, and let it remain in cold water with a teaspoonful of salt in it for an hour; put ½ lb. of suet dripping into a frying pan, and while boiling, dip the parsley in three times; it should be crisp and green.

Ingredients
4 oz. fine bread crumbs
1 teaspoonful of salt
1 saltspoonful of white pepper
1 tablespoonful of parsley
2 beaten eggs
1 large bunch of parsley
1 teaspoonful of salt

11.—Lamb Cutlets with Cucumbers.

Peel the cucumbers; cut them into two, split each piece

LAMB.

Ingredients for Lamb Cutlets with Cucumbers.

3 Cucumbers
1 quart of water
1 tablespoonful of salt
1 wineglassful of vinegar
¼ lb. of good butter
2 dessertspoonsful of dried flour
1 grain of cayenne
1 teaspoonful of sifted loaf-sugar
1 gill of stock, (No. 2)
The strained juice of a small lemon
8 lamb cutlets
1 saltspoonful of salt
½ ,, ,, pepper
1 dessertspoonful of parsley
¼ lb. of dissolved butter

into three, and remove the seeds; put the cucumbers into a quart of water with the salt and vinegar, and let them remain three hours; drain off the water. Knead the butter with the flour, cayenne and sugar, put it into a degchee and shake over the fire till of a pale yellow color; then put in the cucumber, and simmer very gently for 20 minutes; shake the pan frequently; add the stock, and continue to simmer for ten minutes. Add the lemon-juice, and serve poured over the cutlets, which cook as follows:—Trim the fat off the cutlets, and bare the bone about one inch. Mix the salt, pepper and parsley (finely chopped); season the cutlets, and fry them a pale brown color in the butter. They will require eighteen minutes to fry slowly.

12.—Lamb Cutlets.

Ingredients

8 cutlets
1 saltspoonful of salt
½ ,, ,, pepper
1 dessertspoonful of parsley
Bread-crumbs
Beaten egg
2 oz. of clarified butter

Trim the fat and gristle off the cutlets, bare the bone one inch, and season with pepper, salt and finely chopped parsley; dip them into beaten egg, crumb them over, and put the crumbs on closely; then dip each cutlet in dissolved butter, crumb them again, and pat them into shape with a knife. Broil them over a clear fire till of a golden-brown color, and dish them up with either stewed mushrooms or chestnuts, or any thick puree of vegetables in the centre.

13.—Lamb Pelau.

Chop up the onions, garlic and raisins; knead the curry-

Ingredients of Lamb Pelau.
3 onions
¼ clove of garlic
¼ lb. of Sultana raisins
2 tablespoonsful of curry powder
2 oz. of butter
5 lamb cutlets
1 teaspoonful of salt
¾ lb. of rice
1 pint of stock
3 oz. of butter
1 saltspoonful of salt
The grated rind of ½ lemon
¼ saltspoonful of mixed herbs
1 gill of thick cream
The strained juice of a lemon

powder with the butter, and fry the raisins, garlic and onions for ten minutes. Trim the fat off the cutlets, put them with the onion, add the salt, and simmer for ¾s of an hour. Wash the rice and put it with the stock, and boil slowly for quarter of an hour; drain off the gravy. Add the butter to the rice and the salt; stir till it becomes a bright yellow color; then put in sufficient gravy to moisten it, the grated rind, and the herbs; simmer and stir till the rice is quite tender, (a quarter of an hour) and every grain separate. Add the cream; lay half the rice on a hot dish; add the lemon-juice to the cutlets; lay them with their sauce on the rice, cover them over with the remainder of the rice, and serve immediately.

14.—Stewed Lamb and Peas.

Cut a neck of lamb into small chops; season with salt,

Ingredients.
1½ saltspoonful of salt
1   „   „   pepper
1 dessertspoonful of flour
2 oz. of butter
2 shalots
4 white lettuce leaves
1 teaspoonful of sifted loaf-sugar
2 tarragon leaves
1 teaspoonful of chopped parsley
¾ of a pint of stock or water
1 pint of peas
½ saltspoonful of salt
1 teaspoonful of loaf-sugar

pepper and flour, and fry in 1 oz. of butter till of a pale-brown color on both sides (eight minutes). Chop the shalots and lettuce leaves, quite small, put them in a degchee with 1 oz. of butter, the sugar, tarragon and parsley (chopped). When the butter is dissolved, put in the chops and stock, and simmer very gently for twenty minutes. Add the peas, salt and sugar, continue to simmer for quarter of an hour. Place the lamb neatly on a hot dish, pour over the peas, and serve at once.

15.—Sweetbreads Roasted with Green Peas.

Ingredients.
2 raw yolks
Some bread crumbs
3 oz. of butter

Trim off the pith and skin, and put the sweetbreads into boiling water for five minutes, and then into cold water for an hour; dip a paste brush in two raw yolks of egg beaten, brush the sweetbreads all over and roll them in bread-crumbs; then dip them in 1 oz. of clarified butter and roll them in bread-crumbs; put them into a tin dish with 2 oz. of butter, and set them in a quick oven to bake for half an hour; baste them frequently with butter from the pan. When they are done a light golden brown color, dish them up with white sauce (No. 2) and stewed peas.

16.—Lamb's Head and Pluck.

Ingredients.
1 onion
½ clove of garlic
1 carrot
1 turnip
1 small bunch of sweet herbs
3 cloves
1 tablespoonful of salt
5 pints of cold water
1 saltspoonful of salt
2 ,, ,, pepper
1 grain of cayenne
2 tablespoonsful of baked flour
¼ lb. butter
1 tablespoonful of mushroom-ketchup
1 tablespoonful of Harvey sauce
1 teaspoonful of soy
Some beaten egg
Some bread-crumbs
3 oz. of dissolved butter

Well wash the head and pluck; put them in a large degchee with the onion, garlic, carrot, turnip, herbs, cloves, salt and water.; boil up quickly, skim and simmer for one hour. Take them out of the degchee; split the head, take out the tongue and brains, and fold the head in a clean cloth to dry; mince the liver, heart, half the lights, the tongue (take off the skin) and the brains; season the mince with the salt, pepper, cayenne and flour; put it into a degchee with the ¼ lb. of butter, ¾ of a pint of the liquor strained, the ketchup, sauce and soy; stir frequently, and simmer gently for half an hour; brush the head over with beaten egg; strew it with fine bread crumbs and bake in a moderate oven ¾ of an hour; baste frequently with the dissolved butter; place the mince on a hot dish and the head (which should be of a pale brown color) in the centre, and serve at once.

MUTTON.

1.—Saddle of Mutton Roasted.

Dredge the saddle with dried flour; put it in a sheet of paper thickly spread with sweet dripping; hang it before a good fire, quite close for 20 minutes, then at a distance until done. A quarter of an hour before serving, take off the paper; put half a saltspoon of salt into a teacupful of boiling water; pour it over the mutton; then baste till slightly browned. Pour off the fat, and serve the dripped gravy in the dish. Send to table *very hot* with a pot of red currant jelly turned out on a plate.

Note.—A saddle of mutton will require seven minutes to the pound to be underdone; with the gravy in ten minutes.

2.—Leg of Mutton Roasted

Is done in precisely the same manner as a saddle.

3.—Leg of Mutton Boiled.

Put the mutton into a big degchee, and cover it well with cold water; boil up quickly; skim; add a handful of salt, a few carrots and turnips, and simmer gently till done, allowing a quarter of an hour to the pouud. Dish it up with a cut paper ruffle on the shank bone. Mash the turnips, mix them with a dessertspoonful of flour, a pat of butter, and a wineglass of milk with the yolk of one egg beaten up in it, and a pinch of pepper and salt. Mould the mashed turnips in the shape of large eggs with two tablespoons, and place them in a circular row round the dish with a piece of boiled carrot in between. Pour a little gravy under the mutton, and serve with caper sauce, (*see* recipe) in a separate dish.

Note.—Reserve the liquor in which the mutton was boiled for Economical Soup No. 2.

4.—Leg of Mutton with Anchovy Sauce.

Ingredients.
Some lean ham or bacon
2 tumblers of stock
1 saltspoonful of salt
1   ,,   ,, pepper
1 clove of garlic
1 scrape of nutmeg
1 bay leaf
1 sherry glass of brandy
6 anchovies
3 oz. of butter

Prick the leg with garlic and lard it thinly with pieces of lean ham, the thickness of a little finger. Put it into a degchee with the stock; add the salt, pepper, garlic, nutmeg, bayleaf and brandy; simmer until it is done, allowing a quarter of an hour to a pound of meat. Bone the anchovies, pound them and incorporate with the butter. When the leg is ready, take it off the fire, strain the sauce in which it has been boiled; put the sauce back into the degchee, and add the anchovy butter. Simmer for five minutes and then put in the leg and leave it in to keep hot until wanted.

5.—Caper Sauce.

Ingredients.
4 oz. butter
1½ oz. of flour
A grate of nutmeg
1 saltspoonful of salt
½   ,,   ,, pepper
A small piece of glaze
½ pint of the liquor in which the mutton has been boiled
1 tablespoonful of capers
1 teaspoonful of white vinegar

Knead 3 oz. of the butter, flour, nutmeg, salt and pepper well together; put them into a small saucepan with the glaze and liquor; stir over the fire until the sauce begins to boil: then stir in the remaining ounce of butter; add the capers, and serve at once. The sauce should be very thick and smooth.

6.—Roast Shoulder of Mutton.

Cut out the vein from the underpart; allow sixteen minutes to the pound; hang it before a good fire, and baste constantly. Half an hour before serving, dredge it with a little dried flour, sprinkle over half a saltspoonful of salt, and continue to baste; pour off all the fat; add a teacupful of boiling water to the gravy that has dripped from the mutton, pour it on the dish; serve with onion sauce (No. 4), which may be served separately if desired.

7.—Boiled Shoulder of Mutton.

This is done in the same way as a leg of mutton, and smothered in onion sauce (No. 4).

8.—Loin of Mutton Roasted.

Place it before a quick bright fire, quite close for ten minutes; draw it back and roast slowly at a distance for an hour. A few minutes before serving, dredge it with baked flour and half a saltspoonful of salt; baste it well from the beginning. Pour off the dripping, and serve in its own gravy, with a little boiled water added to it in the dish.

9.—Loin of Mutton stuffed and served with rich Gravy.

Ingredients.
- ¼ lb. of mutton suet
- ½ oz. of sweet almonds
- 1 oz. of bread-crumbs
- 1 teaspoonful of chopped parsley
- 1 saltspoonful of mixed sweet-herbs
- ½ saltspoonful of pepper
- 1 grain of cayenne
- 2 yolks of eggs
- 1 white of egg
- 1 black onion, (*see* page 3)
- 1 shalot

Bone a fine loin of mutton, trim off some of the fat, and beat the meat with a rolling pin to flatten it and make it tender. Make a stuffing with the suet chopped fine, the almonds, (boiled ten minutes and pounded to a paste) the bread-crumbs, parsley, herbs, pepper, salt, cayenne

Ingredients of Stuffed Lion of Mutton.

1 piece of garlic, the size of a pea
½ carrot
½ head of celery
1 pint of water
1 tablespoonful of flour
1 dessertspoonful of ketchup
1 teaspoonful of soy
½ saltspoonful of salt
1 wineglassful of port wine

and eggs; mix these well together, and spread the stuffing equally over the inner side of the mutton; roll it neatly lengthways, skewer it up, and roast it before a good fire, at a distance, one hour, basting continually. Put the bones into a saucepan with the onion, shalot, garlic, carrot, celery and water, and stew three hours. Strain, add the flour, ketchup, soy and salt; boil up for ten minutes; add the wine; pour the gravy over the mutton, and serve very hot.

10.—Barley Broth and Sheep's Head with mashed Potatoes.

Well wash the head; put it into a degchee with the vege-

Ingredients.

1 sheep's head
2 onions
1 turnip
1 carrot
1 leek
 } sliced
2 oz. of barley
1 dessertspoonful of salt
1 saltspoonful of sugar
2 sprigs of parsley
1 „ „ thyme
1 „ „ marjoram
 } tied together
2 quarts of water
8 potatoes
3 oz. of dripping
A teacupful of milk
1 saltspoonful of salt
½ „ „ pepper
1 tablespoonful of fine bread-crumbs

tables, barley, salt, sugar, pepper, parsley and herbs; pour over two quarts of water; stir the barley from the bottom frequently and skim with care; simmer 2½ hours. Take out the head; skin the tongue; mash eight potatoes with a wooden spoon; add two oz. of dripping and the boiling milk; place the potatoes on a flat dish; put the head on the potatoes, sprinkle over with salt, pepper and bread-crumbs. Put one oz. of dripping cut into small pieces on the head to baste it; put it into a quick oven, and bake half an hour. Serve in the same dish it is baked in. The potatoes and bread should both be a nice brown color. Take out the herbs, skim off all the fat, and serve the barley broth in a tureen.

11.—Mutton Steak and fried Potatoes.

Cut two steaks half an inch thick off the thick end of a leg of mutton. Put them on a gridiron over a quick bright fire for eight minutes; serve on a hot dish; mix half a teaspoonful of chopped parsley with one oz. of butter. Rub quickly over both sides of the steak, sprinkle with a little salt and pepper, and serve at once with fried potatoes round the dish.

Reserve the remainder of the leg to be served as follows :—

Ingredients.
2 onions chopped
3 saltspoonful of salt
1 teaspoonful of sugar
1 quart of water
1 lb. of rice
Some sliced lemon

Put the piece of mutton from which you have cut two steaks into a degchee with the onions, salt, sugar and water; boil up and skim carefully. Simmer very gently for ¾ of an hour, skimming frequently. Wash the rice, put it with the mutton, and simmer half an hour. Serve very hot, garnished with slices of lemon.

12.—Irish Stew

Ingredients.
A loin of mutton (or beef)
2 lbs. of potatoes
8 oz. of onions
1 teaspoonful of flour
1 saltspoonful of pepper
1 quart of cold water

Cut the potatoes into lumps (not sliced) and put a layer of them in the bottom of a degchee, with the onions sliced, the pepper and salt; then another layer of potatoes, and so on. Put the meat, cut into pieces on the *top*, sprinkle the flour over, pour over the cold water, and stew gently for eight hours.

13.—Sheep's Head.

Ingredients.
1 head and pluck
1 carrot
1 onion
1 head of celery
1 bunch of parsley
6 cloves
1 blade of mace
1 tablespoonful of salt
1 saltspoonful of salt
2 " " pepper
1 grain of cayenne
2 tablespoonful of flour
7 oz of butter
1 tablespoonful of ketchup
1 teaspoonful of Harvey sauce
1 teaspoonful of Soy
1 yolk of egg beaten
Some fine bread-crumbs

Split the head in halves and remove the brains; steep in water and wash thoroughly. Put the head, lights and liver in a degchee with the carrot, onion, celery, parsley, cloves, mace and salt; moisten with five pints of water: boil up and simmer slowly for 1½ hours. Take the head, &c. out carefully, and place them on a dish; strain the broth, remove all the grease. Trim the two halves of the head; mince the liver, lights, heart, tongue (having taken off the skin) and brains; season the mince with the salt, pepper, cayenne and flour, put it into a degchee with the strained broth, quarter ℔. of butter, ketchup, sauce and soy; stir frequently and simmer gently for an hour; brush the head over the beaten egg; strew it with fine bread-crumbs, and bake in a moderate oven for ¾ of an hour; baste frequently with dissolved butter; place the mince on a hot dish and the head (which should be of a pale brown color) in the centre, and serve at once.

14.—Sheep's Liver and Bacon.

Ingredients.
1 lb. sheep's liver
½ lb. bacon
1 desertspoonful of dry flour
¼ saltspoonful of salt
1 grain of pepper

Cut the bacon into thin slices, and the liver into slices ⅓ of an inch thick. Put the bacon into a frying pan and fry both sides brown; place it round a dish before the fire. Dredge both sides of the liver with flour, and fry it till brown (twenty minutes.) Place it neatly in the middle of the dish

MUTTON.

Pour away the fat, and dredge the dessertspoonful of flour into the frying pan, pour in a gill of boiling water, add the pepper and salt; shake the pan till the gravy thickens and browns; pour it over the liver, and serve at once.

(Another way.)

Cut the liver into slices two inches long and a quarter of an inch wide; wrap each piece in a sage leaf and then fold it in a thin slice of bacon, and fry in a frying pan. When they are done a light brown, stick them on silver skewers, six on each, and serve.

15.—Sheep's Brains with White Sauce.

Ingredients.
1 teaspoonful of vinegar
2 oz. of butter
Some flour
1 beaten egg
Some fine berad-crumbs
1 gill of new milk
The thin peel of one lemon
½ shalot
½ saltspoonful of salt
2 yolks of eggs
½ teaspoonful of lemon-juice
4 drops of Tarragon vinegar

Four sets of brains; lay them in hot water and put in the vinegar; steep half an hour; well wash them in cold water and dry in a cloth. Dip the brains in the butter (dissolved), and dredge them with flour; then dip them in beaten egg and strew them with the bread-crumbs. Fry in *plenty* of boiling lard slowly till of a light brown color, for 20 or 25 minutes. Serve neatly placed round the dish, with the following sauce in the centre:—

Boil the milk with the lemon-peel, shalot and salt; let it simmer ten minutes; beat the yolks, strain the milk, stir in the eggs; add the strained lemon-juice and the vinegar, and serve.

16.—Sheep's Kidneys, broiled.

Take off the skin and cut the kidneys in half; put them on an iron skewer, dip them into oiled butter, and sprinkle lightly with pepper and salt; put them on a gridiron over a bright fire, and broil for eight or ten minutes; withdraw the skewer, and serve on a very hot dish.

17.—Sheep's Kidneys stewed in Port Wine.

Ingredients.
8 *fresh* kidneys
½ saltspoonful white pepper
1 grain of cayenne
½ saltspoonful of salt
1 saltspoonful of parsley } finely
1 ,, ,, shalot, } chopped
1 tablespoonful of flour
3 oz. of butter
2 tablespoonsful of stock, No. 1
1 teaspoonful of red currant jelly
1 claret glassful of port wine

Trim off the pith and skin, and cut each kidney into four pieces; season with the pepper, cayenne, salt, parsley, shalot and flour. Put the butter into a small degchee, and when it begins to dissolve; put in the kidneys; shake the pan over a moderate heat until they are slightly browned; then add the stock, jelly, and port wine; put on the lid and do not remove it again; shake the pan and simmer gently for twenty minutes; turn out on a hot dish, and serve at once.

ENTREES OF MUTTON.

1.—Mutton Chops, plain.

Season with pepper and salt; heat the gridiron; lay on the chops, and broil over a clear fire (about ten minutes); turn frequently, and serve with a little chopped shalot and a pat of butter under each chop.

2.—Mutton Chops.
(Another way.)

Mince an onion and some parsley very fine, put this in a little oil and rub the cutlets well with the mixture, leave them to soak two hours, season with a little pepper and salt, and broil as directed above.

3.—Mutton Cutlets, Bread-crumbed.

The cutlets must be from the best end of a neck of mutton; each cutlet must have a bone in it and the meat should not be thicker than the bone; trim them neatly, scrape all the sinew off the bone so as to leave it bright and clean, and beat the cutlets flat with a chopper. Season the bread-crumbs with the salt, pepper and cayenne; dip the cutlets into the bread-crumbs, then into the beaten egg, then into the bread-crumbs again; broil in plenty of boiling fat till of a *pale* brown color, fifteen or twenty minutes. Serve with either a purée of potatoes or thick

Ingredients.
2 oz. of fine bread-crumbs
1 saltspoonful of salt
1 beaten egg,
(or 1 oz. of oiled butter)

purées of turnips, spinach, onions, carrots, chestnuts or Jerusalem artichokes in the centre.

Note.—It is very rare to see cutlets well prepared; they must be very carefully trimmed and thickly covered with bread-crumbs, so as to appear a smooth compact shape when they are served. The large, loose, untidy dark-brown sodden-looking cutlets which are usually served under that name are most unappetising.

4.—Mutton Cutlets with Portuguese Sauce.

Ingredients.
1 onion
1 large apple
½ clove of garlic
6 Sultana raisins
1 wineglassful of vinegar
1 teaspoonful of moist sugar
1 tablespoonful of gravy
4 pepper-corns
1 clove
1 wineglassful of port wine

Prepare the cutlets as directed above, place them in a circle round the dish with the following sauce in the centre:— Peel and chop the onion, the apple, the garlic and raisins; put them into a saucepan with the vinegar, sugar, gravy, pepper-corns and clove; simmer twenty minutes; add the port wine; rub through a sieve, and serve as directed.

5.—Mutton Cutlets with white Mushroom Sauce.

Ingredients.
Lemon juice
1 teaspoonful of salt
1 small teaspoonful of white pepper
The grated rind of ½ lemon
3½ oz. of butter
   Mushroom sauce
⅓ pint of new milk
1 shalot
¼ clove of garlic
1 small piece of thin lemon peel
3 sprigs of parsley
20 button mushrooms
1 pint of boiling water
1 teaspoonful of salt
The juice of one lemon
1 yolk of an egg
½ gill of cream

Have six or seven cutlets off the best end of a neck of mutton, trim off the fat, pith and gristle, and bare the bone one inch from the end. Rub each cutlet with lemon-juce, and season the whole with the salt, pepper, and lemon-rind; put them into a bright tin dish with the butter, and bake in a slow oven for ¾ of an hour. Put the milk into a bright saucepan with the shalot, garlic, peel and parsley; boil ten minutes and strain.

Peel the mushrooms; put them into the boiling water, with the salt and lemon-juice; boil up fast for ten minutes; drain. Beat the yolk with the cream, stir it into the milk; add the mushrooms; boil up for two minutes. Serve the sauce over the cutlets, which must be neatly placed on the dish, the ends of the bones meeting in the centre.

6.—Mutton Cutlets braised.

Ingredients.
1 teaspoonful of salt
1 saltspoonful of pepper
Some dried flour
Some garlic
2 oz. of butter
1 teacupful of good gravy

Prepare the cutlets as in the foregoing receipts, season with the salt and pepper, and dredge each cutlet with flour. Make a bright degchee hot, rub it four times across the bottom with garlic; put in the butter to dissolve; then put in the cutlets and brown both sides slowly; add the gravy, and simmer as gently as possible for half an hour. Serve with any purée of vegetables poured round; the cutlets being in the centre with the ends of the bones raised in the middle of the dish.

7.—Fillets of Mutton.

Ingredients of Pickle.
1 quart of water
1 pint of vinegar
4 cloves
4 pepper-corns
1 teaspoonful of salt
1 onion
1 carrot } sliced
¼ head of celery
1 bunch of parsley
1 ,, ,, thyme

Remove the fillet or meaty part wholly from the bone of a loin of mutton; pare away all the fat and sinew, and divide it across in the middle into two equal parts; sub-divide these *lengthways* into four fillets; if properly cut they will not require trimming. Put all the ingredients for the pickle into a basin, lard the fillets with fat bacon, lay them in the pickle, cover them over and leave them for four hours. Drain them and lay them in a bright tin dish with half oz. of butter under each and a gill of the clear pickle poured over them, and put them, in a quick oven to bake for quarter of an hour. Hold a salamander over them for a moment, and dish them up in a circle with any purée of vegetables or white mushroom sauce in centre.

SECOND DRESSINGS OF MUTTON.

1.—Saddle of Mutton à la Polonaise.

Ingredients.
½ pint of brown sauce or gravy
1 sprig of parsley
1 shalot chopped
1 saltspoonful of pepper
1 teaspoonful of salt
1 dessertspoonful of Oude sauce
12 potatoes
2 oz. of butter
2 yolks of eggs
1 saltspoonful of salt
½ ,, ,, pepper
Some bread-crumbs
1 white of an egg
4 eggs

Cut all the meat from a cold saddle and mince it fine; put it into a degchee with the gravy, parsley and shalot (chopped), the pepper, salt and Oude sauce; stir over the fire for ten minutes. Boil and mash the potatoes and stir them over the fire for a few minutes with a wooden spoon, adding the butter, two yolks, salt and pepper, until it becomes a firm paste. Fill up the bone of the saddle with this, leaving only a little space for the mince in the centre; when this is filled up the saddle should have assumed its original shape. Egg over the potato crust, strew the mince thickly with bread-crumbs, bake in the oven for half an hour till of a light brown color; poach the four eggs, place them on the saddle, pour a little gravy or sauce round the base, and serve.

Note.—This is a most excellent dish, and looks very nice.

2.—Mutton hashed Venison fashion.

Ingredients.
1 saltspoonful of salt
½ oz. of white pepper
1 desertspoonful of baked flour
¼ of a pint of strong gravy

Cut some slices of cold mutton ⅓ of an inch thick; trim off the skin and browned fat. Season with the pepper, salt and baked flour. Make

Ingredients for Mutton hashed Venison fashion.
1 kidney
1 shalot
½ carrot
2 oz. of sheep's liver
1 tablespoonful of red current jelly
½ wineglassful of port wine

some gravy with the bones and trimmings of the mutton and the kidney, shalot, carrot, and olive (all chopped)'; strain it, and put it with the mutton into a small degchee; put it over a slow fire and let it *scarcely* simmer for 1½ hours. Stir the red current jelly, add the wine, and serve immediately with a dish of French beans.

Plain Hashed Mutton is prepared in the same way as the above, omitting the jelly and wine. Serve with small sippets of toast round the dish, and the bones grilled.

3.—Fillet of Mutton.

Cut a neat compact piece (about 1½ lbs.) off a cold roast leg of mutton; put it into a degchee with the onion and mushrooms; knead the flour with the butter, put it into the degchee and add the lemon-juice, salt, pepper and gravy; simmer very gently for ¾ of an hour; shake the stewpan frequently, baste the mutton with the gravy, skim off all the fat, add the marsala, and serve at once.

Ingredients.
1 onion } finely
3 large mushrooms } chopped
1 oz. of butter
1 dessertspoonful of flour
The strained juice of a lemon
1 teaspoonful of salt
1 saltspoonful of pepper
1 teacupful of gravy
1 small wineglassful of marsala

4.—Pounded Mutton Cutlets with Tartar Sauce.

Cut half a pound of cold roast mutton, free it from skin and fat, put it into a mortar with the ham and garlic and pound it into a paste; season with the pepper, butter and gravy; mix well and let it stand in a cool place for an hour. Divide it into six parts, lay each in a

Ingredients.
1 oz. of cooked ham (or tongue)
1 piece of garlic the size of a pea
1 saltspoonful of pepper
1 oz. of dissolved butter
3 tablespoonsful of mutton gravy

piece of oiled paper and fold in the form of a cutlet and fry twelve minutes. Serve in the paper with Tartar sauce (No. 12) in a separate dish.

5.—Minced Mutton Cutlets with Tomato Sauce.

Cut one ℔. of cold mutton into thin slices, remove all fat and gristle; mince as fine as possible; season with salt, pepper, cayenne and shalot; put the isinglass into the mutton gravy to dissolve it; add it to the mince; put in the dissolved butter and stir until firm. Form the mince into seven or eight cutlets; dip them first into beaten egg and then into flour, and let them stand in a cool place for an hour. Dip them again into beaten egg and flour, and fry them in plenty of boiling fat over a quick fire for eight minutes. Serve the cutlets round the dish and the tomato sauce (No. 34) in the centre.

Ingredients.
1 teaspoonful of salt
1 ,, ,, pepper
1 grain of cayenne
½ shalot (chopped)
4 tablespoonsful of mutton gravy
1 drachm of isinglass
1 oz. of dissolved butter
1 beaten egg
Some flour

These cutlets may also be served with any purée of vegetables instead of the tomato sauce, or with celery or Soubise sauce (*see* recipe.)

6.—Minced Mutton with Macaroni.

Chop the mutton quite fine and season with the salt, pepper and flour; rub a degchee three times across the bottom with garlic; put in the mutton and add the gravy, ketchup, sauce, pickle and brandy; simmer gently and stir occasionally for half an hour. Boil the ma-

Ingredients.
¾ lb. of cold mutton
1 saltspoonful of salt
1 ,, ,, pepper
1 tablespoonful of flour
1 teacupful of gravy
1 dessertspoonful of walnut ketchup
1 tablespoonful of Oude sauce
1 dessertspoonful of walnut pickle
1 desertspoonful of brandy or rum
½ lb. of macaroni

M

Ingredients for Minced Mutton with Macaroni.
1 quart of water
½ pint of new milk
1 oz. of butter
½ saltspoonful of salt
1 ,, ,, mustard (made)
¼ grain of cayenne

caroni in the water for half an hour; drain; put it into a saucepan with the milk, butter, salt, mustard and cayenne, and simmer very gently till tender (about a quarter of an hour or twenty minutes.) Place it round the dish in the form of a wall, put the mince in the centre, and serve.

7.—Mutton with Mushrooms.

Cut the mutton into neat slices a quarter of an inch thick,
Ingredients.
1 lb. of cold roast leg
1 onion
3 oz. of butter
1 teaspoonful of salt
1 saltspoonful of pepper
¼ grain of cayenne
4 large mushrooms
½ teacupful of mutton gravy

and trim off the fat and gristle; rub a pie-dish four times across the bottom with garlic; chop the onion quite fine; put it into the dish with one oz. of the butter; season the meat with the salt, pepper and cayenne; put half of it into the dish; peel the mushrooms, cut them into slices, lay them on the meat; add one oz. of the butter in four pieces; put in the rest of the meat, add another ounce of butter; pour over the mutton gravy; cover closely with another dish, and bake in a slow oven for ¾ of an hour. Serve very hot.

VEAL.

1.—Chump end of the loin of Veal stuffed and roasted.

Ingredients.
4 oz. of suet
1 oz. of lean ham
1 egg, hard-boiled
1 oz. of fine bread-crumbs
1 saltspoonful of white pepper
1 teaspoonful of chopped parsley
1 teaspoonful of mixed herbs
Grated rind of ½ lemon
2 raw eggs
2 oz. of butter
1 dessertspoonful of flour
½ saltspoonful of salt
Some cut lemon

If possible keep the veal three or four days. Make a stuffing by chopping the suet and the yolk of the hard-boiled egg quite fine; add the ham pounded, the bread-crumbs, pepper, parsley, herbs, and lemon rind; mix all well together; add two yolks well beaten and *one white ;* with sharp knife loosen the skin round the thick part of the joint; put in the stuffing; secure it with skewers. Butter a sheet of white paper, fasten it over the veal and hang it *close* to a good fire for twenty minutes; then withdraw it to a distance and roast slowly till done, allowing 26 minutes to the pound; baste frequently; half an hour before serving remove the paper that the veal may become nicely browned. Knead the two ounces of butter with the flour, and stir into ⅓ of a pint of boiling water; add the salt, and boil ten minutes; pour off the dripping; stir the veal gravy into the melted butter; place the veal on a hot dish, the broad side downwards, pour the gravy over, and serve at once with the cut lemon on a plate.

2.—Loin of Veal à la Creme.

Get the kidney end of the loin of veal; wrap it securely in

buttered paper fastened with some string; hang it close to a good fire for twenty minutes, then at a distance for 1½ hours; then put a clean dish under it and baste it all over continuously with a pint of cream; as the veal turns round and round, this will form a delicate light brown crust; when removing the veal to serve it up great care must be taken not to knock this crust off. Knead two ounces of butter with one dessertspoonful of flour, and stir into ⅓ of a pint of boiling water; simmer ten minutes. Cut a round of bread ⅓ of an inch thick, take off the crust, toast a pale brown color; place the veal on the toast; pour off the dripping; add the gravy to the melted butter and pour it round the veal, *not over* it. Twelve button mushrooms or one pint of peas may be added to the sauce.

Note.—All joints of veal may be dressed in this fashion.

3.—Small Fricandeau of Veal.

Have about three lbs. of veal, either the middle of the loin or the best end of the neck; cut it off in one compact piece; trim off the skin and fat, and lard it thickly with the bacon; rub the bottom of the degchee across three times with the garlic; place in the veal with all the ingredients except the wine or brandy; cover the larding with writing paper, thickly buttered; simmer it as gently as possible for three hours; take off the paper, baste the veal, and continue to simmer half an hour longer. Take out the veal, skim off all the fat, and rub the gravy and vegetables through a hair

Ingredients.
Some fat bacon
Some garlic, fresh cut
1 onion }
1 small carrot } sliced
1 mushroom, chopped
½ lettuce
2 cloves
1 small blade of mace
¼ allspice
1 saltspoonful of salt
½   ,,   ,, pepper
1 teaspoonful of moist sugar
¾ pint of cold water
1 tablespoonful of good brandy,
or 1 wineglassful of sherry

sieve or coarse cloth; add the brandy or wine, and serve the gravy over the veal.

Note.—The cold Fricandeau makes an excellent Mayonnaise—*see* receipt for Mayonnaise of fowl.

A large Fricandeau is cut from the prime piece of the fillet, six inches long and four broad. Proceed exactly as in the above, but instead of the wine add the strained juice of one lemon, and serve with a purée of either spinach, sorrel, or young green peas and a cupful of the gravy.

4.—Stewed Breast of Veal with White Sauce.

Ingredients.
Some fresh cut garlic
2 shalots
1 blade of mace
The thin rind of ½ lemon
1 sprig of thyme
3 ,, ,, parsley
1 teaspoonful of salt
1 saltspoonful of white pepper
2 yolks of eggs
½ gill of thick cream

Heat a small degchee and rub it four times across the bottom with garlic; have a neatly cut square piece of breast of veal, about three ℔s., place it in a degchee; tie the shalots, mace, lemon-peel, thyme and parsley in a muslin bag; put them into the degchee also; add a pint of water; boil up quickly, skim; add the salt and pepper, and simmer as gently as possible for 3½ hours. Beat the yolks with the cream; take out the muslin bags; skim every particle of fat off the veal, stir in the egg and cream and serve at once.

Note.—It is a good addition to boil 1½ pints of green-peas, and put them into the sauce five minutes before serving.

5.—Stewed Breast of Veal with Oysters.

Ingredients.
2½ lbs. of veal
1 large onion
2 cloves
1 blade of mace

Get a nice piece of breast of veal cut in a neat square; put it in a degchee with the onions, cloves, mace, cinnamon, parsley and thyme all tied up

Ingredients for Stewed Breast of Veal with Oysters.

1 inch of cinnamon
1 sprig of parsley
1 small sprig of thyme
The juice of 1 large lemon
The liquor of 3 dozen oysters
3 yolks of eggs
1 gill of cream
3 dozen oysters

loosely in a muslin bag; strain in the lemon-juice and oyster liquor; simmer very gently for three hours, and skim often. Take out the bag; beat the yolks with the cream; put in the oysters, simmer five minutes, stir till the sauce thickens, and serve.

6.—Galatine of Veal.

Have a piece of the breast of veal twelve inches long and

Ingredients.

1 dessertspoonful of sifted sugar
1 ,, ,, salt
1 onion,
1 lettuce,
1 carrot,
1 turnip,
} all sliced
12 eggs
1 teaspoonful of Anchovy sauce
1 saltspoonful of white pepper
The grated rind of 1 lemon
2 teaspoonsful of chopped parsley
1 ,, ,, mixed herbs in fine powder
3 oz. of dissolved butter
½ lb. of mild lean ham
4 truffles
1 piece of fresh cut garlic
½ saltspoonful of salt
The strained juice of a lemon

seven broad; put it into a degchee which will just hold it and sufficient water to cover it well; add the sugar, salt, and sliced vegetables; boil up quickly, skim; simmer gently for two hours. Boil the eggs hard, pound the yolks; add the Anchovy sauce, white pepper, grated rind, parsley, herbs and butter, mix well.

Cut the ham into strips half inch broad and three inches long, and as thin as possible; slice the truffles. Take out the veal, remove the bones and gristle and lay it flat, the skin downwards; rub the surface with the garlic, three times across; sprinkle over the salt, rub in the lemon-juice; spread the egg paste equally over; lay on the ham and truffles in lines; roll up the veal as lightly as possible; sew it up in a strong cloth; put it back into the pot with the bones and pieces and simmer *very* gently three hours longer. Take out the veal, place it between two boards, with a heavy weight on the upper one; when cold remove the cloth. May be glazed or garnished with savoury jelly.

Note.—Reserve the liquor for soup in an uncovered earthen pan.

7.—Veal and Ham Pie.

Ingredients.
1½ lbs. of veal cutlets
¼ lb. of mild ham
4 button mushrooms
1 shalot
1 saltspoonful of salt
1½ ,,   ,,   white pepper
1 oz. of butter
1 dessertspoonful of Harvey sauce
1 gill of veal broth or cold water
1 tablespoonful of flour
The strained juice of 1 lemon
4 eggs

Paste.
½ lb. of flour
½ gill of cold water
The juice of ½ large lemon
7 oz. of butter

Have the cutlets free from skin and bones, cut it into 1½ inch pieces; cut the ham as thin as it can be cut, and then into 1½ inch pieces; chop the mushrooms and shalot and fry them with butter in a small degchee; add the pepper and salt, the sauce, broth and flour, and stir over the fire till it boils; then add the lemon-juice. Butter the edge of a 10-inch pie-dish; put in the veal and ham in layers; pour in the sauce, and finish with a layer of hard-boiled eggs. Make a paste as follows:—Moisten the flour with the water and lemon-juice; press the paste out on a slab; put the butter in the centre; cover it up; roll out four times, then let it stand for two hours in a cool place or on ice; then take a sixth part of the paste; roll it out thin and line the edge of the dish with it; moisten with cold water; roll the remainder out the size of the dish; put it over, press the edge to make it adhere; trim round with a sharp knife and notch at inch distances; make a hole in the centre for the steam to escape, ornament to fancy, and bake in a moderate oven for two hours. Serve with cut lemon.

Note.—If ham cannot be obtained streaky bacon may be substituted.

8.—Veal Cutlets.

Ingredients.
1¼ lbs. of fillet of veal
8 oz. of butter
Some baked flour
Fine bread-crumbs
1 dessertspoonful of baked flour
The strained juice of 1 lemon
½ saltspoonful of salt
½ gill of water
12 button mushrooms
9 thin rashers of bacon

The fillet should be about ⅓ of an inch thick; cut it into nine oblong pieces, all of the same size; trim off the skin, fat, and corners; dip each piece into t oz. of dissolved butter and dredge it lightly with flour; let them stand ten minutes; then dip them again into butter and strew them on both sides with bread-crumbs; fry in the remainder of the butter, eight oz., *boiling*, at some distance from the fire for twenty minutes; they must be of a *pale* brown color on both sides. Strain the butter, mix in the flour, lemon-juice, salt, and water (boiling) and mushrooms; boil up, skim, and simmer ten minutes (in the frying pan). Roll the rashers, put a skewer through them and roast before the fire while the cutlets are frying; place the veal and bacon alternately round the dish, and the sauce in the centre. Serve very hot.

9.—Veal Cutlets à la Maintenon.

(In paper.)

Ingredients.
1 oz. of bread-crumbs
2 ,, ,, fat bacon
1 small shalot
1 sprig of parsley
A large mushroom (or a truffle)
Grated rind of ½ a lemon
One tenth of a nutmeg
A saltspoonful of mixed sweet herbs
½ a saltspoonful of salt
½ a ,, ,, pepper

Chop very finely the bacon, bread-crumbs, shalot, parsley, and mushroom (or truffle). Mix them together, add the grated lemon, rind, nutmeg, sweet herbs, salt and pepper. Cut three chops off the best end of the neck of veal; take off the skin and the chine part of the bone; cover three sheets of foolscap paper with three ounce of butter; dissolve two ounce of butter, dip the cutlets into it, and then into the seasoned crumbs; lay each on a sheet of paper, roll the edge tightly round, preserving the shape of the cutlet, and boil slowly in plenty of lard for an hour, drain on a sieve before the fire, and serve in the paper.

10.—Veal Cutlets, braised with fresh Tomatos.

Ingredients.
1½ lbs. of veal cutlet
¼ lb. of butter
1 dessertspoonful of baked flour
3 anchovies
½ a clove of garlic
1 oz. of mild lean ham
1 small onion
6 fine ripe tomatos
⅙th of a nutmeg grated
½ of a saltspoonful of white pepper
1 grain of cayenne
1 dessertspoonful of lemon juice
1 saltspoonful of vinegar
2 tablespoonsful of marsala or sherry

Trim the skin off the veal and cut it into eight neat pieces; place the cutlets and butter in a stewpan; when the butter dissolves dredge over the flour, and let them very slowly become a pale brown colour on both sides. Clean and pound to paste the anchovies, garlic and ham; peel and slice the onion and tomatos, and the nutmeg, white pepper, cayenne, lemon-juice, vinegar, marsala or sherry; put all these ingredients into the stewpan with the cutlets and simmer as slowly as possible for an hour and a quarter; skim frequently, and shake the stewpan to prevent burning at the bottom. Serve quite hot.

11.—Sweetbreads, with Truffles.

Ingredients.
Sweetbreads
¼ of a lb. of butter
Some baked flour
6 truffles
1 gill of marsala
1 saltspoonful of salt
1   ,,   ,, white pepper
1 dessertspoonful of lemon-juice
1 gill of stock, (No. 2)
1 dessertspoonful of baked flour
2 oz. of butter

Blanch the sweetbreads in boiling water five minutes and in cold for an hour; remove the fat, skin and pith; dry them, and dredge them lightly with baked flour; place them on a tin dish and baste well with the dissolved butter; bake till nicely browned, about half an hour.

Peel and slice the truffles; put them into a stewpan with the marsala, salt, white pepper, and lemon-juice; simmer ten minutes, and add the stock. Knead the baked flour and butter, and stir in for five minutes; put in the sweetbreads, and continue to simmer half an hour longer; then serve.

Note.—For other ways of dressing sweetbreads, *see* Lamb sweetbreads.

12.—Croûstade of Sweetbreads, Mushrooms, and Potato Balls.

Ingredients.
A 2 lb. loaf, one day old
½ lb. of oiled butter
2 sweetbreads
A dessertspoonful of baked flour
Garlic
2 oz. of butter
1 teaspoonful of salt
1 saltspoonful of white pepper
⅙th of a grated nutmeg
Thin rind of ½ a lemon
4 sprigs of parsley
Half a blade of mace
2 cloves
Strained juice of a lemon
2 tablespoonsful of white wine
A teacupful of veal stock, (No. 2)
The yolks of 2 eggs
A gill of thick cream
20 button mushrooms
1 saltspoonful of salt
The juice of a lemon
4 potatoes
½ a saltspoonful of salt
1 oz. of fresh butter
¼ of a gill of cream
One well beaten egg
Some milk

The loaf to be baked in an oval cake-tin. Cut off the top above the tin; scoop out the crumb, leaving ¾ of an inch all round and at the bottom; pare off the crust, dip the case into the oiled butter, and put it into the oven for twenty minutes; redip it in the butter, and let it remain in the oven till of a pale bright brown colour. (Or a paste case may be used, *see* note.) Cut off the pith and skin of the sweetbreads, and blanch them in boiling water for five minutes. Cut into equal sized pieces, and throw them into cold water for an hour; take them out, wipe them dry, and dredge over the baked flour. Rub a bright stewpan four times across the bottom with garlic, put in the butter, sweetbreads, salt, white pepper, nutmeg, rind of lemon, parsley, mace, cloves, lemon-juice, white wine, and veal stock; boil up quickly, skim; then simmer gently for three quarters of an hour.

Take out the sweetbreads; skim and strain the sauce; add the eggs beaten up with the cream; boil two minutes. Skin the mushrooms; throw them into a pint of boiling water, with the salt and lemon-juice; boil fast for twelve minutes, and drain on a sieve. Boil the potatoes, add the salt, butter, cream and beaten egg and put them into fast boiling milk for two minutes; then drain on a sieve. Put the sweetbreads, mushrooms, and potato-balls in alternate layers into the bread case, and pour the sauce over; serve quite hot, with a neatly rolled napkin on the dish.

Note.—Make a paste (*see* Veal Patties), roll it out, the last time an inch and a quarter thick; cut it with a vol-au-vent cutter six inches in diameter. Make an incision a quarter of an inch deep, with a cutter an inch smaller; bake about three-quarters of an hour. Take out the centre, and proceed as directed.

13.—Veal Patties.

Ingredients.

The juice of a lemon
1 gill of cold water
¾ lb. of sifted flour
¾ lb. of fresh butter
½ lb. of lean veal
2 oz. of ham
The grated rind of ½ a lemon
One tenth of a grated nutmeg
½ saltspoonful white pepper
½ „ „ salt
1 teaspoonful of Parmesan cheese grated
1 tablespoonful of baked flour
Some veal stock
Strained juice of ½ a lemon
½ a gill of thick cream

Put the lemon-juice in the water, and stir in sufficient to moisten the flour; knead to a smooth paste; lay it on a slab, and spread the butter over it; turn over the four sides; dredge it with flour, and roll out. Do this four times; then fold it in three, and let it stand in a cool place for two or three hours. Roll out again twice, the second time a third of an inch thick. Have ready two circular patty cutters; one 2½ inches across, and the other 1½ inch. Dip the cutters into flour, and cut out eight of the larger size; press the smaller size on the centre of each piece of paste, cutting it ⅛th of an inch deep. Roll out the remainder of the paste, and cut out eight of the smaller size. Place them all on a baking tin, and bake in a quick oven till of a pale brown colour, about twenty minutes. Take them out, and with a sharp penknife remove the centre paste from the larger pieces; fill the vacancy with veal prepared as follows, then place the smaller piece over the centre, and serve immediately. Mince quite small the veal and ham, season with the lemon rind, nutmeg, white pepper, salt, cheese and baked flour. Put it in a saucepan with sufficient veal stock to well moisten it, and simmer gently; stirring constantly for a quarter of an hour. Add the strained juice of half a lemon, and the cream; then fill the patties as directed.

14.—Calf's Head, boiled, with White Sauce.

Ingredients.

A calf's head
A teacupful of vinegar
A tablespoonful of salt
A pan of cold water
A sage leaf
A sprig of parsley
¼ oz. of butter
½ a saltspoonful of salt
2 grates of a nutmeg
A cut lemon
3 oz. of butter
2 tablespoonsful of baked flour
¼ a gill of thick cream
Strained juice of ½ a lemon
15 button mushrooms or a dessertspoonful of finely chopped parsley.

Put the vinegar and salt into a pan of cold water and soak the head in it for about twenty minutes; then well wash it in fresh water; trim off the rough black pieces from the mouth; take out the tongue and brains and put them in cold water. Put the head into a big degchee, the split side downwards, and entirely cover it with cold water. Boil up quickly, then skim, and simmer very gently till done. Be careful to keep the head well covered with water. Half of a *very* small head will require an hour and three quarters from the time of boiling up; a moderate size, two hours and twenty minutes. Tie the brain in a piece of muslin with the sage leaf and parsley.

Put in the tongue and brains three quarters of an hour before the head is done. Rub the brains through a sieve or coarse cloth; put them into a saucepan with half ounce of butter, half saltspoonful of salt, and two grates of nutmeg. Skin and trim the tongue; put it on a small dish, and pour the brains over it. Lay the head upon a hot dish, the split side downwards, and serve immediately with a cut-lemon upon a plate and a white sauce (*see* Sauces) poured over it, with either the mushrooms or parsley.

Note.—Reserve the liquor in an earthen pan uncovered for stock or soup.

15.—Calf's Head Brawn.

Get the half of a fine large calf's head with the skin on. Take out the brains, and bone it entirely; rub a little fine salt over it, and leave it to drain for twelve hours. Wipe it dry; mix the saltpetre, salt, and bay salt, and powder them very fine; rub this well into every part of the head; leave it in this pickle for four or five days, turning it daily, and rubbing in a little of the pickle each time; then pour the treacle over it; continue to turn it every day and baste it with the brine for a month. Then hang it up for a night to drain; wrap it in brown paper, and send it to be smoked where wood only is burned, from three to four weeks. When wanted for table wash and scrape it very clean but do not soak it; lay it with the rind downwards in a saucepan which will hold it easily; cover it well with cold water as it will swell considerably in the cooking; let it heat rather slowly; skim it when it first begins to simmer, and boil it as gently as possible for two hours, or even more should it not be *thoroughly* tender all

Ingredients of the Pickle.
¾ of an oz. of saltpetre
4 oz. of common salt
3 oz. of bay salt
4 oz. of treacle

through. When the fleshy side of the head is done, which will be twenty miuutes or half an hour sooner than the outside, pour some of the water off it, leaving only enough to cover the gelatinous part, and simmer this until it is *quite* tender.

This head will be found most delicious eating with Oxford Brawn sauce (*see* recipe.)

16.—Calf's Feet with Sharp Sauce.

Ingredients.

2 feet
2 oz. of fine bread-crumbs
1 saltspoonful of salt
½ ,,   ,, white pepper
2 grates of nutmeg
½ clove of garlic, chopped fine
2 beaten eggs
Salad oil ⅓ of a pint or 6 oz. of dissolved butter

Boil the feet for four hours in sufficient water to cover them; simmer and skim occasionally; split them, and trim off any rough pieces, and roll them in a cloth to dry; season the bread-crumbs with the salt, pepper, nutmeg and garlic; mix these ingredients well. Dip the feet into the beaten egg, then in the crumbs; let them remain a quarter of an hour; then redip them and fry either in the oil or butter about ten minutes till of a pale brown color. Serve very hot with the sharp sauce on a separate dish.

Sharp Sauce.

Two tablespoonsful of vinegar, one dessertspoonful of brown sugar, one teaspoonful of mustard, mix well.

17.—Calf's Brains, fried.

Ingredients.

1 gill of vinegar
1 dessertspoonful of salt
2 tablespoonful of baked flour
2 eggs
1 claret glass of cream
½ lb. of butter
1 bunch of parsley

Two sets of brains; take off the skin; wash them in cold water, and cut them into thin slices, then throw them into two quarts of boiling water, with the vinegar and salt; let them remain an hour; wash them again in cold water, and roll them in a cloth to dry.

Make the batter with the flour, eggs and cream, and beat with a wooden spoon for twenty minutes. Dissolve the butter in the frying pan; dip each piece of brain into the butter and fry to a pale yellow color over a gentle fire; serve with fried parsley.

Wash a bunch of parsley, dip it in the boiling butter for three minutes and dry on a sieve before the fire; place it in the centre of the dish with the brains round it. Serve very hot.

Note.—May also be served with Mayonnaise Sauce. An excellent dish.

18.—Calf's Brains with White Sauce.

Ingredients.
2 sets of brains
1 onion sliced
4 sprigs of parsley
½ pint of veal broth
1 lemon
1 saltspoonful of salt

Clean and branch the brains as in the preceding receipt, and cut each into four pieces, put them into a small saucepan with the onion, parsley and broth; simmer for three-quarters of an hour. Take out the brains, strain the sauce and prepare white sauce (*see* Sauces) with it. When it is ready put in the brains with the juice strained, and the salt, simmer ten minutes, and serve.

Note.—The brains may also be served with Dutch Sauce.

19.—Calf's Brains with Brown Sauce.

Ingredients.
2 sets of brains
2 tablespoonsful of vinegar
1½ teaspoonful of salt
1 clove of garlic

Take off the skin; wash the brains well in cold water; put them into a stewpan with a quart of water, one tablespoonful of vinegar, one teaspoonful of

Ingredients of Calf's Brains with Brown Sauce.
2 oz. of butter
Some baked flour
2 shalots
2 mushrooms
1 tablespoonful of rum
⅓ of a nutmeg grated
1½ grain of cayenne
1 teaspoonful of loaf sugar
1 saltspoonful of curry powder
1 oz. of butter
1 dessertspoonful of baked flour
1 claret glass of stock (No. 1)

salt, the garlic, and boil for a quarter of an hour; drain on a sieve. Dissolve the butter; dip in the brains, dredge with the flour; place them on a tin dish and bake in a moderate oven three-quarters of an hour; baste frequently with the butter. Chop the shalots and mushrooms, put them into a saucepan with a tablespoonful of vinegar, the rum, nutmeg, cayenne, sugar, and curry powder, and stir over the fire for ten minutes. Knead the ounce of butter with the dessertspoonful of baked flour, add the stock, simmer and stir for quarter of an hour. Place the brains on a hot dish, pour over the sauce, and serve.

20.—Kabobes and Kedcheree.

Ingredients.
1½ lbs. of veal cutlets
1 wineglassful of vinegar
1 saltspoonful of Tarragon vinegar
1 teaspoonful of salt
¼ clove of garlic bruised
½ pint of split peas
¼ lb. of rice
3 onions
6 oz. of butter
1 teaspoonful of salt
¼ of a saltspoonful of cardamoms
⅛ of a nutmeg grated
2 beaten eggs
1½ tablespoonful of curry powder
¼ of a lb. of butter
1 lemon

Cut the cutlets a third of an inch thick; and then into neat pieces two inches square; put them into ¾ of a pint of water with the two kinds of vinegar, salt and garlic. Let them remain an hour. Wash the split peas, and boil them for 2½ hours in a pint of water; add the rice (well washed) and continue to boil for 25 minutes, stirring frequently to keep it from burning. Chop the onions, fry in eight ounces of butter till slightly browned; drain off the water, add the peas and rice to the onions, season with the salt, cardamoms and nutmeg. Stir and fry till the butter is all absorbed, and the whole is of a pale brown color; then stir in the water drained from the rice and peas. Wipe the veal dry, dip each piece in a beaten egg, then in the curry powder, and fry slowly in a quarter of a pound of butter till nicely browned on both sides (about 25 minutes.) Lay in the centre of a hot dish, pour over the strained juice of the lemon, place the **kedcheree** round it, and serve at once.

21.—Potted Veal and Tongue.

Ingredients.
¾ of a lb. of cold roast or braised veal
¼ lb. of cold tongue
2 tablespoonsful of veal gravy
1½ teaspoonful of anchovy sauce
½ mustardspoonful of fresh made mustard
1½ saltspoonful of white pepper
3 grates of nutmeg
7 oz. of dissolved butter
Garlic

The meat must be quite free both from bone, skin, fat and gristle. Mince and then pound in a mortar, till in soft paste; add the gravy while pounding; season with the sauce, mustard, pepper and nutmeg. Cross the bottom of the pestle once with garlic, continue to pound until the seasoning and meat are well mixed, then add five ounces of dissolved butter. When the whole is soft and smooth press it into a raised pie-dish or large gallipot, flatten the top with a knife, and pour over two ounces of dissolved butter.

PORK.

1.—Roast Loin of Pork, seasoned.

Ingredients.
1 large onion
1 saltspoonful of finely powdered sage
½ saltspoonful of white pepper
2 ,, of flour of mustard
Some butter and salt

Score the skin with a very sharp knife at half inch distances. Soak the onion in cold water and plenty of salt for an hour; then chop it quite fine; add the sage, pepper, and mustard; mix this seasoning well together and rub it over the pork; spread a sheet of white paper with butter, fold it round the pork, and roast before a brisk fire at a distance allowing half an hour to the pound, and basting frequently; half an hour before serving take off the paper and continue to baste till the pork is nicely browned and the skin crisp. Pour off the fat; add a gill of boiling water or thin stock to the gravy dripped from the meat. Pour it into a hot dish, place the pork on it, skin uppermost, and serve with a tureen of apple or tomato sauce. (*See* Sauces.)

2.—Loin of Pork, French fashion.

Ingredients.
A small loin of pork
A gill of salad oil
2 teaspoonsful of salt
A saltspoonful of white pepper
A small onion
Half a clove of garlic

Put a small loin of pork (about 3½ lbs.) into a pie-dish, with the salad oil, salt, white pepper, onion (finely chopped), garlic (chopped), sweet herbs, chopped parsley, and grated

Ingredients of Loin of Pork, French fashion

A teaspoonful of mixed sweet herbs
A teaspoonful of parsley
⅙th of a nutmeg

Ingredients of Sauce.

One sour apple
2 shalots
The juice of a lemon
A teaspoonful of moist sugar
¼ of a grain of cayenne
A mustardspoonful of fresh made mustard
½ a saltspoonful of salt
⅓ of a pint of stock (NO. 1.)
A tablespoonful of brandy

nutmeg; rub the ingredients well into the pork; cover the dish and let it stand for two days; then hang it before a good fire, and roast at a distance for two hours; baste constantly, either with salad oil or dissolved butter.

Serve with gravy made as follows:—Peel and mince the apple and two shalots; put them into a saucepan, with strained lemon-juice, moist sugar, cayenne, mustard, salt, and stir over the fire until browned; add the stock and boil for a quarter of an hour; stir in a tablespoonful of brandy; strain and serve in the dish, but not poured over the pork.

3.—Fillets of Pork, with Apple Sauce.
(Second dressing.)

Cut up about ¾ of a pound of cold roast pork into slices

Ingredients.

¾ lb. of cold roast pork
3 oz. of fine bread-crumbs
A saltspoonful of white pepper
A grain of cayenne
A saltspoonful of salt
⅙th of a nutmeg
2 oz. of butter
3 shalots or a small onion

the sixth of an inch thick; season the bread-crumbs with the white pepper, cayenne, salt, and nutmeg (grated); dissolve the butter slightly (not to oil); dip the pork into the butter, then into the crumbs, lay it in a tin dish; chop the shalots or onion, and strew over; pour the remainder of the butter over, and bake in a moderate oven for ¾ of an hour. Serve with Apple or Tomato sauce; lay the pork tastefully round the sauce. (*See* Sauces.)

4.—Pork Cutlets with Mushroom Sauce.

Cut six or eight chops, the width of the bone from the

Ingredients of Pork Cutlets with Mushroom Sauce.

The strained juice of a lemon
1 teaspoonful of salt
1 saltspoonful of white pepper
1 small onion
2 sprigs of spersley (*finely chopped.*)
1 tablespoonful of good oil

Ingredients of Sauce.

12 button mushrooms
½ saltspoonful of salt
1 grain of cayenne
1 grate of nutmeg
1 teaspoonful of tarragon vinegar
The juice of ½ lemon
1 oz. of butter
3 tablespoonsful of stock
1   ,,   ,, marsala

foreloin of small pork; trim off the fat and bare the end of the bone about one inch. Mix all the ingredients together; rub them well over the cutlets and let them remain two hours; dip each one into beaten egg and then into fine bread-crumbs. Dissolve some fat in a bright frying pan and fry the cutlets in it till of a pale brown color; (about twenty minutes); drain on a sieve before the fire, pour the following sauce over, and serve instantly.

Peel, clean and chop the mushrooms; season them with the salt, cayenne, nutmeg, vinegar and lemon-juice; put them into a small saucepan with the butter, and stir over the fire for ten minutes; add the stock, boil up quickly for five minutes, stir in the marsala, and serve at once.

5.—Bath Chap.

Soak the chap for twelve hours in cold water; scrape and wash it; put it into a saucepan with plenty of cold water, and boil gently for 2½ hours. Take off the skin, trim off the rough parts, and serve either with broad beans, brussels sprouts, or young greens, as a garnish.

6.—Roast Sucking Pig.

Ingredients.

4 fine onions
1 dozen sage leaves
2 oz. of butter
½ lb. of fine bread-crumbs

Chop the onions and sage leaves; fry them in the butter over a slow fire for ten minutes; then add the bread-crumbs, yolks, salt and pepper. With this stuff

Ingredients of Roast Sucking Pig.
2 yolks of eggs
3 saltspoonsful of salt
2 ,, ,, pepper
Some brown sauce and melted butter

ing fill the paunch of the sucking pig; sew it up securely, and roast it before a bright fire for two hours; close for ten minutes and then at a distance, basting frequently with a paste brush dipped in salad oil. When the pig is done, and before removing it from the spit, cut off the head and divide the pig in half by sawing it straight down the spine. Dish it up with brown gravy; put some more in a sauce-boat, and put in a little of the stuffing reserved for the purpose, the brains and a few spoonsful of melted butter.

7.—Roast sucking Pig with Chestnuts.

Prepare as above, but prepare the stuffing as directed for roast turkey and chestnuts. *(See* recipe.*)*

8.—To boil a Ham.

Soak the ham in plenty of cold water for 24 hours; put it into a large pot with plenty of *cold* water; boil up *slowly;* skim; then simmer very gently until done, allowing 28 minutes to the pound; take it up by the knuckle, to avoid putting a fork into the thick part and so letting out the juice; pull off the skin; trim off any rough brown pieces, and powder the ham over with brown baked bread-crumbs. Cut a frill of white paper three inches deep; roll it round the knuckle, and send it to table on a dry warm dish.

Note.—If the ham weighs more than 12 lbs. allow a quarter of an hour for each pound beyond that up to 16 lbs.; and beyond that weight ten minutes for each pound.

9.—Ham boiled in the French way.

Soak as directed above, and put into the water in which

it is to be boiled one quart of cider and a pint of vinegar with a large bunch of sweet herbs. When it is two-thirds done, skin it, cover it with brown baked bread-crumbs and set it in an oven, until it is done, (about 1½ or two hours). Decorate with a frill, and serve with or without spinach or greens as a garnish.

10.—Another French recipe for boiling Ham

After soaking, cleaning and trimming the ham, wrap it in a little very sweet, clean hay, and tie it up in a thin cloth; place it in a pan or ham kettle, as nearly its own size as possible, and cover it with two parts of water and one of white wine or cider; boil up and skim; then add five carrots, three onions, a large bunch of savoury herbs, and a clove of garlic. Let the whole simmer for four or five hours, or longer should the ham weigh over 16 lbs. When quite tender take off the skin, sprinkle with baked brown bread-crumbs, decorate with a frill, and serve.

11.—Baked Ham.

Ingredients.
1 large onion
3 carrots
1 head of celery
1 turnip
1 handful of parsley
4 cloves
10 peppercorns
1 blade of mace
1 clove of garlic
2 tablespoonsful of moist sugar

Ingredients of Paste.
2 lbs. of dripping
3 lbs. of flour
3 pints of bran

It should be a York Ham which has been kept about a year, and should weigh about 14 lbs. Soak it one night in cold water; scrape and well wash it; put it in an iron pot with the onion, carrots, celery turnip, parsley, cloves, peppercorns, mace, garlic, moist sugar, and enough water to cover it; boil up gently; skim; then simmer for two hours. Make a paste as follows:—Rub the dripping into the flour and bran; add enough hot water to make a firm paste; roll it out about one inch thick; put in the ham; press the paste round it that it may perfectly adhere and keep in the juice; place it on a tin dish and bake in a gentle oven for 6½ hours.

If it is to be served cold, let it remain in the paste until perfectly cold; then crack the paste, pull off the skin, wipe the fat with a soft clean cloth; bush it over thickly with glaze (*see* recipe); put a frill round the knuckle; garnish with savoury jelly or parsley, and serve. If it is to be used hot, garnish with spinach, brussels sprouts, mashed turnips or carrots.

Note.—Hams are far better if they are left to remain in their own liquor until cold, as this renders them far more succulent; but in small families this plan does not answer as they will not keep so long; and the same objection exists to serving ham upon, or closely garnished with savoury jelly, as it becomes unfit for the table far sooner than the hams themselves.

12.—Brawn.

Get a medium sized pig's head; split it open and remove the brains and all the bones; strew it thickly inside with salt, let it drain until the following day. Cleanse the ears and feet in the same manner; wipe them free from all brine, lay them (head, ears and feet) in a large pan, and rub them well with the saltpetre and sugar, mixed; leave them for twelve hours, then add six ounces of salt; leave them until the following day; then pour the

Ingredients of Pickle.
Some salt
1½ oz. of saltpetre
6 oz. of sugar
¼ of a pint of vinegar

Ingredients of Cooking.
1 large grated nutmeg
1½ teaspoonsful of mace
½ ,, ,, ,, cayenne
½ ,, ,, ,, cloves
1 large bunch of savoury herbs
2 moderate-sized onions
1 small head of celery
4 carrots
1 teaspoonful of peppercorns

vinegar over them, and leave them in the pickle for a week, turning them every day. Then wash the ears and feet and boil them for one and a half hours; bone the feet while they are warm, and trim the gristle from the large ends of the ears. When these are ready mix the nutmeg with the mace, cayenne and cloves. Wash, but do not soak the head; wipe and flatten it on a board; cut some of the flesh from the thickest parts; season the head, ears, and feet with the spices, and lay the head on its thickest part; fit in the ears and feet, roll it up very tight and bind it firmly with broad tape; fold a thin cloth quite closely round it and tie it securely at both ends. Place it in a pot or pan which will just hold it; put in the bones and trimmings of the feet and ears, together with the bunch of herbs, onions, celery, carrots, and peppercorns, and sufficient water to cover it well; boil very gently for four hours, and leave it till nearly cold in the liquor in which it was boiled. Then take it out, take off the cloth, and put the brawn between two dishes, with a heavy weight on the upper one. The next day take off the tape, and serve with Oxford brawn sauce. (*See* recipe.)

13.—Mock Brawn.

Ingredients.
Ears, eyepieces, feet and tongue of a medium-sized pig
1 ℔. of common salt
¼ oz. of saltpetre
2 ox-feet
Some savoury herbs
2 onions
2 carrots
½ teaspoonful of peppercorns

Clean the ears, eye-pieces, feet and tongue; rub them with the salt and saltpetre, and leave them for five days; put them in a pan with cold water, and boil them gently until they are quite tender; pull out the bones and cut the meat into pieces, the size of a walnut. Boil the ox-feet until perfectly tender; take out the bones and all the meat, leaving only the skin; press the skin flat on a board; cut up the nice part of the meat and mix with the pork. Place the meat on the skin; roll it up quite tight; put it into a strong cloth, sew it up; boil it for two hours, then press it into a round pan or mould which will just hold it; put a heavy weight on it, and let it remain until next day. Then turn out. Serve with Oxford brawn sauce, (*see* recipe.)

14.—Sausages and Chestnuts.

(An excellent French entrée.)

Ingredients.
40 fine chestnuts
Some butter
1 large teaspoonful of flour
½ pint of strong stock
2 glasses of white wine
1 small bunch of savoury herbs
1 saltspoonful of salt
¼   „   „   pepper
¼   „   „   cayenne

Roast and peel the chestnuts; fry the sausages gently in butter; when they are well browned take them out and pour the fat in which they have been fried into a bright degchee or saucepan; mix the flour with it; then pour in by degrees the stock and wine; add the herbs, salt, pepper and cayenne; boil up; lay in the sausages round the pan and the chestnuts in the centre; stew *very gently* for an hour; take out the herbs; dish the sausages neatly and pile up the chestnuts in the centre, strain the sauce over them, and serve very hot.

POULTRY.

1.—Boiled Turkey with Celery Sauce.

Chop the beef suet;

Ingredients of stuffing.
¼ lb. of beef suet
2 oz of fine bread-crumbs
1 tablespoonful of fresh chopped parsley
1 saltspoonful of salt
½ ,, ,, white pepper
⅛ of a nutmeg grated
The rind of ½ lemon grated
The strained juice of a lemon
½ saltspoonful of mixed sweet herbs
½ saltspoonful of thyme
2 well beaten fresh eggs
2 tablespoonsful of cream

mix it with the bread-crumbs and parsley, and season with the salt, pepper, nutmeg, lemon rind and juice, sweet herbs and thyme; add the eggs and cream. Put this stuffing into the b as of the turkey; fasten the skin loosely over it; rub the turkey with a cut lemon; cover the breast with thin slices of fat bacon; tie it over with a clean white cloth; put it into a large pot with sufficient water to cover it; boil up quickly, then *simmer gently* till done. A turkey weighing ten pounds will take two hours, one of fifteen pounds two hours and a half. Take it out of the cloth, remove the bacon, and pull out the skewers. Place the turkey on a hot dish; pour half a pint of the celery sauce (*see* recipe) over the breast; put the rest of the sauce in a tureen, and serve immediately.

2.—Boned Turkey served with Tongue and Forcemeat.

Cut the legs off the turkey; scald, trim, and set them aside; bone the turkey without removing the wings; prepare a veal forcemeat (*see* recipe) and nearly fill the inside of the turkey with it; boil a small pickled tongue slowly for two and a half hours; skin it and trim off the root, leaving only a portion of the fat; thrust it into the middle of the forcemeat; fasten the skin loosely over it, and then follow the preceding recipe in every particular.

Note.—Turkeys dressed in this fashion and covered with a thick Bechamel sauce (*see* recipe) instead of Celery sauce, and garnished with truffle, tongue, and aspic jelly (*see* recipe) make an excellent dish for ball suppers.

3.—Turkey stuffed and roasted.

Prepare the stuffing as follows:—Scrape the pork, veal, ham and suet; rub the bread crumbs to fine powder: add the parsley and mix well together. Season with the nutmeg, lemon-peel, pepper, cayenne, loaf sugar, salt and sweet herbs. Put the whole into a mortar and pound to a smooth paste; add the beaten eggs and lemon-juice; when well mixed, fill the crop of the turkey with it; fasten the skin loosely over it and put the remainder into the body; cover it over with sheets of white paper thickly buttered. Hang the turkey before a large fire, near for the first twenty minutes, then at a distance till done; baste frequently. A

Ingredients of stuffing.

½ lb. of lean pork
¼ lb. ,, ,, veal
2 oz. ,, ,, ham
½ lb. of beef suet
2 oz. of bread-crumbs
1 tablespoonful of chopped parsley
⅙ of a nutmeg grated
The peel of a lemon grated
1 saltspoonful of white pepper
1 grain of cayenne
1 saltspoonful of loaf sugar
1½ ,, ,, salt
2 ,, ,, sweet herbs
2 ,, ,, fine powder
3 well beaten eggs
The strained juice of a lemon

Gravy.

Some garlic
2 oz. of butter
1 onion
1 carrot
½ head of celery, sliced
1 lb. of lean beef
½ lb. ,, ,, veal
1 oz. ,, ,, ham
2 mushrooms
2 truffles
1 clove
¼ of an inch of mace
4 white peppercorns
1 teaspoonful of loaf sugar.
1 saltspoonful of flour of mustard

Ingredients of Gravy for Roast Turkey
1 saltspoonful of salt
4 sprigs of parsley
1 quart of water
1 tablespoonful of baked flour
1 wineglassful of white wine

turkey weighing nine pounds will require two and a quarter hours, and beyond that allow ten minutes more for every additional pound. Half an hour before serving take off the paper; dredge the turkey slightly with baked flour, and baste with dissolved butter until done. Make a gravy as follows:—Rub the degchee twice across the bottom with garlic; put in the butter, with the onion, carrot and celery sliced; add the beef, veal, ham, mushrooms, truffles, clove, mace, peppercorns, sugar, mustard, salt and parsley. Let it stand by the fire for an hour to brown the meat and extract the gravy; add the warm water, and simmer gently (skimming frequently) for three and a half hours. Mix the flour with the white wine and stir in. Boil fast and skim for twenty minutes; then strain; place the turkey on a hot dish; pull out the skewers; pour some of the gravy into the dish (not over the turkey) and the remainder into a tureen; garnish with some fried sausages, and serve at once.

Note.—Fried plantains are delicious eaten with Roast Turkey.

4.—Roast Turkey with Chestnut stuffing.

Prepare the stuffing as follows:—Scald, peel, and scrape

Ingredients.
50 Chestnuts
1 pint of milk
2 oz. of butter
1 teaspoonful of salt
1 lb. of sausage meat
2 saltspoonsful of pepper
1 grain of cayenne

the chestnuts; boil them in the milk for twenty minutes with the butter and salt; drain them dry; mix them with the sausage meat, pepper and cayenne. Fill the body of the turkey with this stuffing and proceed in every particular as in the preceding recipe; only garnish with whole stewed chestnuts instead of sausages (about twenty).

5.—Roast Turkey with Pâté de foie gras Stuffing.

Ingredients.
1 lb. of *fresh* Pâté dé foie gras
3 oz. 3 drachms of sweetbread
6 oz. 6 drachms of bread-crumbs
The yolks of five eggs

Mince the sweetbread very fine; mix the *pâté* with the sweetbread and bread-crumbs and bind it together with the yolks. Fill the body of the turkey with this stuffing and proceed in every particular as in the recipe for roast turkey.

6.—Turkey's Legs broiled.
(Second dressing.)

Ingredients.
1 saltspoonful of white pepper
¼ ,, ,, cayenne
1 mustardspoonful of fresh made mustard
1 saltspoonful of salt
1 piece of garlic, the size of a split pea
The strained juice of a lemon

Score the meat of the legs at half inch distances, and three-quarters of an inch deep. Mix the pepper, cayenne, mustard, salt, garlic, and lemon-juice well together; rub this seasoning well into the divisions and all over the legs. Place them on a gridiron over a bright fire, and broil for twenty minutes at a distance; turn them that they may be nicely browned all over. Place them on a hot dish, rub over each half an ounce of butter, and send to table very hot.

7.—Pulled Turkey.
(Second dressing.)

Ingredients.
½ an onion
½ turnip
1 small head of celery
3 oz. of butter
1 saltspoonful of salt
1 ,, ,, white pepper
1 tablespoonful of flour
Some garlic
1 tablespoonful of sherry

Pull the meat off the bones of a cold turkey, in strips, by using two forks; make a gravy with the bones, onion, and turnip fried in one ounce of the butter until browned. Season the meat with the salt, pepper and flour. Put two oz. of butter into a bright saucepan, rub the bottom once across with garlic; put in the meat, and shake the pan till the butter is all absorbed; then add enough of the gravy (strained) to moisten it. Simmer ten minutes, stir in the sherry, and serve with fried sippets.

If a white dish be preferred stew the bones and vegetables (fried but *not browned*) in milk, and substitute two tablespoonsful of cream for the sherry; garnish with slices of lemon.

Note.—For other modes of dressing the remains of turkey, see *Second dressings of fowl* which may be followed in every respect.

8.—Roast Fowl with Gravy and Bread-sauce.

Ingredients.
2 oz. of fresh lard
4 ,, ,, ,, butter
1 onion (sliced)
4 slices of carrot
3 ,, ,, celery
1 teaspoonful of moist sugar
¾ of a ℔. of gravy beef (or ½ pint of stock)
1 saltspoonful of flour of mustard
1 saltspoonful of salt
1 clove
1½ pints of warm water
1 dessertspoonful of flour
1 teaspoonful of soy

Spread a sheet of paper thickly with the lard (or the same quantity of butter) and wrap it round the fowl: hang it before a good clear fire, *close* for ten minutes and then at a distance until done; baste frequently; ten minutes before serving take off the paper and baste with two ounces of dissolved butter until done. Chickens require half an hour, a moderate sized fowl fifty minutes, and a capon an hour and a quarter. Place the fowl on a hot dish, pull out the skewers, and serve with the gravy in the dish and the breadsauce (*see* rceipe) in a tureen. Make the gravy as follows :—Put one ounce of butter, the onion, carrot, celery, sugar and gravy beef into a small stewpan; simmer gently over the fire until nicely browned; then add the mustard, salt, clove and water; simmer (skimming often) very gently until reduced to half the quantity. Knead the remaining ounce of butter with the flour; stir into the gravy, and add the soy. Boil ten minutes, strain and serve.

Note.—All poultry is immensely improved by being stuffed with as many mushrooms as you can put in, 2 oz. of butter, a saltspoonful of salt, and one grain of cayenne; well basted; put a round of toast under and serve on the toast.

9.—Boiled Fowls.

Ingredients.
1 pair of fowls
3 quarts of milk

Truss the fowls for boiling; place them in the degchee and cover them with the milk; boil up quickly, and then simmer till done. Chickens require sixteen minutes; fine fowls twenty-five minutes, capons from forty to fifty minutes.

Serve with white, parsley, green, or celery sauces (*see* recipes) according to taste.

Note.—Reserve the milk in which the fowls were boiled in an earthen pan for soup, and serve for any of the white soups. *See* recipes.

10.—Braised Fowl with Tomatoes.

Ingredients.
1 fowl
3 oz. of butter
A piece of fresh cut garlic
½ pint of strong veal gravy
6 large ripe tomatoes
1 shalot
1 teaspoonful of salt
1 saltspoonful of white pepper
1 grain of cayenne
⅙th part of a nutmeg, grated
⅛ saltspoonful of mustard
½ ,, ,, ginger
The strained juice of 2 lemons
1 wineglassful of marsala

Truss a fine young fowl as for boiling; spread a sheet of paper thickly with the butter and wrap the fowl in it. Heat a stewpan and rub it three times across the bottom with garlic; put in the fowl, pour the gravy over it; boil up quickly, and put the pan where it will only just simmer. Slice the tomatoes; chop the shalot; season with the salt, pepper, cayenne, nutmeg, mustard and ginger; add the lemon-juice and marsala. Baste the fowl with the gravy frequently, and when it has simmered three-quarters of an hour put in the tomatoes. Stir and boil up; then continue the slow simmering and basting for another hour and a quarter. Take the paper off the breast; lay the fowl on a hot dish; pour the sauce over, and serve immediately.

11.—Chicken and Onions.

Ingredients.
A fine chicken
Some small onions
A teaspoonful of salt
A little bacon
8 large onions
A saltspoonful of pepper
A quart of milk
2 tablespoonsful of flour
2 oz. of fresh butter
A grain of cayenne pepper

Truss the chickens for boiling, fill the body with small onions which have previously been parboiled in milk and a teaspoonful of salt. To the milk in which they were boiled, add the remainder of the quart, put in the head, giblets and feet of the chicken and bacon, and boil for one hour. Then put the chicken into the stock and simmer for three-quarters of an hour. Then take out the chicken, reduce the stock to one pint by boiling, strain it, mix two tablespoonsful of flour or arrowroot in three of cold milk and stir into the sauce, mixing one way, until it is perfectly smooth like cream; add the butter and cayenne, and stir over the fire until it is well mixed, taking care it does not boil; then pour it over the chicken and serve.

Note.—Mushrooms can be used instead of onions and make a most palatable dish.

12.—Two Chickens for eight persons.

Cut up one of the fowls; the leg and thigh into two

POULTRY. 121

Ingredients.
2 fowls
1 Spanish (or other) onions
2 oz. of butter
1 saltspoonful of salt
½   ,,   ,, cayenne
1 teaspoonful of garlic or French vinegar
1 pint of button mushrooms
1 teaspoonful of salt
1 saltspoonful of pepper
2 tablespoonsful of arrowroot
1   ,,   ,, mushroom ketchup .

pieces, the back into three pieces, and the breast into two pieces, which, with the merry thought, will be fourteen pieces.

Cut up the onion small, and put it into the saucepan with the butter, cayenne and salt; let it stew gently for about an hour, until it is in a complete pulp; add the chicken, stew half an hour, and just before serving add the vinegar.

Cut up the other fowl in the same way as the first one.

Pick and scald the head and necks of both fowls, and stew them in half a pint of water for an hour; strain the liquor and put it in a saucepan with the button mushrooms, pepper and salt; put in the pieces of fowl and simmer for half an hour; then thicken with the arrowroot. Just before serving add the mushroom ketchup.

Pigeons, grouse, partridges and turkey are all delicious, served in the same way.

13.—Braised Fowl and White Sauce with Braised Beef and Chestnuts.

Mix one tablespoonful of salad oil, with the strained juice of a lemon, one saltspoonful of salt, one saltspoonful of white pepper, one grain of cayenne, one saltspoonful of flour of mustard, three grates of nutmeg, a piece of garlic, the size of a pea (bruised), and three tablespoonsful of "Cre-fydd sauce," (*see* note.)

Ingredients.
1 fowl
1½ lbs. of the upper side of the round of beef an inch thick
6 rashers of bacon ¼ inch thick without bone or skin
Some butter milk, garlic, shalots
1 gill of cream
1 carrot
1 head of celery
15 chestnuts
2 lemons
Oil, sugar, pepper, salt, &c
2 oz. of butter
1 tablespoonful of flour or arrowroot

Q

Rub this well into the beef, and let it remain closely covered for 24 hours. Clean, and cut up small the heart of the celery, the carrot and two shalots. Put them into a saucepan with an ounce of butter. Lay in the beef, pour the sauce over it, and three-quarters of a pint of cold water. Place the fowl on the beef with two ounces of butter spread on the slices of bacon laid over that. Peel the chestnuts with a sharp knife, and lay them round the fowl. Boil up quickly, baste the fowl with the gravy, then simmer as gently as possible for two and half hours. Mix a tablespoonful of baked flour into half a pint of a new milk, boil ten minutes; add the cream; place the fowl on a hot dish with the bacon round it, and pour the white sauce over. Lay the beef on a hot dish, pour over the gravy and vegetables; add the strained juice of a lemon, and send both dishes to table immediately.

Note.—If you have no Cre-fydd sauce, use instead a tablespoonful of port wine, a teaspoonful of soy, a teaspoonful of brandy, and a saltspoonful of chutney.

14.—Chickens with Green Peas.

Ingredients.
1 pint of green peas
¼ oz. of butter
1 bunch of parsley
4 *small* onions
1 dessertspoonful of flour
½ tumbler of gravy
1 teaspoonful of salt
½ ,, ,, sugar

Boil the chickens, cut them into pieces, and put them in a saucepan with the peas, butter, parsley and onions; put on the fire for four minutes and then add the flour and gravy; simmer for twenty minutes, stir in the salt and sugar, and serve very hot.

15.—Mayonnaise of Fowl.

Boil a fine fowl as in recipe No. 9, and when it is cold cut it up into neat pieces. Wash two fine lettuces, or any salad in season, and four spring onions; leave them in water for two hours. Prepare the Mayonnaise sauce, (*see* recipe) and leave it to stand in a cool place or on ice for an hour. Wipe each salad-leaf, and break it into pieces; cut up the onions quite small; put half the salad in the bowl or on the dish; on that lay half the fowl; then half the sauce; then the remainder of the fowl; the rest of the salad over that; pour the sauce over all, sprinkle with the chopped onions, and garnish with slices of alternate beetroot and cucumber if you have any.

16.—Fricasseed Fowl, white.

Ingredients.
A young fowl
Some baked flour
¾ pint of milk
A shalot
1 sprig of thyme
2 leaves of tarragon
1 inch of thin lemon-peel
¼ ,, ,, mace
1 clove
1 teaspoonful of salt
1 ,, ,, loaf sugar
The strained juice of a lemon

Cut up the fowl into joints, and put it into cold water for an hour to blanch; wipe it dry and dredge each piece with flour; put it into the stewpan with the milk and the shalot, thyme, tarragon, lemon-peel and clove tied in a bit of muslin; add the salt and sugar; boil up quickly; then simmer very gently for three quarters of an hour; take out the bag, place the fowl on a hot dish, and pour it over the lemon-juice.

Prepare white sauce (*see* recipe) or melted butter for vegetables (*see* recipe) with the liquor in which the fowl was boiled; pour it over the fowl, and serve at once.

17.—Fowl Pie.

Ingredients.
6 mealy potatoes
1 saltspoonful of salt

Prepare the fowl in all respects as above; when it is ready to serve make a paste as follows:—Mash the potatoes; fla-

Ingredients of Fowl Pie.
3 oz. of butter
½ gill of cream (or milk)
1 well beaten egg
Some slices of bacon or ham

vour with the salt; add the butter, cream, and egg, and beat with a wooden spoon till quite light; line a pie dish with about one-third of the potato; lay in a layer of bacon, then the fowl; pour over the sauce; cover with another layer of bacon; lay over the remainder of the potato; smooth it over with a knife and bake in a moderately heated oven for three quarters of an hour.

Note.—Two hard-boiled eggs cut in halves are an improvement. This dish can also be prepared with cold fowl, and if there be no white sauce use instead some veal gravy, or stock.

18.—Fowl Fricasseed in Oil.

Cut up the fowl into joints and put it into cold water for

Ingredients.
1 young fowl
1 pint of good salad oil
1 teaspoonful of oil
2 mushrooms
3 truffles (if you have them)
1 shalot
1 sprig of thyme
14 sprigs of parsley
1 bay leaf
2 button mushrooms
2 shalots
1 truffle
1 saltspoonful of salt
1 ",,   ,, loaf sugar
The juice of 1 lemon
¼ gill of marsala

two hours; wipe it quite dry; put the salad oil into a stewpan, and when warm put in the fowl with the mushrooms, truffles, shalot, thyme, parsley, and bay leaf. Boil up quickly; then simmer until the fowl is done a pale yellow color (about three quarters of an hour.) Make the following sauce:—Clean the mushrooms, chop the shalots and truffle; put them into a small saucepan with enough of the oil in which the fowl was cooked to moisten them; stir over a quick fire for ten minutes. Add the salt, sugar, lemon-juice, and marsala. Drain the fowl on a cloth to take off the fat, put it on a hot dish; pour the sauce over, and serve at once.

19.—Timbale of Macaroni with Fowl.

Ingredients.
1 boiled fowl
1 lb. of macaroni
Some veal forcemeat
Onion
Pepper
Salt
A little fat bacon
Some butter

Prepare some veal forcemeat (*see* recipe—about quarter the quantity given will do). Boil the macaroni until it is quite tender, but not so soft that it will break or stick together. Cut it all up into pieces one-third of an inch long. Butter a pudding basin or a round mould and stick in the little pieces of macaroni upright, so that when turned out the shape will look like a honey-comb. They must touch each other, and the sides of the basins or mould must be covered up to the very top. Dip a metal spoon in hot water, and scoop out some of the veal forcemeat, and lay a thin layer of it over the macaroni as you proceed. When the mould is thus lined fill it with the fowl (boiled as in recipe No. 9) finely minced and seasoned with a little choped onion, salt, pepper, and bacon. Pour in two tablespoonsful of white sauce, prepared from the bones of the fowl and the milk in which it was boiled (*see* recipe). Cover the fowl in with a layer of forcemeat about half an inch thick; cover the bowl over with a round piece of buttered paper, lay a plate on that, and steam for an hour. Turn out carefully, and serve with the remainder of the sauce poured round it.

Note.—A few button mushrooms are a great improvement to the sauce, and this dish may be made with any kind of white meat.

20.—Fowl with Savoury Macaroni.

(Second dressing.)

Put the macaroni into the water and leave it to soak

Ingredients of Fowl with Savoury Macaroni.

6 oz. of Genoa macaroni
3 pints of cold water
The remains of a cold fowl
1 onion (sliced)
1 carrot
3 sprigs of parsley
1 clove
1 teaspoonful of salt
1   „   „ flour of mustard
1 dessertspoonful of grated cheese
1 piece of garlic, the size of a pea
1 quart of cold water or stock
3 oz. of butter
¾ of a lb. of cold fowl
1 saltspoonful of salt
1   „   „ white pepper
Some baked flour
1 gill of olive oil or ¼ lb. of butter
½ wineglassful of marsala

for two hours. Cut up the cold fowl and put the bones and trimmings into a saucepan with the onion, carrot, parsley, clove, salt, mustard, cheese and garlic. Pour in the water or stock; boil for two hours; strain; lay the macaroni carefully in a stewpan with three ounces of butter; pour over the gravy, and *simmer* till tender, about 1½ hour. Season the fowl with the salt and pepper; dredge it lightly with flour, and fry to a nice yellow color in the oil or butter. Lay the macaroni round the dish in the form of a wall; add the marsala to the gravy; place the fowl in the centre; pour over the gravy, and serve at once.

21.—Quenelles of Fowl.

Prepare some chicken forcemeat with the flesh of a fowl as described in quenelle forcemeats of veal (*see* recipe), using half the quantities given, and finish by incorporating with it two tablespoonsful of thick white sauce (*see* recipe). Form this forcemeat into egg-shaped quenelles with two tablespoons, and poach them for ten minutes in boiling broth or water; serve them dished up in a circle, with some rich Bechamel sauce (*see* recipe) poured over and round them, and garnish with green peas, truffles, or mushrooms.

22.—Chickens à la Tartare.

Draw, singe, trim, and split the chickens into halves; season with pepper and salt, and fry them with butter until done on both sides; then press them between two dishes until half cold; dip them in egg and then in bread-crumbs; sprinkle with a little clarified butter and crumb them again. Twenty minutes before they are wanted broil the two halves over a clear fire until they are a light golden brown; place them on a dish containing some Tartar sauce (*see* recipe); garnish with pickles, and serve.

Note.—All kinds of poultry and game are delicious, served in this way.

23.—Devilled Fowl.

Take the legs of either boiled or roasted fowls; score the flesh deeply and rub over the following mixture; melt the butter and mix in the chutney, cayenne, pepper, and salt; put the legs on a gridiron over a slow fire, and take care they do not burn; cook slowly for a quarter of an hour, turning them frequently; take them off and pour a little more dissolved butter over each; shake a little pepper over, and serve at once.

Ingredients.
1 oz. of butter
1 teaspoonful of chutney
1 pinch of cayenne
1 ,, ,, pepper
1 ,, ,, salt

24.—Aspic of Fillets of Chicken or Game.

Melt the jelly and pour some into the mould, (about half an inch thick); leave it to settle; when it is firm lay in some of the hard-boiled eggs, (whites and yolks) gherkins and beetroot and arrange them according to taste; pour in some more jelly and leave it to settle; then put in the fillets neatly cut into shapes; add some jelly, enough to set but not to cover the chickens, leave it to settle; pour round and over some

Ingredients
Aspic jelly (*see* recipe)
Cold fillets of 2 or 3 chickens
4 hard-boiled eggs
Some truffles, gherkins and beetroot
Mayonnaise sauce (*see* recipe)

Mayonnaise sauce, and cover this well over with *cold* aspic, otherwise it would if liquid mix with the sauce and get muddy. Then fill the mould with liquid aspic as full as it will hold, and put it on-ice or in a very cold place to settle. When ready to serve dip a cloth in hot water; wrap it round the outside of the mould, and turn the jelly out on a dish.

25.—Curried Fowl.
(Second Dressing.)

Ingredients.
About ½ ℔. of cold fowl
1 large onion
3 oz. of butter
1 tablespoonful of curry powder
1½ saltspoonsful of salt.
1 desertspoonful of baked flour
1 sherry glass of thick cream
The strained juce of a lemon
6 oz. of rice

Cut up the cold fowl; stew the bones in a pint of water for ¾ of an hour, slice the onion; mix the butter with the curry powder, and fry the onion in it until it is of a pale brown color and quite tender; put in the fowl; strain the gravy (about a teacup), from the bones; add it to the fowl and put in the baked flour; simmer, stirring frequently for twenty minutes; stir in the cream and lemon-juice, and serve at once with a wall of rice round.

Wash the rice; put it into a quart of cold water and boil for half an hour; drain on a sieve before the fire, and stir with a wooden fork to separate the grains.

26.—Fowl Curry.
(Another way.)

Ingredients.
1 cabbage
2 apples
The juice of 1 lemon
1 saltspoonful of black pepper
1 large tablespoonful of Mr. Arnott's curry powder, (*see* recipe)

Take the heart of a cabbage, pull away all the outside leaves until it is about the size of an egg; chop it fine, and add the apples sliced fine, the lemon-juice, pepper and curry powder; mix

Ingredients of Fowl Curry.
3 onions
½ clove of garlic
2 oz. of butter
2 tablespoonsful of flour
1 pint of strong gravy

well; put the onions into a stewpan with the butter, and fry a light brown color; then add to it the cabbage, apples, lemon-juice and curry powder; add the chopped garlic, flour and gravy, and stew well together.

Then put in a cold roast fowl nicely cut up; simmer for twenty minutes, and serve at once with plain boiled rice (*see* preceding recipe.)

Pork or mutton chops, kidney, lobster, the remains of a calf's head, all are excellent, served as above.

27.—Minced Fowl with Savoury Rice.

(*Second dressing.*)

Cut all the white meat off the fowl; put the bones, skin and rough pieces into a stewpan with one quart of water, onion, carrot, garlic, sugar, salt and pepper; boil for two hours; wash the rice, put it into a quart of cold water and boil for a quarter of an hour; strain dry; mince the fowl; season it with the salt, white pepper, parsley, flour, mushroom and lemon-juice; put the mince into a stewpan with enough gravy to moisten it well, and simmer very gently, stirring frequently for eighteen minutes. Put the rice into a stewpan with the butter, and stir over the fire for five minutes; add the remainder of the gravy, and simmer, stirring constantly for ten minutes; lay the rice round the dish and the mince in the centre; serve very hot.

Ingredients.
The remains of a fowl
2 quarts of water
1 onion
½ carrot
1 piece of garlic, the size of a pea
1 teaspoonful of loaf sugar
1 ,, ,, salt
1 saltspoonful of pepper
½ lb. of best rice
1 quart of water
1 lb. of minced fowl
1½ saltspoonsful of salt
1 ,, ,, white pepper
1 dessertspoonful of chopped parsley
1 tablespoonful of baked flour
1 large mushroom (chopped)
The juice of ½ lemon
2 oz. of butter

28.—Croquets of Fowl.
(Second dressing.)

Ingredients.
2 oz. of butter
6 oz. of dried flour
The yolks of 2 fresh eggs
4 tablespoonsful of cold water
½ lb. of cold fowl
1 piece of garlic
½ pint of water
2 oz. of ham or tongue
⅙ of a nutmeg
½ saltspoonful of white pepper
The grated rind of ¼ lemon
½ saltspoonful of flour of mustard
⅛ ,, ,, salt
1 lb. of clarified dripping
Some parsley

Rub the butter into the flour; beat the yolks of the eggs with the water, and stir into the flour until it is a stiff paste; knead till quite smooth; roll it out twice; then let it stand in a cool place (or on ice) for six hours; cut up the cold fowl and free it from all skin; put the bones and trimmings into a saucepan with the half pint of cold water, the garlic (about the size of a pea), and stew it for gravy. Pound the fowl to a paste, add the ham or tongue pounded, the nutmeg, pepper, lemon, mustard and salt; add enough of the gravy to moisten it. Continue to pound until the ingredients are well mixed; roll out the paste ⅛ of an inch thick; divide it into eight equal pieces about three inches square; brush over the surface with cold water; put ⅛ part of the pounded meat into each piece in the form of a sausage; fold the paste over; press the edges to make them adhere; then fry in the boiling lard till of a pale yellow colour; drain on a sieve before the fire, and serve with or without fried parsley in the centre.

29.—Chicken Legs en Papillotes.
(Second dressing.)

Remove the bones from some cold legs of chicken or fowl.

Ingredients.
1 oz. of butter
Some chopped parsley
Some boiled bacon
Pepper and salt

Dissolve the butter and season it with a little chopped parsley, pepper, and salt; dip in the pieces of chicken; wrap them in some thin slices of boiled bacon; then fold in some slices of buttered paper; double over the edges neatly; lay them on a gridiron over a slow fire for ten minutes, turning them twice, and taking care they do not burn.

Pulled Fowl.
(Second dressing.)

(*See* Pulled Turkey.)

30.—Roast Goose with stuffing and Apple or Gooseberry Sauce.

Ingredients.

4 onions
2 dessertspoonsful of fine bread-crumbs
½ saltspoonful of powdered sage
1 ,, ,, salt
1 ,, ,, loaf sugar
½ ,, ,, flour of mustard
1 teaspoonful of brandy
1 oz. of dissolved butter

Ingredients of Gravy

1 tablespoonful of flour
¾ of a pint of stock (No. 1)
1 teaspoonful of soy
3 grain of cayenne
½ saltspoonful of salt
The strained juice of ½ lemon

Boil the onions in plenty of water for a quarter of an hour; drain and chop them small; mix them with the bread-crumbs, sage, salt, sugar, mustard, brandy and dissolved butter; mix well and put this into the body of the goose; cover its breast with a slice of thick fat bacon, or a sheet of paper spread with one ounce of butter; roast before a brisk fire for one and a half hours, basting constantly; ten minutes before serving take off the bacon (or paper); dredge slightly with flour, and baste until done; serve with the following gravy:

Mix the flour with the stock; add the soy, cayenne and salt; boil fast for twenty minutes; add the gravy dripped from the goose and the strained lemon-juice. Serve in a tureen. Make some apple sauce (*see* recipe), and serve in a tureen. If you have no apples, the following is a good substitute:

Gooseberry Sauce.

Ingredients.
1½ pints of bottled gooseberries
½ gill of water (or syrup)

Boil the gooseberries and water (or syrup) until they are quite soft; then rub them through a sieve, and serve in a tureen.

Note.—Roast gosling may be served in the same way, (it will take fifty minutes) and is a far more delicate dish.

31.—Roast Goose with Tomatoes and Chestnuts.

Prepare the goose in every way as above; add thirty cleaned and roasted chestnuts to the stuffing and fill the inside of the goose with it; continue as in previous recipes, and when dished up garnish with a border of stuffed tomatoes. (*See* recipe.)

32.—Roast Ducks and Ducklings stuffed.

Ingredients.
2 oz. of bread-crumbs
3 shalots
2 sprigs of parsley
1   „   „ thyme
2 sage leaves
1 clove
¼ saltspoonful of white pepper
½   „   „ salt
1   „   „ loaf sugar
1 inch of lemon-peel
⅛ of a nutmeg grated
½ pint of water
2 oz. of butter
1 saltspoonful of chopped parsley

Make a stuffing as in the recipe for roast goose; the quantity given will be sufficient for two ducks, or the following receipt may be preferred:—Put the bread-crumbs into a saucepan with the shalots, parsley, thyme, sage-leaves, clove, pepper, salt, loaf sugar, lemon-peel, nutmeg and water; boil and stir for twenty minutes until the water is all absorbed; then add the butter, and stir it through a sieve; when cold add the parsley, and with this mixture stuff the ducks; roast before a quick fire, basting constantly till done. Ducklings require thirty-five minutes, and ducks fifty minutes. They must be sent to table hot and with gravy as directed for goose in the preceding recipe.

33.—Braised Duck, with Turnips.

Ingredients.

10 small turnips
1 desertspoonful of sugar
8 oz. of butter
1 onion chopped
2 dessertspoonsful of flour
1 teaspoonful of soy
1 saltspoonful of salt
½   ,,   ,, pepper
¼ of a pint of any good stock
1 wineglassful of marsala
The strained juice of a lemon

Peel the turnips; sift the sugar over them; dissolve six ounces of the butter and fry the turnips to a light brown color in a stewpan; add the two remaining ounces of butter and the chopped onion; put in a fine duck, breast downwards, and let it remain to brown twenty minutes. Take out the duck; stir the flour into the butter; add the soy, salt, pepper and stock; boil fast and skim off the fat; add the marsala and lemon-juice; put in the duck, breast uppermost, and simmer gently for twenty minutes more. Place the duck on a hot dish, the turnips round it and the gravy poured over. Serve instantly.

34.—Braised Duck, with Green Peas.

Ingredients.

4 spring onions
2 sage leaves
4 sprigs of parsley
½ saltspoonful of salt
½   ,,   ,, pepper
One tenth of a nutmeg grated
4 oz. of butter
Some lettuce
¾ of a pint of stock

Chop the onion, sage and parsley, quite small; season with salt, pepper, and nutmeg; knead these with one ounce of butter, and put into the body of the duck; spread three ounces of butter over the bread; lay on the bottom of a degchee four large leaves of fresh cut lettuce: place the dish on them, cover closely, and let it simmer till of a pale brown color (about half an hour); then add one quarter of the stock (or plain veal gravy). Continue to simmer for twenty minutes; then take out the duck, and serve very hot.

35.—Stewed Giblets.

Ingredients.
1½ saltspoonsful of white pepper
2 „ „ „ salt
1 grain of cayenne
1 grate of nutmeg
2 chopped shalots
1½ tablespoonsful of flour
Some garlic
¼ lb. of butter
1½ pints of good stock
1 wineglassful of white wine
1 tablespoonful of mushroom ketchup
1 dessertspoonful of Harvey sauce

The giblets must be well cleaned and soaked in warm water for an hour. Wipe them dry and cut them into neat pieces two inches long; season with the pepper, salt, cayenne, nutmeg, shalots and flour. Rub a small degchee twice across the bottom with garlic, put in the giblets with butter, and fry over a gentle fire till slightly browned; then add the stock, wine, ketchup and sauce; boil up slowly, skim, then simmer gently for two and a half hours, skimming occasionally. Serve very hot.

Note.—Truffles (sliced), button mushrooms, or button onions are a great improvement.

36.—Roast Pigeons.

Ingredients.
2 oz. of butter
2 dessertspoonsful of fine dried bread-crumbs
1 grain of cayenne
¼ saltspoonful of salt
¼ „ „ pepper
1 „ „ chopped parsley
1 grate of nutmeg
1 small shalot, finely chopped

Knead together the butter, bread-crumbs, cayenne, salt, pepper, parsley, nutmeg and shalot. Have two young pigeons, and put half the the stuffing into each; lay a thick slice of fat bacon over the breast of each, and roast before a quick fire for fifteen minutes, basting constantly with butter; ten minutes before they are done take off the bacon and continue to baste till of a nice brown color. Serve with some gravy, or on toast.

37.—Stewed Pigeons.

See recipe for stewed Patridges with bacon and cabbage.

38.—Broiled Pigeons.

Ingredients
- 1 oz. of butter
- 1 dessertspoonful of flour
- 1 teaspoonful of chopped chives
- ½ ,, ,, ,, parsley
- ½ saltspoonful of salt
- ¼ ,, ,, pepper

Ingredients of Sauce.
- Some garlic
- 1 oz. of butter
- 1 dessertspoonful of flour
- ¼ saltspoonful of pepper
- 1 gill of stock
- 1 tablespoonful of mushroom ketchup
- 1 tablespoonful of marsala
- The strained juice of a lemon
- 2 pickled gherkins, finely chopped

The pigeons must be trussed flat. Knead the butter, flour, chives, parsley, salt and pepper together; stir over the fire for five minutes; take it off for a minute; dip in the pigeons, and continue to do so until all the mixture adheres to them and they are well covered with it. Let them stand for an hour, then broil over a bright fire for eighteen minutes. Serve with the following sauce poured round them:—Rub the bottom of a small saucepan twice across the bottom with garlic; put in the butter, flour and pepper; stir till well mixed; then add the stock, ketchup, marsala, lemon and gherkins; boil fast for eight minutes, then serve as directed.

39.—Boiled Pigeons, with Celery or Soubise Sauce.

(*See* recipe for Partridges.)

40.—Pigeons à la Tartare.

(*See* Chickens à la Tartare.)

41.—Pigeon Pie.

Ingredients.
- 2 young pigeons
- 1 lb. of rump steak
- 4 fresh eggs
- 2½ saltspoonful of salt
- 2 ,, ,, pepper
- 1 gill of gravy
- Some lard or butter

Cut the pigeons into quarters, and the rump steak, which should be about half an inch thick, into six pieces; boil the eggs for ten minutes; season the whole with the salt and pep-

Ingredients of Paste.
9 oz. of flour
½ gill of cold water
The juice of half lemon
¼ lb. of good butter

per. Lay the steak at the bottom of a ten inch pie dish, the pigeons upon it, the yolks of the eggs at equal distances; add the gravy. Rub the edge of the dish with lard or butter; line it with strips of paste one-sixth of an inch thick; moisten it with cold water; cover it with paste; press round to make it adhere; trim with a sharp knife; notch at inch distances; make a hole in the centre; ornament to taste, and bake in a moderate oven for two hours and a quarter. The paste is made as follows :—Moisten the flour with the water and lemon-juice; knead flat; put the butter in the centre; fold over; roll out four times; dredge flour over each time. Let it stand in a cool place two or three hours; then use as directed.

GAME.

1.—Guinea-fowl, larded and roasted.

Lard a young guinea-fowl thickly and deeply with fat bacon; spread a sheet of white paper with three oz. of butter; wrap the guinea-fowl in it and roast before a quick fire for 35 minutes, basting frequently; ten minutes before serving remove the paper and baste with dissolved butter till of a light brown color, and serve with the following gravy in the dish (not poured over the bird), and bread-sauce (*see* recipe) in a tureen.

Gravy.

Ingredients of Gravy.
- 1 onion
- 1 oz. of butter
- 1 tablespoonful of flour
- ½ saltspoonful of salt
- ½ ,, ,, pepper
- ½ ,, ,, sugar
- ½ ,, ,, mustard
- ¾ of a pint of stock
- 1 tablespoonful of mushroom ketchup
- 2 tablespoonsful of port wine

Slice the onion and fry it in the butter until it is of a nice brown color; add while frying the flour, salt, pepper, sugar and mustard; stir in the stock, ketchup and port, boil fast for 25 minutes, and then strain into a tureen.

Note.—The recipes for pheasants may be followed for guinea-fowl.

2.—Roast Pheasant.

The hen is the nicer bird. Lay a thick slice of fat bacon over the breast; stuff the bird with as many mushrooms as it will hold, two oz. of butter, one saltspoonful of salt, and a grain of cayenne. Baste it constantly, and roast for half an hour. Ten minutes before serving take off the bacon that the bird may be nicely browned. Serve with gravy and bread-sauce as in the previous recipe.

Note.—Pheasant is also delicious served with sage and onion stuffing (*see* recipe for *Goose.*)

3.—Boiled Pheasant with Celery Sauce.

Truss the pheasant like a fowl for boiling. Put it into a small degchee and cover it with new milk (about three pints); boil up quickly, then simmer as gently as possible until done; a small bird will take thirty minutes, a large one fifty minutes, and an old one an hour, from the time of boiling up. Serve hot with a little celery sauce (*see* recipe) poured over it, and the rest in a tureen.

Note.—The same recipe may be followed substituting *Soubise Sauce* (*see* recipe) for celery.

4.—Braised Pheasant with Beef and Chestnuts

(*See* recipe for Braised Fowl with beef and chestnuts.)

5.—Pheasant with Truffles.

Ingredients.
6 large truffles
½ clove of garlic
1 lb. of fresh lard
3 sprigs of parsley
1 ,, ,, thyme
1 bay leaf
1 saltspoonful of salt
4 peppercorns
⅓ of a nutmeg grated
1 clove
3 slices of carrot
1 wineglassful of rum
Some butter
1 teacupful of stock
1 dessertspoonful of baked flour
½ saltspoonful of salt
½ ,, ,, loaf sugar

Wash, peel and slice the truffles; put them into the body of a nicely trussed pheasant; pound the peel and parings of the truffles with the garlic, and knead it with the lard. Put the pheasant into an oval deep dish or pan; cover it with the lard; add the parsley, thyme, bay leaf, salt, peppercorns, nutmeg, clove, carrot, and rum; cover it over closely and put it into a moderate oven for ¾ of an hour; then leave it for two or three days to imbibe the flavour of the truffles. When required take it out of the fat; envelope it in paper thickly spread with butter, and bake in a moderate oven for ¾ of an hour. Strain the gravy, add the stock, flour, salt and sugar; boil ten minutes; take the paper off the pheasant; add the dripped gravy and butter to the sauce. Place the pleasant on a hot dish, remove the skewers, pour over the gravy, and serve at once.

6.—Salmi of Pheasant.

Ingredients of Sauce.
3 dessertspoonsful of salad oil
½ glass of claret
A pinch of salt, pepper, and cayenne
The strained juice of a lemon

Roast a pheasant; when it is nearly cold divide it into pieces and take off the skin; put the oil, claret, salt, pepper, cayenne and lemon-juice into a small saucepan; lay in the pieces of pheasant, toss them over the fire until the whole is very hot, and serve at once.

Note.—A dozen mushrooms are a great improvement.

7.—Cold Pheasant with Balbirnie Sauce.

Ingredients.
1 small shalot
1 saltspoonful of mustard
1 tablespoonful of oil
1 pinch of salt and pepper
1 tablespoonful of vinegar
2 tablespoonsful of ketchup

Chop the shalot very small and mix with it all the other ingredients. When well incorporated, serve with cold pheasant on a separate dish.

8.—Pulled Pheasant.

(*See* Pulled Turkey.)

9.—Roast Partridges.

Hang the birds before a brisk fire; baste constantly with plenty of butter (¼ of a ℔. for a brace) and roast for about eighteen minutes. Serve garnished with fried breadcrumbs and with bread sauce (*see* recipe) and the following gravy in tureens :—

Ingredients of Gravy.
1 pint of stock
1 teaspoonful of Soy
1 tablespoonful of Harvey sauce
1 tablespoonful of flour
½ saltspoonful of salt
½   ,,   ,, flour of mustard
1 grain of cayenne
1 tablespoonful of port wine

Put the stock into a saucepan with the Soy, Harvey sauce, flour, salt, mustard and cayenne; boil quickly (uncovered) till reduced to about ⅓ (twenty minutes); add the port wine, strain and serve.

10.—Braised Partridges.

Truss the partridges as a fowl for boiling. Slice the carrot, onion and celery and put them with the parsley into a stewpan; add the butter; lay in the partridge (breast uppermost) and cover with some slices of fat bacon; add the stock and simmer very slowly for two hours. Put the round of buttered bread into the oven to brown; add more butter if required. Lay the partridges on the bread; rub the gravy and vegetables through a fine sieve; add the marsala, boil up, pour over the birds, and serve immediately.

Ingredients.
1 small carrot
1 onion
1 small head of celery
4 sprigs of parsley (chopped)
1 oz. of butter
Some fat bacon
½ pint of good stock
A round of bread *thickly* spread with butter
1 wineglassful of marsala

11.—Braised Partridges with Cabbage.

Trim the cabbage and wash it well; put it into cold water with the tablespoonful of salt and let it remain three hours; put it in *cold* water and boil *uncovered* for twenty minutes; drain and press out all the water.

Ingredients.
1 small cabbage
1 teaspoonful of salt
3 oz. of butter
1 teaspoonful of loaf sugar
1 saltspoonful of pepper
     ,,   ,, salt
The strained juice of lemon

Braise the partridges as directed in the preceding recipe, adding the cabbage, butter, sugar, pepper and salt; if the birds be old 2½ hours will not be too long to simmer them. Add the strained lemon-juice over the cabbage, and serve it round the dish; the bacon in the centre and the birds on it.

12.—Stewed Partridges with Celery or Soubise Sauce.

(*See* recipe for Pheasants.)

13.—Partridges with Tomato Sauce.

Ingredients.
2 tablespoonsful of oil
1 clove of garlic
1 saltspoonful of salt
Some cloves

Truss two partridges as for boiling; fry them in a small stewpan with the oil, garlic and salt; when they are browned add some Tomato Sauce (*see* recipe); put in ten olives (cleaned, soaked and stoned) simmer for ten minutes, and serve.

Note.—Partridges are also delicious, served with sage and onion stuffing (*see* recipe for *Goose* and use half the quantities given) and also potted (*see* recipe for *Snipe*.)

14.—Roast Quail.

Truss the quail for roasting; cut some thin layers of fat bacon just large enough to cover the quail; spread a 'vine leaf over each, cut it to their size and tie it round. Run an iron skewer through the birds, and roast them before a brisk fire for ten minutes; dish them up with water-cresses round them, and serve with gravy and toast under them, and bread-sauce (*see* recipe) in a separate dish.

15.—(Another way.)

Cut a strip of crumb-bread, the size of the number of birds you have to send to table; toast it a pale brown color;

lay the birds on the toast, baste them with dissolved butter, and bake on a tin dish in a very hot oven for fourteen or eighteen minutes, basting constantly. Serve on the toast with or without the following gravy :—

Knead the butter with the flour, cayenne and mustard. Rub the bottom of a small saucepan twice across the bottom with the garlic; put in the stock; stir in the butter and boil fast for quarter of an hour; add the marsala and lemon-juice, and serve at once in a tureen.

Ingredients of Gravy.
2 oz. of butter
1 dessertspoonful of flour
½ grain of cayenne
¼ of a saltspoonful of flour of mustard
A piece of fresh cut garlic
½ pint of stock
2 tablespoonsful of marsala
The strained juice of ½ lemon

16.—Snipe and Woodcock.

Cover the birds with layers of bacon and tie them round with string; roast them before the fire for twenty minutes, basting constantly with butter, and place some toasted bread under the birds to receive the droppings from the trail. Dish them up on the toast with water-cresses round them and some plain butter sauce in a separate boat.

17.—Snipe Pudding á l'Epicurien.

Plunge, singe, and divide the snipe in halves; remove the gizzard and reserve the trail for use hereafter; season the birds with cayenne and lemon-juice, and a pinch of salt; set them aside till wanted. Slice the Portugal (or other) onion and fry it in the butter, till of a light brown color; add the flour, mushrooms, parsley, garlic and herbs; moisten

Ingredients.
6 snipes
Cayenne, lemon-juice and salt
A Portugal onion
1 oz. of butter
1 tablespoonful of flour
12 chopped mushrooms
4 sprigs of parsley
1 piece of garlic, the size of a pea
1 pinch of aromatic herbs
½ pint of wine
Some slices of truffle
Some suet paste

with the wine; stir the whole over the fire to boil for about ten minutes; strain through a sieve; line a basin with a thin crust of suet paste, put in the birds, sauce and sliced truffles; cover in with the paste; steam for 1½ hours; turn it out with care, and serve (or serve in the basin.)

18.—Potted Snipe.

The birds used for this purpose must be perfectly fresh.

Ingredients.
6 or 8 snipes
Some fat bacon
Some black pepper and salt
Some clarified fresh butter
Some flour and water paste

After being plucked, cut off their wings and legs; remove the gizzard with the point of a knife, leaving the trail undisturbed; split the birds in half and place them on a dish. Take an earthenware oval pie pan; (such as Yorkshire pies or potted meats are made in) line the bottom and sides of this with very thin layers of fat bacon; arrange the snipe therein in neat rows, and season with the pepper and salt; when the pan is nearly full pour in enough clarified butter to cover over the birds. (The quantity will depend on the number of birds and the size of the dish.) Put the lid of the pan on, and cover in the edge with some flour and water paste to keep the steam in while baking. Bake in a moderate oven for two hours, and when *quite* cold remove the paste, take off the cover and use when required.

19.—Salmi of Snipe.

(Second dressing.)

Divide the birds into joints and lay them aside on a plate.

Ingredients.
3 cold roast snipes
The juice of 4 lemons
Some salt, white pepper and cayenne

Break up the livers and trails on the silver dish (on which you are going to serve the birds) and

Ingredients of Salmi of Snipe.
2 spoonsful of French mustard
½ glass of white wine
1 teaspoonful of olive oil

squeeze the lemon-juice over them. Season the birds with salt, pepper and cayenne; and lay them on the dish; add the mustard and wine. Put the dish over a spirit lamp and keep moving each piece about so that the seasoning may penetrate and become well mixed. Do not allow it actually to boil, but just as it comes to it put out the lamp, sprinkle over a little olive oil, stir for a moment, and serve.

Note.—All sorts of game are delicious dressed in this way.

20.—Wild Duck.

Rub the liver over the breast till it is red; roast before a brisk fire from 16 to 25 minutes, basting liberally with butter; send to table with a rich brown gravy. On the table, close to the carver, should be a deep silver dish with hot water or a spirit burner under it; put into this one oz. of butter, two glasses of port wine (or claret); one of Harvey's sauce, the juice of a lemon, a sprinkle of salt, and a pinch of cayenne; the carver should put the pieces of bird into this as he carves them; add the gravy, stir it round, and let the guests help themselves.

21.—Widgeons and Teal.

Prepared as above, only ten to fifteen minutes will be enough time to roast them.

22.—Salmi of Wild Fowl.

Cut up the remains of wild duck, widgeon or teal; put
Ingredients.
Some good gravy
3 shalots, chopped

the trimmings and bones into a small saucepan with enough

GAME. 145

Ingredients of Salmi of Wild Fowl.
1 tablespoonful of flour
The strained juice of a lemon
A pinch of cayenne, pepper and salt
A wineglassful of port wine or Madeira

gravy or broth to moisten it, and the chopped shalots. Simmer for half an hour; strain; thicken with the flour; put in the pieces of duck and add the lemon-juice, cayenne, pepper, salt and wine. Warm the birds slowly, and serve at once.

Note.—Christopher North's Own Sauce (*see* recipe) is a great improvement to this or any other kind of hash or stew.

23.—Roast Hare.

Fry the liver and kidney with the shalot in one oz. of butter, till firm; then chop them small; chop the beef suet; add to these the bread-crumbs, parsley and ham and mix well together; add the herbs, nutmeg, lemon-rind and juice, pepper, salt and sugar, wine and beaten eggs; mix all these well together and put this stuffing into the body of the hare; sew it up with a needle and thread; lay slices of fat bacon on the back and fold the whole in a sheet of paper; hang it before a clear hot fire, and roast for $1\frac{1}{4}$ to $1\frac{1}{2}$ hours; baste constantly; half an hour before serving remove the paper and bacon; dredge slightly with flour, and baste with the dissolved butter till done. Make some rich brown sauce (*see* recipe); stir into it two tablespoonsful of red currant jelly and a glass of port wine, and serve at once a little on the dish with the hare and the rest on a tureen.

Ingredients of Stuffing.
The liver and kidneys
1 shalot
1 oz. of butter
½ lb. of beef suet
3 oz. of bread-crumbs
1 tablespoonful of chopped parsley
1 oz. of lean ham (or bacon chopped)
1 saltspoonful of mixed sweet herbs
⅙ part of a nutmeg (grated)
The grated rind of ½ lemon and its juice
1 saltspoonful of white pepper
1 ,, ,, salt
1 ,, ,, loaf sugar
1 wineglassful of port or marsala
1 beaten egg
Some slices of bacon
Some baked flour
¼ lb. of dissolved butter

LEVERETS are roasted in the same way, using ½ the quantities given for the stuffing, and roasting for ¾ of an hour.

24.—Braised Hare.

Make a stuffing as for Roast Hare (*see* recipe); put it into the body of the hare, and sew it up with a needle and thread. Peel and slice the shalots, carrots and mushrooms; put them into a stewpan with the bacon; lay the hare in, back uppermost; add the stock, marsala and butter; simmer very gently for 2½ hours; baste frequently with the gravy; take out the hare; rub the gravy and vegetables through a fine sieve, mix the flour with it, put it back into the stewpan with the hare; simmer twenty minutes more, then serve with currant jelly.

Ingredients.
4 shalots
2 small carrots
6 mushrooms
2 slices of bacon
1 pint of stock
1 gill of marsala
4 oz. of butter
2 dessertspoonsful of baked flour

25.—Braised Leveret.

See preceding recipe; using half the quantities given, and 1¾ hours as the time for stewing.

26.—Jugged Hare.

Have a fine young hare cut into joints; wash and wipe each piece, and dredge it over with dry flour. Peel, wash and slice the onions, mushrooms, carrot, celery, and parsley; put them into a stewpan with the cloves, mace, thyme and bacon; lay the hare on the vegetables; divide the butter into three slices; and lay them on it. Stand the

Ingredients.
1 onion
4 mushrooms
1 carrot
½ head of celery
6 sprigs of parsley
2 cloves
½ inch of mace
1 sprig of thyme
2 thin slices of bacon
6 oz. of butter
2 saltspoonsful of salt
1½ ,, ,, pepper
1 teaspoonful of moist sugar
1 pint of good stock
1 tablespoonful of flour
¼ of a pint of port wine

Ingredients of Forcemeat Balls.

The liver of the hare
½ oz. of lean cooked ham (or bacon)
3 oz. of veal suet
1 dessertspoonful of chopped parsley
2 oz. of bread-crumbs
2 saltspoonsful of mixed sweet herbs.
1 saltspoonful of pepper
1 ,, ,, salt
1 ,, ,, loaf sugar
½ ,, ,, flour of mustard
The grated rind and strained juice of ½ lemon
1 tablespoonful of brandy
2 beaten eggs
Some baked flour and butter

stewpan by the side of the fire, and let it simmer gently until the hare is firm and well flavoured with the ingredients; shake frequently. Take out the hare, strain the gravy, and skim off all the butter; lay the hare again in the stewpan (leaving out the liver); season with the salt, pepper and sugar; put in the gravy; add the stock mixed with the flour and port wine; cover closely; shake the stewpan constantly and simmer *very gently* for an hour; then lay in the forcemeat balls which make as follows :— Chop the liver, ham, suet and parsley as fine as possible; add the bread-crumbs, herbs, pepper, salt, sugar, mustard, lemon-rind and juice, brandy and beaten eggs; beat with a wooden spoon until well mixed; then make it up into balls a little smaller than a walnut; dredge them well with baked flour, and fry in the butter skimmed off the gravy until they are slightly browned; lay them in a stewpan with the hare and continue to simmer for forty minutes. Serve very hot, with plenty of currant jelly on a plate.

27.—Boiled Rabbit.

Ingredients.

1 carrot
2 onions
A bunch of parsley
6 peppercorns
1 teaspoonful of salt
2 sprigs of thyme
Half a clove of garlic

Wash the rabbit well, soak it in milk and water (equal parts) for two hours. Truss it with two wooden skewers and some string, and put it on the fire with enough of the milk and water in which it was soaked to cover it; add the carrots, onions, parsley, peppercorns, salt, thyme and garlic; boil up and simmer gently for 35 or 45 minutes. Take out the skewers, and serve with some fried bacon and any of the following sauces:

Either rich white sauce, (*see* recipe) in which case mix with it the livers parboiled and pounded, and well seasoned with cayenne and lemon-juice; or else onion sauce, (*see* recipe) ·or celery sauce, (*see* recipe) or white mushroom sauce (*see* recipe).

28.—Rabbit á la Tartare.

(*See* Fowl á la Tartare.)

29.—Brown Fricassee of Rabbit.

Ingredients.
1 young rabbit
1 clove of garlic
Some baked flour
12 button onions
20 ,, mushrooms
¼ lb. of butter
1 saltspoonful of pepper
1 ,, ,, salt
1 ,, ,, sugar
1 teaspoonful of chopped parsley
½ saltspoonful of mixed sweet herbs
1 tablespoonful of Harvey's sauce
¾ of a pint of any stock
¼ lb. of good streaky bacon
1 wineglassful of marsala
The juice of one lemon

Cut the rabbit into joints, and put it into cold water with the garlic; let it remain one hour; wipe it dry and dredge each piece with flour. Peel the onions and mushrooms and fry them in the butter until they are slightly browned, then drain. Fry the rabbit in the same butter till of a pale brown colour, then drain. Mix into the butter one tablespoonful of the flour, the pepper, salt, sugar, parsley, herbs, sauce and stock; boil fast for ten minutes: then stand it aside for the butter to rise; skim and strain. Cut the bacon into pieces the size of an inch, put it into the gravy with the rabbit, and simmer gently for 25 minutes; then add the mushrooms, onions, sherry and lemon-juice; simmer for fifteen or twenty minutes. Serve very hot.

30.—Rabbit fried in Batter.

Ingredients.
1 sliced onion
4 sprigs of parsley
1 sprig of thyme
1 saltspoonful of salt
1   ,,   ,, pepper
1 tablespoonful of oil
1   ,,   ,, white vinegar

Cut up the rabbit into joints and put it in a basin with the onion, parsley, thyme, salt, pepper, oil, and vinegar; leave it for three hours, turning the rabbit occasionally in order that it may become thoroughly impregnated with the sauce. A quarter of an hour before dinner take the rabbit out of the sauce, dip each piece in batter (*see* recipe) and drop it into boiling butter or lard; fry a light brown color, (fifteen minutes) and when the pieces are crisp, drain them on a sieve before the fire and dish up with fried parsley in the centre, and some Maitre d' Hotel sauce, (*see* recipe) or Tartar sauce (*see* recipe) in a sauce boat.

31.—Rabbit Curry.

Ingredients.
3 good sized onions
2 tablespoonsful of any curry powder (*see* recipes) or Capt. White's curry paste
1 dessertspoonful of dried flour
3 oz of good butter
¼ of a clove of garlic
Some stock
The strained juice of a lemon
½ gill of cocoanut milk (or good cream)
½ lb. of good rice

Peel and slice the onions; dredge them with the curry powder and dried flour, and fry them in the butter until they are of a pale brown color. Put them into a stewpan with the rabbit, cut into small pieces, the garlic, and enough stock to moisten; simmer very gently, stirring frequently for 1½ hours; add the lemon-juice and cream, and serve at once with a separate dish of boiled rice. Wash the rice, put it into three pints of cold water, and boil for half an hour; drain on a sieve before the fire or in the oven; separate the grains by stirring with a wooden fork.

32.—Rabbit Pudding.

Ingredients.
1 piled saltspoonful of pepper
1 ,, ,, ,, salt
1 grain of cayenne
3 oz. of bacon (cut into strips)
½ lb. of beef suet
½ ,, ,, flour
1 pinch of salt
½ gill of cold water
1 teaspoonful of stock (or water)

Cut up the rabbit, and season it with the pepper, salt and cayenne. Make a paste as follows:—Chop the beef suet and knead it into a stiff paste with the flour, suet and water; grease a basin, roll out the paste (keeping a small piece for the top); line the basin; lay in the rabbit and bacon; add the stock; roll out the piece of paste for the top; wet it and press it round so as to make both edges adhere; dip a cloth into boiling water, dredge it with flour, tie over the pudding, put it into plenty of boiling water, and boil 3½ or 4 hours. Loosen the edge with a knife, turn out carefully, and serve at once.

CURRIES.

Note.—In all cases where ghee is given in the recipe butter or *good salad oil* may be substituted. The latter will be found far the most wholesome ingredient in hot weather.

1.—Fish Curry.

Ingredients.
2 lbs. fish
4 oz. ghee
4 oz. curds
8 oz onions
1 teaspoonful { dried chillies / green chillies / green ginger / garlic
1 oz. salt
1 dessertspoonful { Mathee Bajee seeds / ginger
1 oz. tamarind
½ oz. turmeric
½ oz. coriander seed
A few leaves of green coriander

Pound the chillies in a mortar; mix the ginger, garlic, mathee bajee seeds, turmeric, coriander seed, and 4 oz. of onions with the chillies and pound them well together; fry the remainder of the onions in the ghee till they are well browned. Express the tamarind juice and mix it with the dhye, ghee, browned onions, coriander leaves and chillies; fry the fish in the ghee with the onions; add all the other ingredients and simmer until done—about 20 minutes.

2.—Another Fish Curry.

Ingredients.
2 lbs. of fish
8 oz. of ghee or oil
8 oz. of curds
4 oz. of gram (chenna) flour
4 oz. of Thillee oil
10½ oz. of onions
2 oz. of tamarind

Clean the fish and cut it up in pieces; prick it then with the point of a fork, and rub it with the flour; mix the salt and turmeric in the oil; dip the pieces of fish in it, and leave them to soak for an hour; take them out

Ingredients of Fish Curry.

½ oz. { green ginger / coriander seed (roasted) / garlic / aniseed / zeera }
1 oz. of salt
20 grains of cinnamon
10 grains of { cloves / cardamons / capsicum }
1 oz. of turmeric
The juice of a lemon

and rub them again with the flour and the tyre; wash this off with the lemon-juice; grind the aniseed and zeera in water; rub it into the fish. Grind all the spices; sprinkle them over the fish; put the ghee on the fire in a saucepan and when it is hot throw in the pieces of fish; shake them gently; grind the tamarind and pour it over the fish; simmer it gently for few minutes; cover the saucepan and cook over a slow fire till done, giving it an occasional shake to keep the fish from burning.

3.—Egg Curry.

Boil the eggs till they are quite hard; take off the shells

Ingredients.

10 eggs
10½ oz. of ghee, butter, or oil
1 tablespoonful of salt
10 grains of saffron
½ oz. of turmeric
2 teaspoonsful of cinnamon
2 ,, ,, cloves
2 teaspoonsful of cardamons
1 teaspoonful of black pepper
1 lime
6 onions

and separate the whites from the yolk; cut the whites into slices; grind up all the spices; take half and mix them with 2 oz. of the ghee, slice three of the onions and fry them brown in the ghee; add the eggs (yolks and whites) and fry them together; mix the remainder of the onions and spices with a little water; add the eggs, &c; boil the whole for a few minutes; add the lime-juice and serve.

4.—Fowl Curry.

Cut the fowl in pieces; sprinkle it over with half of the

Ingredients.

1 fowl
¼ lb. Kabul gram
½ lb. onions
½ oz. coriander seed (roasted)
1 oz. salt

onions sliced, the green ginger, salt and coriander seed, (all well ground.) Wash the gram and

CURRIES.

Ingredients of Fowl Curry.
40 grains cinnamon
,, ,, cloves
,, ,, cardamons
20 ,, of black pepper
½ oz. of green ginger
4 oz. of ghee

boil it in a little water until it becomes tender; pour it over the fowl; drain the gravy into a saucepan; add all the remainder of the spices except the cloves; put ½ the ghee into a saucepan with the cloves, add the gravy and fry for a few minutes; put the fowl into another stewpan with some ghee and fry it for 10 minutes; add the gravy and simmer gently till tender.

5.—Partridge Curry.

Ingredients.
4 partridges
2 lbs. of mutton
½ lb. of ghee or butter
¼ lb. of onions
½ oz. of garlic
1 oz. of coriander seeds
1 pint of cream
¼ lb. of blanched almonds
1 oz. of salt
1 drachm of turmeric
40 grains of cinnamon
40 ,, ,, cloves
40 ,, ,, cardamom
¾ oz. of ginger
2 oz. of gram flour
1 lemon
A little rice water

Cut the mutton in slices and put it in a sauce-pan with half of the onions, half of the green ginger and coriander seeds, pounded, and half the salt; simmer till the meat is quite tender and separates from the bones. Put 3 oz. of the ghee with the cloves in a saucepan; strain in the gravy and give it a good stir on the fire till it is well mixed. Cut the partridges down the middle length ways; wash them well; prick the pieces all over with a fork; rub in the flour and then wash it off; cut up two of the onions; rub them well over the partridges, and then wash the pieces again; fry them in the ghee with the remainder of the onions sliced and the juice of the rest of the ginger (bruised); grind the spices with a little salt; mix all together and boil with some of the gravy until it is tender and nearly dried up; then fry and sprinkle over with the juice of the lemon and the garlic; add the rest of the gravy and boil gently for ¼ of an hour. Grind the almonds with the rice water; add the cream; stir well and pour over the partridges, simmer for 20 minutes and serve.

6.—Meat, Egg and Vegetable Curry.

Ingredients.
2 lbs. of mutton
5 eggs
½ lb. of butter
½ lb. of onions
¾ oz. of green ginger
20 grains of capsicum (ground)
20 ,, of turmeric
¼ lb. of turnips
½ lb. ,, carrots
¼ lb. of Bengal beet or spinach
¾ oz. of green gram
½ oz. of coriander seed
1 oz. of salt
40 grains of cinnamon
40 ,, ,, cardamom

Mix all the ground spices except the turmeric with the butter; cut the meat in pieces and fry it in the butter; add water enough to moisten it, and set it on the fire to boil; clean the vegetables and add them to the meat and butter. When tender take the saucepan off the fire and strain off the gravy; take out the beetroot, mash it in the gravy, stir it round over the fire; add the meat and vegetables and simmer till done; boil the eggs hard, cut them in halves and when the curry is all but ready add the eggs and turmeric powder, simmer for 5 minutes and serve.

7.—Kid Curry.

Ingredients.
2 lbs. of kid's meat
10½ oz. of butter
½ lb. of curds
¼ lb. of onions
¾ oz. of green ginger
¾ ,, ,, salt
4 oz. of blanched almonds
4 oz. of cream
¾ oz. of *dhall*
½ oz. of turmeric
½ oz. of garlic
40 grains of cardamoms
40 ,, ,, cinnamon
40 ,, . ,, cloves
Some rice water
The juice of 1 lime

Slice half the onions, garlic and ginger; put them in the frying-pan with 4 oz. of butter and fry till brown; strain the butter into a sauce-pan and stand it near the fire where it will keep hot; cut the meat in small slices and season it with half the curry stuff, onions and ginger; mix them together with some of the curds, rub it over the meat and fry it for 3 minutes in the butter; add the dhall and the rest of the curds and boil till it is dried up; fry it well, add a little water and simmer till the meat is tender. Grind the almonds with the rice water, mix it with the cream, stir well and pour over the meat; then add the onions fried with the rest of the curry stuff to it; pour the lime-juice over it, simmer gently for 10 minutes, and serve.

8.—Kid and Egg Curry.

Ingredients.

2 lbs. of kid's meat
7 eggs
1 lb. of butter
¼ „ „ onions
1 oz. of garlic
¾ oz. of salt
1 drachm of turmeric
½ oz. of green ginger
20 grains { cinnamon, cardamom, black pepper, cloves

Wash the meat well and cut it into the shape of dice; pound the ginger, half the onions, and garlic; squeeze the juice into a basin; add the salt; rub the meat with this; fry the remainder of the onions sliced in the butter; give the meat a stir round in it; add a little water and boil fully till the mixture is all dried up; then fry it well; take the whites of the eggs, put them in a basin with a little water, and warm over the fire, stirring with a spoon all the time; add to the meat and simmer with a little water for a quarter of an hour; add the curry spices, ground, simmer for a few minutes, and serve.

9.—Mutton, Egg and Vegetable Curry.

Ingredients.

2 lbs. of mutton
5 eggs
½ lb. of butter
¼ lb. of onions
¾ oz. of green ginger
20 grains of capsicum

Pound all the spices except the turmeric; mix them with the butter; cut the meat in pieces, and fry it with the spices and butter; add a little water and put it on to boil; clean the

Ingredients of Mutton, Egg and Vegetable Curry.

20 grains of turmeric
¼ lb. of turnips
½ lb. of carrots
¼ lb. of paluk (beet) leaves or spinach
2 oz. of moong (green gram)
½ oz. of coriander seed
1 oz. of salt
40 grains of { cinnamon / cardamom }

vegetables and moong, and add them to the meat; when tender take off the fire and strain off the gravy; wash the moong in it and give the whole a fry; add the meat and vegetables and boil for a few minutes; boil the eggs hard, cut them in half; when the curry is done add the eggs and the turmeric, (ground) simmer for a few minutes, and serve.

10.—Mutton, Eggs and Pistachio Nut Curry.

Cut the meat in pieces; slice the onions, and put them

Ingredients.

2 lbs. of mutton
5 eggs
½ lb. of butter
¼ lb. of onions
¼ oz. each of { green ginger / coriander seed / salt }
1 oz. each of { pistachio nuts / blanched almonds / raisins }
40 grains of cinnamon
20 grains of cloves
20 „   „ cardamom
20 „   „ turmeric
The juice of a lime

with the salt, green ginger, and ground coriander into the butter and fry; when it is done take out ½ lb. of the meat; lay it aside; add a little water to the remainder; boil till the meat is tender; strain off the gravy; give the meat a quick stir over the fire; stir in a little flour and water and the spices, except the turmeric, ground to a paste; boil gently. Take a quarter of the meat laid aside; stir the white of the eggs in a little water; add it to the meat; set it on the fire; when it is done add the remainder of the meat; stir well and when thoroughly done stir in the lime-juice, sprinkle with the powder of turmeric and serve.

11.—Mutton and Mangoe Curry.

Cut the meat in small pieces; heat a saucepan on the fire

Ingredients of Mutton and Mangoe Curry.

2 lbs. of mutton
½ lb. of ghee or butter
1½ lbs. of unripe mangoes
¼ lb. of onions
½ oz. of salt
¼ „ green ginger
½ „ coriander seeds
20 grains of black pepper
20 „ „ cardamom
20 „ „ cloves
40 grains of cinnamon
¼ lb. of sugar
¾ oz. of raisins
20 grains of turmeric
The juice of 2 limes
A little rice milk

and put in half the ghee and the onions sliced; fry until they are brown; add the meat and fry until the gravy is well mixed with the ghee; add the salt; pound the coriander seeds and a little water; boil till the meat is nearly done. Strain the gravy into another sauce-pan; put some cloves in the remainder of the ghee; fry the meat in it again; clean and stone the raisins; add them to the meat. Take half the mangoes, clean and cut them into small slices and boil in water till tender. Make a syrup with the sugar and lime-juice and pour it over the mangoes; let it stand for an hour, pour off the syrup; boil the remainder of the mangoes, wash them and add the syrup; pour this over the meat; boil for a few minutes. Add the preserved mangoes, curry stuff and the turmeric ground in the rice milk. Simmer for a few minutes stirring well, and serve.

12.—How to boil Rice for Curries.

Spread it on a table or cloth, and pick out all the stones, gravel and dirt; wash it in 2 or 3 different waters, rubbing the grains well between the hands; add a little lime-juice or alum powder to whiten it; drain off the rice and throw it into plenty of water; boil it gently and simmer till tender; throw it into a cullender and let it drain for a few minutes; then put it back into the sauce-pan uncovered, spread a cloth over the top, stand it close to the fire till it has steamed quite dry so that every grain is separate; then serve an once.

PELAUS.

1.—Fish Pelau.

Ingredients.
2 lbs. fish
1½ lbs. of meat
1 lb. of rice
¾ lb. of ghee
½ lb. of onions
4 oz. green ginger
¾ oz. of coriander seeds
2 oz. of blanched almonds
1 drachm of cinnamon
½ ,, ,, cardamom
½ ,, ,, cloves
½ ,, ,, black pepper
1½ oz. pounded raw gram flour
2 oz. of sweet oil
1 ,, ,, salt
¼ oz. of garlic
¼ lb. of curds
Some rice water

Clean the fish well; cut it into slices and dip it in the salad-oil; leave it for half an hour; wipe it; rub it over with the pounded gram flour and wash it in water; prick the fish with a fork; bruise some of the onions, a little of the ginger, salt and spices with the curds, and cover the fish with this. Fry it in some of the ghee to a nice brown color; fry some of the onions sliced in a little ghee, and give the fish a quick turn in this; fry some more sliced onions separately in ghee with a little garlic and a few cloves, the almonds and some coriander seeds (ground), and a little rice water and turmeric till it forms a sauce; stand it off the fire. Cut the meat in slices, wash it well, put it in a saucepan with a little water, the rest of the onions, green ginger, salt and pounded coriander seeds; boil till thoroughly done. Put the meat and gravy into a coarse cloth; strain out the gravy into a basin; put some ghee and cloves into a saucepan, add the strained sauce and give it a quick turn over the fire. Parboil the rice; mix it with the gravy, and boil till the rice is thoroughly done; put the rice in another saucepan, add the spices; cover the sauce-pan and let it stand on the fire for a few minutes; put the fish and gravy on the top and serve.

2—.Fowl and Egg Pelau.

Ingredients.
A fine fowl
5 eggs
1½ lbs. of mutton
1½ ,, ,, rice
1½ ,, ,, ghee
1 drachm of cinnamon
¼ ,, ,, cardamom
½ ,, ,, cloves
2 drachms of black pepper
¾ of an oz. of coriander seeds
20 grains of turmeric
¾ of an oz. of salt
¼ lb. of onions
¾ oz. of green ginger
¼ lb. of curds

Mince ½ lb. of mutton very fine with some salt and coriander seeds; fry in some of the ghee and set on one side. Chop the rest of the mutton up fine; add ¼ of the ginger with a little of the spices and salt to the whites of the eggs well beaten up; put the whole into a mortar and pound it to a paste; make it up into small balls and fry them in ghee; beat up the yolks with some sliced onions, ground ginger, spices, and a little ghee; heat in a frying-pan and put the mixture in. Dress it as you would an omelet; sprinkle the turmeric over and set it aside.

Clean the fowl, rub it with some salt and the juice of some of the onions and green ginger; put in the minced meat as stuffing and tie it up close; put the fowl on the spit; mix some of the turmeric, cloves and cardamom (well ground) with the curds; smear some of this over the fowl, and keep on basting it with the remainder until the fowl is properly roasted. Parboil the rice in water with some cinnamon, cloves, cardamom and black pepper. Take another sauce-pan; put in the rice, balls, and fried eggs, with some gravy from the fowl and ghee; cover the saucepan closely and let the mixture simmer till the rice is done; then serve it on a dish with the roast fowl in the centre.

3.—Meat and Egg Pelau.

Take 1½ lbs. of the meat and cut it into slices; put it

Ingredients of Meat and Egg Pelau.

2 lbs. of meat
5 eggs
10 ½ oz. of butter or ghee
½ lb. of onions
½ oz. of green ginger
1 „ „ dried apricots
1 „ „ pistachio nuts
1 „ „ almonds
1 „ „ raisins
40 grains of cinnamon
20 „ „ cloves
20 „ „ cardamons
20 „ „ black pepper
20 „ „ cummin seed
2 lbs. of rice

into a saucepan with the onions and ginger, sliced, some salt, coriander seeds (ground in a little of the butter); boil till the meat is tender. Strain off the gravy into another saucepan; add a little butter and cloves to the meat and give it a quick fry over the fire; pound the cummin seeds and half the spices and add them to the meat. Parboil the rice in plain water add it to the gravy and boil till the rice is done; put it and some of the butter into the saucepan with the meat; cover closely; simmer gently for an hour. Mince the remainder of the meat and give it a quick fry with some butter; add some salt and pounded coriander seeds and a little water; boil gently; when it is done and the ghee and gravy are well mixed put in the raisins, pistachios, apricots, blanched almonds, and spices, with the whites of the eggs well beaten up, and let it all stand beside the fire till it is quite done; fry the yolks of the eggs in a little butter; put the rice on a dish, the minced meat on it, the fried eggs on the top, and serve.

4.—Meat and Plantain Pelau.

Cut the meat in slices; put it into a saucepan with some

Ingredients.

3 lbs. of meat
2 „ „ rice
1 „ „ ghee
10 plantains
½ lb. of onions
3 „ „ limes
1½ lbs. of sugar
½ oz. of salt
40 grains of cinnamon
20 „ „ cloves
20 „ „ cardamons
¾ oz. green ginger
½ „ coriander seeds
20 grains of cummin seeds

water, sliced onions, green ginger, pounded, salt and coriander seeds and a little ghee; boil till the meat is done; strain the gravy into a separate saucepan, add a little ghee and some cloves to the meat and give it a quick fry; make a clear syrup with 1 lb. of the sugar, a little water, and the juice of 2 limes; add this to the gravy. Put the meat into another saucepan with the corianda seeds, spices and a little of the gravy; mix well and boil till the gravy is reduced. Parboil the rice in water, stir it into the gravy, and boil till it is tender; add it to the meat and boil together for 10 minutes; add some more ghee; cover the saucepan close and simmer over a gentle fire. Make some more clear syrup with the remainder of the sugar, a little water, and the juice of a lime; cut each plantain length-wise in 4 pieces, and boil these in the syrup till done. Serve the pelau with the plantains and gravy on the top.

VEGETABLES.

1.—Boiled Potatoes.

They should be as nearly the same size as possible; wash off the earth and rub them with a clean cloth, but neither scrape them nor take off the eyes. Rinse them in cold water, and put them into a saucepan *close together*, so that they may not lie loose, and a small quantity of water will suffice to cover them. Pour this in cold, and when it boils throw in a tablespoonful of salt, and *simmer* the potatoes until they are nearly done; then boil *quickly* for three or four minutes. When they are quite tender (which may be known by probing them with a fork), pour off all the water, tip up the lid so as to let the steam escape, and put the saucepan close beside the fire for ten minutes. They must be sent to table *instantly* either peeled or in their skins, and should be served on a hot napkin. Some potatoes are done in twenty minutes, some take one hour or more, it depends on the size and also on the kind of potato.

Note.—This common vegetable which is so delicious when properly cooked, is generally prepared in such a manner as to be perfectly uneatable, sodden and heavy, and many people who find it disagree with them attribute the fault to the vegetable instead of to the manner of cooking. Dressed as above, served in their skins and eaten with a little fresh butter, they afford in themselves an almost sufficient meal.

Note 2.—Potatoes are better boiled in salt water than in fresh.

2.—New Potatoes.

Rub off the skins with a rough cloth: let them stand half

an hour in cold water; put them into boiling water with one saltspoonful of salt, and boil ten minutes. Pour off the water, steam for ten minutes, and serve on a hot dish with one ounce of fresh butter in the centre, or on a hot napkin, neatly folded.

3.—Fried Potatoes.

Pare the potatoes and cut them into thin slices or quarters; let them stand in cold water ten minutes; drain and wipe them quite dry; throw them into a sauce-pan *half filled* with boiling fat, and fry to a light brown colour. Take them out with a slice, and put them on a sheet of white blotting paper (or brown paper) on a sieve, before the fire, to absorb the fat before serving.

Note.—The secret of good fried potatoes is to put them into *plenty* of boiling fat. The wire baskets recommended for whitebait may be advantageously used for all kinds of frying.

4.—Mashed Potatoes.

Boil as directed, and rub them while quite hot through a sieve; put the pulp into a saucepan with two ounces of butter, three saltspoonsful of salt, one of pepper, and one gill of cream heated (or the same quantity of milk with one yolk beaten in it). Beat vigorously over the fire with a wooden spoon to make them light, and serve at once.

5.—New Potatoes in Butter.

Rub off the skins with a coarse cloth; wash the potatoes and wipe them dry, and put them with three ounces of butter into a small saucepan; simmer them *gently* for half an hour over the fire, shaking them all the time; when they are half done sprinkle a teaspoonful of salt over them ; serve *very* hot on a hot dish.

Note.—A little chopped parsley sprinkled over them when the salt is put in is a great improvement.

6.—Potatoes, à la Maitre d'Hotel.

Ingredients.
1 spoonful of broth, (or white sauce,)
4 oz. of butter
Some pepper and salt
1 teaspoonful of chopped parsley
1 dessertspoonful of lemon juice

Boil the potatoes as directed. If they are large, cut them in slices about quarter of an inch thick; if new, serve them whole. When done put them into a small saucepan with all the ingredients, and toss them gently over a clear fire until they are quite hot. Serve instantly.

7.—Potatoes, à l'Italienne.

Ingredients.
1 tablespoonful of cream (or milk)
1 oz. butter
2 eggs
Some salt

Boil the potatoes as directed, peel them, put them through a sieve into a saucepan; sprinkle with a little salt, put in the yolks of the eggs, the cream and milk, and stir them over the fire with a wooden spoon. Beat the whites to a strong froth and mix them in lightly with the potatoes; pile them up in a rocky form on a dish and brown before the fire or in an oven; or else press them into a mould well buttered and strewed with fine bread-crumbs, turn them out and brown in the oven.

Note.—If any of this potato is left it is delicious formed into balls dipped in beaten egg and fine bread-crumbs, and fried brown in butter.

8.—Baked Potatoes.

Scrub and wash them exceedingly clean; wipe them very dry, and either bake them in front of the fire, placing them at a distance from it and turning them constantly, or bake them in a moderate oven. Serve *very hot* with some cold butter. They will take from one and three quarters to two hours.

9.—Potato Snow.

Boil the potatoes as directed, and when they are done press them through a wire sieve, previously heated, into the hot dish on which they are to be served.

10.—New Potatoes, à la Creme.

Boil the potatoes as directed, cut them into slices and put them into a stewpan with the ingredients. Toss them for a few minutes over the fire, and serve them with sippets of fried bread round the dish.

Ingredients.
½ gill of cream
2 oz. of fresh butter
½ saltspoonful of salt
½ ,, ,, pepper
The juice of half lemon

11.—Potatoes, à la Proveneale.

Cut up the potatoes into rounds a quarter of an inch thick; fry them in boiling oil till of a light brown color; season them with the parsley, shalot, pepper and salt, and pour over the lemon-juice.

Ingredients.
6 boiled potatoes
1 oz. of salad oil
1 teaspoonful of chopped parsley and shalot
1 saltspoonful of salt
½ ,, ,, pepper
The juice of half lemon

Note.—A small piece of glaze about two inches square is a great improvement.

12.—Potato Croquets.

Bake the potatoes; rub their pulp through a sieve; put

Ingredients of Potato Croquets.
6 potatoes
1 oz. of butter
3 yolks of eggs
1 saltspoonful of salt
½ ,, ,, pepper
Some beaten eggs
Some bread-crumbs

it into a stewpan with the butter the three yolks, salt and pepper; stir over the fire until the paste ceases to adhere to the sides of the stewpan; turn it out on a plate, put another over it, and let it stand till cold. Then shape it into balls, dip each into beaten egg, and then into bread-crumbs, and fry to a light brown color in boiling fat.

13.—Potato Salad.

Cut some cold boiled potatoes into slices; add some beetroot and celery and some lettuce leaves, cress or endive; season with oil, vinegar, pepper, salt, chopped parsley and shalot, and serve.

14.—Potato Hash.

Put some cold chopped potatoes into a frying-pan with one ounce of butter, or two slices of bacon cut into little pieces; stir over the fire for five minutes; add some cold meat minced and seasoned with pepper and salt, and fry gently until hot all through. Serve at once, with or without fried sippets.

15.—Kale Cannon.

Take some mashed potatoes and the remains of cabbage

Ingredients.
Pepper and salt
½ oz. of butter
2 tablespoonsful of cream or milk
1 onion

or brussels sprouts; chop the latter a little; mash these well together and season with a little pepper and salt, the butter and milk. Put a raw onion into the middle of the mash, stir over the fire until it is very hot; take the onion out, and serve the Kale Cannon at once on a very hot dish.

16.—Spinach, plain.

Pick off the stem of each leaf and avoid using any that are old or discolored; wash the spinach in several waters, and put it into a quart of water with a dessertspoonful of salt; press it down with a wooden spoon, and let it boil rapidly (uncovered) for fifteen minutes; drain it through a sieve, and press out all the water; mince it quite fine, and put it into a small stewpan with a pat of butter and a little pepper and salt; stir for two or three minutes, and serve at once with some fried sippets of bread.

17.—Spinach Purée.

Prepare the spinach as above; when the water has been pressed out, rub the spinach through a coarse wire sieve, and put it into a stewpan with all the ingredients; stir it over the fire with a wooden spoon for six minutes, and serve piled up on a hot dish garnished with fried sippets.

Ingredients.
2 oz. of butter
1 saltspoonful of salt
½ ,, ,, pepper
1 teaspoonful of white sugar
1 piece of glaze (or a little strong broth)

18.—Spinach Purée with Cream.

Prepare as above, but at the moment of serving stir in a tablespoonful of thick cream.

Note.—Turnip tops may be dressed as above and are an excellent substitute for spinach, and the young leaves of dandelions dressed in the same way are a delicious and most wholesome dish.

19.—Spinach and Poached Eggs.

Prepare and dress spinach as for spinach purée with cream. Break four fresh eggs into separate cups; have a small bright omelet pan full of boiling water; put in a salt spoonful of salt and teaspoonful of vinegar; pour in carefully one egg at a time; as one sets, put in another; they will require three minutes; take them out with an egg slice, drain off the water, and place the eggs neatly on the spinach. Serve at once.

20.—Sorrel.

Sorrel is dressed in the same way as spinach, and all the recipes may be used for it.

21.—Stewed Sorrel.

Ingredients.
½ ounce of butter
1 spoonful of white sauce
1 saltspoonful of salt
1   ,,   ,, sugar

Wash the leaves clean; boil them tender in water and rub through a hair sieve into a saucepan; add the butter and white sauce; sprinkle over the salt and sugar; stew for a few minutes, and serve with sippets of toast.

22.—Stewed Endive.

Ingredients.
½ pint of veal broth
A slice of ham (or bacon)

Choose a piece of nice white endive, pick it and blanch it in boiling water, put it into cold water; take it out and squeeze it well; chop it with a knife; put it in a saucepan with the broth and bacon. Let it simmer over a gentle fire until it gets thick; remove the ham, and serve at once.

23.—Stewed Lettuces.

Ingredients.
1 saltspoonful of salt
½   ,,   ,, pepper
1 oz. of butter
A little flour
A teacup of broth

Strip off the outer leaves and cut away the stocks; wash them very carefully and throw them into water with a tablespoonful of salt. Boil for twenty

Ingredients of Stewed Lettuces.
A lemon-juice, little white vinegar, or thirty minutes, and when they are quite tender take them out and press all the water out of them; chop them (not very small) and put them into a clean saucepan with the pepper, salt and butter; then dredge them with a little flour, add the gravy, and boil quickly until they are nearly dry; stir in the lemon-juice or vinegar, and serve instantly with fried sippets round them.

24.—Green Peas, plain.

The peas must be young, fresh gathered, and fresh shelled.

Ingredients.
1½ pint of peas
3 pints of water
1 tablespoonful of sugar
1 ,, ,, salt
1 sprig of mint
1 oz. of fresh butter

Dissolve the sugar and salt in the water, and while it boils rapidly put in the peas and mint; boil fast, uncovered, for fifteen or twenty minutes; drain, take out the mint, turn the peas on to a hot dish, put the butter in the centre, and serve.

25.—Green Peas, à la Francaise.

Pull the heart of the lettuce apart, and put it into a stew-

Ingredients.
The heart of one lettuce
2 spring onions
1½ pint of peas
2 tablespoonsful of loaf sugar
1 teaspoonful of salt
1½ oz. of fresh butter
1 teacupful of water

pan with the onions, peas, sugar and salt, half an ounce of butter and the water; simmer gently for half an hour, shaking constantly. Take out the lettuce and onions, drain off the water, and put in one ounce of butter; *shake* till well mixed with the peas, and serve very hot.

26.—Peas, à la Crême.

Boil the peas as directed, drain them and put them into a

Ingredients.
1 oz. of butter
1 saltspoonful of salt

small degchee with all the ingredients; toss them over the fire till

W

Ingredients of Peas, à la Crème.
1 saltspoonful of pepper
1 " " sugar
1 wineglassful of cream
Or one tablespoonful of white sauce

well mixed, and serve very hot, either with cutlets, or as a vegetable separate.

27.—French Beans, plain.

Strip off the strings by breaking off each end; cut the beans into shreds one and half inches long and the sixth of an inch thick; throw them into water with one teaspoonful of salt in it, and let them remain one hour; drain and put them into fast-boiling water with one tablespoonful of salt, and boil fast, uncovered for twenty minutes. Drain and serve at once.

Note.—French cooks hold that we lose the flavor of the bean by cutting it so thin, and thus allowing all the juice to escape, that it is better when the beans are very young not to cut them, and only to cut them in half (lengthwise) when they are older.

28.—French Beans, stewed.

Boil as directed above for *ten* minutes; drain and put them into a small degchee with two tablespoonsful of broth, one ounce of butter rolled in a tablespoonful of flour, and half a tablespoonful of pepper; stew gently, ten or fifteen minutes till tender, and serve very hot.

29.—Fried French Beans.

Boil them either whole, or cut as above; drain off the water, and fry them in dissolved butter until they are slightly browned; sprinkle over a little pepper, and serve. Cold beans are quite as good as fresh boiled, dressed thus.

30.—French Beans, à la Francaise.

The beans must be quite fresh and young; strip off the

VEGETABLES.

*Ingredients of French Beans,
à la Francaise.*
1 lb. of beans
1 dessertspoonful of salt
3 oz of butter
1 tablespoonful of chopped parsley
1 saltspoonful of chives
The strained juice of a lemon

strings and ends and put them into cold water for one hour; drain and throw them into a saucepan of boiling water with the salt, and boil uncovered for one quarter of an hour ; drain quite dry. Knead the butter with the parsley and chives ; put the beans and butter into a degchee and fry till tender (about fifteen minutes) ; add the lemon-juice, and serve at once.

31.—Puree of Green Peas for Garnish.

Ingredients.
1 pint of green peas
2 spring onions
1 oz. of butter
1 oz. of glaze
½ saltspoonful of salt
½   ,,   ,, pepper
1 pinch of sugar

Boil the peas for twenty minutes with the mint and onions ; drain off the water; bruise the peas in a mortar, and rub them through a sieve or coarse cloth ; put the pulp in a small stewpan with the butter, glaze, pepper, salt and sugar; stir over the fire until quite hot, and pile up in the centre of the cutlets.

Note.—A little spinach-juice improves the color.

32.—Asparagus.

Scrape off the outer skin, cut off the end of the stalk leaving the asparagus about seven inches long ; tie it up into bundles with tape ; let it remain in cold water about two hours. Put it into plenty of boiling water with salt, and boil uncovered for twenty or thirty minutes ; take it out the *moment* it is tender. Cut a round of bread half an inch thick, take off the crust, toast the bread, pour over it while on the fork a cupful of the water in which the asparagus is boiling, spread it with butter on both sides, lay it on a hot dish, take the tape off the asparagus and serve it on the toast, with melted butter, or German sauce (*see* recipe) in a tureen.

33.—German Sauce.

Ingredients.
1 tablespoonful of baked flour
½ pint of cream
1 beaten yolk
2 oz. of butter
¼ of a saltspoonful of white pepper
¼ „ „ „ salt
1 teaspoonful of white vinegar

Mix the baked flour with the cream and stir it over the fire until it begins to thicken; then add the beaten yolk, butter, salt and vinegar; stir all together three minutes, and serve as directed.

34.—Asparagus Salad, cold.

Boil the asparagus as directed above, and let it get cold. Put it into a long deep dish; mix one tablespoonful of vinegar, two of oil, one saltspoonful of salt, half saltspoonful of pepper, one saltspoonful of minced parsley, and pour over the asparagus.

35.—Asparagus Toast.

Ingredients.
1 bundle of asparagus
3 spring onions
1 handful of parsley
1 dessertspoonful of salt
1 oz. of butter
1 dessertspoonful af flour
½ saltspoonful of salt
¼ „ „ pepper
1 oz. of glaze (if at hand)
1 saltspoonful sugar

Scrape and wash the asparagus, soak it in cold water for two hours; put it into plenty of boiling water with the onions, parsley and salt, and let it boil for half an hour. Drain off the water and remove the onions and parsley. Bruise the asparagus in a mortar, and rub it through a sieve; put the pulp in a small saucepan with the flour, butter, salt, pepper, glaze and sugar; stir over the fire for five minutes, pour over some toast, and serve.

36.—Sea-Kale.

Is tied in bundles and dressed in precisely the same as

asparagus, and served with either melted butter, or German sauce (*see* recipe.)

37.—Broad Beans, with Parsley Sauce.

Ingredients.
8 pints of beans
3 quarts of water
2 tablespoonsful of salt

The beans must be young and fresh shelled. Put them into the boiling water with the salt, and boil (uncovered) twenty-five minutes; drain and serve with parsley sauce (*see* recipe).

38.—Broad Beans, à la Francaise.

Ingredients.
¼ lb. of butter
1 dessertspoonful of chopped parsley
1 teaspoonful of chopped chives
4 gill of new milk
1 yolk
½ gill of thick cream

Boil the beans as directed in the preceding receipt; put them in a degchee with the butter, parsley, chives, and milk, simmer (shaking the stewpan frequently) for quarter of an hour; beat the yolk with the cream, stir it carefully into the beans, and serve immediately.

39.—Haricot Beans.

Ingredients.
1 saltspoonful of salt
1   ,,   ,, pepper
1 teaspoonful of parsley chopped
1   ,,   ,, chives
1 tablespoonful of lemon-juice
3 oz. of butter
2 tablespoonsful of cream

Soak the beans all night; put them on the fire in a degchee of cold water and let them boil slowly for two or three hours, till tender; drain off the water, and stir in the salt, pepper, parsley, chives, lemon-juice and butter, put on the lid of the saucepan and simmer half an hour, shaking constantly; add the cream and serve.

These beans are most delicious cooked as above, with the substitution of one gill of good gravy for the cream, and served with a roast leg of mutton.

40.—Artichokes.

Ingredients.
1 wineglassful of vinegar
1 tablespoonful of salt
2 quarts of water

Take off some of the outer leaves, trim the stem and cut off the points of the leaves with a pair of scissors; wash the artichokes and leave them in water for an hour. Put the vinegar and salt into the water, when it boils; put in the artichokes, and boil uncovered for three quarters of an hour. Drain off all the water, and serve on a napkin with melted butter (*see* recipe) in a tureen.

41.—Jerusalem Artichokes.

Ingredient.
1 teacupful of vinegar

Pare them and wash them in cold water with the vinegar in it; boil in plenty of water (boiling) for twenty minutes; drain them on a sieve, and serve with white sauce (*see* recipe) poured over them, or melted butter (*see* recipe).

42.—Jerusalem Artichokes, fried.

Ingredients.
2 yolks of eggs
2 oz. of fine bread-crumbs
1 grain of pepper
1 pinch of cayenne
1 tablespoonful of grated parmesan cheese

Boil them as in the foregoing receipt; beat the eggs, season the bread-crumbs with the pepper, cayenne, and Parmesan; dip the artichokes in the egg and strew them over with bread-crumbs; fry in butter to a pale brown color eight minutes, and serve at once.

43.—Mushrooms, baked.

The mushroom must be perfectly fresh and of a moderate size. Peel them and pull out the stems; wash them quickly in cold water, and wipe them quite dry; fill the black sides with butter, and on that sprinkle a grain of salt, a grain of pepper, and a pinch of cayenne, *on each mushroom.* Place the mushrooms, butter uppermost on a dish, and cover them with another dish; bake in a quick oven about twenty minutes; and serve very hot with their own gravy poured over them.

Another way.

Prepare them as above. When they are seasoned put them on rounds of toast, about six on a round; cover them with finger bowls, and bake as directed. Serve them with the finger bowls still on so that they may be *very* hot.

44.—Fried Mushrooms.

Prepare as in the foregoing receipt and cook on a gridiron, or in a frying-pan with the butter uppermost, for a quarter of an hour.

45.—Stewed Mushrooms.

Ingredients.
2 oz. of butter
1 tablespoonful of water
1 teaspoonful of vinegar
1 saltspoonful of pepper
1 teaspoonful of salt
½ gill of cream

Take off the skins and stems, wash them and put them in a small saucepan (an earthen stewpan is best), with the butter, water, vinegar, pepper, and salt; simmer for twenty minutes, throw in the cream, and serve very hot.

46.—Grilled Mushrooms.

Ingredients.
Some mushrooms
Oil, pepper, and salt
A little broth
Some chopped parsley
Three young onions
The yolk of an egg
Two tablespoonsful of cream

The mushrooms should be large; if fresh skin them and remove the stalks; lay them on a dish with a little oil, and sprinkle some salt and pepper over them; let them stand an hour, then broil on a gridiron over a clear fire; serve them dry on toast, or with the following sauce:—Mince the stalks, or any spare pieces of the mushrooms fine, put them into a small stewpan with the broth, chopped parsley, and onions; beat the yolk in the cream, stir it in, beat all thoroughly together, and pour round the mushrooms.

47.—Mushroom Toast.

Ingredients.
20 button mushrooms
The juice of a lemon
½ oz. of butter
Some pepper and salt
3 cloves
Small onions, parsley, and sweet savory
A little flour
Some veal broth
2 yolks of eggs
3 tablespoonsful of cream

Skin and clean the mushrooms and put them into a small stewpan with the lemon-juice, butter, pepper and salt; tie the cloves, onions, parsley and savory in a piece of muslin and put them in also; stew gently until nearly dry; dust in a little flour, add enough of broth to moistens, and stew gently for a quarter of an hour. Take out the herbs: beat up the eggs and cream, add them to the mushrooms; make some good buttered toast, put the mushrooms and sauce on it, and serve at once.

48.—Cucumber.

Ingredients.
1 dessertspoonful of salt
½ saltspoonful of white pepper
½ grain of cayenne
2 tablespoonsful of good oil
2 dessertspoonsful of vinegar

Pare the cucumber and cut it into slices one eighth of an inch thick; put it on a plate and strew the salt over it; let it remain for two hours; throw it into a quart of cold water, and drain immediately on a napkin. Place the slices (which will have become quite thin) on a dish neatly, sprinkle over them the pepper and cayenne, and add the oil and vinegar.

49.—Stewed Cucumbers, white.

Ingredients.
2 large cucumbers
1 quart of water
1 tablespoonful of salt
½ pint of veal stock
1 dessertspoonful of white vinegar
1 teaspoonful of sifted white sugar
2 yolks of eggs
1 gill of cream

The cucumbers should be fresh cut; peel them and cut each into four pieces lengthways, and again each piece into two, slanting the knife that the ends may be pointed. Put them into the cold water with the salt in it, and let them remain an hour; drain them, take out the seeds, and put the pieces of cucumber in a stewpan with the stock; vinegar, and sugar; simmer gently for half an hour. Beat the yolks with the cream; take out the cucumber and place them on a dish; stir the eggs and cream into the sauce for two minutes; pour it over the cucumbers, and serve at once.

50.—Stewed Cucumbers, brown.

Ingredients.
2 shalots
1 teaspoonful of brown sugar
½ saltspoonful of white pepper
1 tablespoonful of brown vinegar
1 saltspoonful of salt
2 oz. of butter
⅓ pint of stock

Prepare cucumbers as in the foregoing receipt, place them in a stewpan with the shalots, chopped, the sugar, pepper, vinegar, salt, butter and stock; simmer gently for an hour, and serve.

Note.—Eight small onions will be found a great improvement.

51.—Turnips, plain.

The turnips should be moderate sized; pare them neatly and put them into cold water to blanch for an hour; throw them into boiling water with a dessertspoonful of salt, and boil for half an hour, or until quite tender; drain and serve very hot.

Note.—Some people think that they are of a better flavour if boiled and pared afterwards.

52.—Mashed Turnips.

Prepare and boil the turnips as directed for plain turnips

Ingredients.
6 turnips
½ saltspoonful of salt
1 oz. of butter
1 gill of thin cream, (or new milk)

press out all the water and rub them through a wire sieve with a wooden spoon; put them into a stewpan with the salt, butter, and cream; stir over the fire until they have absorbed all the moisture, and serve boiling hot.

Note.—A little good white sauce if you have it at hand, is a great improvement to this excellent receipt.

53.—Turnips Glacés, with Sugar.

Trim the turnips in the shape of small pears, (if they

Ingredients.
2 dozen young turnips
½ oz. of butter
2 oz. of pounded loaf sugar
1 saltspoonful of salt
½ pint of good broth

are quite young, which is best, leave them their own shape); put the butter, sugar, and salt into a deep saucepan, moisten with the broth, and lay in the turnips carefully; simmer very gently over a moderate fire for twenty minutes; remove the lid, set the pan on a brisk fire to reduce the sauce to a glaze, rolling about the turnips with great care to avoid breaking them. Dish with the sauce poured over.

54.—Turnips stewed in Butter.

The turnips must be young and finely grained; wash, wipe

Ingredients.
1½ lbs. of turnips
3 oz. butter
½ teaspoonful of salt
½   ,,   ,, white pepper

and pare them; slice them half an inch thick and divide them into dice. Dissolve the butter in a saucepan and lay in the turnips; stew very gently for an hour; when they are half done, season with the salt and pepper. Serve either in the centre of cutlets or by them-

55.—Carrots.

Rub the carrots with a coarse cloth and cut off the ends; put them into boiling water with the salt, sugar, and parsley; boil about half an hour if they are young, an hour if they are old; drain and serve with the hot cream poured over them.

Ingredients.
1 dessertspoonful of salt
1 tablespoonful of loaf sugar
1 sprig of parsley
1 gill of hot cream

56.—Carrots with Butter.

Prepare the carrots as above, but instead of the hot cream, put them into a saucepan with all the ingredients and toss them very gently until they are well covered with the sauce, which must never be allowed to boil. Serve very hot.

Ingredients.
2 oz. of butter
1 teaspoonful of minced parsley
1 saltspoonful of salt
½ ,, ,, white pepper
A pinch of cayenne

Note.—Cold carrots may be re-dressed in this way.

57.—Carrots à la Francaise.

Scrape the carrots; cut the small ends into two and the large ends into eight pieces; boil in water with the salt and sugar for one hour; drain on a cloth; place them on a stewpan with the butter, stew until the butter is nearly absorbed by the carrots; pour in the milk, and simmer gently for an hour. Beat the yolks; place the carrots on a hot vegetable dish; stir the eggs into the milk; simmer two minutes; pour the sauce over the carrots, and serve.

Ingredients.
1 dessertspoonful of salt
2 tablespoonsful of sugar
2 oz. of butter
½ pint of new milk
The yolks of two eggs

58.—Purée of Carrots.

Ingredients.
3 lbs. of fine carrots
2 oz. of butter
½ teaspoonful of salt
1 dessertspoonful of pounded sugar
½ pint of cream

Boil the carrots till quite tender, press the water from them and rub them through a fine sieve; put them into a clean stewpan and dry them thoroughly over a gentle fire, taking great care they do not burn; add the butter, and when this is well dissolved and mixed with them, strew in the sugar and salt; stir in the cream by degrees, and when the purée is thick and not too moist serve garnished with sippets of toast.

59.—Stewed Celery, with White Sauce.

Ingredients.
fine heads of celery
of a pint of veal stock
2 yolks of eggs
1 gill of cream

Cut off all the coarse outer leaves of the celery, trim the stem, cutting it across, one inch down; wash well and let it remain in water with a little salt in it for several hours; put it into a stewpan with the stock; simmer very gently an hour and a half. Take out the celery and stir into the gravy the beaten yolks of two eggs and the cream; when set (two minutes will suffice), pour the sauce over the celery and serve.

60.—Stewed Celery, with Brown Sauce.

Ingredients.
2 oz. of butter
2 dessertspoonsful of dried flour
1 teaspoonful of sifted sugar
1 saltspoonful of salt
One twelfth part of a nutmeg
1 saltspoonful of pepper
1 pint of stock (No. 1)
The strained juice of a lemon

Wash and trim the celery as directed in the foregoing receipt; put it in a stewpan with the butter, and simmer till slightly brown. Dredge over the flour, sugar, salt, grated nutmeg and pepper; shake the pan and pour in the stock by degrees; simmer gently for an hour and a half; add the strained lemon-juice, and serve.

61.—Salsifis.

Ingredients.
1 wineglassful of vinegar
1 teaspoonful of salt
2 oz. of butter
1 tablespoonful of dry flour
½ pint of boiling milk
½ gill of thick cream

Scrape and cut the ends off each; throw them into cold water with the vinegar and salt, and let them remain ten minutes; then boil them in the same water for about twenty minutes. Serve with white sauce or melted butter *(see* recipe) poured over.

62.—Fried Salsifis.

Ingredients.
2 eggs
½ pint of milk
3 tablespoonsful of flour
Some butter or oil

Make a batter with the eggs, milk, and flour, well beaten together for twenty minutes; dip each (cold boiled) salsifis into the batter and fry until of a light brown color either in butter or oil. Serve very hot.

63.—Parsnips, plain boiled.

Ingredients.
1 teaspoonful of salt
1 ,,   ,, sugar

Scrape and wash the parsnips; cut out every speck or blemish; cut off the small end, and divide the thick end into four or six pieces lengthways; put them into boiling water with the salt and sugar; boil moderately fast for three quarters of an 'hour, and skim the water all the time. Serve with salt fish or boiled pork. They are very good mashed, *(see* recipe for Mashed Turnips).

64.—Fried Parsnips in Batter.

Ingredients.
2 eggs
½ pint of milk
3 tablespoonsful of flour.
Some butter or oil.

Cut up some cold boiled parsnips; dip the pieces in a batter made of the eggs, milk and flour, (well beaten for twenty minutes) and fry in butter or oil till of a pale brown color; serve very hot.

65.—Fried Parsnips, plain.

Boil some parsnips until they are about half done; when they are cold wipe them in a cloth, slice them thickly, sprinkle with salt and pepper, and fry in butter till of a pale brown color. Can be served separately, or with roast meat.

Ingredients.
Salt, white pepper, butter

66.—Vegetable Marrow.

Pare the marrows very neatly; cut them into quarters lengthway; take out the seeds and wipe the marrows with a coarse clean cloth; put them into boiling water, with a teaspoonful of salt, and boil for ten or fifteen minutes. Toast a round of bread, without crust; pour over a cupful of the vegetable water, and butter the toast. Serve the marrows upon it with either melted butter or white sauce (*see* recipes.)

67.—Vegetable Marrow, fried.

Prepare as above, dip into eggs and fine bread-crumbs and fry in plenty of butter until of a pale brown color.

68.—Stuffed Vegetable Marrows.

Have two moderate sized fresh cut marrows; rub the skin with a coarse cloth; cut off each end about half an inch deep; scoop out all the seeds and fill the vacancy with pork sausage meat pressed tightly in; rub the bottom of a stewpan six times across with the fresh-cut garlic; lay in the marrows; add the stock and all the other ingre-

Ingredients.
Some pork sausage meat
Some fresh-cut garlic
½ pint of stock (No. 1)
1 finely chopped shalot
The juice of 6 large tomatoes
1 tablespoonful of vinegar
½ grain of cayenne
1 saltspoonful of pepper
1   ,,   ,, salt
½ of a nutmeg, grated
2 oz. of butter

dients, laying one ounce of butter on each marrow; simmer gently for four hours; baste the marrow frequently with the sauce; skim off the fat, and serve with the sauce poured over the marrows.

Note.—Any white mince may be used instead of the pork sausage meat; game is especially good, and the bones of the birds may be used to make the stock. This dish makes a delicate *entrée*.

69.—Portugal Onions, stewed.

Peel the onions and place them in a stewpan; knead the butter and sugar; put it on the onions and let them slowly become slightly browned; then pour over each the tomato sauce and stalk; simmer gently for three hours, basting the onions frequently with the gravy. Serve very hot.

Ingredients for each Onion.
½ oz. of butter
1 saltspoonful of sifted sugar
1 teaspoonful of tomato sauce
1 tablespoonful of gravy

70.—Portugal Onions, boiled.

Peel the onions and boil them in salt and water for ten minutes; throw them into cold water for half an hour; then put them into a saucepan, cover them with cold water, and let them boil gently for one hour. Drain and serve with melted or dissolved butter over them.

71.—Portugal Onions, roasted.

Peel the onions and place them in a Dutch oven before a good fire; baste them frequently with dissolved butter (an ounce for each), and roast for an hour and a half. Serve with or without their own sauce.

72.—Portugal Onions, fried.

Peel and slice the onions quite thin; fry them in plenty

of boiling butter or olive oil till of a pale brown color, fifteen to twenty minutes. Drain on a sieve before the fire for five minutes.

73.—Portugal Onions, stuffed.

Ingredients.
2 large Portugal onions
Some pork sausage meat*
2 apples chopped fine
1 tablespoonful of baked flour
2 oz. of butter
½ pint of stock (No. 1)
The strained juice of 2 lemons
1 tablespoonful of brandy

* Any white mince will do, and if you use game the stock can be made from the bones of the birds.

Peel the onions; scoop out the centre, making a hole two inches across; fill them with the sausage meat and place them in a stewpan; pare, core and chop the apples very fine; knead the flour with the butter; put half on each onion; put in the apples and stock; simmer very slowly for three and a half hours; baste the onions frequently with the gravy; pour the lemon-juice and brandy over the onions, and in five minutes skim off the butter and serve, with the sauce poured over the onions.

74.—Boiled Leeks.

Ingredients.
1 tablespoonful of salt
1 dessertspoonful of vinegar

Trim off the root and the outer leaves; cut the green ends off, leaving the leeks six inches long; wash them well, put them into boiling water, with the salt and vinegar, and boil, uncovered, for three quarters of an hour. Serve upon hot buttered toast without crust, and pour either white sauce or melted butter *(see* recipes) over them.

75.—Stewed Leeks.

Ingredients.
1 pint of stock (No. 1)
1 tablespoonful of vinegar

Trim and wash the leeks as in the preceding, recipe, and stew them in the stock for an hour and a half; add the vinegar and serve.

76.—Beetroot boiled.

Wash the roots delicately clean, but neither scrape nor cut them, and do not take off even the fibres until they are boiled or you will spoil the color. Throw them into boiling water and boil from one and a half to two and a half hours, or even longer, according to their size, which varies greatly. Pare and cut into thick slices, and serve with melted butter (*see* recipes) poured over them.

77.—Beetroot, baked.

Wash and wipe the beetroot very dry, but neither cut nor break *any* part of it; lay it in a warm earthen dish and bake it in a gentle oven from two to four hours, according to size. When cold take off the skin and serve it in any of the following ways:—

78.—Cold Beetroot with French Sauce.

Ingredients.
2 tablespoonsful of oil*
1   ,,   ,, vinegar
1 small teaspoonful of sifted sugar
1 saltspoonful of salt
1   ,,   ,, pepper
1 pinch of cayenne

Cut the cold beetroot into slices: mix all the ingredients and pour them over it. Serve with cold meat, fish or cheese.

* Cream used instead of oil will be found a great improvement.

79.—Stewed Beetroot.

Ingredients.
½ pint of any stock
1 saltspoonful of salt
1   ,,   ,. pepper
1 pinch of cayenne
1 shalot, chopped
2 sprigs of parsley, chopped
1 wineglassful of vinegar

Bake the beetroot one hour, and when cold take off the skin; cut it into slices a quarter of an inch thick; put it into a stewpan with the stock, salt, pepper, cayenne, shalot and parsley; simmer three quarters of an hour; add the vinegar, and serve.

80.—Beetroot and Onions with sauce Piquante.

Ingredients.

2 or 3 beetroots
2 or 3 dozen button onions
1 ordinary-sized onion
1 oz. of butter
½ pint of good stock
1 tablespoonful of arrowroot
1 gill of good cream
1 dessertspoonful of chili vinegar
1 saltspoonful of pepper
1 teaspoonful of salt

Boil the beetroots till tolerably tender with the button onions; let them remain till cold, then pare the beetroots; slice them and lay them in a stewpan. Prepare the following sauce:— Chop the onion, fry it brown in the butter, thicken with the arrowroot; stir in the cream; stew the beetroot ten minutes in this sauce, and as you take it off the fire add the vinegar, pepper and salt. Serve the onions in the centre, the beetroot and sauce round.

81.—Cauliflower, plain.

Choose a cauliflower that is white and firm, but not hard; trim off the stem and the outer leaves; leave it in a pan of cold water with a handful of salt in it for three hours: wash it very thoroughly and examine it well to see that no insects remain in any part of it. Put it into plenty of boiling water with a tablespoonful of salt, and boil (uncovered) for twenty-five minutes; drain on a sieve. Serve with melted butter (*see* recipe) in a tureen, or poured over it.

82.—Cauliflower with Parmesan Cheese.

Ingredients.

2 oz. of Parmesan cheese grated
1 teaspoonful of flour of mustard
1 saltspoonful of white pepper
1 pinch of cayenne
2 oz. of dissolved butter

Boil the cauliflower as directed in the preceding recipe: divide it into pieces the size of a walnut, leaving out the stem and leaves. Season the grated cheese with the mustard, pepper and cayenne; dip each piece of cauliflower into the cheese and place them close together on a flat dish; strew the

VEGETABLES. 187

remainder of the cheese over the top, baste with the dissolved butter and bake in a quick oven for a quarter of an hour. Serve immediately.

83.—Stewed Cauliflower.

Ingredients.
½ pint of veal stock
¼ oz. of butter
1 dessertspoonful of flour
1 squeeze of a lemon

Prepare cauliflower as directed for plain boiling, and when it is about half done take it out of the water and put into a small saucepan with the stock and simmer till tender. Take out the cauliflower and put it on a hot dish; set the saucepan on a quick fire, roll the butter in the flour, stir it into the sauce for two minutes, add a squeeze of a lemon, pour the sauce over the cauliflower, and serve at once.

84.—Brocoli.

Brocoli is prepared in exactly the same way as cauliflower, and may be served according to any of the preceding recipes.

85.—Brussels Sprouts.

Free them from all discolored leaves, cut off the stems and wash them thoroughly. Throw them into a saucepan of boiling water with a tablespoonful of salt and boil them quickly from eight to ten minutes; drain them well and serve upon thick rounds of buttered toast with or without melted butter (*see* recipe) in a separate dish.

86.—Brussels Sprouts, French way.

Ingredients.
2 oz. of butter
1 saltspoonful of salt

Boil the sprouts; put them into a saucepan with the butter, salt and pepper; toss over the fire for three minutes. Add

Ingredients of Brussels Sprouts, French way.
½ saltspoonful of pepper
A few drops of lemon-juice
2 tablespoonsful of white sauce or veal broth

the lemon-juice and white sauce or broth, stir for a minute, and serve very hot with a border of sippets.

87.—Cabbage.

Trim off the outer leaves and stem and divide the cabbage into four quarters; wash carefully and leave it in cold water with a handful of salt in it for two hours. Put it into fast boiling water with a tablespoonful of salt, and boil rapidly (uncovered) for twenty minutes, if a small cabbage, forty minutes, if a large one; drain on a sieve, press out the water with a plate, and serve very hot either plain or with melted butter (*see* recipe) poured over.

88.—Stewed Cabbage.

Ingredients.
1 oz. of butter
1 saltspoonful of salt
½ ,,   ,,   pepper
1 tablespoonful of flour
1 cup of thick cream or some veal broth

Cut out the stalk entirely and slice a firm fine cabbage or two in thin strips; after they have been well washed and drained; throw them into a large pan of boiling water ready salted and skimmed, and when they are tender, (in about ten or fifteen minutes) pour them into a sieve or strainer; press the water thoroughly from them, and chop them slightly. Put the butter into a very clean saucepan, and when it is dissolved add the cabbage; sprinkle over the salt and pepper and stir it over a clear fire until it appears tolerably dry; then shake in the flour lightly, turn the whole well, and add the cream or broth by slow degrees. Serve very hot.

89.—Stuffed Cabbage.

Ingredients.
½ of a lb. of pork sausage meat.*
¼ „ „ beef or veal ⎫ chopped
suet ⎬
4 shalots ⎭
4 sprigs of parsley
The peel of half a lemon (grated)
⅛ of a nutmeg (grated)
1 tablespoonful of mixed herbs (powdered)
½ tablespoonful of salt
½ „ „ flour of mustard
1 well beaten egg
¾ of a pint of any stock or gravy
2 oz. of butter
The strained juice of two large lemons

* Any kind of white minced meat will do

Take a moderate-sized firm young cabbage, trim and well wash it; put it into warm water with one handful of salt and a wineglassful of vinegar, and let it remain two hours. Make a stuffing as follows:—Mix all the ingredients down to the well beaten eggs (inclusive) well together; cut the stem off the cabbage, and with a sharp knife, scoop out sufficient of the heart to make space for the stuffing; press in the stuffing; bind the cabbage with a piece of tape; put it into the stewpan with the gravy and butter (or the cabbage); simmer gently for three and a half hours; add the strained lemon-juice, take off the tape, and serve at once with the gravy in the dish.

90.—Roast Tomatoes.

Choose them of nearly the same size; take off the stalks, and roast them gently in a Dutch oven, or put them at the edge of a dripping pan, taking care that no fat from the roasting joint shall fall on them, and keeping them turned so that they shall be equally done. Serve with roast mutton, or beef, or veal.

91.—Stewed Tomatoes.

Arrange the tomatoes in a stewpan in a single layer; pour over them as much gravy as will reach to half their height; stew them very gently until the under sides are

92.—Stuffed Tomatoes.

Ingredients.
3 oz. of cold fowl or veal
1 oz. of cooked ham (fat and lean)
1 teaspoonful of chopped parsley
½ ,, ,, mixed sweet herbs
¼ ,, ,, salt
½ ,, ,, white pepper
1 small shalot
The yolk of one hard boiled egg
1 anchovy (cleaned and boned)
1 oz. of butter dissolved to a cream
Some cut lemons and cayenne

Make a forcemeat with all the ingredients down to the anchovy (inclusive); pound them to a paste, then add the dissolved butter. Wipe each tomato, cut off the stem, scoop out the seeds, and fill the tomatoes with the forcemeat. Bake on a tin dish in a quick oven from ten to fifteen minutes, place them on a hot dish, and serve with cut lemons and cayenne pepper on a plate.

93.—Tomatoes à la Provencale.

Ingredients.
4 or 6 large ripe tomatoes
1 gill of salad oil
1 dozen button mushrooms
1 handful of parsley
1 shalot
2 oz. of scraped fat ham or bacon
1 saltspoonful of pepper
1 ,, ,, salt
1 ,, ,, chopped thyme
3 yolks of eggs
Some fried bread-crumbs
¼ pint of brown sauce

Rub the skin of the tomatoes with a soft cloth; cut off the part of the tomato next the stalk, and scoop out the seeds, without breaking the sides of the tomatoes; place them in circular order in a stewpan; pour in the salad oil; chop up the mushrooms, parsley and shalot; put them into another saucepan with the chopped ham; season with the pepper, salt, and thyme; fry these together for about five minutes, then add the beaten yolks; fill the tomatoes with this preparation: shake the bread-crumbs over them, and place over a brisk fire, hold ing a red hot salamander over them for about ten minutes, by which time they will be done; dish them up with some brown sauce poured round them, and serve.

94.—Purée of Tomatoes.

Ingredients.
1 dozen fine ripe tomatoes
1 small mild onion
½ pint of good gravy
½ saltspoonful of cayenne
1 teaspoonful of salt
¼ of a pint of good cream
1 teaspoonful of flour

Cut the tomatoes in half, take off the stalks and scoop out the seeds, lay them in a stewpan with the onion and gravy; simmer for one hour; when they begin to boil add the cayenne and salt; take out the tomatoes, press them through a sieve, put them back into the stewpan, heat them again; mix the cream with the flour, and boil for five minutes; stir it into the tomatoes, and simmer gently for a few minutes, until the purée is nice and thick. Then serve very hot, either as an accompaniment to veal cutlets, calf brains, pork, beef, or roast goose or else as a vegetable by itself.

65.—Tomato Toast.

Ingredients.
4 or 6 large ripe tomatoes
2 oz. of fresh butter
1 grain of cayenne
½ saltspoonful of white pepper
1   ,,   ,, salt
⅛ of a nutmeg grated
The strained juice of a large lemon
Some hot buttered toast

Rub the skin of the tomatoes with a soft cloth; divide them in halves; take out the seeds; knead the butter with the cayenne, pepper, salt, and nutmeg. Place the tomatoes on a baking dish; fill each with the butter; bake in a quick oven for twenty minutes; add the lemon-juice, and serve upon the buttered toast *very* hot.

96.—Truffles, a la Serviette.

Select some very fine truffles; wash and brush them

Ingredients of Truffles a la Serviette.

Some bacon
1 bunch of parsley } Tied to-
Green onions and thyme } gether
½ dozen cloves
1 cloves of garlic
Some rich veal gravy
½ pint of champagne

well with cold water; line a small stewpan with slices of fat bacon; lay in the truffles with the bunch of parsley, onions, and thyme, the cloves and garlic; pour in enough veal gravy to cover them; add the champagne; boil very gently for an hour, draw them aside and allow them to cool in the gravy. Heat them afresh when they are wanted for table; lift them out, and drain on a very clean cloth, and send them up to table on a beautifully white napkin to show off their color.

97.—Truffles, à l' Italienne.

Wash and wipe the truffles, and pare them carefully

Ingredients.

1 oz. of fresh butter
Minced eschalot and } 1 teaspoon-
parsley } ful
1 saltspoonful of salt
1 ,, ,, pepper
The juice of 1 lemon
1 pinch of cayenne
½ pint of rich brown sauce

(reserving the trimmings for flavoring); slice them about the size of an 8 anna piece; put them into a frying pan with the butter, eschalot and parsley, salt and pepper; fry over the fire, stirring carefully for ten minutes; add the lemon-juice, cayenne and brown sauce; stir over the fire for two or three minutes, and serve very hot.

98.—Truffles, à la Piedmontaise.

Clean and pare the truffles and cut them in halves; lay

Ingredients.

½ lb. of truffles
2 tablespoonsful of Lucca oil
Chopped parsley }
 ,, thyme } 1 table-
1 clove of garlic } spoonful
Mignionette pepper }
1 saltspoonful of salt
1 gravyspoonful of rich brown sauce

them in a small saucepan with the oil, flavorings, and salt; fry them over a brisk fire for five minutes; remove the garlic, then add the brown sauce, glaze, and lemon

Ingredients of Truffles à la Piedmontaise.
1 small piece of glaze
The juice of ½ lemon
2 French rolls
2 oz. of butter

juice; toss the whole over the fire; have ready the hollow crusts of two French rolls from which a round piece of crust at the top has been removed; spread it thickly with butter, put it in the oven for ten minutes to brown, and then pour in the truffles and serve at once.

99.—Curried mixed Vegetables

May be made of any of the following vegetables mixed in about equal quantities: peas, beans, cauliflower, carrots, turnips, tomatoes, asparagus, leeks, artichokes, brocolis, haricot beans, celery, sprouts, and greens.

Boil and cut up the vegetables into neat pieces. Slice the onions, knead the curry powder with the salt and butter, put it into a frying pan with the onions, and fry till slightly browned; then stir in the vegetables and fry until well saturated with the curry; stir all the time (about ten minutes). If you have the cream stir it in as soon as done, and serve at once with or without some plain boiled rice (*see* recipe.)

Ingredients.
Vegetables
3 onions
1 tablespoonful of curry powder
1 teaspoonful of salt
3 oz. of butter
(1 tablespoonful of cream is a great improvement)

100.—Chartreuse of Vegetables.

Boil and blanch the carrots and cut them and the turnips into shapes with a cutter; boil the onions. Boil and chop the spinach, cauliflower, and asparagus heads; line a mould with the slices of bacon; arrange the car-

Ingredients.
3 dozen pieces of carrots
3 doz. pieces of turnips
2 ,, button onions
A handful of spinach
1 cauliflower
1 dozen asparagus heads
Some slices of bacon

rots, turnips, &c., round the bottom and sides in any pattern you fancy; press the spinach well over them to keep them in shape and fill up the remainder of the shape with any vegetables you may have. These should be stewed in broth and seasoned with salt and pepper. Set the mould in a pan of hot water (taking care there is not enough water to boil over into the mould;) boil for an hour; serve with brown sauce.

Note.—The mould may, if preferred, be put in an oven and baked for an hour. This is a very delicious dish.

101.—Macedoine of Vegetables.

Ingredients.
2 dozen asparagus tops
12 button onions
2 turnips
2 carrots
12 new potatoes
20 French beans
A little broth
1 oz. of butter
2 saltspoonsful of salt
2   ,,   ' pepper
2 tablespoonsful of thick white sauce
1 teaspoonful of sugar

Scrape and clean the vegetables and cut the turnips, carrots and potatoes with a cutter, boil all the vegetables in the broth with the butter, salt and pepper, till done; stir in the white sauce and sugar; toss lightly over the fire and serve very hot, either alone or in the centre of a side dish.

Note.—Any vegetables which happen to be in season, peas, cauliflower, brussel sprouts, &c., may be used either in addition to or instead of those given.

SALADS.

In order to ensure a good salad it is essential that the lettuce should be perfectly fresh and crisp, that the oil should be really good, (a very rare thing in India) and that the dressing should not be poured over the salad until just before it is wanted.

After rinsing, all lettuces should be carefully wiped in a clean cloth or shaken dry in a salad basket, and then *broken up* with the fingers into small pieces.

1.—An English Salad.

Ingredients.
2 tablespoonsful of salad oil
1   „   „ vinegar
1 teaspoonful of sugar
2 saltspoonsful of salt
1   „   „ pepper

Never let the lettuce soak in water; rinse it and wipe it immediately in a soft clean cloth; split it down the stalk and divide each leaf into four pieces; add water-cress, beetroot, radish, and shalots if you have them; mix the ingredients of the sauce together carefully, stir in, and serve at once.

2.—A French Salad.

Ingredients.
Only *one* kind of lettuce
1½ tablespoonful of fine salad oil
    „   „   „ tarragon vinegar
1   „   „   „ French vinegar
1 teaspoonful of salt
1 saltspoonful of pepper
Some chopped chervil & chives

Rinse and dry the lettuce as in the foregoing recipe; break it into small pieces; mix the sauce carefully, stir it in lightly, and serve at once.

3.—Another English Salad.

Ingredients.

1 lettuce
1 head of endive
1 " celery (shred)
Some slices of beetroot
1 " " cucumber
2 hard-boiled yolks
1 teaspoonful of salt
1 " " mustard
1 saltspoonful of loaf sugar
½ " " pepper
1 good tablespoonful of thick cream
1 good tablespoonful of salad oil
2 " " " vinegar
6 drops of tarragon vinegar

Put the lettuce, endive, celery, beetroot and cucumber in a salad bowl; make the salad mixture as follows: put the cold yolks into a basin with the salt, mustard, sugar and pepper; bruise the yolks with a wooden spoon and add the cream by degrees; when it is well incorporated, stir in the oil and vinegar; mix well and pour over the salad.

Note.—A little Anchovy or Worcester sauce is considered by some epicures as an improvement to the above sauce.

The above salads may, if preferred, be served with Tartar or Mayonnaise sauce (*see* recipe.)

4.—Flemish Salad.

Ingredients.

The fillets of four salt herrings
1 beetroot (ready cooked & cold)
4 boiled potatoes
2 apples, peeled, and shred*
Some Brussel sprouts
A head of celery
A few small onions

* These may be omitted

Cut the herrings into small pieces, slice the beetroot and potatoes and chop the onions. Put all the ingredients in a salad bowl, season with oil, vinegar, pepper and salt.

Note.—Any dried or pickled fish may be substituted if preferred.

5.—Lobster Salad.

Lobster, salmon, or crab salads may be made with lettuce, endive, cucumber, cress, &c., and serve with Mayonnaise or Tartar sauce. (*See* recipes.)

6.—Tomato Salad.

Mix one drop of extract of garlic with a teaspoonful of

vinegar; spread it over a flat dish. Wash and dry the tomatoes; slice them and lay them on the dish; sprinkle liberally with fine salt; shake a little pepper over; pour a few drops of oil and a teaspoonful of vinegar over each slice, and serve This salad should be prepared an hour before it is used.

7.—Russian Salad.

Ingredients.
6 hard boiled eggs
Beetroot
Lettuce
Anchovies
Cold potatoes
Onions
Apples
Some cold chicken or any white meat

All the ingredients are to be chopped fine. Put some of the chopped whites and yolks (separately) aside, also some beetroot and lettuce, (about three tablespoonsful of each.) Mix the remainder of the ingredients with oil, vinegar, tarragon, sugar, pepper, and salt; when the mixture is well saturated and soft pile it up on a dish, smooth with a spoon. Then cover it over in sections with the yolks and whites of eggs, the chopped beetroot and lettuce alternately, so that the different colors contrast prettily. Then garnish round the edge with slices of beetroot, eggs, tomatoes, &c.

Note.—This is a delicious dish and particularly adapted for cold luncheons, pic-nics, and ball suppers.

8.—Cold Meat Salad.

Mince any cold meat—game is the best, and add equal quantities of sliced beetroot and chopped celery. Season with oil, vinegar, pepper and salt.

9.—Hot Vegetable Salad.

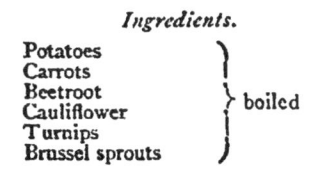

Ingredients.
Potatoes
Carrots
Beetroot
Cauliflower } boiled
Turnips
Brussel sprouts

Break up the vegetables quickly with a wide pronged fork; add the pepper, salt, onion, and

Ingredients of Hot Vegetable Salad.

1 Spanish onion (raw)
2 tablespoonsful of chopped parsley
8 ,, ,, Lucca oil
5 ,, ,, tarragon vinegar
1 teaspoonful of salt
1 saltspoonful of white pepper
Some slices of cucumber
A few spring onions

parsley; put in the cucumber and onions chopped; stir in the oil, and lastly the vinegar. Mix well, and serve in a salad bowl.

EGGS.

1.—Boiled Eggs.

The eggs should be perfectly fresh and must be cooked in sufficient water to cover them completely. The water must be *boiling* when they are put in and then the time required will be: underdone, three minutes; to render the whites firm, three and half to four minutes; hard, eight to ten minutes.

Eggs cooked in the shell without boiling, for invalids: Put some boiling water into a strong basin—a slop basin; let it remain a few seconds; pour it out; lay in the egg or eggs, and roll them over to take off the chill; then pour in over the egg *quite boiling* water from a kettle, till the egg is well covered; put a plate over the basin instantly and let it remain on the table for twelve minutes, when it will be found beautifully cooked, so as to be palatable even to people who cannot eat eggs dressed in the usual way.

2.—Poached Eggs.

Half fill a bright frying pan with boiling water; add one and a half saltspoonsful of salt and two teaspoonsful of vinegar; break each egg separately into a cup; pour them carefully into the water, while *boiling;* with a small slice throw the white over the yolk; when done, drain for half a minute, then serve either on hot buttered toast or on spinach, or sorrel.

3.—Poached Eggs with Anchovy Toast.

Prepare the eggs as above, and pour a little Anchovy sauce on the toast in which the eggs are to be served.

4.—Eggs and Bacon.

Cut some thin rashers of bacon; cut off the bones and skin; lay them in a frying pan, and fry both sides brown. Break as many eggs as you have rashers, each in a separate cup and fry one at a time. Tilt the pan and pour the egg carefully into the fat, and with an egg slice constantly throw the boiling fat over the egg; three minutes will suffice for each egg. Place an egg on each rasher, and serve very hot.

5.—Eggs au plat.

Take any dish which will bear the heat of fire. Cut a slice of butter and melt it in it; break some fresh eggs into separate cups and lay them in the butter one by one; strew a little pepper (mignionette if you have it) and salt over each egg, and place the dish over a gentle fire until the whites are quite set. Hold a salamander over the top for a moment, and serve at once in the same dish.

6.—Buttered Eggs.

Put two ounces of fresh butter into a frying pan; break six eggs into a basin; sprinkle in some pepper and salt; break the eggs slightly with a fork; when the butter is boiling, lift the frying pan off the fire; pour in the eggs and stir them quickly with the fork until they set; great care must be taken that they are not allowed to become hard; have ready a round of buttered toast, pour the eggs over, and serve at once.

7.—Buttered Eggs with Truffles.

Ingredients.
6 new laid eggs
2 oz. of butter
1 ,, ,, truffle
2 tablespoonsful of cream
A little mignionette pepper
Some salt

Put the butter into a frying pan with the eggs and the truffles (cut into small slices); add the cream, pepper and salt. Stir quickly with a wooden spoon or a fork over the fire until the eggs begin to thicken; then take the frying pan off and continue to work the eggs until they become firm but do not harden. Serve very hot either in a dish by themselves, or on buttered toast; or else prepare some sippets, stand them in a circle on a dish, stick them together with a little white of egg, dish up the eggs in the centre, and serve at once.

8.—Eggs in Paper Cases.

Ingredients.
2 oz. of butter
Some stale bread-crumbs
A little minced parsley
Some salt
Some cayenne pepper

Make some small paper cases. Mix the butter with the bread-crumbs, parsley, salt and pepper. Butter the bottom of the boxes; put in some of this mixture; break an egg into each box; cover it over with bread-crumbs; the boxes must be well filled up; put them over the gridiron for two or three minutes; pass a salamander over the top, and serve.

9.—Eggs à la Bonne femme.

Ingredients.
4 eggs
A middle-sized onion
½ oz. of butter
1 teaspoonful of vinegar
Some bread-crumbs
Some pepper and salt

Cut the onion into dice; fry them in a stewpan with the butter a light brown; add the vinegar; butter a tin dish sprinkle the onions over it, break, the eggs into it, and put the dish in the oven; mix a little pepper and salt with the bread-crumbs, fry them, and sprinkle over the eggs when done. Serve at once.

10.—Eggs grated.

Ingredients.
8 eggs
3 oz. of butter

Boil the eggs hard (which will take ten minutes), separate them from the whites; put a large round of buttered toast on a hot plate or dish; put a sieve over this; rub the yolks of the eggs through the sieve on to the toast; serve at once.

11.—Eggs with Cheese.

Ingredients.
2 oz. of fresh butter
Some Gruyére cheese
8 eggs
Some mignionette pepper
Some salt
1 gill of thick cream

Spread the bottom of a silver, porcelain (fire-proof), or tin dish with the butter; cover this with thin slices of the cheese; break in the eggs carefully, so as not to disturb the yolks: season with pepper and salt, pour the cream over the top; strew two ounces of grated cheese over this; set the dish in the oven and bake about ten minutes; pass a hot salamander over the top, and serve at once with some very thin toast separately.

12.—Eggs à la Tripe.

Ingredients.
6 eggs
3 small onions
A little milk
2 spoonsful of good white sauce
1 pinch of pepper
The juice of a small lemon
Some fresh cut garlic

Boil six eggs hard; immerse them in cold water for three minutes, take off the shells and cut them into thick slices. Slice the onions and divide them in the folds of the rings; parboil them in water; drain it off, and boil for five minutes in a little milk; then drain upon a sieve or cloth. Rub the saucepan twice across the bottom with garlic, lay in the eggs and the onions, the sauce (*see recipe*), pepper and lemon-juice; toss over the fire, and when quite hot, serve with sippets of toast round the dish.

13.—Eggs au Gratin.

Boil, peel and slice the eggs as above. Put the sauce, cheese, butter, pepper, salt, yolks and lemon juice into a saucepan; stir over the fire till it begins to thicken, then withdraw it; lay the eggs in circular rows on the dish; spread some of the sauce between each layer; cover with the remainder of the sauce; strew over the fried bread-crumbs mixed with a little grated Parmesan, put some sippets of toast round the base, put into the oven for ten minutes, and serve.

Ingredients.
16 eggs
1 tablespoonful of white sauce
12 oz. of grated Parmesan cheese
½ small pat of butter
½ saltspoonful of pepper
½   ,,   ,, salt
4 yolks
The juice of half lemon
Some fried bread-crumbs

14.—Eggs with Nutbrown Butter.

Put two ounces of the butter into a frying pan over the fire; as soon as it begins to frizzle break the eggs into it without disturbing the yolks; season with pepper and salt; fry the eggs over the fire for five minutes; remove carefully into a hot dish; put the remaining two ounces of butter into the pan; fry till it is brown; add the vinegar; boil together for two minutes; pour over the eggs, and serve at once.

Ingredients.
2 oz. of butter
5 eggs
Salt and pepper
2 tablespoonsful of vinegar

15.—Eggs aux fines herbes.

Put the butter into a stewpan; when melted, stir in the

Ingredients of Eggs aux fines herbes.
2 oz. of butter
½ pint of new milk
Some salt and pepper
6 eggs
1 dessertspoonful of chopped parsley

milk with a pinch of salt and pepper. Break in the eggs and stir with a whisk or fork briskly over the fire for two minutes, taking care it does not adhere to the bottom or get too hard; add the parsley, and continue stirring until the eggs begin to set; take off the fire, whisking all the time, and the moment they are thick, of the consistency of thick Devonshire cream, and rather lumpy, pour them over a round of buttered toast and serve at once.

16.—Eggs and Mushrooms.

Trim and cut the mushrooms, put them into a stewpan

Ingredients.
12 button mushrooms
1 oz. of butter
6 eggs
Some bread-crumbs, pepper and salt

with the butter and a pinch of butter and salt, and stew till tender; when done put them in a shallow tin dish and break the eggs over them, taking care to keep them whole. Strew fine bread-crumbs and some pepper and salt over the top, put them into a sharp oven for five minutes, or until the eggs are well set. Serve at once with fried sippets round the dish.

17.—Asparagus Eggs.

(*Entremets.*)

Take the asparagus heads, cut the green tops into pieces

Ingredients.
2 tablespoonsful of cream
2   ,,   ,, good gravy
2 oz. of butter
A little salt and pepper
6 eggs
2 doz. heads of small asparagus

the size of large peas, and throw them into boiling water with plenty of salt, and when tender drain them on a sieve. Put the cream, gravy, butter, salt and pepper into a stewpan; break in the eggs, and when they begin to set, throw in the asparagus heads; stir over the fire for half a minute, pour them on a hot dish, and garnish with fried sippets.

18.—Turkey's Eggs, forced.
(An excellent entremets.)

Ingredients.
6 Turkey eggs
2 oz. of fresh butter
1 saltspoonful of salt
1 grate of nutmeg
1 pinch of cayenne
1 hen's egg
1 dessertspoonful of rich cream

Boil the Turkey eggs gently for twenty minutes in plenty of water, which should cover them entirely, and when done lift them into a large pan of water to cool. When *perfectly* cold roll them in a cloth, pressing lightly to break the shells; peel them off and cut the eggs evenly in half, lengthwise. Take out the yolks carefully, and pound them to a smooth paste in a mortar or bowl with the butter, salt, nutmeg and cayenne. Blend these ingredients thoroughly; whisk the raw yolk of the hen's eggs; stir it in by degrees; add the cream and continue whisking for a few minutes; the mixture should now be like thick batter; fill the whites with it, (cutting a tiny slice from the bottom of each to make it stand evenly on the dish) full and high; smooth over with a knife; put the eggs on a dish, and place them on a very gentle oven for a quarter of an hour; serve instantly with brown sauce and mushrooms.

19.—Curried Eggs.

Ingredients.
6 or 8 eggs
3 oz. of good butter (or oil)
3 dessertspoonsful of curry powder
2 onions
¾ pint of gravy
1 gill of good cream
2 teaspoonsful of arrowroot

Boil the eggs quite hard, as for salad, and when they are quite cold take off the shells. Mix the butter and curry powder; put it into a stewpan and shake over the fire for some minutes; chop the onions fine and throw them in; when they are tolerably soft add by degrees the broth, and stew slowly till the whole is reduced to a pulp; mix the arrowroot smoothly into the cream, stir into the curry and simmer the whole until the raw taste of the thickening is gone. Cut the eggs in half; heat them quite through in the sauce without boiling them, and serve at once with curry rice (*see* recipe) in a separate dish.

20.—Scotch Woodcock.

Ingredients.
6 anchovies
2 eggs
1 tablespoonful of good cream
Some grated ham or tongue or hung-beef

Wash, scrape, and split the anchovies; bone them and warm them on a plate before the fire; whisk the eggs, (yolks and whites) with the cream; put them in a saucepan and stir over a gentle fire till they thicken. Have a round of buttered toast ready; lay the anchovies on it, put them close to the fire, and when *quite* hot, pour over the boiled eggs; sprinkle the grated ham, tongue, or hung-beef on the top, and serve at once.

OMELETS.

The frying pan in which an omelet is to be made should be *very* small, or the omelet will spread and be too thin, and so get burnt. An omelet should be light and thick, and only brown on one side; as the eggs *begin* to set roll the omelet into the form of an oval cushion.

1.—A common Omelet.

The eggs must be very fresh; break them carefully and whisk them until they are very light; whiie beating add the pepper and salt; dissolve the butter in a *very small* frying pan; pour in the eggs, and when it is well risen and nearly firm in the centre, roll it into the form of an oval cushion, and serve instantly.

Ingredients.
6 eggs
½ teaspoonful of salt
¼ ,, ,, pepper
2 oz. of butter

2.—A good Omelet.

Break the eggs into a basin; add the cream, the small pat of butter broken up, salt and pepper, to taste; put the butter into a very small frying pan on the fire; while it is melting whip the eggs, &c., well together till they froth; as soon as the butter frizzles pour the eggs in the pan and stir the omelet; when they set and seem firm, roll the omelet into the form of an

Ingredients.
6 eggs
1 tablespoonful of cream
1 small pat of butter broken up
2 oz. of fresh butter
Salt and pepper

oval cushion; allow it to acquire a golden color on one side, turn out on a hot dish and serve at once.

3.—Savoury Omelet.

Add one dessertspoonful of chopped parsley and one teaspoonful of chopped shalot to the above recipe, and put them into the eggs while you are beating them.

4.—A very light Omelet.

Ingredients.
¼ pint of cream
6 eggs
1 pinch of cayenne
Some shalot and parsley
Some salt
1½ oz. of butter

Beat the cream, the yolks of the eggs, cayenne and salt together; chop very fine the shalot and parsley; add about one teaspoonful to the eggs, mix well; whip the whites separately and add them to the omelet; melt the butter in a frying pan and pour in the eggs; when they set and begin to get firm fold over in the form of a cushion, and when one side is golden brown, turn it out on a hot dish. Serve either with or without gravy.

5.—Omelet with Cheese.

Make the omelet according to any of the above recipes, and add two ounces of grated Parmesan (or other cheese) and some mignionette pepper.

6.—A Ham, Tongue, or Hung-beef Omelet.

Prepare an omelet as directed, and add four tablespoonsful of either of the above grated, and a teaspoonful of mustard, and omit the other seasoning.

7.—Kidney Omelet.

Prepare the omelet according to any of the foregoing

recipes. Have ready some ready-cooked kidneys (*see* recipes); chop them and add them to the omelet when it is ready, just before folding up. Serve with brown sauce.

8.—Oyster Omelet.

Prepare the oysters as for "stewed-oysters" (*see* recipe) and lay them in the omelet (prepared according to recipe) just before folding up.

MACARONI, CHEESE, SAVOURY RICE, TOASTS, &c.

1.—Savoury Macaroni with Cheese.

Ingredients.
8 oz. of macaroni (Genoa)
3 pints of cold water
1 quart of stock (No. 2)
2 oz. of butter
6 oz. of grated Parmesan (or other) cheese
2 teaspoonsful of flour of mustard
2 grains of cayenne
1 saltspoonful of white pepper

Put the macaroni, salt, and water into a saucepan, simmer very gently for twenty minutes, and drain on a sieve. Then put the macaroni again into a saucepan with the stock, and simmer till quite tender, (about one and three quarters of an hour); stir in one ounce of the butter, three ounces of the cheese, the mustard, cayenne and pepper; lay it on a dish, and sift the remainder of the cheese thickly over it; break one ounce of butter in small pieces, spread it over the top; bake in a quick oven or before the fire till of a pale brown color (twelve to fifteen minutes), serve very hot.

2.—Savoury Macaroni.
(Another way.)

Ingredients.
6 oz. of macaroni (Naples)
2 quarts of boiling water
1 tablespoonful of salt
3 oz. of butter
1 quart of new milk
1 teaspoonful of flour of mustard
1 saltspoonful of white pepper
1 grain of cayenne
1 grate of nutmeg
6 oz. of grated cheese
2 fresh eggs
1 gill of fresh cream

Blanch the macaroni in the boiling water with the salt in it; let it remain till cold; then drain on a sieve. Put it into a saucepan with two ounces of the butter and stir over the fire until it is absorbed; add the milk and simmer very gently till tender (one and a half hours); add the mustard, pepper, cayenne, nutmeg, three ounces of the cheese, and eggs (beaten with the cream); place on a dish, sift the grated cheese over; lay one ounce of butter on the top, in small pieces; bake in a quick oven or before the fire till of a pale brown color (twelve to fifteen minutes), and serve at once.

3.—Macaroni with Bread-crumbs.

Ingredients.
2 oz. of macaroni
1 pint of seasoned stock
1 oz. of butter
Pepper and salt
Bread-crumbs

Blanch the macaroni as in the foregoing recipes (using half the quantity of water and salt), drain and put into a saucepan with the stock; simmer for an hour; add the butter, pepper and salt, to taste; stir well together; put on a dish, cover thickly with bread-crumbs, brown in the oven, or before the fire, and serve.

4.—Macaroni with Bacon.

Prepare the macaroni as above; boil two ounces of streaky bacon, cut it into slices, and add before browning.

5.—Savoury Macaroni Pudding.

Ingredients.
2 oz. of macaroni
1 pint of seasoned stock
½ pint of milk
1 egg
Pepper, salt, shalot
Chopped parsley
1 shalot minced, fine

Blanch the macaroni; put it into a saucepan with the stock and simmer gently for an hour. Make a custard with half a pint of milk and an egg; season with pepper and salt, chopped parsley and shalot; stir into the macaroni, and bake in a slow oven for half an hour.

6.—Macaroni à la Reine.

Prepare the macaroni as directed in recipe No. 2; cut

Ingredients of Macaroni à la Reine.
6 oz. of macaroni
6 " " rich *white* cheese
½ pint of rich cream
Salt, cayenne
½ saltspoonful of pounded mace
2 oz. of butter
Bread-crumbs fried and dried

the cheese in slices; boil the cream, and dissolve the cheese in it gently, add the salt, cayenne and mace; when it is *perfectly* mixed and smooth put in the macaroni, (well drained and dry). Pour it into a hot dish, sprinkle over some bread-crumbs, and serve at once.

Note.—Bechamel sauce may be used instead of the cream, and is a great improvement to this excellent dish.

7.—Cheese Soufflée or Fondu.

Grate the cheese; put it into a saucepan with the mus-

Ingredients.
6 oz. of rich cheese (Cheddar or Parmesan,
1 teaspoonful of flour of mustard
1 saltspoonful of white pepper
1 grain of cayenne
1 grate of nutmeg
2 oz. of butter
2 tablespoonsful of baked flour
1 gill of new milk
6 eggs

tard, pepper, cayenne, nutmeg, butter, flour and milk; stir it over the fire until it becomes like smooth cream (but it must not boil); add the yolks of the eggs well beaten; beat the whites of the eggs to a stiff froth; add them and quickly pour the mixture into a tin or card-board mould, and bake at once in an oven for twenty minutes. Serve inmediately.

Note.—The reason a good fondu is so rare in India is that it is not baked the moment it is mixed, and is not served the moment it is ready.

8.—Cheese Soufflée or Fondu.
(Another way.)

Mix the flour and milk to a smooth batter; boil the cream,

Ingredients.
¼ of a pint of new milk
2 oz. of potato-flour, or arrow-root
¾ of a pint of cream (or milk)

and add it boiling to the batter; stir well together and add the butter in small pieces; when this is

Ingredients of Cheese Soufflé or Fondu.
2 oz. of butter
5 eggs
½ teaspoonful of salt
1 pinch of cayenne
3 oz. of cheese (grated)

well mixed and looks like thick smooth cream, add the yolks of the eggs, well beaten, the salt, cayenne and cheese; whisk well, stir in the whites (beaten to a stiff froth) gently without whisking; pour it into the mould, (which it should half fill), put it into a gentle oven, shut the door *at once* and do not open it again for twenty minutes when it will be ready. Serve at once.

9.—Bread and Cheese Pudding.

Ingredients.
6 oz. of rich cheese
4 ,, ,, fine bread-crumbs
2 ,, ,, dissolved butter
1 teaspoonful of flour of mustard
1 saltspoonful of white pepper
1 pinch of cayenne
1 grate of nutmeg
1 gill of new milk
3 beaten eggs

Mix all the ingredients together and beat with a wooden spoon for ten minutes; put the mixture in a pie dish, and bake in a moderate oven for three quarters of an hour. Serve very hot, with hot dry toast handed round.

10.—Stewed Cheese.

Ingredients.
¾ lb. of rich cheese
1 teaspoonful of flour of mustard
½ saltspoonful of white pepper
¼ ,, ,, cayenne
1 wineglassful of sherry
1 oz. of butter
The yolks of 2 eggs well beaten

Pare off the rind and cut the cheese in slices; season it with the mustard, pepper, and cayenne; put it into a pie dish; pour over the sherry; cut the butter into small pieces and sprinkle over the top; bake in a quick oven until the cheese is dissolved (twelve minutes); add the yolks; mix well, pour into a tin dish and bake for ten minutes, or till the top is of a pale brown color. Serve very hot, with fresh made hot dry toast on a rack.

11.—Welsh Rabbit.

Cut a round of bread half an inch thick off the bottom of

Ingredients of Welsh Rabbit.
½ lb. of rich cheese
1 teaspoonful of flour of mustard
1 grain of cayenne
½ oz. of butter

a loaf; trim off the crust; spread it thickly with butter; cut the cheese in *thin* slices; knead together the mustard, cayenne, and flour; stir it before the fire till of a creamy substance; lay half the cheese on the bread, pour half the butter equally over it; put the remainder of the cheese on that; cover with the remainder of the butter. Place it in a cheese toaster, or a Dutch oven, before the fire, or on a tin dish in the oven for about twenty minutes. Serve very hot.

12.—Cheese Toast.

Ingredients.
3 oz. of cheese (single Gloucester if possible)
Yolks of 2 eggs
4 oz. of bread-crumbs
3 ,, ,, butter
1 teaspoonful of mustard
1 saltspoonful of salt
½ ,, ,, cayenne

Grate the cheese; mix it with the eggs, bread-crumbs and butter; add the mustard, cayenne and pepper, and beat the whole well together. Toast some bread, cut off the crust, and cover the slices thickly with the mixture; put it into the oven. When brown serve as quickly as possible.

13.—Boiled Cheese.

Ingredients.
½ lb. of Cheshire or Gloucestershire cheese
2 yolks, 1 white of egg
½ pint of cream

Cut the cheese into thin slices; pound it well in a mortar add the well beaten yolks and white of egg; stir in the cream; mix all the ingredients well, bake on a dish, ten or fifteen minutes; serve very hot with dry toast.

14.—Cheese Ramakins.

Beat the yolks and whites of the eggs separately; mix all

Ingredients of Cheese Ramakins.
6 oz. of Gruyére or Parmesan cheese, grated
6 fresh eggs
1 oz. of fresh butter
1 pinch of cayenne
1 saltspoonful of flour of mustard

the other ingredients well, add the yolks; when well mixed add the whites, and continue baking for ten minutes. Put the mixture either into small paper cases, or buttered tins, and bake in a quick oven fifteen to twenty minutes.

15.—Cheese Canapees.

Ingredients.
Some clarified butter
Some cheese, mustard, and pepper

Cut some slices of bread, rather thin, stamp them out with a plain cutter, round or oval, fry them in clarified butter; spread with a little mustard, lay some slices of cheese on each, and sprinkle with pepper; put them in a brisk oven, or before a clear fire, and as soon as the cheese is melted, serve hot.

16.—Cheese Biscuits.

Ingredients.
¼ lb. of fresh butter
¼ ,, ,, baked flour
5 oz. of rich cheese (Chedder or Parmesan)
1 teaspoonful of flour of mustard
1 saltspoonful of cayenne
The yolks of 2 eggs
2 tablespoonsful of cold water

Beat the butter to a cream; stir in all the other ingredients, and knead to a firm paste roll it out one eighth of an inch thick and cut it into biscuits three inches long and one inch broad; bake in a quick oven for twelve minutes. Serve very hot.

17.—Cheese Straws.

Ingredients.
½ lb. of dried flour
¼ ,, ,, butter
¼ ,, ,, grated Parmesan or Gruyére cheese
1 teaspoonful of flour of mustard

Rub the butter into the flour; add the cheese, mustard, cayenne and salt; mix well together. Beat the whites of the eggs with the water, and stir in enough to form a thick paste;

knead it well, and roll it out about one-eight of an inch thick ; cut it into strips about five inches long and one-eighth of an inch wide. Bake in a quick oven till of a *pale* brown color, about five minutes. Pile nicely on a dish, and serve hot or cold. Keep them in a dry place.

Ingredients of Cheese Straws.
1 saltspoonful of cayenne
1 „ „ salt
2 whites of eggs
¼ pint of cold water

18.—Savoury Rice Pudding.

Boil the rice in the stock with the onion. Make a custard with the milk and egg; season with pepper and salt, shalot and parsley. Mix with the rice, pour into a pie dish, and bake in a slow oven.

Ingredients.
1 teacupful of rice
1 pint of good stock
1 onion
½ pint of milk
1 egg
Some pepper and salt
Some chopped shalot and parsley

19.—Savoury Rice.

Wash the rice and boil it in one quart of water for ten minutes; drain; put it into a stew-pan with the butter, sugar, pepper, nutmeg, lemon-rind, (grated) juice, gravy, and chutney; stir and simmer till the gravy is entirely absorbed, (about quarter of an hour). Serve immediately.

Ingredients.
½ lb. of rice
2 oz. of butter
1 teaspoonful of salt
1 „ „ loaf sugar
½ saltspoonful of white pepper
1 grate of nutmeg
The rind of half lemon
The strained juice
½ pint of good gravy
1 teaspoonful of chutney sauce

Note.—Minced ham or bacon, or morsels of fried lamb or mutton, may be added to this, and make a nice breakfast dish.

20.—Rice and Haddock.

Wash the rice and boil it in one quart of water for ten minutes; drain; fry it with the butter and some pepper and salt. When quite hot, add the whites

Ingredients.
½ lb. of rice
1 grate of nutmeg
Some pepper and salt
2 oz. of butter

Ingredients of Rice and Haddock.
3 hard-boiled eggs
1 dried haddock
A little grated Parmesan cheese

of the eggs shred fine; divide the haddock with a fork into small pieces and add these; pile the mixture up lightly on a hot dish, rub the yolks of the eggs through a wire sieve, mix with the Parmesan, and strew this lightly over the pile of rice; garnish with fried croûtons; put it into the oven for five minutes, just so as slightly to colour the surface a golden hue, and serve at once.

21.—Rice, Polish fashion.

Wash the rice and boil it in one quart of water for ten minutes; drain; cut the onion into thin slices and fry with the butter; add the rice and ham; season with the cayenne and cheese, stir lightly over the fire until very hot, and serve at once.

Ingredients.
½ lb. of rice
1 large onion
2 oz. of butter
2 ,, ,, cooked ham or bacon cut into shreds
1 pinch of cayenne
1 dessertspoonful of grated cheese

22.—Rice, Piedmontese fashion.

Clean the rice and boil it in one quart of water for ten minutes; drain. Chop the onion very fine and fry it in a small stewpan with the butter; season with the cheese, cayenne and salt. Pile up the rice on a hot dish, strew the fillets of anchovies or sardines over the top, and serve at once, very hot.

Ingredients.
¼ lb. of rice
1 small onion
1 oz. of butter
3 baked potatoes
1 oz. of grated Parmesan
1 pinch of cayenne
 ,, ,, salt
Some cleaned fillets of anchovies or sardines

23.—Rice, Florentine fashion.

Wash the rice and boil it in one quart of water for ten

Ingredients of Rice, Florentine fashion.

½ lb. of rice
1 onion
1 dessertspoonful of salad oil
½ pint of shrimps or prawns *
1 dessertspoonful of curry powder
1 tablespoonful of grated Parmesan

* Any kind of dressed fowl, game, tongue, ham, truffles, salmon, or any cold fish may be used instead

minutes; drain. Chop the onion and fry it in the salad oil; add the shrimps and curry powder, and fry for a few minutes; add the boiled rice and Parmesan, stir well together over the fire, and serve very hot.

24.—Rice, Spanish fashion.

Wash the rice, and boil it for ten minutes in a quart of water; drain. Fry it in a stewpan with the oil until of a light golden colour; add the tomato sauce; season with the cheese, pepper and salt; pile up on a hot dish and garnish with the fried ham.

Ingredients.

½ lb. of rice
1 dessertspoonful of salad oil
1 tablespoonful of tomato sauce
1 dessertspoonful of grated cheese
Some pepper and salt
Some slices of fried ham, bacon, sausages, or salmon

25.—Rizzoletti.

Wash the rice, boil it for ten minutes in one quart of water; drain. Put it in a stewpan with the sauce, three yolks of eggs, nutmeg, pepper and salt; stir over the fire until the eggs begin to set; put it aside to cool; when cold, take a tablespoonful of it, spread it out with a teaspoon, lay in a teaspoonful of any kind of mince; wrap it up in the rice so that it forms a ball; dip in egg and bread-crumbs; fry in a frying pan with the butter till of light golden colour; dish up garnished with fried parsley, and serve very hot.

Ingredients.

½ lb. of boiled rice
2 dessertspoonsful of good white sauce
3 yolks of eggs
1 grate of nutmeg
Some pepper and salt
Bread-crumbs
Mince of any kind
3 oz. of butter

26.—Kedgereé.

Ingredients.
4 oz. of rice
4 ,, ,, cold fish
2 ,, ,, butter
Some cayenne and salt
2 eggs

Boil the rice as for curry (*see* recipe), and when it is drained and cold put it into a saucepan with the fish (which must be divided into small flakes with a fork). Add the butter in pieces, and plenty of cayenne and salt; put over a clear fire and stir until it is very hot; beat the eggs slightly, add them to the rice, and mix quickly. The rice must not *boil* after the eggs are added, but must be served just as they are beginning to set. Serve with chutney.

Note.—In the hot season when it is desirable to use as little butter as possible so as not to have *rich* dishes, use two more eggs instead of the butter.

17.—Casserole of Rice.

Ingredients.
½ lb. of best rice
1 quart of veal broth or stock No. 1
4 oz. of butter
Some rich white mince, or fricassee, or oysters prepared as for oyster sauce (*see* recipe)

Wash the rice, drain it on a hair sieve and put it into a stewpan with the broth; simmer *very* gently *near* the fire until it begins to swell, then put it on the fire and simmer as gently as possible for about half an hour or until it begins to be tender; add the butter, and continue simmering until it is dry and quite tender enough to be easily crushed with a wooden spoon. Work it to a smooth paste by crushing it against the sides of the saucepan; press the rice into a well-buttered mould and leave it to cool. When it is cold, dip the mould quickly into hot water which will loosen the contents. Turn out the rice and reverse it again, in a tin or dish, and with the point of a knife mark round the top a rim of about an inch wide. Brush some clarified butter over the whole pudding, and put into a quick oven to colour a pale golden brown; when it is ready, draw it out, raise the cover carefully where it is marked: scoop out the rice from the inside, leaving only a crust of about one inch in thickness in every part, and fill with the white mince or fricassee.

28.—Dresden Patties.

Ingredients.
Bread, milk, eggs, rich white mince or stewed oysters or mushrooms (*see* recipes), some butter.

Pare the crust neatly either from French rolls or bread and divide the bread into circular pieces, three inches in diameter and two inches deep; hollow them out in the centre to the depth of one inch; dip them into milk; lay them on a drainer, and pour milk over them at intervals till they are well soaked but do not let them break; brush them with egg, rasp the crust of the rolls over them, fry a light brown colour and drain them well; fill them with the mince, mushrooms, or oysters (which must be ready prepared beforehand), and serve *very hot* upon a napkin.

29.—Kanapees.

Ingredients.
A large loaf, some oil, hard-boiled eggs, capers, cucumbers, tarragon, chives, some fillets of cleaned anchovies, salad oil, vinegar, pepper and salt

Cut the bread into slices three quarters of an inch thick, then cut into circles with a cutter; fry a good golden brown in the salad oil. Have ready some hard-boiled eggs (6); chop them fine; also the tarragon and chives; put them into a basin, season with oil, vinegar, pepper and salt; pile this preparation on the toasts when they are ready; drain the anchovies well, scrape off the skin, divide them into fillets, and lay these like lattice-work over the top of the canapees. Serve at once.

30.—Savoury Toasts.

Ingredients.
Some bread, butter, cayenne, and mustard
4 tablespoonsful of English cheese, (or 6 tablespoonsful of Gruyére or Parmesan)
4 tablespoonsful of grated ham
Seasoning of mustard and cayenne *
Some good butter

* Truffles minced, seasoned and stewed tender in butter with one or two eschalots may be served on fried toasts, and will be much liked

Cut some slices of bread free from crust, about half an inch thick; butter the tops thickly; spread some mustard on them, and then cover with a deep layer of grated cheese, and of ham seasoned rather highly with cayenne; fry them in good butter, but do not turn them in the pan. Lift them out and put them for a few minutes in a Dutch oven or before the fire, to dissolve the cheese. Serve very hot.

31.—Anchovy Toast.

Prepare some very thin dry toast, spread it with anchovy butter (*see* recipe), and upon this place some fillets of anchovies, cleaned, scraped, and with the bones taken out. Serve on a napkin.

32.—Roties d'Anchois.

Ingredients.
Anchovies, a little oil, a little rasped lemon-peel, some shalots, parsley and tarragon
The yolk of a hard-boiled egg
Two spoonsful of oil, one of lemon-juice, mustard and pepper

Cut some bread half an inch thick, toast it and soak it in a little *good* oil. Mince the anchovies, shalots, parsley, tarragon and yolks; add the rasped lemon-peel, and mix well together. Drain the toasts from the oil; spread the mixture on thick, arrange on the dish on which they are to be served; make a sauce of the oil, lemon-juice, mustard and pepper, pour over and serve.

33.—Curried Toasts, with Anchovies.

Ingredients.
Some bread, butter or good oil
Curry paste, anchovies, and cayenne

Cut some slices of bread about half an inch thick and two and-a-half inches square; free them from crust; fry them in butter (or oil); lay them on a dish and spread a layer of Captain White's curry-paste (not very thickly) on the top; place them in a gentle oven for three or four minutes. Lay some fillets of anchovies (cleaned and boned) across them, replace in the oven for two minutes, sprinkle lightly with cayenne, and serve at once.

34.—Delicate Trifles.

Ingredients
¼ lb. of any cold game (partridge, snipe, rabbit, &c)
A little ham (or tongue)
1 truffle
Mushrooms
Parsley and shalots
Nutmeg, pepper and salt
1 tablespoonful of good white sauce *
4 eggs

* This may be made with the bones of the game (*see* recipe for white sauce)

Cut the cold game up into little squares, and fry in the butter with the ham, truffle, mushrooms, parsley and shalots; season with nutmeg, pepper and salt; when colored brown put in a mortar with the white sauce, and pound thoroughly; rub through a wire sieve, and place the purée in a *small* stewpan; add the yolks of the eggs; whisk three of the whites to a substantial froth; mix in lightly, and with this preparation fill a dozen little paper cases; brush over the tops with a paste brush dipped in the remaining beaten white of egg; push them into a *moderate* oven, and bake for twelve minutes. When done serve instantly on a napkin; if they are kept waiting they will be spoiled.

35.—Sardine Toast.

Skin four sardines and mix them to a paste with a piece

MACARONI, CHEESE, SAVOURY RICE, TOASTS, &C.

Ingredients of Sardine Toast.
- 2 oz. of butter
- 2 dessertspoonsful of anchovy sauce
- 1 dessertspoonful of flour
- 1 teaspoonful of milk
- 1 wineglass of water
- 1 grain of cayenne pepper
- 4 sardines
- 2 slices of bread

of butter (the size of a walnut) the red pepper, and a few drops of the sauce. Put the flour, one spoonful of the anchovy sauce, the water and milk into a small saucepan and stir it into a thick sauce. Fry the bread in the remainder of the butter. Add the paste to the sauce in the saucepan, stir over the fire for five minutes, put over the toast, and pour on the remainder of the anchovy sauce.

36.—Kidneys on Toast.

Ingredients.
- 2 veal kidneys
- 2 oz. of butter
- Some salt
- 2 or 3 minced onions
- 1 oz. of butter
- 1 dessertspoonful of flour
- A little broth or stock
- 5 eggs
- Some finely minced parsley
- A little grated nutmeg
- Some French roll (or light bread)
- Some hot oil or clarified butter
- A little milk

Cut the kidneys into small pieces, and put them in a small stewpan with one ounce of butter, a pinch of salt, and a teaspoonful of minced onion; stew till tender. Put one ounce of butter, the flour and the broth into another stewpan; reduce it till it is thick; put in the kidneys, four of the eggs (whole), and the minced parsley; stir well over the fire for a few minutes, and let it get cold. Cut two slices of bread (stale), dip them in the milk with one egg beaten up in it. Spread the mince over very thick; fry in butter, or clarified butter, and serve very hot.

37.—Egg and Cress Sandwiches.

Ingredients.
Brown bread, butter, hard-boiled eggs, small salad or cress, cleansed fillets of anchovies

Cut some thin slices of brown bread and butter; between two slices place layers of thinly sliced hard-boiled eggs, small salad or cress and anchovies; cut the slices into oblongs, and serve them on a napkin.

38.—Chicken or Game Sandwiches.

Ingredients.
White bread and butter
Cold roast fowl or game
Shred lettuce leaves
Fillets of anchovies

Cut some slices of bread and butter (from rolls, if you have them), and between two slices place very thin slices of the fowl, lettuce leaves, and anchovies. Dish on a napkin and serve.

39.—Sandwiches of Game and Tartar Sauce.

Ingredients.
Some thin crisp toast
Cold roast game
Shred celery
Tartar sauce

The toast must be very thin and crisp; between two slices, place alternate layers of the game *very* thinly sliced, celery and Tartar sauce. Dish on a napkin.

40.—Fish Sandwiches.

Ingredients.
Brown bread and butter
Cold fish and Tartar sauce
Lettuce leaves
Cold boiled eggs and sliced gherkins

Cut some slices of thin bread and butter, and between two slices put layers of cold fish; spread these over with Tartar sauce, strew with gherkins, then some slices of cold boiled eggs; sprinkle with shred lettuce leaves, cover with another slice of bread, press it well down, cut into squares, dish on a napkin, and serve.

41.—Minced Sandwiches.

Ingredients.
Bread, oil, ham or tongue
Any sort of cold game or poultry
Pickled gherkins and olives
Vinegar, oil, mustard, sugar

Cut some thin slices of bread, and fry them a light brown color in oil; mince the game, gherkins, and olives, fine, and mix well; make a sauce of a little vinegar, oil, mustard and sugar, and moisten the mince with it; incorporate well; spread the mixture thickly on the toast, and lay some more toast on the top: cut into neat oblong pieces, and serve on a napkin.

42.—Yarmouth Bloaters.

Cut off the head and tail, split the bloater down the back, spread it out flat, and broil on both sides over a clear fire; send to table on a hot dish with a pat of fresh butter and a Captain's biscuit, heated in the oven or before the fire.

43.—Grilled Kippered Salmon.

Broil the salmon, rub it over with a pat of butter and a little cayenne and lemon-juice, and serve very hot.

44.—Dried Haddocks.

Dip them in scalding water to enable you to remove the skin; boil them over a clear sharp fire, rub them over with fresh butter or little rich cream, lemon-juice and cayenne, and serve very hot.

45.—Sardines.

Take them carefully out of their box, lay them neatly on a dish, garnish with capers or chopped parsley, pour a little fresh salad oil over them, and serve with thin bread and butter.

Note.—Olive farcies served with them are a great addition.

46.—Anchovies.

Wash, wipe, and scrape the anchovies; split them down the backs; place the fillets in neat rows in a dish; garnish with slices of hard-boiled eggs; pour over a little fresh salad oil, and serve.

47.—Devilled Biscuits.

Take some plain thin biscuits, soak them in pure oil, strew

thickly with cayenne and salt on both sides, and toast over the fire on a gridiron.

48.—Devilled Biscuits, dry.

Take some plain cheese bicuits, dip them twice in warm water, dredge with cayenne (one saltspoonful for six) and bake till quite crisp in a slow oven. Serve piled on a napkin.

49.—Devilled Biscuits, buttered.

Ingredients.
1½ oz. of butter
1 saltspoonful of cayenne
1   ,,   ,, flour of mustard
Some warm milk

Take some devilled biscuits; dip them into the warm milk; knead the butter, cayenne, and mustard together; spread it over the biscuits, and bake in a slow oven till crisp. Serve hot.

50.—Devil Mixture.

For any kind of Grill, and also for seasoning Steaks, Butter, Sauce, &c.

Ingredients.
1 spoonful of mustard (French or English)
1 spoonful of Oude sauce, or chutnee
1 spoonful of anchovy sauce
2 spoonsful of salad oil
½ spoonful of cayenne

Mix all these ingredients well together, score the meat or fish you wish to grill, deeply, cover it well with the sauce, and grill brown.

51.—Devilled Salmon, Sardines, Bloaters, &c.

Prepare some devilled biscuits (*see* recipe No. 41); rub some thin slices of kippered salmon with devil's mixture (*see* No. 44); lay them on the biscuits; salamander them, or place them in a hot oven or before the fire. Serve quite hot.

52.—Cheese Biscuits.

Ingredients.
¼ lb. of fresh butter
¼ lb. of baked flour
5 oz. of rich cheese, grated
1 teaspoonful of flour of mustard
6 saltspoonsful of cayenne
The yolks of two eggs well beaten
2 tablespoonsful of cold water

Beat the butter to a cream, add the flour, cheese, mustard, cayenne, and yolks; mix well; knead to a fine paste; roll it out one-eight of an inch thick, and cut into biscuits with a circular cutter about two inches in diameter, or cut into slices one inch wide and three inches long; bake in a quick oven for twenty minutes. Serve very hot.

35.—Pulled Bread.

Take the crust off a new *warm* loaf; pull the crumb into rough pieces about two inches long; lay them on a sheet of paper, and bake in a slow oven till crisp through and a golden brown color. Serve with butter and cheese.

MILK, CREAM, CREAM-CHEESE, CUSTARD.

1.—Curded Milk.

Boil one quart of new milk and let it cool sufficiently for the cream to be taken off; rinse an earthen jar *well* with buttermilk, and before the boiled milk cools pour it in and add the cream which was taken off it *gently* on the top. Let it remain 24 hours (or 12 in very hot weather); turn it out into a deep dish, mix with pounded sugar, and serve with or without cream. The milk by this process becomes a very soft curd, slightly acid, and is a most refreshing and wholesome dish in hot weather. It can also be eaten with stewed fruit.

2.—Devonshire Cream.

Strain the milk into large shallow pans; let it stand twelve hours. Carry the pans carefully and put them near the fire; leave them there till the milk is scalding hot but it must *on no account* either simmer or boil. When it is ready, rings and small bubbles of air appear on the surface. Carry it back to the dairy and leave it there twelve hours more. Butter made of this cream is excellent and merely requires to be beaten with the hand in a shallow wooden tub, which is the usual method of making butter in Devonshire.

3.—Rennet, for making Curds.

Essence of Rennet can be purchased at a Chemists, but

in case there is none at hand, rennet can be prepared in the following manner :

Take the stomach of a fresh killed calf (we have heard that a kid will answer as well); scour it well with water, inside and out; stretch it out to dry on strong wooden skewers; it should be hung in the corner of the kitchen near the fire in a paper bag, and portions cut off as it is wanted.

4.—Curds and Whey.

Cut off a small piece of rennet, put it in a teacupful of water and soak for two hours; put a quart of warm new milk in a dish with one dessertspoonful of the rennet liquor out of the cup, and keep it in a warm place until the curd separates from the whey. Serve with powdered white sugar, and Devonshire, or other cream.

There are china moulds made on purpose for curds with little holes in them, which are best for setting the curds in.

5.—Devonshire Junket.

Prepare the curds and whey as above, sweeten and cover with cream.

6.—Cream Curds.

Ingredients.
1 quart of cream
6 eggs
3 quarts of water
Some salt
1 tablespoonful of vinegar, or 1 pint of thick sour buttermilk

Mix the cream and eggs well together; put the water with a little salt in it to boil on the fire; when it boils put in the vinegar or buttermilk; then stir in the eggs and cream, and as the curd rises sprinkle a little cold water on it with your hand. When it stops rising take it off the fire; let it stand for a little while; lay a wet cloth over a wire sieve;

skim off the curds and lay them on it; put them in a cool place; next day turn out on a dish and serve with powdered sugar.

7.—Curds and Cream, without Rennet.

Put two quarts of the previous day's milk (unskimmed) into a cool oven, and let it remain until a fine curd is formed; take it out, set it to cool, and when quite cold strain it through muslin; tie it up tight and put it under a heavy weight to press out the whey; let it remain two hours. Two hours before it is required put it on a dish and pour three quarters of a pint of good sweet cream over it. Powder with sugar and serve.

Note.—This is a very nice accompaniment to fruit of any kind.

8.—Cream Cheese.

Skim one pint of thick cream; let it stand twelve hours; add a little salt; dip a napkin in salt and water, fold it four times, pour the cream into it and hang it up for twelve hours to drain. Lay it on a plate; cover it with nettles or vine leaves; lay another plate on the top; it will be ready to cut next day. It may also be made in the morning and eaten in the evening, but in that case put no nettles on it, and serve as soon as it is made.

9.—Another Cream Cheese.

Let twelve quarts of milk stand two days, or until it is quite thick; skim it, dip a linen cloth in salt and water; tie the cream up in it and hang it up to drain. When it has done dripping, put the cheese in a soup plate with a clean wet cloth under it, so arranged that you can turn the cheese from time to time till it dries; then put it on another plate, cover it with nettles, put a plate on the top, leave it six or twelve hours, and use.

10.—Another Cream Cheese.

Dip a linen cloth in salt water; lay it in a square shape on a plate; pour' in the thickest cream you have and leave it untouched one day; then turn it into a dry cloth and put a four pound weight upon it; the next day change the cloth, leave it for twelve hours more. Then use.

Note.—In hot weather it will be well to stand the cream-cheese on ice while it is in process of manufacture.

11.—Custard.

Ingredients.
1 pint of new milk
3 oz. of loaf sugar
The rind of half a lemon
8 eggs
¼ pint of good cream
20 drops of vanilla

Let the lemon-peel stand half an hour in the milk, then put them on the fire with the sugar; boil for three minutes; take it off the fire for five minutes. Take out the lemon-peel; beat the eggs, leaving out four of the whites; add the milk to the eggs, stirring quickly as you pour it gently in. Put the custard back into a small saucepan and stand this in another saucepan half full of boiling water; stir over the fire until it begins to thicken; add the cream and the vanilla, or the same quantity of essence of lemon, or two tablespoonsful of either brandy, maraschino, or rum.

12.—Queen's Custard.

Ingredients.
12 new-laid eggs
1½ pints of cream
3 oz. of sugar
1 pinch of salt

Beat and strain the eggs; boil the cream and sweeten it with the sugar; add it to the eggs, stirring quickly; add the salt, thicken as above, and flavour with a wineglass of noyau, maraschino, or curaçao.

13.—Chocolate Custards.

Ingredients.
2 oz. of chocolate
¼ pint of water
1 pint of new milk
The peel of half a lemon
3 oz. of sugar
½ pint of cream
8 yolks of eggs

Dissolve the chocolate gently in the water by the side of the fire; boil it till it is quite smooth. Put the lemon-peel in the milk for half an hour; add the milk *very* gradually to the chocolate stirring carefully all the time; add the sugar; beat and strain the eggs, and when the milk is boiling pour it on to them gradually. Strain the mixture through a fine sieve, and pour it into the cups. Stand them in a preserving pan containing about two inches deep of boiling water, cover close and strew the cover with hot charcoal to prevent steaming inside. Let them boil thus for a quarter of an hour. Stand aside till cold; then serve.

Note.—If you have no large flat preserving pan, put the custard into a jar or jug, set it in a pan of boiling water, and stir it without ceasing until it is thick. Do not put it into the glasses or dish till it is cold.

This can be made into a mould by dissolving half an ounce of isinglass in the milk, and essence of coffee, or a coffeecup of good strong coffee or tea may be substituted for the chocolate.

PASTRY, TARTS, &c.

Everything used in making pastry should be delicately clean, and the ingredients of the very best kinds. Some practice is necessary to accomplish the more delicate sorts, but if all the directions are minutely followed, perfection may be attained by anyone. In mixing paste, the water should be added very gradually, and the whole gently drawn together with the fingers, and when it is damp enough it should be kneaded till it is as smooth as cream, bearing in mind however that the more expeditiously the finer kinds of paste are made and despatched to the oven, and the less they are touched the better. The temperature of the oven is an important matter, it should be hot enough to raise the paste, but not so fierce as to color or burn it before it is done. This experience alone teaches.

When carelessly kneaded, the paste is often covered with small dry lumps and crumbs, or the water is poured in so quickly that more than the quantity given in the recipe has to be added to make the flour workable; this must be avoided by care, or the disproportion in the ingredients will spoil the paste. In the hot season ice must be used for the lighter kinds of paste.

1.—Fine French Puff Paste.

In very hot weather harden the butter in ice, and if neces-

Ingredients of Fine French Puff Paste.

1 lb of the *finest* flour
1 ,, ,, good fresh butter
2 yolks of eggs
1 small teaspoonful of salt
About half pint of water

sary lay the paste between the intervals of rolling on a sheet of tin over some ice for a few minutes.

Put the flour on a paste-board or slab, make a hollow in the centre, break a few small bits of butter; put them in the centre with the salt and yolks of eggs; now add about two-thirds of the water, pouring it in the centre—*not* on the flour. Push in the flour gently from the sides until it is all well incorporated, sprinkle a few drops of water on it, and work the sponge of paste to and fro on the board for two minutes, after which it should be elastic, soft and smooth as satin. Now take the butter, press it in a soft thin cloth to extract all the moisture there may be remaining in it, and form it quickly into a ball. If it is soft from the heat, set it on ice for a couple of minutes. When it is ready roll the paste out square, big enough to cover the butter well; lay on the ball of butter, flatten it down a little with the palm of the hand, fold the crust well over it, sprinkle a little butter on the board and roller and roll it out quickly *very* thin; this is called giving pastry *one turn;* lay this on a baking sheet over ice in the ice-box; leave it ten minutes; take it out; sprinkle the board and rolling pin lightly with flour; roll the paste out as thin as possible; fold it in three; press the folds together by running the rolling pin very lightly across it; turn it round; roll it out again the reverse way in the same manner as before; fold it in three again; fasten the folds by running the rolling pin over them, and set the paste back on the ice for eight minutes; give it two more turns in the same way, rolling it each time very lightly to the full length it will reach, always taking great care that the butter shall not break through the paste. Set it on the ice again for ten minutes, roll it out twice more as before, then give it half a turn by folding it once only and it will be ready for use. When properly made it will rise during baking from one inch to six inches in height, and is used principally in *vol-au-vents* patties and tartlets.

Note.—The juice of one lemon may be added with the eggs and water.

2.—English Puff Paste.

The flour must be very fine and must be carefully dried and sifted; break eight ounces of the butter into it; add a pinch of salt and enough cold water to make a paste.

Ingredients.
2 lbs. of flour
2 ,, ,, butter
A little salt
Some water

Work it quickly and lightly until it is smooth and pliable, then level it with the paste roller until it is three quarters of an inch thick, and place upon it six ounces of the butter broken into small bits, at regular intervals; fold the paste over into the shape of an omelet, roll it out again, lay in six ounces more butter; repeat the rolling, dusting a little flour over the board and roller each time; add six ounces more butter, and roll out the paste thin three or four times, folding the ends into the middle.

3.—Very good Light Paste.

Mix the lard with the flour and make them into a smooth paste with cold water; press the butter in a clean cloth and make it into a ball by twisting the cloth

Ingredients.
1 lb. of flour
6 oz. of lard
10 ,, ,, butter
A little salt

round it. Roll out the paste, put in the ball of butter, close it like an apple dumpling, and roll it lightly until it is less than an inch thick, fold the ends into the middle, dust a little flour over the board and roller, and roll the paste thin a second time; set it aside for a few minutes on ice or in a cool place; roll it out, fold it over; roll again; do this twice; lay it on the ice again; roll it out twice more, folding it each time in three. Then use it *at once* for whatever purpose you need it. If it is allowed to lie before baking it will be tough and heavy.

4.—Common Suet Crust for Pies.

Ingredients.
2 lbs. of flour
12 or 16 oz. of beef or kidney suet
Salt: for fruit pies ¼ teaspoonful; for meat pies 1 teaspoonful

Chop the suet very small and add it to the flour with the salt; mix these with cold water to a firm paste and work it very smooth. Roll it out and use as required.

5.—Excellent Suet Crust.

Ingredients.
1 lb. of flour
1 lb. of suet
4 oz. of butter (or oil)
1 saltspoonful of salt

Strip the skin off some fresh veal and kidney suet; chop it; put it in a mortar with the butter, and pound perfectly smooth; then use it for making the crust in the same way the butter is used in making puff paste (*see* recipe), and it will form an excellent substitute for *hot* pies or crusts.

Note.—For a *short* crust, use eight ounces of suet, two ounces of butter, and half a saltspoonful of salt.

6.—Very rich Short Crust for Tarts.

Ingredients.
8 oz. of butter
½ lb. of flour
1 pinch of salt
2 oz. of sifted sugar
A little milk

Crumble the butter very lightly into the flour, breaking it quite small. Mix well; add the salt and sugar, and by degrees enough milk to make it into a very smooth stiff paste. Bake it slowly and do not let it get colored. It is a most excellent crust and will rise well if properly made.

7.—Cream Crust.

Ingredients.
1 lb. of flour (dried and sifted)
1 small teaspoonful of salt
¾ pint of rich cream*
6 oz. of butter

* For a less rich crust 4 ounces of butter, and half a pint of cream will suffice

Stir the salt into the flour and mix the cream gradually with it so as to form a smooth paste; give the paste a couple of *turns*, put the butter in the middle, fold the paste over it, roll it out, use it for fruit tarts, puffs, or good meat pies.

8.—French Crust, for hot or cold Meat Pies.

Ingredients.
2¼ lbs. of flour
1 lb. of butter
1 small teaspoonful of salt
The yolks of 4 eggs
½ pint of water

The flour must be dried and sifted, break the butter into little bits and work it into the flour with the fingers until it is like fine crumbs of bread; add the salt; beat the eggs with the water; strain it; add it by degrees to the flour and make into a firm paste until it is perfectly smooth. Roll out and use as required.

9.—Vol-au-Vent.

Prepare some puff paste (*see* recipe for French or English puff paste); roll it out one and a quarter inches thick; cut it into the right shape with a round tin cutter about six inches in diameter, pressing it down quickly and firmly so as to take off the raw edges; press another cutter, one inch smaller, gently down on the paste, so as to make a round mark inside the edge of the *vol-au-vent*, about half an inch deep; egg it over with white of egg if for a sweet dish; brush it over with yolk of egg if for an *entrée*; put it on a baking tin and put immediately into a brisk oven that it may rise but not be scorched. Take it out, insert the point of a knife in the mark made with the smaller cutter, and lift out the cover which will come out quite easily. Scoop out all the soft unbaked crumbs from underneath, and turn it out on a sheet of white paper to drain. If for an *entrée*, fill and use at once as directed (*see* recipe); if for a sweet dish, sift some white sugar over, and glaze by holding a salamander or red-hot shovel over it when it is drawn from the oven; lay it on a sheet of white paper to drain and cool; fill it either with a rich marmalade of apples, or stewed fruit or peaches, greengages, apricots or plums, compotes, (*see* recipes), or any kind of bottled fruit, and heap well-whipped rich cream over the fruit.

This, if well made, is a most delicious dish.

10.—Puff Paste Patties, or Vols-au-Vents.

Prepare the puff paste (*see* recipe), let it rest on ice for three minutes (in hot weather) and cut out with a plain patty cutter (the cover of a cornflour tin will do) just dipped in hot water as many patties as you require; moisten a baking sheet or tin with a brush dipped in water, press down each patty in its place, brush over the surface with yolk of egg, and with another cutter, smaller than the first one, dipped in hot water, make an incision round the centre of the patties; push the sheet into a brisk oven and bake about twenty minutes until well risen but not scorched; lift out the centre with a sharp pointed knife; scoop out the loose unbaked crumb from the inside and fill with any kind of white mince-meat or fish, prepared with white sauce according to recipes, or with mushroom, lobster, oyster, or shrimp-sauce (*see* recipes); put on the covers, or cover with fried bread-crumbs, and serve at once.

If the patties are wanted for tartlets, sprinkle them with white powered sugar, and glaze with a salamander as you take them out of the oven, and set them on a sheet of white paper to drain and cool. Fill with any kind of jam or jelly, or put a preserved plum, greengage or peach in each, and if you like a spoonful of whipped cream, very stiff, on the top.

11.—Bread and Butter Pastry.

Prepare some puff paste (*see* recipe) (using half the quantities given) and roll it out a quarter of an inch thick; cut into bands three inches wide, and then again into strips half an inch wide, and place them on a baking tin in rows about two inches apart. Bake in a sharp oven, and just before they are done, sprinkle with white sugar and hold a red hot salamander over them to glaze them; spread with jam and lay together like bread and butter jam sandwiches; dish on a napkin, or lay round a dish with some rich whipped cream in the centre.

12.—Polish Puffs.

Prepare the puff paste (*see* recipe); roll it out very thin (a quarter of an inch); cut it up into square pieces about two and a half inches square; wet the centre and turn in the four corners so that they meet in the middle; place a dot of paste in the centre, pressing it down with the finger; egg over and bake in a quick oven, a fine bright light color; just before they are done sift over some finely powdered white sugar, pass a red hot salamander over to glaze them, and decorate with apple, currant or quince jelly.

13.—Plaits.

Prepare some puff paste (*see* recipe), giving it nine turns instead of six and half; roll it out one-eighth of an inch thick and cut it into bands five inches wide; divide these into narrow strips a quarter of an inch wide; take four of these strips, lay them over one another at one end with a little white of egg or water between each to fasten them; plait loosely but neatly together; when finished fasten the ends in the same way. As each plait is ready, place it on the baking sheet, brush over with white of egg and bake a light color; glaze with powdered white sugar, salamander, and decorate with jelly or greengage jam.

14.—Pastry or Almond Paste Sandwiches.

Ingredients.
Puff paste
Any jelly or jam

Take some puff or almond paste (*see* recipes), divide it in two and roll it out square and as thin as possible; butter a tin well, lay one-half of the paste on it and spread lightly with jelly; lay the remaining half closely over; press a little with the rolling-pin to make it adhere well. Mark it in divisions, and bake from fifteen to twenty minutes in a moderate oven.

15.—Lemon Sandwiches.

These are made as above, only substituting lemon or orange cheese-cake mixture (*see* recipes) for the jelly.

16.—Meringue Tart.

Ingredients.
Some pastry (*see* recipe)
Some stewed fruit

Lay a band of fine crust (*see* short crust for Tarts) round the edge of a Tart dish; fill the dish with any kind of fruit (fresh

Ingredients of Meringue Tart.
The whites of four eggs
Three tablespoonsful of sifted sugar

or bottled) with half their weight of sugar; roll out the remainder of the paste very evenly; brush the edges with water, lay it over the fruit, press round the edge of the dish with the thumb, and trim off the edges close to the dish with a knife; make an incision at each end to let the steam escape. Beat the whites of the eggs to a *stiff* froth, stir the sugar in gently and quickly, pile this up on the tart. Put it into a moderately brisk oven, and when the crust has risen well and the ring is set, either lay a sheet of writing-paper lightly over it, or put it in a part of the oven where it will not be too much colored. It should be faintly tinted a golden color.

17.—Apple Tart.

Ingredients.
1½ ℔s. of apples
Some English puff paste (*see* recipe)
4 oz. of pounded sugar
The grated rind and strained juice of a lemon
2 cloves

Lay a band of the paste round the edge of the Tart dish; pare and core the apples; weigh them; dip them in water and lay them compactly in the Tart dish, higher in the centre than at the sides; add the sugar, lemon-rind, juice and cloves. Cover over with the remainder of the paste rolled out thin; press round the edges, pare with a knife round the dish; ten minutes before it is done (it will take about one hour), brush over with white of egg well beaten and sift loaf sugar over that. Serve with custard (*see* recipe) or whipped cream.

Note.—Any kind of fruit may be substituted for apples using rather more than half their weight of sugar.

18.—Mince-meat.

Wash the currants, pick and well dry them; chop one

Ingredients of Mincemeat.

2 lbs. of currants
2 ,, ,, raisins
¾ ,, ,, mixed candied peel
1 ,, ,, fresh beef suet
¾ ,, ,, the undercut of sirloin of beef (roasted), or fillet of veal
} chopped.

The grated rinds and strained juice of 2 lemons
1 orange
1½ lbs. of moist sugar
½ nutmeg, grated
½ teaspoonful of powdered cinnamon
½ saltspoonful of powdered ginger
1 cayenne spoonful of cloves
1 pint of brandy

pound of them; stone and chop the raisins; mix them with all the ingredients except the brandy well together, then stir in the brandy; put the meat into stone jars, tie over with a bladder and keep in a dry cool place till needed. Mince-meat should not be used for six weeks after it has been made, and will keep a year.

Note.—One pound of unsalted ox-tongue fresh boiled and cut free from the rind may be substituted for the roast beef.

19.—Mince Pies.

Butter some patty pans well, and line them with some puff paste (*see* recipe) rolled thin; fill them with mincemeat (about two tablespoonsful to each), moisten the edges with water, close carefully with the remainder of the paste, trim carefully, make a small hole in the centre, and bake in a moderately heated oven for twenty-five or thirty minutes. If when they are partially done they seem to take too much color, lay a paper over them.

20.—Mince Pies, with Egg Icing.

Ingredients.

½ lb. of mince-meat
2 oz. of pounded sugar
The grated rind and strained juice of 1 lemon
Some fine paste (*see* recipes)
4 tablespoonsful of pounded sugar

Add the sugar, lemon-rind and juice, butter and yolks of eggs to the mince-meat; beat well together. Line some patty pans with the paste; put them into a moderate oven, and when the insides are just set, ice thickly with the whites of eggs whipped to a stiff froth and mixed quickly with four tablespoonsful of sugar; set immediately in the oven again and bake slowly a fine light brown.

21.—Cheese Cakes.

Line some tartlet tins or patty pans with fine puff paste *(see* recipe and use half the quantities) rolled very thin; fill them with any of the following mixtures; ornament with narrow strips of paste laid on in cross-bars or with pastry leaves tastefully arranged, and bake in a moderate oven half an hour.

22.—Lemon Cheese Cake mixture.

Ingredients.
1 lb. of loaf sugar
3 large lemons
3 tablespoonsful of brandy
½ lb. of fresh butter
8 eggs

Dissolve the sugar in the lemon-juice (strained) and the brandy; stir in the butter until dissolved but not oiled; add the lemon-rind (grated), the yolks of all the eggs, and the whites of four, well beaten; stir rapidly over a gentle fire till the mixture is of the consistency of honey. Put it in a jar, and when cold, tie it over with thick writing-paper, and keep in a cool place.

23.—Orange Cheese Cake mixture.

Ingredients.
4 oranges
2 lemons
2 quarts of milk
¾ lbs. of fine new honey
The yolks of eight eggs
6 oz. of fresh butter
⅙ of a nutmeg
1 wineglassful of brandy

Strain the juice of the oranges and lemons into the milk, and put it into a gentle oven until a solid curd is formed; when cold strain off the whey; pound the curd with the honey; add the grated rind of two of the oranges, the yolks (beaten), the butter (beaten to a cream), the nutmeg and brandy; beat the mixture until it becomes of the consistency of thick cream; put it into a jar, tie it down, and keep it in a cool place.

24.—Almond Cheese Cake mixture.

Ingredients:
¼ lb. of sweet almonds
½ ,, ,, loaf sugar
6 oz. of fresh butter
2 tablespoonsful of ratafia
The yolks of 6 eggs (beaten)

Blanch the almonds; dissolve the sugar, butter and ratafia; mix together, and stir till cold, but not set; pound the almonds to a soft paste, add them to the other ingredients, beat the eggs and stir together over a gentle fire; when the mixture begins to thicken, take it off and rub it through a fine sieve; put it in a jar, and when cool tie it down and keep it in a cool place.

25.—Common Lemon Tartlets.

Ingredients.
4 eggs
4 oz. of pounded sugar
1 dessertspoonful of cornflour
3 oz. of butter
1½ large lemon

Beat the eggs until they are very light; add the sugar to them gradually; whisk together for five minutes; strew in the cornflour lightly; dissolve the butter, and when it is *lukewarm* add it to the mixture; beat the whole well, add the lemon-juice, strained, and the rind, grated. Line some patty pans with fine puff paste (*see* recipes) rolled very thin, fill them two-thirds full with the mixture, and bake about twenty minutes in a moderate oven.

Note.—A few macaroons or ratafias powdered may be substituted.

26.—Pastry Cream.

Ingredients.
1 oz. of flour
2 yolks of eggs
¾ pint of cream
1½ oz. of butter, (clarified)

Beat the yolks of the eggs, add them to the flour; boil the cream, stir it to the eggs and flour very gradually; put it into another stewpan, and stir it over

Ingredients of Pastry Cream.
2 oz. of white sugar
Some rasped lemon-rind
1½ oz. of ratafias

a gentle fire until it is quite thick; take it off and stir well, up and round; replace it on the fire and simmer from six to eight minutes; pour it into a basin; add the sugar, butter, and a lump of sugar rubbed on a lemon and pounded, and the ratafias crushed to powder with a paste-roller. Make some small *vol-au-vents* (*see* puff paste patties). When they are ready glaze the edges by sifting fine sugar thickly over them and holding a red-hot salamander or shovel over them until the sugar melts and forms a pale barley-sugar glaze. Have the pastry cream ready, hot; fill the *vol-au-vents* with it, and send to table at once.

27.—Jelly Tartlets or Custards.

Put the jelly into a basin, stir the beaten eggs in gra-
Ingredients.
4 tablespoonsful of fine fruit jelly
12 beaten eggs

dually. Line some tartlet pans with thin puff paste (*see* recipes); fill them with the custard, and bake ten minutes.

28.—Strawberry Tartlets.

Take off the stalks of the strawberries and crush them;
Ingredients.
1 pint of fresh strawberries
2½ oz. of powdered sugar
4 eggs (well whisked)

mix them with the sugar; stir in the eggs by degrees; beat well; line some patty pans with fine paste (*see* recipes); fill three parts full with the mixture, and bake from ten to twelve minutes.

SWEET OMELETS, SOUFFLÉS, FRITTERS, AND PANCAKES.

1.—Omelet with Preserve.

Ingredients.
7 eggs
3 tablespoonsful of thick cream
1 oz of fresh butter
Some jam or marmalade

Beat all the yolks of the eggs with four of the whites; add the cream; dissolve the butter in a small omelet pan over a very slow fire; pour in the eggs and stir quickly until they begin to set; let them continue over a *very slow* heat for three minutes; lay the preserve over the upper side; fold over the omelet; dredge with finely powdered sugar; pass a red-hot salamander or shovel over the sugar to glaze it, serve instantly.

2.—Sweet Omelet.

Follow the preceding recipe, adding to the eggs while beating them the grated rind of half a lemon with its strained juice, and two tablespoonsful of loaf sugar. Serve as directed, omitting the jam.

3.—Potato Omelet.

Ingredients.
3 oz. of mealy potatoes, boiled and mashed
2 oz. of loaf sugar

Beat the eggs separately, and all the other ingredients together; then add the eggs and beat for a quarter of an hour; fry in a small omelet pan till of a

Ingredients of Potato Omelet.
¼ of a saltspoonful of powdered cinnamon
The strained juice of 2 oranges
¾ pint of new milk
3 fresh eggs

golden color. Serve either plain with sifted sugar, glazed with a salamander, or with preserve.

4.—Omelet Soufflé.

Break the eggs and put the yolks into one basin and the

Ingredients.
10 eggs
5 oz. of very finely pounded sugar
The grated rind of half a lemon
20 drops of essence of vanilla

whites into another; add to the yolks the sugar, lemon-rind, and vanilla; beat fast for ten minutes; beat the whites to a stiff froth; add them to the yolks, &c., and continue to beat for ten minutes. Put the mixture into a soufflé dish, or into a plain round cake mould, well buttered; bake instantly in a *very* quick oven for twelve minutes; sift loaf sugar over the top; roll a napkin round the tin, and serve at once, holding a hot salamander over it till it reaches the dining-room to prevent its falling in.

5.—Rice Flour Soufflé.

Mix the rice to a perfectly smooth batter with a little of

Ingredients.
1½ pints of new milk or cream
4 oz. of flour of rice
2 ,, ,, fresh butter
2½ ,, ,, pounded sugar
6 eggs
1 pinch of salt
The rind of 1 lemon

the milk or cream; put the remainder into a very clean saucepan; when it boils stir in the rice; *simmer* for ten minutes, stirring it all the time (it must be very thick); then mix in the butter, sugar, and lemon-rind; stir for three minutes; take the saucepan off the fire, beat in the yolks of the eggs carefully and by degrees; whisk the whites to a firm froth; butter the pan, and when all is ready for the oven, stir the whites in gently to the other ingredients; pour immediately into the soufflé pan or mould (buttered), and put into the oven. It will take about thirty minutes in a slow oven, but it is impossible to tell exactly; when it has risen very high and is a fine golden brown color it will be ready. Serve at once, and hold a hot salamander over it till it reaches the dining-room.

Note.—The soufflé may be flavoured with vanilla or orange flowers, and arrowroot, tapioca, sago, or any other farinaceous substances may be used instead of rice-flour.

6.—Potato-flour Soufflé.

Ingredients.
The rind of half a citron or of an orange
2½ oz. of sugar
1 pint of cream
2 oz. of potato-flour
¾ pint of milk
The yolks of 7 eggs
1 pinch of salt

Pare off the rind in the thinnest possible strips and infuse it in the cream by the side of the fire; blend the potato-flour with the milk; take the lemon-peel out of the cream; boil it and stir it boiling into the milk; stir the mixture in a large basin until it thickens; add the salt, butter (just dissolved in a small saucepan) and the sugar. Beat the yolks, stir them into the mixture by degrees; beat the whites to a stiff froth, and stir *gently* in; fill the soufflé pan or mould (buttered) less than half full; set it instantly in a gentle oven; close the door and do not open it for fifteen minutes; in about thirty minutes the soufflé will be ready; serve at once.

7—Coffee Soufflé.

Ingredients.
6 oz. of flour (plain, potato, or rice)
10 oz. of sugar
1 pinch of salt
2 oz. of butter
½ pint of strong coffee
½ ,, ,, cream
6 eggs

Blend the flour to a perfectly smooth batter with some of the cream. Put the remainder of the cream with the sugar, salt, butter (just dissolved), and coffee into a saucepan; when it boils, stir in the flour; simmer for ten minutes stirring all the time; beat the yolks; stir them into the mixture off the fire; whisk the whites to a stiff froth; butter the pan, and when all is ready, add the whites gently; put the mixture into the pan, and bake instantly in a gentle oven for about thirty or forty minutes. Serve *at once.*

Note.—Chocolate soufflés are made as above, substituting four ounces of chocolate and half a pint of milk for the coffee.

8.—Fruit Soufflé.

Ingredients.
1 dozen ripe apricots
½ lb. of sugar
½ pint of water
4 oz. of flour
2 ,, ,, butter
1 pint of cream
6 eggs

Take the stones out of the apricots; put them in a stewpan with the sugar and water; boil, stirring with a wooden spoon until the fruit is dissolved; rub through a sieve; then mix the fruit with the flour, butter and cream; stir over the fire till it is nice and thick; add the yolks of the eggs beaten; mix gently; beat the whites to a stiff froth; stir in as lightly as possible; turn into a soufflé dish and bake instantly; it will take thirty or forty minutes in a gentle oven.

Note.—Any other fruit may be used in the same way.

9.—Brown Bread Soufflé.

Prepare as for potato-flour soufflé, using two ounces of grated and sifted brown bread-crumbs instead of the flour, and one ounce of picked and washed currants.

10.—Cream Soufflé.

Mix the flour smoothly with some of the cream; add the

edients of Cream Soufflé.
gs
blespoonsful of flour
" " maraschino
1 pint of cream

maraschino and three yolks; beat well; put in the cream; beat the whites of the four eggs to a stiff froth, and stir them in; bake in a small tin or paper-case; sift pounded sugar over, and serve.

11.—Soufflé Pudding.

Blend the ground rice with a little of the milk till it is

Ingredients.
3 oz. of ground rice (or arrow-root or tapioca)
4 oz. of powdered sugar
2 " " butter
6 eggs
1 stick of vanilla or 20 drops of essence of vanilla
½ pint of milk or cream, or both mixed

quite smooth; put the milk on the fire with the vanilla stick in it; simmer till it boils; take out the vanilla and pour the milk over the flour; add the butter (stirring well; then the sugar; then the yolks of eggs (well beaten). Butter a mould, tie buttered paper round it reaching about six inches above the mould; add the whites of eggs beaten to a stiff froth; pour the mixture *instantly* into the mould, and steam for an hour. If you have not a proper steamer put a saucer upside down in a large saucepan, stand the mould on it; the water in the saucepan (which should be boiling when you put in the pudding) must reach about half-way up the mould. Serve *at once* with the following sauce poured over.

Note.—This is a most delicious pudding, and strawberry or raspberry cream (*see* recipe) may be substituted for the strawberry sauce.

12.—Strawberry Sauce.

Pass the strawberry jam through a hair sieve; put it into

Ingredients.
1 pot of strawberry jam
1 tablespoonful of powdered loaf sugar

a *bain marie* (that is, a saucepan in another larger one half filled with boiling water) with the sugar;

SWEET OMELETS, SOUFFLES, FRITTERS, & PANCAKES.

Ingredients of Strawberry Sauce.
1 dessertspoonful of sherry with two drops of *good* cochineal in it

add the sherry colored with the cochineal. Let it get thoroughly hot, and then pour it over the pudding.

Note.—Great care should be taken to get really good pure cochineal. It is a magnificent color, and a couple of drops of it are more effective than twenty of the stuff ordinarily sold. It is perfectly harmless.

13.—Pancakes.

Ingredients.
3 fresh eggs
3 tablespoonsful of dried flour or cornflour
¾ of a pint of new milk
4 oz. of butter or olive oil

Beat the eggs; stir in the flour till you have a smooth paste; add the milk; beat with a *wooden* spoon for fifteen minutes; stand the batter in a cool place for two hours; beat again and fry in butter (one ounce for each pancake) till of a pale brown color on each side; shake the pan to keep the pancake loose, and turn it by tossing it up so that it comes down on the other side; four minutes for each side will be enough. Serve at once either plain, with sugar and lemon separate, or with apricot jam laid inside and the sides folded over.

Note.—Served with rich raspberry or strawberry cream (*see* recipe) in a separate dish, these form a most delicious sweet *entremets*.

14.— Light French Pancakes.

Ingredients.
7 eggs
½ pint of cream
1 oz. of butter
3 tablespoonsful of flour

Beat the yolks; add the cream and the butter broken up into small pieces and mixed with the flour; when they are well mixed, add the whites of the eggs beaten to a stiff froth; mix gently; fry in a little butter, as thin as possible; do not turn them in the pan, but as they are done turn them out one on the top of the other, sifting sugar between.

15.—Rice Pancakes.

Ingredients.
¼ lb. of rice
2 oz. of powdered sugar
½ pint of cream
½ ,, ,, milk

Boil the rice till quite tender in milk; strain and pound it in a mortar; add the cream; beat the eggs and stir them in; mix all together, and fry as above.

16.—A Rich Pancake.

Ingredients.
1 pint of cream
5 eggs
2 oz. of flour
The rind of one lemon
1 lump of loaf sugar
2 oz. of pounded sugar
2 ,, ,, clarified butter
A few powdered ratafias

Whisk the eggs well; add a quarter of the cream and strain through a fine sieve; add the flour gradually; stir in the remainder of the cream; beat with a wooden spoon; put it aside for two hours; just before using rasp the lemon-rind on to the sugar, powder it, add it to the batter; mix in the two ounces of sugar, the butter and ratafia powder. Put some butter in a small frying pan; pour in some of the batter, *very* thin, just to cover the frying pan; do not turn the pancakes; pile on a dish, and serve at once, with or without clouted cream.

17.—French Batter.

Ingredients.
¼ of a pint of boiling water
¾ of a pint of cold water
½ ounce of fine dry flour
1 pinch of salt
The whites of two eggs beaten to snow

Cut the butter into small pieces; pour rather less than the quarter of a pint of boiling water on to it; when the butter is dissolved, add the cold water so that the mixture should not be quite as warm as new milk; stir in the flour by degrees so that it is very smooth, and add the salt; stand it aside for an hour. Just before using, stir in the whites of eggs beaten to a solid froth. If the batter seems too thick add a little cold water before mixing in the eggs. This is a very light crisp batter.

18.—Frying Batter.

Ingredients.
¾ lb. of fine dry flour
2 oz. of butter (dissolved)
1 teaspoonful of salt
3 eggs
½ pint of tepid water

Mix the flour, butter, salt, and two yolks together with a wooden spoon, adding by degrees the tepid water; work it well until it presents the appearance of smooth cream; set it aside for an hour; just before using stir in the whites of the three eggs beaten to a stiff froth; then use as directed.

Note.—Many varieties of batter may be prepared by adding one wineglassful of any white wine or liquor to the tepid water. If the wine is very light half a pint may be substituted for the water, and two tablespoonsful of good salad oil used instead of the butter.

19.—Plain Fritters.

Ingredients.
3 eggs
3 tablespoonsful of flour
A little more than half pint of milk

Beat the eggs well; add the milk; strain through a fine hair sieve (or any clean cloth). Add them very gradually to the flour, and add as much more milk as is needed to bring it to the consistency of cream; stand it aside for two hours, then beat thoroughly; pour it into a jug and drop small portions of it into a frying pan with boiling butter in it (or lard which is better, if it is very good and fresh). When lightly colored on one side turn, drain them well as they are lifted out, and serve with powdered sugar sifted over them, and lemons.

Two or three ounces of well washed and dried currants may be added to the batter just before using.

20.—Apple Fritters.

Prepare the batter as directed in the preceding recipe.

Ingredients of Apple Fritters.
3 eggs
3 tablespoonsful of flour
½ pint of milk
3 apples
3 oz. of sifted sugar
1 lemon

Pare the apples; cut them into slices three quarters of an inch thick; scoop out the core neatly by making a round hole in the centre of each slice; lay them in a stewpan with the sugar, the strained juice and grated rind of the lemon, and simmer (uncovered) for ten minutes; place them on a plate; pour the syrup over them and leave them to absorb the sugar for several hours; then wipe each piece, dip it into the batter and fry in butter or oil till of a golden color; drain on a sieve before the fire; sift sugar over, and serve on a neatly folded napkin. Send to table very hot.

21.—Orange Fritters.

Pare three of the oranges; free them entirely from the white skin; divide each into slices; take out the pips with a penknife. Dissolve the sugar in

Ingredients.
4 large ripe oranges
3 oz. of sugar
1 tablespoonful of rum or brandy

the juice of the remaining orange and the rum (or brandy), boil in a very small saucepan till in a thick syrup, and pour it over the oranges; let them stand for two hours; drain on a sieve, dip each in batter, and proceed as in the foregoing recipe.

22.—Peach Fritters.

Prepare as above, only substituting a glass of noyeau for the rum. Apricot fritters are prepared in the same way.

23.—Rice Fritters.

Wash and drain the rice; put it into a saucepan with

SWEET OMELETS, SOUFFLES, FRITTERS, & PANCAKES.

Ingredients of Rice Fritters.
3 oz. of good rice
3 ,, ,, sugar
The thin rind of half a lemon
1 inch of cinnamon
Nearly a pint of milk
3 eggs

the sugar, lemon-rind, cinnamon and milk; boil (stirring frequently) for three quarters of an hour; rub through a fine wire sieve. Beat the yolks and white of the eggs separately; add the yolks to the mixture which had passed through the sieve; beat for ten minutes, then add the whites; beat five minutes more; then fry in butter (in a small omelet pan) till of a golden color on both sides. Drain before the fire, and serve on a neatly folded napkin with fine loaf sugar sifted over.

Note.—This is a delicious dish if served with strawberry or raspberry cream (*see* recipe) in separate dish.

24.—Custard Fritters.

Ingredients.
1 pint of milk
1 inch of cinnamon
The thin rind of half a lemon
1 oz. of flour
1 grain of salt
6 eggs

Boil the milk with the cinnamon and lemon; add the sugar, flour, salt and eggs; beat well together; butter a mould; pour in the custard and steam until firm. When it is quite cold cut carefully into square pieces; dip each separately in frying batter or French batter (*see* recipes,) and fry separately in boiling butter or lard a light golden color. Drain and serve very hot with sugar sifted over.

Any kind of cold custard puddings, such as cabinet, ground rice, arrowroot, &c., can be prepared as above.

25.—Cake and Pudding Fritters.

Cut a plain pound rice cake, or rich seed cake into small square slices half inch thick; dip them in batter, (*see* recipe) and fry as directed in preceding recipes. When they are ready spread over a layer of apricot or strawberry jam, and serve immediately.

Cold plum pudding sliced in the same way and dipped in French batter (*see* recipe) makes a very nice variety of fritter.

26.—Potato Fritters.

Ingredients.
7 oz. of potatoes
1½ ,, ,, butter
3 eggs
3 oz. of sugar
The grated rind of one lemon
A pinch of salt

Boil the potatoes; strain them; mash perfectly smooth while hot; add the butter, eggs, salt, and lemon-rind; drop small portions into boiling butter, and fry a light golden brown on both sides. Sift sugar over and serve with or without red currant, apple, or quince jelly on each fritter.

27.—Lemon Fritters.

Ingredients.
6 oz. of fine bread-crumbs
4 ,, ,, beef suet
4 ,, ,, powdered sugar
1 small tablespoonful of flour
4 eggs
The grated rind of two small lemons and their juice
2 dessertspoonsful of cream

Chop the suet as fine as possible; mix with it the bread-crumbs, sugar, flour, the eggs (lightly whisked), the lemon-rind, cream, and last of all the lemon-juice. Mix well, and fry in butter for five minutes. Serve very hot.

BOILED AND BAKED PUDDINGS.

PRELIMINARY REMARKS.

All the ingredients for Puddings must be fresh and of good quality, and it is false economy to try and use inferior articles or those which have been long stored. Eggs should always be broken into a cup separately before they are used, in order that a bad one may be detected and set aside, and they should always be strained through a sieve after they are beaten. The whites of eggs should be beaten in a deep bowl, and it is best to whisk a small quantity either with the wire spoons sold for the purpose, or a knife, which is better than a fork. While any liquid remains at the bottom of the bowl they are not sufficiently beaten; when a portion of them taken up with the whisk and dropped from it remains standing in points, it is ready and should be used at once.

If milk is not perfectly sweet it will curdle in use and spoil the pudding, and if it is too quickly baked the milk will turn to whey instead of mixing with the eggs in a rich custard on the top. It is generally best to pour the milk boiling on to the eggs, which must then be beaten together.

A *very* little salt improves all sweet puddings and brings out their flavour, but its presence must never be perceptible.

Pudding cloths should be steeped in water the moment they are taken off, and dried in the open air after they have been well washed.

How to clean Currants.

Put them into a cullender *(see kitchen utensils)*; strew a handful of flour over them; rub gently with the hand to separate the lumps and detach the stalks; work them round in the cullender; shake it well and the small stalks and stones will fall through. Pour plenty of water over the currants, drain them and spread them on a clean soft cloth; press it over them to absorb the moisture, and leave them to dry. When they are perfectly dry take off the remaining stalks, and any stones which may have remained among them.

To Steam a Pudding in a common Saucepan.

When the mould is filled, tie it over first with a well buttered paper, and then with a small piece of thin muslin well floured; gather up the corners and tie them carefully so that no part of the muslin or paper touch the water. Put a saucer upside down into a saucepan; pour in enough water to cover the saucer to a depth of three inches, and when it boils put in the mould, press on the cover of the saucepan, and boil gently without ceasing until it is done. More boiling water must be added as that in the pan evaporates, and it must be poured carefully in without touching the pudding.

1.—A Christmas Plum Pudding.

Ingredients.
½ lb. of beef suet, chopped fine
10 oz. of fine raisins, stoned
½ lb. of fresh currants, washed
6 oz. of mixed candied peel, chopped
½ lb. of moist sugar

Mix the suet, raisins, currants, peel, sugar, lemon-rind, cinnamon, cloves, nutmeg, flour, and bread-crumbs well together; add the lemon-juice and brandy; stir for five minutes; add the

Ingredients of a Christmas Plum Pudding.

- The grated rind of a large lemon
- 1 cayennespoonful of powdered cinnamon
- 1 cayennespoonful of powdered cloves
- ⅛ of a nutmeg, grated
- 6 oz. of sifted flour
- 2 oz. of sifted bread-crumbs
- The strained juice of one lemon
- 1 sherryglass of brandy
- 4 beaten eggs
- ¼ pint of new milk

eggs and milk. Beat the mixture with a wooden spoon for twenty minutes; put it into a quart basin or mould well rubbed with butter; tie it over with a clean cloth dredged with flour; put it into plenty of boiling water and boil fast for six hours; or else tie closely in a stout cloth well buttered and floured, lay a plate in the bottom of the saucepan to keep the pudding from burning, and boil as directed. Serve with either of the following sauces, or with German sauce (*see* recipe).

2.—Brandy Sauce.

Knead the butter with the flour and stir it into the boiling water; add the sugar, simmer ten minutes; add the brandy, and serve at once in a tureen.

Ingredients.
- 3 oz. of fresh butter
- 1 tablespoonful of baked flour
- ¾ of a pint of boiling water
- 1 tablespoonful of moist sugar
- 1 claretglass of brandy

3.—A very rich Sauce.

Dissolve the sugar in the milk; boil quickly for ten minutes; beat the yolks with the cream; add them to the sugar, whisking briskly; continue to whisk until smooth; add the brandy; serve instantly.

Ingredients.
- 4 oz. of loaf sugar
- ½ wineglass of new milk
- The yolks of four fresh eggs
- ½ pint of cream
- 1 claretglass of brandy

4.—An excellent Plum Pudding.

Mix and beat the ingredients well together in the order in which they are given. Continue to beat with a wooden spoon for about twenty minutes; butter and

Ingredients.
- 8 oz. of flour
- 3 " " bread-crumbs
- 6 " " beef-kidney suet

Ingredients of Plum Pudding.

6 oz. of raisins (weighed after stoning)
6 ,, ,, currants (well washed)
4 ,, ,, minced apples
5 ,, ,, sugar
2 ,, ,, candied peel
½ teaspoonful of spice
A pinch of salt
1 sherryglass of brandy
3 eggs

flour well a stout cloth; tie the pudding up lightly in it; put a plate in the bottom of a saucepan of boiling water, and boil three and a half hours. Serve with Punch sauce or German sauce (*see* recipe).

5.—Punch Sauce.

Ingredients.

2 oz. of sugar
¼ of a pint of water
The rind of half a small lemon
The ,, ,, quarter orange
1½ oz. of butter
1 teaspoonful (not heaped) of flour
½ glass of brandy
⅓ ,, ,, white wine
¾ ,, ,, rum
The juice of half an orange
The ,, ,, ,, a small lemon

Dissolve the sugar in the water; add the lemon and orange rind; boil very gently from fifteen to twenty minutes; strain out the rinds; thicken the syrup with the butter and flour; add the brandy, wine, rum, lemon, and orange juice; stir over the fire, but take care it does not boil, and serve at once very hot.

6.—Small Plum Pudding.

Ingredients.

3 oz. of the crumb of a stale loaf
¼ of a pint of boiling milk
6 oz. of suet, finely minced
1 ,, ,, dry bread-crumbs
10 ,, ,, stoned raisins
1 pinch of salt
The grated rind of a small orange
3 yolks of eggs
2 whites

Grate the three ounces of bread-crumbs and soak in the milk. Add all the ingredients in the order in which they are named; beat well together with a wooden spoon for fifteen minutes; butter and flour a stout cloth; tie up the pudding lightly in it; put a plate in the bottom of a saucepan of boiling water, put in the pudding, and boil for two hours. Serve with Sweet sauce.

7.—Sweet Sauce.

Knead the butter and flour together; stir into the boiling

BOILED AND BAKED PUDDINGS.

Ingredients of Sweet Sauce.
1 oz. of butter
1 tablespoonful of flour
½ of a pint of boiling milk
2 tablespoonsful of moist sugar
2 ,, ,, cream

milk; add the sugar; boil ten minutes; stir in the cream, and pour the sauce round the pudding at once.

8.—Vegetable Plum Pudding.

Ingredients.
1 lb. of smoothly mashed potatoes
½ lb of carrots boiled and beaten to a paste
1 lb of flour
½ ,, ,, suet
¾ ,, ,, sugar
1 ,, ,, currants
1 ,, ,, raisins
½ nutmeg, grated
1 pinch of salt
2 eggs

Mix the ingredients well together in the order in which they are given; beat with a wooden spoon for twenty minutes; flour and butter a warm pudding cloth; tie the pudding up in it closely, and boil for four hours. Serve with Wine sauce

Note.—This pudding is large enough for sixteen persons, so that half the ingredients would suffice for an ordinary dinner. It is very cheap and is excellent cold.

9.—Wine Sauce.

Ingredients.
The very thin rind of a small lemon
1½ oz. of sugar
1 wineglassful of water
1 oz. of butter
½ teaspoonful of flour
1½ wineglassful of sherry or madeira

Dissolve the sugar in the water; add the lemon-rind, and boil gently together for ten minutes; take out the lemon-rind; knead the butter smoothly with the flour, put it into the syrup, and stir over the fire for one minute; add the wine, heat but do not boil the sauce, and serve at once.

Note.—Port wine sauce is made in the same way, substituting Port wine for Sherry, and adding the juice of a lemon or an orange, a little grated nutmeg and more sugar.

10.—Fig Pudding.

Put the figs and suet into a basin, add the bread-crumbs,

Ingredients.

½ lb. of figs, chopped fine
½ ,, ,, suet
½ ,, ,, powdered loaf sugar
½ ,, ,, fine bread-crumbs
4 yolks of eggs, well beaten
½ wineglass of sherry
1 teacup of milk
2 grates of nutmeg

sugar, yolks, sherry, milk and nutmeg. Knead well with the hands so that the figs may be well incorporated with the other ingredients; butter a mould thickly, put in the mixture, tie over a piece of well-buttered paper, then a well-floured cloth, and steam for four hours. Serve with German sauce.

11.—German Sauce.

Ingredients.

½ oz. of butter
3 yolks of eggs
1 oz. of powdered sugar
A little cream
½ glass of sherry

Put a white jar in a saucepan half filled with boiling water over the fire; put in the ingredients except the sherry and whisk them all together over the fire until the sauce thickens; then add the sherry and pour over the pudding. It should be well thickened and highly frothed, and is a most delicious sauce.

12.—Cabinet Pudding.

Ingredients.

8 oz. of stale sponge cake
1 ,, ,, ratafias
7 ,, ,, candied fruit
8 fresh eggs
½ pint of new milk
1 wineglassful of cream
1 ,, ,, curaçao
2 oz. of loaf sugar

Boil the sugar in the milk; beat the eggs; add them to the milk while it is warm but not boiling; let it get cold; then add the curaçao and cream. Cut the cake into thin pieces; butter a quart mould, line it tastefully with three ounces of the candied fruit; lay in the cake, fruit, ratafias and custard in the order in which they are named, until it is quite full. Let it stand for an hour that the cake may soak in the custard; then cover it with buttered writing paper, tie a cloth over that, fasten up the ends on the top so that they do not touch the water, and steam over fast boiling water for an hour and a half. Turn out carefully and serve with the following sauce in the dish.

13.—Curacao Sauce.

Boil the sugar and lemon-rind in one wineglassful of water; moisten the arrowroot with the remainder of the water and add it to the sugar; stir over the fire for three minutes; add the curaçao; take out the peel, and serve as directed.

Ingredients.
3 oz. of loaf sugar
The rind of half lemon
2 wineglassesful of water
1 dessertspoonful of arrowroot
1 wineglassful of curaçao

14.—A very rich Cabinet Pudding.

Butter a plain quart mould or basin thickly and ornament it tastefully with the dried cherries; cut the sponge biscuits in slices, lay them lightly in the basin, intermingle the ratafias. Put the cream into a small saucepan; add the sugar in lumps and the vanilla; heat and strain this; beat the yolks and whites of the eggs well together; pour the cream hot on to them, and when the mixture is cold, add the brandy by degrees; pour it gently into the mould, cover with butter and paper, and steam the pudding very gently for one hour. If it is boiled quickly it will be destroyed. Serve with Wine sauce (*see* recipe).

Ingredients.
4 oz. of dried cherries
¼ lb. of sponge biscuits
4 oz. of ratafias
¾ pint of thin cream
3 oz. of loaf sugar
30 drops of vanilla or half a pod
6 yolks of eggs
2 whites   ,,
1 wineglassful of brandy

15.—Pineapple Pudding.

Rub the stale cake to powder; cut the pineapple into

Ingredients of Pineapple Pudding.
6 oz. of stale pound cake
6 ,, ,, preserved pineapple
6 fresh eggs
1 oz. of sifted loaf sugar
½ claretglass of new milk
½ ,, ,, cream

quarter inch pieces; beat the eggs; mix these ingredients together; add the sugar, milk and cream; beat well for fifteen minutes; butter a mould, put in the mixture, tie it over with buttered writing paper, and steam over fast-boiling water for one and a half hours. Turn out carefully, and serve with the following sauce poured round it.

16.—Pineapple Sauce.

Put the syrup, jelly, sugar and water into a small saucepan; moisten the arrowroot with a little water; boil the syrup; when it boils, add the arrowroot; stir over the fire two minutes; add the rum and serve.

Ingredients.
4 tablespoonsful of pineapple syrup
2 ,, ,, apple jelly
1 teaspoonful of sifted white sugar
1 wineglassful of cold water
1 teaspoonful of arrowroot
1 tablespoonful of rum

17.—Chestnut Pudding.

Boil the chestnuts in water till they feel tender; dry them in the oven; take off the shells and skins and pound the nuts to powder. To six ounces of chestnuts add the butter beaten to a cream, the sugar, eggs and milk. Butter a mould; stick it tastefully over with dried cherries; put in the pudding mixture; butter a piece of writing paper, tie it over the pudding, and steam over fast-boiling water for one and a half hours; or else bake in a quick oven from twelve to fifteen minutes; turn out carefully, and serve with Victoria sauce (*see* recipe).

Ingredients.
30 chestnuts
4 oz. of butter
3 ,, ,, loaf sugar
6 fresh eggs
1 gill of new milk
Some dried cherries or raisins

18.—Victoria Sauce.

Ingredients.
3 oz. of loaf sugar
1 wineglassful of water
The yolks of three eggs
1 claretglass of cream
1 sherryglass of brandy

Dissolve the sugar in the water; boil it to a syrup; beat the yolks with the cream, pour in the brandy; add them to the syrup, whisking rapidly; serve at once. The sauce should have the appearance of thick cream.

19.—Chestnut Pudding, iced.

Ingredients.
½ pint of new milk
¼ lb. of loaf sugar
2 inches of stick vanilla
¼ lb. of chestnuts in powder
1 gill of new milk
7 yolks of eggs
1 pint of cream

Boil the milk with the sugar and vanilla until well flavoured; prepare the chestnuts as in the foregoing recipe, and when they are powdered, moisten with the gill of milk; strain the sweetened milk over this, put the mixture in a saucepan, and stir over the fire until quite smooth; beat the yolks, add them and continue to stir for three minutes. When nearly cold, add the cream, beat for ten minutes; put the pudding into a one and a half pint mould, and stand it on the ice until quite firm, about ten minutes. Serve with or without whipped cream round it.

Note.—Vanilla sugar prepared as directed (see *General Directions*) can be used, and the stick of vanilla omitted.

20.—Baked Chestnut Pudding.

Ingredients.
12 oz. of chestnut farina
6 ,, ,, pounded sugar
1 dessertspoonful of vanilla sugar
1 pinch of salt
4 oz. of butter
1 pint of milk
6 eggs

Put the farina into a stewpan, add the sugar, salt, butter and milk; stir this gently over the fire until it thickens, then stir it more quickly until the paste ceases to adhere to the sides of the stewpan; take it off the fire; beat the yolks of the eggs; incorporate them with the mixture;

whip the whites to a firm froth; stir them in gently; butter a mould, put in the preparation, place it on a baking sheet, and bake in a moderate oven for about an hour. When done turn it out carefully and serve with apricot jam round it.

21.—Publisher's Pudding.

Ingredients.
6 oz. of Jordan almonds
12 bitter almonds
¾ of a pint of cream
½ pint of almond cream
4 oz. of fine bread-crumbs
4 ,, ,, macaroons
2 ,, ,, flour
5 ,, ,, beef suet (minced fine)
5 ,, ,, marrow (cleaned carefully from fibre)
4 oz. of dried cherries
4 ,, ,, stoned muscatel raisins
6 ,, ,, pounded sugar
½ pint of candied citron
1 pinch of salt
½ nutmeg, grated
The grated rind of 1 lemon
7 yolks of eggs
1 wineglassful of brandy

Blanch all the almonds; beat them to the smoothest possible paste in a mortar; boil the cream, and pour it very gradually over the almonds; turn them into a cloth, twist it strongly opposite ways, and wring out all the cream. Take a half pint of this cream, heat it, and as soon as it boils pour it over the bread-crumbs; cover it with a plate, and leave it till it is nearly cold. Then mix in the crushed macaroons, the beef suet, the marrow (shredded, not too small), and all the other ingredients in the order in which they are given, stirring well. Pour the mixture into a thickly buttered quart mould or basin, fill it to the brim; lay a sheet of buttered paper over, then a well-floured cloth; tie them down securely, and boil the pudding for four and a quarter hours. Let it stand for two minutes before it is turned out, and serve with German sauce, (*see* recipe).

Note.—When almonds are objected to they may be omitted, and the boiling cream poured at once on the bread-crumbs. In this case two ounces of the sugar used had better be vanilla sugar. (*See* recipe).

22.—Lemon Pudding.

Ingredients.
½ lb. of fresh butter
½ ,, ,, sifted loaf sugar
The grated rind of two large lemons
The strained juice of two large lemons
4 tablespoonsful of Oswego flour
6 fresh eggs

Beat the butter to a cream; add the sugar, rind, lemon-juice, Oswego flour, and eggs; beat together for twenty minutes. Have ready some puff paste, (*see* recipe) roll it out a quarter of an inch thick; line a pie dish with it; ornament to taste; put in the pudding, and bake in a quick oven 35 to 40 minutes. Serve hot or cold.

23.—Another Lemon Pudding.

Ingredients.
The strained juice of 6 lemons
The rind of 3 lemons
6 oz. of bruised ratafias
6 ,, ,, sugar
1 pint of cream
10 yolks of eggs
6 whites, whipped
1 pinch of salt
3 grates of nutmeg

Rub the rind of three lemons off on some lumps of sugar, and put them into a basin with all the other ingredients in the order in which they are given. Work them together for five minutes with a whisk; have ready some puff-paste, line a pie dish with it, put a thin border round the edge of the dish; put in the pudding mixture; strew some bruised ratafias over the surface, and bake the pudding for about half an hour in a quick oven. When ready it should be a light fawn color.

24.—Lemon Suet Pudding.

Ingredients.
8 oz. of bread-crumbs
6 ,, ,, beef suet
3½ ,, ,, pounded sugar
1 large lemon
6 oz of currants
5 eggs

Put all the ingredients into a basin in the order in which they are given, the eggs being well beaten; when they are well mixed pour them into a thickly buttered pudding dish and bake for an hour in a quick oven. When it is colored a fine brown

25.—Ginger Pudding.

Ingredients.
1 pint of milk
6 oz. of sugar
6 ,, ,, butter
½ lb of flour
6 eggs
4 oz of chopped preserved ginger

Put the milk, sugar and butter in a stewpan on the fire to boil; as soon as the milk rises, withdraw it, and throw in the flour; stir it quickly with a wooden spoon to mix it well; stir the paste over the fire for a few minutes until it ceases to adhere to the sides of the pan; withdraw it from the fire; stir in the yolks of the eggs well beaten, and the chopped ginger; when they are well incorporated stir in lightly the whites of the eggs whipped to a stiff froth. Spread a mould thickly with butter, put in the pudding, tie over carefully and steam for one and a quarter hours. Serve with German sauce (*see* recipe, flavoured with one dessertspoonful of the syrup belonging to the ginger.

26.—Prince Albert's Pudding, No. 1.

Ingredients.
½ lb. of fresh butter
½ ,, ,, pounded loaf-sugar
6 fresh eggs
½ lb. of dried sifted flour
½ ,, stoned raisins
The grated rind of one lemon
Some slices of candied peel

Beat the butter to a cream; stir in the loaf sugar by degrees; beat well; add the beaten yolks and then the whites of the eggs beaten to a stiff froth; strew in the flour lightly, add the raisins (weighed after they are stoned); mix well. Butter a mould thickly, lay in the slices of candied peel; put in the pudding; tie a piece of thickly buttered paper and a well-floured cloth tightly over, and boil the pudding for three hours. Serve with Punch sauce (*see* recipe.)

27.—The Young Wife's Pudding.

Ingredients.
5 fresh eggs
2½ oz. of powdered loaf sugar
1 pinch of salt
1 large lemon, or a tablespoonful of lemon-brandy or orange-flour water
1 pint of new milk
Some stale bread
Some butter

Break the eggs one by one into a cup, and with the point of a fork remove the specks; as each is done put it into a large basin; beat them up lightly for four or five minutes; add the sugar by degrees, then the salt; whisk well together; add the grated lemon-rind and stir briskly. Pour in the milk, cold, and pour the pudding into a well buttered dish. Cut the bread in slices rather more than a quarter of an inch thick, and with a small cutter cut enough rounds to cover the top of the pudding. Butter them thickly; lay them on the top of the pudding (the dry side uppermost), sift sugar thickly over them, and put the dish in a Dutch oven about one foot from a moderate fire. Bake very slowly for one hour, and the pudding will be firm throughout. If the recipe fails it will be because the fire was too hot.

28.—Mincemeat Pudding.

Ingredients.
Some slices of French roll
Some butter
Some mincemeat
4 eggs
¾ of a pint of milk
2 oz. of sugar
1 pinch of salt

Have a rather deep tart dish; cut the roll in slices, spread thinly with butter, and cover with a thick layer of mincemeat. Cover the bottom of the tart dish with these; put a second layer lightly on the top of the first; make a custard with the milk, eggs, sugar and salt. Pour it over the bread; let the pudding soak in this for an hour; then put it into a *gentle* oven, and bake from three quarters of an hour to an hour.

29.—Marmalade Pudding.

Ingredients.
Some roll or light bread
,,   orange marmalade
4 eggs
¾ of a pint of milk
1 pinch of salt
2 oz. of sugar
1 tablespoonful of brandy

Cut some slices of roll, butter lightly on both sides, and spread the top thickly with marmalade. Beat the yolks of the eggs separately, add the whites well whipped, sprinkle in the sugar, add the milk (or cream). Put the custard in a tart dish, lay the slices of bread and marmalade on the top; let it stand an hour; put it in a *gentle* oven, and leave it there till it is set; take it out at once and serve. This is a delicious pudding if properly baked, but like all custard puddings it is spoiled if subjected to great heat.

30.—Diplomatic Pudding.

Ingredients.
½ pint of cream
4 oz. of loaf sugar
The grated rind of one lemon
6 oz. of bread-crumbs
1 ,, ,, flour
3 ,, ,, beef suet, } chopped
1 ,, ,, beef marrow
2 ,, ,, Muscatel raisins
2 ,, ,, candied orange-peel
2 ,, ,, currants
1 ,, ,, Sultana raisins
5 fresh eggs
⅙ of a nutmeg grated
1 wineglassful of rum
1 ,,   ,,   ,, orange wine

Put the cream, sugar and lemon-rind into an enamelled saucepan and place it over a gentle fire; when nearly boiling, stir in the bread-crumbs, flour, suet, and marrow; stir over the fire for ten minutes; turn into a basin to get cold. Stone and mince the raisins; chop the orange peel; wash and dry the currants and Sultana raisins; beat the eggs. Mix these ingredients together with the cream; add the nutmeg, rum and orange-wine; mix all together, and beat for a quarter of an hour or longer. Butter a mould thickly; ornament with Muscatel raisins to taste; put in the pudding, tie it closely over, and steam rapidly for three hours, or bake in a moderate oven for two hours. Serve with the following sauce in the

BOILED AND BAKED PUDDINGS.

Ingredients of Sauce.
3 oz of loaf sugar
The strained juice of two oranges
3 tablespoonsful of rum

dish. Dissolve the loaf sugar in the orange-juice; boil till it becomes a thick syrup; stir in the rum, and serve.

31.—Parisian Pudding.

Ingredients.
2 oz. of ground rice
1 pint of good cream
The yolks of 6 eggs
The white of 4 eggs
2 oz. of beef suet }
1 ,, ,, beef marrow } chopped
4 sweet apples, peeled and cored
2 oz. of candied orange peal,
1 oz. of candied citron,
1 oz. of angelica } chopped
1 oz. of sweet almonds, blanched and pounded
1 teaspoonful of vanilla
⅛ of a nutmeg, grated
2 oz. of apricot jam
2 ,, ,, Sultana raisins
2 ,, ,, rusks, pounded
1 wineglassful of maraschino
2 oz. of sifted loaf sugar

Mix the rice with the cream and stir it over a slow fire until it thickens; beat the whites and yolks separately, and add them to the cream while it is warm but not hot. Stand this aside to get cold; then add the remainder of the ingredients in the order in which they are given; beat the mixture for a quarter of an hour; rub a plain mould thickly with butter; put in the pudding; cover with writing paper thickly buttered, tie a cloth (floured) tightly over that, and steam for two and a half hours, or bake in a moderate oven for two hours. Turn out carefully, and serve with the following sauce in a tureen.

Ingredients of Sauce.
3 yolks of eggs
2 oz. of sifted loaf sugar
½ pint of marsala
½ gill of cream

Beat the yolks; stir in the sugar and marsala; stir over a slow fire until it thickens; add the cream, stirring it in by degrees. Serve immediately.

32.—Raisin Pudding.

Ingredients.
¼ lb. of flour
½ oz. of ground rice

Mix these ingredients in a basin in the order in which they are given; beat with a wooden spoon for five minutes; butter a

Ingredients of Raisin Pudding.
½ lb. of beef suet (chopped fine)
¼ „ „ moist sugar
¼ „ „ Sultana raisins
The strained juice of one lemon
The grated rind of one lemon
1 egg (well beaten)
¼ of a pint of new milk

plain mould thickly; put in the pudding, tie it closely down with a sheet of well buttered paper and a well floured cloth; boil rapidly for three hours in boiling water. Serve with sifted sugar on the top.

33.—A Pudding for a Prince.

Ingredients.
2 oz. of sweet almonds
6 bitter almonds
½ of a pint of new milk
5 eggs
½ gill of thick cream
2 tablespoonsful of brandy
6 oz. of stale sponge cake
2 „ „ sifted loaf sugar
Some dried cherries

Blanch the almonds; boil them for twenty minutes in the milk; pound them to a paste; when the milk is nearly cold add the eggs well beaten, the cream and brandy; rub the sponge cake to crumbs; add them to the mixture, and beat for ten minutes, then stir in the sugar. Butter a mould; stick it round in vandykes (or to taste), with the dried cherries; pour in the mixture; tie it over with writing paper, buttered, and steam over fast boiling water for 1¾ hours. Turn out immediately, and serve with the following sauce in the dish.

34.—Cherry Sauce.

Ingredients.
1 teaspoonful of arrowroot
1 tablespoonful of cold milk
1 gill of boiling milk
1 dessertspoonful of sifted loaf sugar
¼ of a lb. pot of cherry jelly (or some cherry syrup)

Moisten the arrowroot with the cold milk, stir it into the boiling milk; stir in the sugar; boil for two minutes. Dissolve the jelly, stir it in by degrees; take it off the fire; continue stirring until it is quite smooth, and serve as directed.

Note.—The sauce should be of the consistency of thick cream and a bright rose color.

35.—Clarence Pudding.

Ingredients.
¾ pint of new milk
5 oz. of loaf sugar
¼ of an inch of vanilla
⅙ of a nutmeg, grated
5 fresh eggs
2 French rolls
2 oz. of butter
½ lb. of Sultana raisins

Boil the milk, sugar, vanilla and nutmeg; when the sugar is dissolved, set it aside to cool. Beat the eggs, pour the milk on to them through a strainer, beating all the time; cut the rolls into thin slices, pare off the crust, and spread both sides with butter; wash the raisins. Butter a plain mould and stick it across with lines of raisins meeting in a point at the top; lay in the bread, butter, raisins, and custard in layers till the mould is full; let it stand for an hour; tie it over with a piece of buttered writing paper and a cloth dredged with flour; put it into fast boiling water, and boil quickly for 1¾ hours. Serve with the following sauce poured over.

36.—Vanilla Sauce.

Ingredients.
2 oz. of loaf sugar
¼ of an inch of vanilla
1 dessertspoonful of arrowroot
2 tablespoonsful of rum

Boil the sugar and vanilla in one-third of a pint of water for twelve minutes; moisten the arrowroot with one tablespoonful of cold water; mix them together and boil for three minutes; add the rum. Take out the vanilla and serve as directed.

37.—Cocoanut Pudding.

Ingredients.
⅓ of a fine new cocoanut, grated
6 oz. muscatel raisins, stoned
¼ of a lb. of fresh beef marrow, chopped
The strained juice and grated rind of a small lemon
⅙ of a nutmeg, grated
3 oz. of loaf sugar

Make a custard by boiling the sugar in the milk; beat the eggs, pour the milk into them while hot but not boiling; add the cocoanut milk, and stir till nearly cold. Cut some very thin slices of bread (about four ounces)

Ingredients of Cocoanut Pudding.
½ pint of new milk
3 fresh eggs
1 tablespoonful of cocoanut milk
Some stale bread

butter a plain mould and stick it with rasins in the form of a cross. Divide all the ingredients into five parts and lay them in the mould in the following order until it is full:—Bread, marrow, raisins, cocoanut, lemon-juice, lemon-peel, nutmeg, custard; finish with bread and custard. Let it stand to soak for half an hour; tie it over closely and boil fast in plenty of water for 3½ hours. Turn out carefully and serve with the following sauce in the dish.

38.—Cocoanut Cream.

Ingredients.
2 oz. of loaf sugar
1 wineglass of water
1 inch of cinnamon
1 clove
2 inches of thin lemon-peel
1 dessertspoonful of Oswego flour
2 tablespoonsful of cocoanut milk
2 tablespoonsful of cream
1   "   "   brandy
5 drops of essence of vanilla

Put the sugar into a saucepan with the water; add the cinnamon, clove, and lemon-peel, boil till in a thick syrup. Mix the Oswego with the cocoanut milk; strain the syrup into it; boil up for one minute; add the cream; stir till cold; add the brandy and vanilla and serve cold.

39.—Spongecake Pudding.

Ingredients.
½ lb. of stale spongecake
5 oz. of butter
½ lb. of marmalade
2 oz. of loaf sugar
½ pint of new milk
4 fresh eggs

Cut the cake into slices a quarter of an inch thick; spread one side with butter and the other with marmalade. Boil the sugar in the milk; beat the eggs; add the milk to the eggs while hot but not boiling. Butter a plain mould which holds one and a half pints; lay in the slices of cake (with the buttered side next the tin) and custard alternately till full. Let it stand half an hour to soak; then bake in a well-heated oven for one hour and ten minutes. Turn out carefully, and serve with the following sauce in the dish.

40.—Orange Cream.

Ingredients.
2 oz. of loaf sugar
2 inches of orange peel
1 sherryglass of water
1 sweet orange
1 tablespoonful of rum
1 gill of thick cream

Boil the sugar and orange peel for ten minutes in the water; add the strained juice of the orange and the rum; boil fast for three minutes; take it off the fire, beat in the cream, and continue beating until nearly cold. It must be very smooth. Serve as directed.

41.—Prince Albert's Pudding, No. 2.

Ingredients.
½ lb. of butter
½ ,, ,, dried flour
¼ ,, ,, sifted sugar
½ ,, ,, raisins (stoned and chopped)
¼ lb. of candied peel (chopped)
½ wineglassful of brandy
The grated rind of half a lemon
1 gill of new milk
4 beaten eggs
3 oz. of sugar
1 wineglassful of water
1 ,, ,, brandy

Beat the butter to a cream; add all the other ingredients in the order in which they are given, and beat for ten minutes. Butter a plain mould, put in the mixture, cover with buttered paper and a well floured cloth tied over, and boil fast for two hours. Boil the sugar in the water for ten minutes, add the brandy, pour the sauce over the pudding, and serve.

42.—Marrow Pudding.

Ingredients.
¼ lb. of baked flour (or biscuit powder)
¼ lb. of sugar
¼ ,, ,, currants (well washed and dried)
1 oz. of sweet almonds, blanched and pounded
The grated rind and strained juice of a lemon
⅛ of a nutmeg, grated
6 oz. of beef marrow, finely chopped
2 beaten eggs
¼ of a pint of milk

Put all the ingredients into a basin in the order in which they are given; beat the mixture for ten minutes; butter a mould; put in the pudding; tie it over firmly with buttered paper and a floured cloth; plunge into fast boiling water, and boil fast for three hours; sift loaf sugar on the top, and serve.

Note—Dried cherries, ginger, raisins, or candied peel (chopped small) may be substituted for the currants.

43.—Zandima Pudding.

Ingredients.
6 oz. of butter
6 ,, ,, dried flour
6 ,, ,, sifted sugar
6 fresh eggs
1 wineglassful of raspberry syrup

Beat the butter to a cream; stir in by degrees the flour and the yolks of the eggs well beaten; when well mixed add the whites of the eggs beaten to a stiff froth and the syrup. Beat for ten minutes. Butter a mould, pour in the mixture, tie over with buttered paper and a cloth, and boil fast for one and a half hours, or bake in a moderate oven for one and a half hours. Serve with raspberry cream poured over the pudding.

44.—Raspberry Cream for Puddings.

Ingredients.
1½ gills of good cream
½ pot of raspberry jam

Whip the cream with the jam, pass it through a sieve, whip again, and serve as directed.

Note.—Strawberry cream may be made in the same way.

45.—College Pudding.

Ingredients.
Some light paste (*see* recipes)
Some jam or marmalade
3 oz. of sweet almonds
6 bitter almonds (blanched and pounded)
6 oz. of sifted sugar
4 ,, ,, dissolved butter
The yolks of 6 eggs
The whites of 3 eggs

Butter a pint pie dish and line it with the paste rolled out, very thin; ornament the edges by clipping them with a paste cutter; spread the bottom with about half an inch thickness of jam; mix the almond powder with sugar and the dissolved butter, add the yolks of the eggs beaten with the brandy; add the whites beaten to a stiff froth; beat the mixture for ten minutes; pour it over the jam, and bake in a quick oven for ten minutes.

46.—Jersey Pudding.

Ingredients.
½ lb. of fresh butter
¼ ,, ,, ground rice
6 oz. of sugar
¼ lb. of raisins (stoned and chopped)
2 oz. of candied orange peel (chopped)
1 oz. of flour
6 fresh eggs (well beaten)
3 tablespoonsful of new milk

Beat the butter to a cream and add by degrees all the other ingredients in the order in which they are given. Beat the mixture for twenty minutes. Butter a basin, put in the pudding, tie it closely over, plunge into fast boiling water, and boil rapidly for one and three quarter hours. Serve with lemon-sauce.

47.—Lemon Sauce.

Ingredients.
2 large lemons
3 oz. of loaf sugar
1 wineglassful of gin
1 ,, ,, water

Rub the rind of the lemons with the sugar; put the sugar into a saucepan with the gin, water, and juice of the lemons, and boil till in a syrup; then serve.

48.—Bakewell Pudding.

Ingredients.
3 oz. of sweet almonds
½ pint of new milk
A French roll
Some jam
6 oz. of fresh butter
6 ,, ,, sifted loaf sugar
6 yolks of eggs
3 whites ,,

Blanch the almonds; boil them in the milk for ten minutes; pound them to a smooth paste. Cut the roll into thin slices without crust, and pour the milk over them. Butter a pie dish, lay in the bread as a lining, and on that spread the jam very thick. Dissolve the butter and stir in the almonds, add the butter, the yolks and whites of the eggs, and beat well for a quarter of an hour. Pour the mixture over the jam, and bake in an oven for fifty minutes or an hour.

Note.—Rich puff paste (*see* recipe) may be substituted for the bread as a lining to the dish.

49.—Currant Pudding.

Ingredients.
½ lb. of currants (well washed and dried)
¼ lb. of moist sugar
½ ,, ,, flour
½ ,, ,, beef suet
½ ,, ,, lemon (the strained juice and grated peel)
2 eggs
1 gill of milk

Mix all the ingredients together in the order in which they are given; beat well for ten minutes and boil in a basin well covered over and tied down for three and a half hours. Serve with sweet sauce.

50.—Sweet Sauce.

Ingredients.
2 oz. of butter
1 tablespoonful of baked flour
½ of a pint of milk
2 tablespoonsful of moist sugar

Knead the butter with the flour; boil the milk and stir in the butter; add the sugar, boil for five minutes, and serve.

51.—Jam Pudding.

Ingredients.
¼ of a lb. of loaf sugar
½ lb. of fresh butter
¾ of a pint of new milk
6 oz of Oswego flour
5 eggs
6 oz. of apricot jam
6 ,, ,, greengage jam

Make a paste as follows:—Boil the sugar and butter in the milk; stir in the Oswego flour; stir (off the fire) for ten minutes; add the yolks well beaten, and last of all the whites beaten to a firm froth. Divide the paste into three parts; butter a mould and lay in the paste and the jam in alternate layers; cover with writing paper spread with butter, and steam over fast boiling water for three quarters of an hour, or bake in a quick oven for three quarters of an hour. Turn out carefully with sugar sifted over, or with the following sauce in a tureen.

Ingredients of Sauce.
3 oz. of loaf sugar
1 gill of brandy
3 oz. of butter

Dissolve the sugar in the brandy; beat the butter to a cream; mix these together and beat until smooth.

52.—Boiled Jam Pudding ("Roley Poley.")

Make a paste with equal quantities of finely chopped beef suet and sifted dry flour;* moisten with cold water and knead to a firm paste; roll it out one-sixth of an inch thick and spread it with jam, leaving a quarter of an inch all round; brush the edge with water; roll the pudding in the form of a bolster; press the edges to make them adhere; roll it tightly in a cloth, tie both ends, put into fast boiling water, and boil rapidly for two hours. Serve with or without rich custard (*see* recipes) cold in a tureen.

53.—Baked Jam Roll.

Ingredients.
½ pint of new milk
4 oz. of butter
6 ,, ,, sifted flour
4 ,, ,, loaf sugar
The grated rind of 1 lemon
4 eggs
Any kind of jam

Put the milk and butter into a saucepan; place it over a slow fire, and when nearly boiling stir in the flour, sugar (in fine powder) and lemon-rind; when well mixed, add the eggs, beaten, and stir till it becomes a paste; turn it out on a paste board and let it get cold. Dredge it with flour; roll it out a quarter of an inch thick. Spread it with any kind of jam (or marmalade), roll it over in the form of a bolster, and bake on a tin in a moderate oven for 20 or 25 minutes. Sift loaf sugar thickly over, and serve either hot or cold and with or without custard.

54.—Potato Pudding.

Ingredients.
4 or 5 mealy potatoes
6 oz. of sifted loaf sugar
The grated rind of a lemon
The strained juice of a lemon

Bake† the potatoes, and as soon as they are done press them out of the skin that the steam may evaporate; when cold rub them through a fine sieve

---

* Or *see* recipes for suet crust.
† Or boil the potatoes very dry. (*See* recipes for mashed potatoes.

Ingredients of Potato Pudding.
2 tablespoonsful of brandy
1 gill of thick cream
4 fresh eggs

with a wooden spoon. Take six ounces of the potato and add the other ingredients in the order in which they are given, (the yolks and whites of the eggs beaten separately); beat for a quarter of an hour; butter a plain mould; stick it with candied peel, cut in thin half circles; put in the pudding and bake in a quick oven for three quarters of an hour, turn out and serve immediately; or steam over fast-boiling water for an hour. Serve with Brandy Cream Sauce.

55.—Brandy Cream Sauce.

Ingredients.
3 oz. of loaf sugar
1 wine glassful of water
1 gill of good thick cream
1 wineglassful of brandy

Dissolve the sugar in the water; boil till in a thick clear syrup; beat in the cream; add the brandy by degrees. Serve over the pudding.

56.—Almond and Potato Pudding.

Ingredients.
¼ lb. of sweet almonds
½ pint of new milk
¼ lb. of fresh butter
6 oz. of loaf sugar
6 ,, ,, cold mealy potatoes
The grated rind of a large lemon
The strained juice of a large lemon
¼ of a nutmeg, grated
5 eggs

Blanch the almonds and boil them in the milk for twenty minutes, then pound them to a soft paste; dissolve the butter and sugar in the milk. Rub the potatoes to a fine powder, add to them all the other ingredients in the order in which they are given (the yolks and whites of the eggs whipped *separately;*) beat for twenty minutes; butter a tin mould, put in the mixture, and bake in a quick oven for forty minutes. Turn out carefully, and serve at once either alone or with raspberry cream, or any of the sauces for puddings. (*See* recipes.)

57.—A rich Potato Pudding.

Ingredients.
14 oz. of mashed potatoes
4 ,, ,, butter
4 ,, ,, sugar
The grated rind of one lemon
1 pinch of salt
1 gill of cream
5 eggs (yolks and whites beaten separately)
1 wineglassful of brandy
1½ oz. of candied peel

Prepare the potatoes as for mashed potatoes (*see* recipe), pass them through a fine sieve, add the ingredients in the order in which they are given; beat well together for ten minutes; butter a mould thickly; ornament with thin slices of candied peel, put in the pudding mixture, and bake in a moderate oven for forty minutes. Pour a little clarified butter over the top, sift plenty of white sugar over it, and serve with or without any of the pudding sauces. (*See* recipes.)

58.—Potato Puffs.

Ingredients.
2 oz. of fresh butter
2 ,, ,, loaf sugar
1 wineglassful of milk
3 oz. of mealy potatoes (boiled)
The grated rind of a small lemon
3 fresh eggs

Dissolve the butter and sugar in the milk; rub the potatoes to a powder; mix these together; add the lemon rind and the yolks of the eggs; beat for ten minutes; beat the whites to a froth; add these; butter five small tin moulds; put one-fifth of the mixture into each, and bake in a quick oven for eighteen minutes. Sift sugar over them, and serve at once.

Any kind of jelly or jam may be served with them.

56.—Hasty Puffs.

Ingredients.
¾ of a pint of new milk
The thin rind of half a lemon
1 inch of cinnamon
3 oz. of flour
3 ,, ,, butter
3 tablespoonsful of sugar
3 eggs

Put the milk, lemon-rind, and cinnamon into a saucepan and boil up; stir in the flour quickly; when well mixed add the butter and sugar; when nearly cold add the eggs, well beaten. Take out the peel and cinnamon; beat for five minutes. Butter six small cups; put one-sixth of the mixture into each, and bake in a quick oven for ten or twelve minutes. Turn out and serve with any kind of preserve round the dish.

60.—Puddings in Haste.

Equal quantities of bread-crumbs, beef suet, chopped, and currants well washed, half the quantity of sugar, eggs and milk. Mix all together and beat well. Dip some small cloths in hot water; wring them dry; dredge well with flour, put a teacupful of the mixture into each, tie them up tightly, put them into boiling water, and boil fast for twenty minutes. Turn out carefully, sift powdered loaf sugar over, and serve at once.

61.—German Puffs.

Ingredients.
2 oz. of fresh butter
2 tablespoonsful of new milk
2 fresh eggs
2 oz. of sifted sugar
2 ,, ,, dried flour

Dissolve the butter in the milk; beat the eggs with the flour; add the milk and all the other ingredients; butter four or five small moulds; rather more than half fill them with the mixture and bake in a quick oven for eighteen or twenty minutes. Serve with the following sauce in the dish, or with clarified sugar.

62.—Maraschino Syrup.

Ingredients.
3 oz. of loaf sugar
4 bitter almonds (blanched and chopped)
The thin rind of quarter lemon
The strained juice of an orange
1 wineglassful of water
1 ,, ,, maraschino

Put the sugar, almonds, lemon-peel, orange-juice, and water into a saucepan; boil and skim till quite bright and thick; strain, add the maraschino and serve.

63.—Cup Pudding.

Beat the butter to a cream; add all the other ingredients in the order in which they are given; beat for ten minutes. Butter six small moulds; three parts fill them, and bake in a quick oven for twenty minutes; turn out and serve with Maraschino Syrup poured over them.

Ingredients
3 oz. of fresh butter
3 ,, ,, baked flour
3 ,, ,, sifted loaf sugar
3 ,, ,, currants or raisins
3 tablespoonsful of cream

64.—Rice Apple Dumplings.

Peel and core the apples without dividing them; dip some small cloths in boiling water, dredge them thickly with flour, spread the rice in six portions on the cloths; lay an apple in the middle of each, tie up the cloths, and boil in boiling water for half an hour. Turn out carefully, sift some brown sugar over them, and serve at once. Or one large dumpling may be made in the same way, but the apples must be quartered. Some good custard may be served with these.

Ingredients.
6 apples
8 oz. of rice

65.—Light Currant Dumplings.

The quantities given are for one dumpling and must be increased according to the number required.

Mix all the ingredients together and add as much milk as will make a very thick batter. Tie the dumplings in well buttered cloths and boil for an hour. Serve with Sweet Wine Sauce.

Ingredients.
3 tablespoonsful of flour
2 ,, ,, suet (finely minced)
1 pinch of salt
Some milk
1 dessertspoonful of currants

66.—Lemon Dumplings.

Mix the bread-crumbs, suet, flour, and lemon-rind well

Ingredients of Lemon Dumplings.
10 oz. of fine bread-crumbs
½ lb. of beef suet (chopped)
1 large tablespoonful of flour
The grated rind of 2 small lemons
The strained juice
4 oz. of pounded sugar
4 large eggs

together; add the eggs (well beaten and strained), and the lemon-juice (strained.) Beat for five minutes; divide into four equal portions; tie in well floured cloths, and boil one hour. Serve with the syrup of preserved ginger.

67.—Baked Apple Dumplings.

Make a paste with the suet, flour and salt, moistened

Ingredients.
¼ lb. of suet (chopped)
¼ ,, ,, flour
½ saltspoonful of salt
5 apples
Some brown sugar

with enough water to make a firm paste; divide it into five parts; roll it out. Pare the apples; scoop out the core; fill the vacancy with sugar; lay each apple in its circle of paste; cover them over, place them in a tin dish, and bake in a moderate oven for three quarters of an hour. Sprinkle moist sugar over, and serve at once.

Note.—These dumplings may be glazed by sprinkling them with sifted loaf sugar and holding a red hot salamander over them for a few seconds.

68.—Apple and Plum Dumplings.

Slice the suet very fine; free it carefully from fibre and

Ingredients.
1 lb of flour
6 oz. of suet
½ saltspoonful of salt
½ pint of water
8 or 10 apples
½ oz. of fresh butter
The juice and grated rind of a lemon
5 oz. of sugar
1 small sherryglass of white wine

mince it fine. Mix it well with the flour, add the salt and as much water as will make it into a firm paste. Roll it thin. Dip a cloth into hot water, wring it dry, shake it out, flour it thickly, and lay it in a basin. Press the paste evenly into the basin upon the cloth, and fill it with the apples pared and quartered. Add the sugar, butter, lemon-rind and juice, and wine. Moisten the edges of the paste, put on the paste-cover, press the edges well together, and fold them over. Gather up the ends of the cloth, tie it firmly close to the pudding, drop it into boiling water, and boil for an hour and a quarter. When it is done lift it out by twisting a fork into a corner of the cloth; turn it gently into the dish in which it is to be served, and *instantly* cut a small hole in the top or the dumpling will be heavy.

Note.—Half a pot of apricot jam is a great addition, put in with the fruit. Rhubarb dumplings are made in the same way.

69.—Paradise Pudding (Apples).

Ingredients.
6 apples
¼ lb of beef suet (chopped)
¼ ,, ,, fine bread-crumbs
8 oz. of moist sugar
The grated rind of an orange
The strained juice
⅛ part of a nutmeg (grated)
4 fresh eggs
1 tablespoonful of rum

Mix all the ingredients in the order in which they are given, and beat with a wooden spoon for ten minutes. Butter a basin, put in the mixture; tie a cloth over it, put it into fast boiling water and boil rapidly for three hours; or bake in a moderate oven for an hour and a half. Serve with the following sauce.

70.—Apple Cream.

Ingredients.
2 tablespoonsful of apple jelly
2 ,, ,, rum
½ gill of thick cream

Dissolve the jelly in the rum and beat it into the cream until smooth. Serve *over* the pudding.

71.—Apple Pudding.

Ingredients.
18 apples
A little water
½ inch of cinnamon
2 cloves

Peel and core the apples and cut them up small; put them into a stewpan which will just hold them with the cinnamon, cloves, lemon peel, and

Ingredients of Apple Pudding.
The peel of one lemon
6 oz. of moist sugar
4 yolks of eggs
1 white ,, ,,
¼ ℔ of good butter
The juice of a lemon

sugar. Stew till they are quite soft; pass through a sieve; add the yolks of the eggs well beaten, the white (well beaten) and all the other ingredients. Beat all well together with a wooden spoon; butter a mould, put in the pudding, tie it over, and bake or boil for half an hour. Serve with Rich Custard.

72.—Charlotte Pudding (Apples).

Ingredients.
Some bread
Some butter
4 apples
A pot of marmalade

Butter a large basin; strew it thickly with moist sugar; cut some slices of bread and butter thin without crust; peel, slice, and core the apples (very thin); put a layer of bread in the basin (butter downwards), then marmalade, then apples; do this till the basin is full; press it well down; put a plate over it with a weight on it; bake in a quick oven for three quarters of an hour. Turn out carefully and serve very hot.

73.—Baked Apple Pudding.

Ingredients.
1 lb. of apples
6 oz. of sugar
1 sherryglass of white wine
3 oz. of butter
The juice and rind of one lemon
Yolks of 5 eggs
1 dessertspoonful of flour, or 3 or 4 Naples biscuits or macaroons crushed small

Weigh the apples after they are cored and pared, and stew them to a perfectly smooth marmalade with the sugar and wine; stir constantly so that they may not stick to the pan. When they are ready and still quite hot, add the butter, lemon-rind and juice, the well beaten yolks and the flour. Put the mixture into a well buttered tin and bake in a moderate oven for half an hour or more. Serve with a little clarified butter on the top with sugar sifted over, or else beat the whites of the eggs to a *firm* froth; mix them with five dessertspoonsful of finely sifted loaf sugar, stir it in very gently a quarter of an hour before the pudding is done; pile the froth on to the pudding, then put it back to finish baking. This is an excellent way of using up any white of eggs you may have over from other dishes.

74.—Brown Bread Pudding.

Ingredients.

- ½ lb. of stale brown bread
- 8 oz. of salt
- 8 „ „ currants
- 3 „ „ sugar
- 2 „ „ candied peel
- ½ saltspoonful of salt
- ⅓ of a small nutmeg
- 5 eggs
- The grated rind of one lemon
- 1 wineglassful of brandy

Mix all the ingredients in the order in which they are given; beat for ten minutes; dip a cloth into boiling water, wring it out, dredge it thickly with flour; boil the pudding in the cloth for three and a half hours. Serve with wine sauce made with port wine. (*See* recipe.)

75.—A rich Bread Pudding.

Ingredients.

- 1 pint of milk
- 4 oz. of fine sugar
- ¼ saltspoonful of salt
- 6 oz. of fine bread-crumbs
- 4 „ „ butter
- 6 eggs
- ½ lb. of currants
- 1 small glass of brandy
- The grated rind of one lemon

Sweeten the milk with the sugar, add the salt, and pour it boiling on to the bread-crumbs; add the butter and cover it with a plate; let the mixture stand half an hour; then stir in the eggs, well beaten, the lemon-rind, currants and brandy; beat well; butter a mould, put in the pudding (which should fill it), tie paper and a cloth tightly over it, and boil for an hour and ten minutes.

76.—A plain Bread Pudding.

Ingredients.

- ½ lb. of bread, powdered
- ¼ „ „ suet (finely chopped)
- 5 tablespoonsful of moist sugar
- ⅙ of a nutmeg, grated

Put any pieces of bread, crust and crumb, into a cool oven and dry these until hard, but not baked brown; pound them to fine dust; mix half a pound of

Ingredients of a Plain Bread Pudding.
½ lb. of currants (or ½ lb. of Sultana raisins)
1 pint of new milk
3 eggs

this powder with all the other ingredients (except the eggs) in the order in which they are given; beat for ten minutes; beat the eggs, add them to the pudding mixture; beat for ten minutes more. Butter a basin, pour in the pudding, tie it well over with buttered paper and a cloth, and boil in plenty of fast boiling water for four hours.

Note.—Half the quantities given will do for an ordinary sized pudding.

77.—Baked Bread Pudding, with Marmalade or Jam.

Ingredients.
6 oz. of bread powder
4 tablespoonsful of brown sugar
¼ of a lb of finely chopped suet
⅛ ,, ,, nutmeg grated
¾ ,, ,, pint of new milk
2 eggs
Some marmalade or jam

Put any pieces of bread, crust and crumb, into a cool oven and dry until hard, but not brown; pound them to fine dust. Mix six ounces of this with the sugar, suet and nutmeg. Pour the milk over this and beat the mixture for ten minutes; beat the eggs, add them to the pudding, beat ten minutes more. Butter a pie dish, put in a layer of the pudding mixture half an inch thick, on that a layer of marmalade, then a layer of pudding, another of jam, and so on until the dish is full, finishing with pudding at the top. Bake it in a slow oven for two hours.

78.—Baked Bread Pudding.

Ingredients.
6 oz. of bread
1 ,, ,, butter
1 pint of milk
3 oz of sugar
5 yolks of eggs
3 whites ,, ,,

Boil the milk and pour it scalding on the bread-crumbs and butter, and let them stand till well soaked; stir in the sugar, eggs (yolks and whites beaten separately), orange peel, (sliced thin), and

Ingredients of Baked Bread Pudding.
2 oz. of candied orange rind
⅛ of a nutmeg, grated
Icing.
3 whites of eggs
3 tablespoonsful of sugar

nutmeg; let the mixture stand until nearly cold, then pour it into a pie dish. For the icing, beat the three whites to a fine froth, stir in the sugar (pounded very fine) gently, pile it lightly on the top of the pudding, and bake in a moderate oven for half an hour. Serve at once.

79.—Plain Bread and Butter Pudding.

Ingredients.
1½ pint of milk
4 oz. of sugar
5 eggs
¼ of a nutmeg, grated
3 ounces of currants
Some bread and butter

Sweeten the milk with the sugar; stir into it the eggs, well beaten; cut some slices of bread and butter, lay them in the dish with currants scattered in between until it is full, pour in the custard, and bake for about an hour. Lemon-rind grated may be substituted for the nutmeg.

80.—Rich Bread and Butter Pudding.

Ingredients.
½ stick of vanilla or the rind of a lemon
1 pint of new milk
¼ ,, ,, cream
4 oz. of sugar (in lumps)
6 eggs (well beaten)
1 pinch of salt
1 sherryglass of brandy
Some bread and butter
4 oz. of currants
1½ oz. of candied orange or lemon-rind

Simmer the vanilla or lemon-rind for fifteen minutes, strain it, and pour in the cream; sweeten it with the sugar and stir in the eggs while it is still hot; add the salt and brandy, stirring briskly the while. Put three layers of well buttered slices of bread in a thickly buttered pie dish and sprinkle the currants and candied peel between; pour over the eggs and milk by degrees, letting the bread absorb one portion before another is added. It should soak for about two hours before being baked. Then put it in a moderate oven for half an hour, and serve.

81.—Common Batter Pudding.

Beat the yolks of the eggs thoroughly; mix them with the milk; add the flour *very gradually*, beating the mixture well as each portion is added to it, or it will not be smooth. Whip the whites to a stiff froth, and just before the pudding is put into the cloth stir them lightly in. Dip a pudding cloth in boiling water, wring it out, flour it well, put in the pudding, leave it room to swell, tie it securely, and put it immediately into fast boiling water. Boil for one hour and ten minutes. Send it to table the *instant* it is ready, either with wine sauce (*see* recipe) or raspberry vinegar heated.

Ingredients.
4 eggs
½ pint of milk
½ lb. of flour

82.—Baked Batter Pudding.

Mix the salt with the flour; whisk the eggs to a light froth; strain them; add them to the flour; beat the batter well and add it to the milk very gradually. Pour the mixture into a buttered dish, put it at once into a brisk oven, and bake for three quarters of an hour. Serve with stewed fruit or prunes.

Ingredients.
6 oz. of flour
1 small saltspoonful of salt
3 fresh eggs
1 pint of new milk

Note.—The same mixture may be baked in buttered cups turned out and served with sugar sifted thickly over them.

83.—Derbyshire Batter Pudding.

Mix the flour with the milk and boil it till it thickens. When quite cold add the butter, sugar, lemon-rind and eggs; beat well. Butter a dish, lay a thin ornamental layer of paste round

Ingredients.
2 tablespoonsful of flour
1 pint of new milk
3 oz. of butter (beaten to a cream)
½ lb. of sifted sugar
The grated rind of 1 lemon

Ingredients of Derbyshire Batter Pudding.
The yolks of 4 eggs }
The whites of 2 eggs } well beaten
A little pastry, (*see* recipe)

the edge; when the pudding is well mixed put it into the dish, and bake it in a quick oven for twenty minutes. Serve either hot or cold, with sifted sugar on the top.

84.—Batter Fruit Pudding.

Butter a 1½ pint basin thickly,
Ingredients.
Some apples or plums
4 tablespoonsful of flour
3 eggs
¼ lb of sugar
½ pint of milk

and fill it nearly to the brim with the apples pared, cored, and quartered, or with plums. Beat the eggs; mix them gradually with the milk; stir in the flour carefully by degrees, beating well. Pour the batter over the fruit; tie a well floured cloth over the basin tightly, and boil for 1¼ hours. Turn it into a hot dish when it is done, and serve *instantly.*

85.—Yorkshire Pudding.

Whisk the eggs well; strain them; mix them gradually
Ingredients.
3 eggs
3 tablespoonsful of flour
1 saltspoonful of salt

with the flour; then pour in by degrees as much milk as will reduce the batter to the consistency of thick cream; beat for a quarter of an hour. Put the tin in which the pudding is to be put under the joint with which it is to be served for about a quarter of an hour; when the batter is ready, pour it into the pan, watch it carefully that it does not burn; it will take 1½ hours; when it is half done cut it down the middle lengthwise and each piece into four, and turn it so that it may be browned on both sides. Serve with the meat.

86.—Family Yorkshire Pudding.

Ingredients.
1 egg
1⅓ pint of new milk
6 tablespoonsful of dried flour
1 saltspoonful of salt

Proceed exactly as in the preceding recipe.

87.—Baked Custard Pudding.

Ingredients.
1 quart of new milk
8 eggs
6 oz. of sugar
1 pinch of salt
Some grated lemon-rind or nutmeg

Beat the eggs and mix them with the milk; strain the mixture through a fine sieve and sweeten it with the sugar; add the salt and pour it into a deep dish, grate the lemon-rind or nutmeg over the top and bake it *very slowly* in a gentle oven from twenty to thirty minutes or longer if it is not firm in the centre. If well made and slowly baked the pudding will be *quite* smooth when cut, and there will be no whey in the dish. The honey-combed appearance these puddings so often have is due to their being subjected to too great heat.

Note.—Instead of grated lemon-rind or nutmeg, sifted sugar may be strewn over the top and burnt by a red-hot salamander being held over it for a few minutes. This is a great improvement.

88.—A finer baked Custard.

Ingredients.
1½ pints of new milk
¼ saltspoonful of salt
The thin rind of a lemon
6 oz. of loaf sugar
The yolks of 10 fresh eggs
The whites of 4 ,, ,,
1 pint of good cream
1 sherryglass of brandy, or maraschino, or noyeau

Boil the milk, salt, lemon-rind and sugar gently together for five minutes. Beat the yolks and whites of the eggs and pour the milk boiling into them by degrees, stirring all the time; strain the mixture and add the cream; let it cool and then flavour it with the brandy; line a pie dish with thin pastry (*see* recipes); pour in the mixture and finish as in the preceding recipe. Serve with or without the syrup of preserved ginger, or with raspberry syrup heated.

89.—Boiled Custard Pudding.

Ingredients.
3 eggs
1 pint of milk
2 oz. of sugar
20 drops of vanilla*

* Or the sugar may be rasped on lemon-rind and then crushed or dissolved in the milk.

Whisk the eggs well; put them into a pint pudding basin; fill up with milk; strain; add the sugar and flavouring; pour it back into the basin, tie it over with buttered paper and a cloth, and boil gently for half an hour. Let it stand a few minutes, turn it out on a dish, and serve either plain or with any of the pudding sauces (*see* recipes), or some preserved fruit.

90.—Oswego Custard Pudding.

Ingredients.
2 large tablespoonsful of Oswego flour
1½ pint of milk
2 oz. of moist sugar
The grated rind of 1 lemon
2 eggs

Mix the flour with a quarter of a pint of the milk; add the remainder of the milk, boiling, the sugar and lemon-rind; stir till nearly cold; add the eggs well beaten. Butter a dish, pour in the pudding, and bake for twenty minutes, or boil in a basin for half an hour.

91.—Boiled Rice Pudding, plain.

Ingredients
½ lb. of rice
¼ ,, ,, moist sugar
¼ pint of new milk
1 egg

Wash the rice; boil it in three pints of water for one hour; drain off the water. Stir the sugar, milk and egg into the rice. Press it into a basin, tie it over with a cloth, and boil for an hour.

92.—A good Boiled Rice Pudding.

Ingredients.
4½ oz. of rice
1½ pints of new milk
2 oz. of butter
4 ,, ,, sugar
1 pinch of salt
4 bitter almonds
The rind of half lemon*
4 eggs

* 20 drops of vanilla may be substituted for the lemon-rind

Put the rice into the cold milk, heat it slowly and simmer for one hour; add the butter, sugar, salt, and lemon-rind, almonds (pounded to a paste); and eggs (well whisked) to the milk while it is still quite hot; let the mixture cool; pour it into a well buttered basin or into a mould which should be quite full; tie buttered paper and a floured cloth over it, and boil exactly an hour; take it out; let it stand for two or three minutes, turn it out and serve with sweet sauce (*see* recipe) or stewed fruit.

93.—Boiled Rice and Raisin Pudding.

Ingredients.
6 oz. of rice
¾ lb. of raisins

Wash the rice, mix it with the raisins, tie them lightly in a well floured cloth, giving them plenty of room to swell; boil 1¾ hours, and serve with Sweet Sauce. (*See* recipe.)

94.—Baked Rice Pudding.

Ingredients.
6 oz. of rice
1 quart of milk
3 oz. of sugar
4 eggs
Nutmeg, cinnamon, or lemon-rind

Put the rice into plenty of cold water and boil it gently for eight or ten minutes; drain well on a sieve or strainer; put it into a clean saucepan with the milk; let it simmer for an hour; sweeten with the sugar; beat the eggs, strain them, add them gradually to the milk, stirring carefully; add the flavouring; put into a buttered pie dish, bake for an hour, and serve.

95.—Baked Rice Pudding without Eggs.

Ingredients.
5 tablespoonsful of rice
4 " " moist sugar
1 quart of new milk
Some nutmeg

Wash the rice well; put it in a buttered pie dish with the sugar and milk; grate a little nutmeg over them and bake in a moderate oven for 2¾ hours.

96.—Richer Rice Pudding.

Ingredients.
4 oz. of rice
1½ pint of new milk
2 oz. of good butter
3 " " sugar
4 eggs
The grated rind of half lemon

Wash the rice very clean; pour the milk on to it and stew it gently till it is tender; while it is still on the fire add the butter and sugar; take it off the fire, and when it is cooled add the eggs well whisked and the lemon-rind. Put the pudding in a well buttered dish and bake in a gentle oven for thirty or forty minutes.

97.—Rice Pudding Meringue.

Prepare the rice exactly as above leaving out the whites of the eggs. Whisk the whites to a stiff froth, stir in lightly five heaped tablespoonsful of *finely* powdered sugar; lay it lightly on the top of the pudding, and bake 1½ hours in a moderate oven.

98.—Ground Rice Pudding.

Ingredients.
5 oz. of ground rice
1 quart of new milk
4 oz. of butter
5 " " sugar
½ saltspoonful of salt
8 yolks of eggs
2 whites
The grated rind of one lemon
1 clearetglassful of brandy

Mix the rice very smoothly with half pint of the milk; boil the remainder of the milk and stir the rice into it; keep stirring it over a gentle fire for ten minutes, and be careful it does not stick to the pan; add the butter, sugar and salt; stir for a few minutes, lift it off and add the beaten yolks, whites, and rind and brandy; lay a border of fine paste (*see* recipes) round a buttered dish, pour in the pudding; strain some clarified butter over the top; moisten the paste with the brush, sift over some sugar and bake in a *very* gentle oven for three quarters of an hour. If preferred the remaining whites of eggs may be used to cover the pudding with meringue. (*See* preceding recipe.)

Note.—This is a very large pudding; half the quantities will do for ordinary use.

99.—Ground Rice Pudding, plain.

Ingredients.
3 tablespoonsful of ground rice
1½ pints of cold milk
3 oz. of vanilla sugar
1 „ „ plain „
3 eggs well beaten

Moisten the rice with half pint of the milk; boil the remainder and pour it on to the rice by degrees, stirring carefully; stir over the fire for a quarter of an hour. Add the sugar; let it get nearly cold; add the eggs. Butter a pie dish, put in the pudding, and bake in a quick oven for twenty-five or thirty minutes.

100.—Ground Rice Cup Pudding.

Ingredients.
2 oz. of ground rice
3 pints of new milk
2 oz. of fresh butter
3 fresh eggs
The grated rind of half lemon
3 oz. of sifted sugar

Moisten the rice with half a gill of the milk; boil the remainder of the milk and stir it into the rice by degrees; stir over the fire ten minutes, then let it get cold. Beat the butter to a cream; beat the eggs, mix these well into the rice; add the lemon-rind and sugar. Beat the mixture for twenty minutes; butter six small moulds (or cups); put an equal quantity into each, and bake in a quick oven for eighteen minutes. Serve immediately with loaf sugar sifted over. If a red-hot salamander is held over each for a few minutes the sugar will glaze into a rich crust.

101.—Gateau de Riz.

Ingredients.
7 oz. of rice
1 quart of milk
3 oz. of fresh butter
5 ,, ,, lump sugar
1 pinch of salt
The rind of one large lemon
6 eggs
2 oz. of clarified butter
Some very fine bread-crumbs

Wash and drain the rice; free it from discolored grains; put it into the milk and place it near the fire to simmer very gently until tender, about three quarters of an hour; add the butter, sugar, salt, and lemon rind, grated; simmer for about an hour until the rice is swollen to the utmost and perfectly tender; take it off the fire, let it cool, and stir in quickly by degrees, the well beaten yolks of the eggs. Take a plain mould, put in the butter and turn it round and round until each part has received a coating of butter; turn it upside down for a moment to let the superfluous butter drain off; throw in the bread-crumbs and shake them entirely over the inside of the mould; shake out those which do not stick. Whisk the whites of the eggs to a stiff froth; stir them gently into the rice; pour the mixture gently into the mould so as not to displace the bread-crumbs; put into a moderate oven *instantly*, and let it remain there an hour. It will, if properly baked, turn out quite brown and firm and looking like a cake. But a hot oven will cause it to break and look unsightly.

It is a great improvement to pour some clear apple, quince, or stawberry jelly (melted) over the rice-cake when it is served.

102.—Gateau de Riz.

(Another way.)

Wash the rice; strain it; put it with the milk and vanilla into an uncovered saucepan on the fire; simmer gently for 1½ hours; stir it occasionally; take it off; take out the vanilla; beat the eggs, add them to the rice; mix well; take a small saucepan or plain mould; put in the lumps of sugar with a little water; put it over the fire; when it bakes and gets brown and thick lift off the saucepan; turn it gently round and round until every part of the inside is covered with syrup; plunge the saucepan into cold water for a few seconds (which causes the coating of sugar to congeal on the saucepan at once). Pour in the rice mixture and put the saucepan (or mould) into another saucepan half full of boiling water; put a little plate with hot charcoal on it on the top and boil for an hour. Turn it out and serve either hot or cold.

Ingredients.
4 tablespoonsful of rice
1¼ pint of milk (or milk and cream)
2 inches of vanilla*
2 eggs
1 tablespoonful of brown sugar
6 lumps of loaf sugar

* Or 20 drops of essence of vanilla.

Raspberry cream will be found a great addition to this refined and elegant pudding.

103.—Sweet Casserole of Rice.

Wash the rice; drain it on a hair sieve; put it into a very clean saucepan with the cold milk; stir well together; place the pan *near* the fire for half an hour; simmer over the fire *very gently* for half an hour more; add the butter, sugar, and lemon-rind, and simmer gently until it is

Ingredients.
½ lb. of rice
1 quart of new milk
2 oz. of butter
2½ ,, ,, pounded sugar
The rind of one lemon, grated, or 25 drops of vanilla
Some clarified butter

sufficiently soft to be easily crushed with a spoon. Butter a tin mould thickly; crush the rice to a smooth paste and pour the mixture into the mould; press it in carefully; smooth the surface and let it stand until cold; dip the mould into hot water, turn out the rice; reverse it again on another dish and with the point of a knife mark round a circular rim about one inch from the edge; brush some clarified butter over the pudding and put into a brisk oven; when it is of a light golden-brown color all over, draw it out, raise the cover carefully where you marked it, scoop out the rice from the inside, leaving only a crust of about one inch thick in every part, and pour into it some preserved fruit (plums, apricots or peaches). Serve with or without whipped cream on a separate dish.

104.—Macaroni Pudding.

Ingredients
2 oz. of macaroni
1½ pints of milk
1 oz. of fresh butter
3 ,, , sugar
3 eggs

Break the macaroni into one inch lengths, soak it in the milk for two hours; put it on the fire in the milk and simmer gently for 1½ hours; stir in the butter and sugar; take it off the fire, and when it is a little cool, beat up the eggs and stir them in. Butter a pie dish; put in the pudding; grate a little nutmeg over the top, and bake in a moderate oven for three quarters of an hour.

Note.—The macaroni may be flavored either with vanilla or lemon-peel and the pie-dish may be lined with puff paste.

105.—Baked Tapioca Pudding.

Simmer the tapioca and lemon-rind in the milk for 1¾

Ingredients of Baked Tapioca Pudding.

3 tablespoonsful of tapioca
The thin rind of a lemon *
1½ pints of new milk
¼ lb. of sugar
3 eggs

* Twenty drops of vanilla may be substituted for the lemon-rind

hours; stir in the sugar; let it get cold; take out the peel; add the eggs, well-beaten; beat ten minutes; butter a pie dish (line the edge with paste if preferred); put in the pudding, and bake in a quick oven for half an hour.

106.—Boiled Tapioca Pudding.

Boil the tapioca gently in the milk for two hours; add the

Ingredients.

4 oz. of tapioca
1½ pints of milk
2 oz. of fresh butter, or half a gill of thick cream
4 oz. of loaf sugar
1 ,, ,, ratafia cakes
5 eggs

butter, sugar, and ratafia cakes; beat well for ten minutes; beat the eggs, stir them in briskly; butter a mould; pour in the pudding; tie over with writing paper spread with butter, and a floured cloth, and steam over boiling water for 1½ hours. Turn out carefully and serve with raspberry syrup warmed and poured over, or serve cold with custard or whipped cream.

Note.—If the whites are whipped separately and stirred into the pudding just before putting it in the shape or basin it will be found to make it lighter.

107.—Semolina Pudding.

Blanch and pound the almonds to a soft paste; put them

Ingredients.

1 oz. of sweet almonds
6 bitter almonds
6 oz. of semolina
5 ,, ,, loaf sugar
1 pint of new milk
2 oz. of butter
5 eggs

into a saucepan with the semolina, sugar and milk; boil gently, stirring constantly for three quarters of an hour; add the butter; stir off the fire for ten minutes; beat the yolks of the eggs, stir them in; butter a mould; beat the whites to a stiff froth; stir them lightly into the pudding, and pour the mixture into the mould; tie it over with writing paper spread with butter; steam over fast boiling water for 1½ hours, or bake in a moderate oven for an hour. Turn out carefully, and serve with raspberry syrup warmed, or any sweet sauce.

108.—Semolina Pudding.

(Another way.)

Ingredients.
½ lb of semolina
6 oz. of sugar
4 ,, ,, butter
1 pinch of salt
1 pint of milk
1 tablespoonful of orange flower water
6 ratafias

Put all the ingredients except the eggs in a stewpan over the fire; stir it till it thickens and ceases to adhere to the sides of the stewpan; beat the eggs, yolks, and whites separately; take the pudding off the fire; add the yolks; beat well; butter a mould; stir the whites lightly into the pudding; pour it into the mould; tie over buttered paper and a floured cloth; steam for an hour; turn out carefully, and serve with custard whip. (*See* next recipe.)

109.—Custard Whip.

Ingredients.
1 oz. of sweet almonds
6 bitter almonds
4 oz. of sugar
1 tablespoonful of orange water
1 gill of cream
The yolks of two eggs

Blanch and pound the almonds; mix them into a smooth paste with the sugar and orange flower water; put them into a small stewpan with the cream, add the yolks whipped, and with a wire whisk whip the sauce over a very gentle heat until it becomes a thick smooth froth.

110.—French Semolina Pudding.

Stand the milk with the lemon-rind in it near the fire for

Ingredients of French Semolina Pudding.
1 quart of new milk
The thin rind of one fresh lemon
5 oz. of semolina
4 ,, ,, sugar
3 ,, ,, butter
1 pinch of salt
4 bitter almonds, blanched and pounded

half an hour; bring it *slowly* to a boil; simmer it for five minutes; take out the lemon-rind. Put in the semolina stirring gently all the time; boil gently for ten minutes; stir in the sugar, butter and salt; boil for three minutes, stirring constantly; take it off the fire, and when it is cool stir in the yolks of the eggs well beaten; add the pounded almonds mixed with a teaspoonful of sugar; prepare a mould as for *gateau de riz* (*see* recipes); beat the whites of the eggs to a stiff froth; stir in gently; pour the pudding into the mould, and bake in a very gentle oven for 1¼ hours.

111.—Soojee Pudding.

Ingredients.
4 oz. of soojee
1½ pints of new milk
3½ oz. of sugar, pounded
2 ,, ,, butter
The rind of one lemon, grated
5 eggs

Boil the milk and drop the soojee into it gradually, stirring well all the time, so that the mixture may be smooth; stir for about ten minutes; add the butter, sugar, lemon-rind; beat the eggs well; take the mixture off the fire, and when it is cooler but still warm stir in the eggs; pour it into a buttered dish; bake half an hour in a moderate oven.

112.—Soojee, Semolina, or Vermicelli Pudding with Apples.

Ingredients.
1 quart of milk
2 oz. of butter
4 ,, ,, sugar, pounded
The grated rind of one lemon

Boil the milk, and proceed exactly as above; when they are in the pudding-dish cover the top over with apples pared, cored, and quartered; press them into the pudding mixture, they will at once rise to the surface again; place the dish in a gentle oven for three quarters of an hour, or until the fruit is quite tender.

113—.Sago Pudding.

Is prepared in the same way as Tapioca and Semolina Pudding.

114.—Rusk Pudding.

Ingredients.
2 rusks
1 egg
½ pint of milk
6 lumps of sugar
The rind of one lemon
Some jam or jelly

Simmer the lemon-rind with the milk and sugar beside the fire for a quarter of an hour; beat the egg; butter a tart dish; lay in the rusks; take the lemon-peel out of the milk, pour it on the egg, beating briskly; pour the mixture over the rusk, and bake *slowly* for an hour. Turn it out on a dish; put a couple of dessertspoonsful of jam or jelly in a teacup in boiling water; when it melts pour it over the pudding.

115.—Biscuit Pudding.

Ingredients.
3 oz. of Huntley and Palmer's Lunch biscuits
½ pint of milk
2 oz. of lump sugar, pounded
2 eggs
The rind of half lemon, grated
1 pinch of salt

Ingredients of Sauce.
2 ounce of lump sugar
¼ of a pint of water
The juice of one lemon
1 tablespoonful of sherry

Soak the biscuit in the milk; when quite soft beat them up quite smooth; add the sugar, eggs (well beaten), lemon-peel, and salt. Butter a basin; put in the pudding; tie it over with buttered paper, and steam for an hour. If the pudding is to be baked one egg may be omitted. Serve with the following sauce. Boil the sugar in the water till it begins to thicken; add the lemon-juice; boil five minutes more; add the sherry, and serve.

116.—Crumb Pudding.

Ingredients.
2 oz. of bread-crumbs
¼ of a pint of milk
2 oz. of sugar
20 drops of essence of vanilla
2 eggs
Some strawberry jam
1 teaspoonful of sifted sugar

Boil the bread-crumbs with the milk; add the sugar and vanilla; when it is quite smooth and thick add the yolks of the eggs well beaten; butter a tart dish, put in the mixture, and bake *slowly* for three quarters of an hour; spread a layer of strawberry jam over the top; beat the whites of the eggs to a stiff forth, stir in the sugar lightly and pile this over the pudding; dip a knife in boiling water, smooth the whites over with it, put the pudding back into the oven, and bake till it is a golden-brown. Serve at once.

117.—Indian Corn Flour Pudding.

Ingredients.
2 oz. of Indian Corn flour
A pint of milk
20 drops of vanilla
2 oz. of sugar
1 egg

This is not "cornflour" as usually sold, but is the flour of maize finely ground, and is an excellent article of diet. Mix the corn flour with a quarter of a pint of the milk; boil the remainder of the milk with the sugar and vanilla and pour it on to the flour; put it into a clean stewpan and stir over the fire until it becomes quite thick; beat the egg; stir it in; butter a tart dish; put in the mixture, and bake very slowly for three quarters of an hour.

118.—Oatmeal Pudding.

Ingredients.
2 oz of oatmeal
¼ pints of milk
2 oz. of sugar
2 ,, ,, sifted bread-crumbs

Mix the oatmeal with a quarter of a pint of the milk; boil the remainder of the milk and add it to the oatmeal; stir in the sugar and stir over the fire

Ingredients of Oatmeal Pudding
1 oz of suet, shredded
2 eggs
20 drops of vanilla, or the grated rind of half lemon

for ten minutes; add the breadcrumbs; stir the mixture till it is stiff; add the suet; beat the eggs, stir them in; add the flavouring. Butter a dish, put in the pudding, and bake slowly for an hour.

SWEET DISHES OR ENTREMETS.

1.—Italian Sweetmeat.

Ingredients.
6 oz. of mixed candied peel,
4 oz. of candied pine apple,
2 oz. of angelica,
¾ lb. of sweet almonds,
12 bitter almonds,
All cut into fine shreds
Blanched & pounded to a paste
16 new laid eggs, (stirred), *not beaten*, and strained
1¼ lbs. of loaf sugar
½ pint of water
3 tablespoonsful of orange water
2 tablespoonsful of brandy

Put the sugar into a saucepan with the water and boil fast, skimming constantly for ten minutes; add the orange flower water and boil five minutes more. Pour off a quarter into a basin to get cold. Take a small tin funnel through which a pea will just pass; hold it over the boiling sugar and drop the strained yolks of the eggs through so as to form small balls; as they set in the sugar take them out and drain on a sieve. When the egg is all prepared, stir the almonds into the sugar and simmer till it forms a soft paste; add the brandy and pass through a sieve. Butter a pie dish, put in the almond paste, candied fruit and egg balls in layers. Beat the whites of five eggs and stir into the clarified sugar; beat to a froth and pour it over the whole; bake in a quick oven for eighteen minutes. Turn out carefully and serve cold.

2.—Russian Pudding.

Ingredients.
¾ pint of cream
3 tablespoonsful of sugar

Put the cream, sugar, and ratafia essence into a bowl and stir one way until the mixture thickens. Butter a plain round

SWEET DISHES OR ENTREMETS.

Ingredients of Russian Pudding.
1 tablespoonful of ratafia essence (vanilla or almond may be substituted)
12 finger biscuits (or slices of sponge cake)
Macaroons
Raspberry or strawberry jam

mould and line it throughtout with sponge cake. Pour in some of the thickened cream, an inch in depth, then put in a layer of macaroons and a layer of jam, then add another layer of cream, another layer of macaroons and jam, and so on until the shape is filled. Let it stand until wanted, dip the mould in hot water for a second, then turn it out and serve.

3.—Gateau à la Crème.

Beat the butter to a cream; stir in the sugar *very* gradually; when well mixed, beat the yolk and stir it in; add the coffee drop by drop, beating all the time with a wooden spoon. The mixture should have the appearance of Mayonnaise sauce. Cut the cake across in slices; lay a slice in the dish, then a layer of cream, and so on till it is finished. Cover with the cream, and serve.

Ingredients.
A rice, sponge, or cornflour cake
4 oz. of butter
4 ,, ,, finely powdered sugar
The yolk of one egg
3 teaspoonsful of essence of coffee

4.—Nesselrode Pudding.

Put the isinglass, sugar, vanilla and milk into an enamelled saucepan; boil gently for ten minutes. Beat the yolks of the eggs and stir into the milk while hot but not boiling; stir over the fire till at boiling heat; strain into a basin. Put the fruits into a small bowl and pour over the curaçao; let it stand half an hour. Beat the cream to a froth;

Ingredients.
1 oz. of good isinglass
5 ,, ,, loaf sugar
2 inches of stick vanilla
1 pint of new milk
6 fresh eggs
4 oz. of preserved pineapple
1 oz. of angelica
2 ,, ,, candied apricots
2 oz. of cherries
2 ,, ,, orange peel
1 ,, ,, ginger
1 wineglassful of curaçao or brandy
1 pint of *very* thick cream

} Cut into half inch squares.

stir it into the custard when nearly cold; put in the fruit, and stir the mixture rapidly for five minutes. Rinse a mould in cold water; pour in the pudding and place it in a pan on, or surrounded by, rough ice; stir it till it begins to set, to prevent the fruit from sinking to the bottom. Let it remain till quite firm, turn it out in a dish, and serve at once.

Note.—This is a very large pudding, and half the quantity will suffice for a small dinner.

5.—Tipsy Cake, or Trifle.

Ingredients.

A 1 lb. sponge cake one day old
¼ lb. of greengage ⎫
¼ „ „ raspberry ⎬ jams
¼ „ „ apricot ⎭
¼ „ „ orange marmalade
½ pint of Madeira or sherry
1 wineglassful of brandy
1 „ „ rum
1 „ „ ginger wine
1 „ „ curaçao
5 oz. of loaf sugar
6 fresh eggs
1 pint of new milk
½ pint of Devonshire cream
5 oz. of blanched sweet almonds
1 „ „ ratafias
Some essence of vanilla

Cut the cake into five slices; put the top slice aside; spread the other four with jam; put two ounces of the sugar into the wine; add the spirits to it; lay the ratafias in a glass dish, and on them the bottom slice of the cake; pour over one-sixth of the wine mixture; do this till the cake is built up; over the top pour the remainder; baste it frequently till the wine is absorbed. Make custard as follows:—

Boil three ounces of sugar in the milk; beat the eggs; add the milk while hot but not boiling; stir over a slow fire till it thickens (about five minutes); stir in the cream; let it get quite cold; add thirty drops of the essence of vanilla; cut the almonds into pointed pieces, stick over the top of the cake tastefully with them; pour half of the custard over three hours before serving; and the remainder at the last moment.

Note.—This Trifle takes about eight hours to make.

6.—Swiss Trifle.

Ingredients.
1 pint of rich cream
6 oz. of lump sugar
The rind of one lemon
1 inch of cinnamon
4 teaspoonsful of fine flour
The juice of two lemons
4 oz. of macaroons
1½ ,, ,, candied citron

Put the lemon-rind and cinnamon into three quarters of a pint of the cream, and stand it *beside* the fire for half an hour; strain it; sweeten it with the sugar; place it over the fire in a *very* clean saucepan; mix the quarter of a pint of cream reserved for the purpose into a smooth batter with the flour; when the cream on the fire boils add this batter to it; simmer three or four minutes, and stir gently without ceasing; pour it out, and when it is quite cold add the strained lemon-juice by degrees. Cover the bottom of a glass dish with a portion of the macaroons, pour in part of the cream, lay in the remainder of the macaroons, add the rest of the cream, and ornament with the candied citron cut thin.

Note.—This dish should be made twelve hours before it is wanted.

7.—Tipsy Cake.

Ingredients.
A Sponge or Savoy cake
Some brandy or white wine
Some blanched almonds
Some rich custard (*see* recipe)

Soak the cake in as much wine as it will absorb; blanch the almonds; cut them into spikes, and stick the cake all over with them. Pour the custard (cold) round it and serve.

8.—Chantilly Basket filled with Whipped Cream and fresh Strawberries.

Ingredients.
Some macaroons
Some barley sugar
Whipped cream
Strawberry syrup
Fresh strawberries

Take a mould of any sort to form a basket in; stick it all over with macaroons held together with melted barley sugar. Take it out of the mould and keep it in a dry place until wanted; whip some cream with the syrup; fill the basket with it and stick fine ripe strawberries over it. It must not be filled until just before it is served.

9.—Charlotte Russe.

Ingredients.
5 yolks of eggs
1¼ pint of good cream
5 oz. of loaf sugar
¾ ,, ,, the best isinglass
¾ pint of good milk
2 oz. of sweet almonds
2 inches of vanilla
Some Savoy (finger) biscuits

Beat the yolks of the eggs and strain them into half-pint of the cream; put this into an enamelled saucepan and stir over a slow fire till it begins to thicken but not to boil. Turn it into a basin to get quite cold. Dissolve the sugar and isinglass in the milk; blanch and pound the almonds; add them and the vanilla to the milk; boil slowly for twelve minutes, rub through a sieve and stir into the eggs while warm; whip the cream, add it to the rest, and stir till it begins to thicken. Trim off the ends of the biscuits; rub a plain quart mould with fresh butter; stick the biscuits round in an upright position close to each other so as to form a wall (the flat side of the biscuits inside); imbed the mould in a rough ice, pour in the cream, cover it over, and let it remain till quite firmly set. When about to serve, dip the mould in hot water, wipe off the droppings, and turn out carefully.

Note—Coffee, strawberry, apricot or chocolate cream *(see recipes)* may be substituted for the above for variety.

10.—Nougat of Almonds.

Ingredients.
2 lbs. of Jordan almonds
1 ,, ,, sifted sugar

Scald and blanch the almonds; remove the skin; wash them and dry them on a napkin; split each almond in half; place them on a baking sheet, and put them in an oven to acquire a very pale fawn color. While they are being colored, put the sugar in a small saucepan and stir it over a slow fire till it melts, stirring it with a wooden spoon. As soon as it is entirely dissolved and begins to bubble, throw in the almonds and mix them gently with the sugar, taking care not to break them. Rub a mould carefully with oil, set it to drain on a plate, and with an oiled lemon spread it out *very quickly* and press it into the mould. When it is set and cool, turn it out on a napkin.

11.—Parisian Nougats.

Ingredients.
8 oz. of pistachio kernels
4 ,, ,, sugar
1 stick of vanilla
1 teaspoonful of cochineal

Scald the pistachios; remove the skins; rub them gently with a napkin to dry them; split each kernel in halves; put them to dry on a baking sheet; pound the vanilla with one ounce of the sugar; sift it and put it with the remainder of the sugar in a small saucepan; stir over the fire with a wooden spoon until the sugar is entirely melted, and as soon as it begins to bubble on the surface add the pistachios; instantly and carefully mix the whole together, taking care not to bruise the pistachios. Oil a baking sheet, spread out the nougat on it in the form of a square about one-eighth of an inch thick; sprinkle it with some roughly broken sugar; before it becomes cold divide it into two bands, and cut these again into a dozen small oblong nougats; pile them up on a napkin, and serve.

12.—Apple Marmalade.

Ingredients.
Some apples
6 oz. of butter
¾ of a ℔. of moist sugar
The strained juice of one lemon

Peel, core, and quarter the apples. Take three pounds and put them in a stewpan with the butter, sugar and lemon-juice; stew over a gentle fire until they form a rich dry dark brown marmalade. Stir constantly to keep it from burning.

Note.—Two or three quinces will be found a great addition to this.

13.—Charlotte of Apples.

Butter a plain mould; cut some slices of bread a quarter of an inch thick; cut out one slice the size of the bottom of the mould and the remainder into long strips like finger biscuits; lay these on a dish; pour over the clarified butter, and when they are well saturated line the mould with them; fill the mould with the apple marmalade press it in; cover over with a dish, and bake in a quick oven for three quarters of an hour. Turn out carefully and serve at once either plain or with apricot or quince jam poured round the base, or melted jelly poured over it. Whipped or thick Devonshire cream served in a separate dish is a great improvement to this delicious dish.

Ingredients.
Apple marmalade (see recipe)
Some stale bread
Some clarified butter
Some apricot or quince jam

Note.—Greengages or apricots boiled to a rich jam with equal weight of loaf sugar may be used instead of apple marmalade.

14.—Apple Hedgehog.

When the marmalade is ready add one ounce of isinglass dissolved in two tablespoonsful of boiling water; rub a mould with sweet almond oil, put in the marmalade, and let it stand in a cool place until firmly set. Cut the blanched almonds into spikes lengthwise and stick the apple mould all over with these till it looks like a hedgehog. Serve with whipped cream or custard in a separate dish.

Ingredients.
Some apple marmalade (see recipe)
Some blanched almonds
Some whipped cream or custard

15.—Méringue of Apples.

When the marmalade is ready and quite cold put it on a dish. Whisk the whites of the eggs to a *stiff* froth ; stir in the sugar gently, and lay the méringue carefully, and lightly over the marmalade. Place it in a moderate oven and bake about half an hour till it is quite crisp and dry and slightly browned.

Ingredients.
Some apple marmalade
4 whites of eggs
4 tablespoonsful of finely sifted loaf sugar

Note.—It is an improvement to this dish to cover the apples with some sweet rice (*see* recipe) before putting on the méringue.

16.—Méringue of Rhubarb, or Gooseberries.

Pare the rhubarb cut it into short lengths ; add the sugar and stew carefully until they form a smooth pulp ; then boil quickly and stir frequently until they are reduced to a dry marmalade. Proceed exactly as above, and serve with or without whipped cream or custard in a separate dish.

Ingredients.
1 lb of young rhubarb or 1½ pint of gooseberries
8 oz of sugar

17.—Méringue of Pears, or other fruit.

Fill a tart dish nearly to the brim with stewed pears, and let them be something more than half covered with their own juice. Whisk the whites of the eggs to a stiff froth, stir in the sugar, and lay the méringue lightly over the fruit. Bake instantly in a moderate oven for half an hour.

Ingredients.
Stewed pears or other fruits
Whites of five eggs
5 tablespoonsful of sifted loaf sugar

18.—Jam or Marmalade Charlotte.

Cut five slices of bread a quarter of an inch thick ; shape

Ingredients of Jam Charlotte.
Some stale bread
6 oz. of butter
Any kind of jam
Some sifted loaf sugar
2 oz. of sweet almonds (blanched and chopped)

them to fit into a circular mould; lay them on a dish; dissolve the butter; pour it over the bread, put it in the oven for ten minutes; when the butter is all absorbed and the bread cold, spread each slice a quarter of an inch thick with jam, and over that sprinkle one teaspoonful of sifted sugar; butter a plain circular mould; strew it with the chopped almonds; lay in the bread and jam; place a dish over and bake in a quick oven for half an hour. Turn out carefully, and serve with or without three quarters of a pint of thick cream or rich custard poured over.

19.—Charlotte à la Parisienne.

Cut the Sponge Cake into horizontal slices half an inch

Ingredients.
A Sponge or Rice cake
3 eggs
4 oz. of fine pounded sugar
1 dessertspoonful of strained lemon-juice

thick; spread each slice thickly with jam; replace the slices into their original form; beat the eggs to a stiff froth; stir in the sugar, add the strained lemon-juice. Cover the cake with this icing and spread it equally over; put it into a very gentle oven to dry. Sift some sugar over it, and serve.

20.—Gertrude à la Crême.

Slice the cake as above and take a round out of the centre

Ingredients.
A Sponge or Rice-cake
3 eggs
4 oz. of fine pounded sugar
1 dessertspoonful of strained lemon-juice
½ pint of cream

of each piece with the cutter; pile the slices in their original form, ice the outside with icing prepared as in the preceding recipe;

put it into the oven to dry. Just before serving fill the centre

SWEET DISHES OR ENTREMETS.

with cream whipped with raspberry or strawberry syrup, or else with coffee or chocolate.

21.—Rhubarb Mould.

Ingredients.
1 quart measure of rhubarb
1¼ lbs. of sugar
The grated rind of half lemon
The strained juice of ,, ,,
12 bitter almonds, blanched and chopped
1 oz. of isinglass
Some Devonshire cream (*see* recipes.)

Skin the rhubarb and cut it into small pieces; weigh after it is skinned and cut; put it into a stewpan with the sugar, lemon-rind and juice, and almonds; boil fast; skim and stir till it becomes a rich marmalade. Dissolve the isinglass in two tablespoonsful of boiling water; add this to the marmalade. Rub a mould with sweet almond oil; put in the fruit and stand in a cool place, or on ice, till it is firmly set. Turn out and serve with Devonshire cream round it.

22.—Greengage Mould.

Follow the preceding recipe, using three pints of greengages instead of the rhubarb, and the kernels blanched instead of the almonds.

23.—Apple Mould.

Peel, core, and cut up twelve good cooking apples; add

Ingredients.
12 apples
¾ lb. of loaf sugar
¼ oz. of isinglass
The grated rind of one lemon
The strained juice of one lemon
1 sherryglass of rum
} To each pound of apple.

the sugar, isinglass, lemon-rind, juice and rum. Boil in a stewpan until it is a rich jam; rub through a wire sieve; rub the mould slightly with salad oil or dissolved butter; press in the apple, smooth over the bottom with a knife and let it stand in a cool place or on ice till quite firm. Turn out carefully, and serve with good custard, (*see* recipe) or whipped cream.

24.—Spongecakes with Apple Snow.

Ingredients.
6 spongecakes
¾ of a pint of cream
2 tablespoonsful of brandy, curaçao or rum, or 20 drops of essence of vanilla
8 large apples
½ lb. of sifted loaf sugar
The strained juice of a lemon
The whites of two eggs

Put the cakes in a glass dish; stir the flavoring into the cream; pour it over the cakes and let them soak for two or three hours. Roast the apples till quite soft; take off the skin and core, and add to half a pound of the pulp the sugar, lemon-juice and eggs. Beat with a whisk until in a snow like forth. Place it on the cakes, and serve.

25.—Vol-au-vent of Fruit.

Prepare a vol-au-vent according to the recipe, (*see* page 237) and fill it at the moment of serving with either greengages, apricots, plums or peaches prepared as for *compotes*. Pour the syrup over and serve with thick whipped cream piled on the top. This dish may be iced and is very delicious.

26.—Rosengrötze.

Ingredients.
1 teacupful of sago
1 quart of milk
1 pot of red currant jelly
½ pint of thick cream

Boil the sago in the milk until it is a jelly; stir in the red current jelly; strain through a tammy sieve into a mould (slightly oiled); leave it to set. Serve with whipped cream round the bottom of the dish.

Note.—Oranges may be used instead of the jelly; the juice of six nd the rind of one, sweetened to taste.

27.—Meringues.

Ingredients.
6 whites of *very* fresh eggs
¾ lb. of fine loaf sugar

Whisk the whites of the eggs to a *very* firm froth; stir in the sugar carefully dried and sifted. Have ready some strips of thick foolscap paper about two inches wide; lay them side by side on a thick wooden board; take a tablespoon and gather it nearly full of the méringue by working it up the side of the bowl in the form of an egg; drop this slopingly on to the bands of paper, at the same time drawing the spoon sharply round the edge of the méringue to give it the smooth rounded look of an egg. Continue this process as quickly as possible till all the egg is used up; strew some coarsely-sifted sugar over them, and allow it to remain three minutes; then lift up the end of one of the strips of paper, shake off the superfluous sugar, lay the band down again, and continue the process till all are done. Bake in a moderate oven for twenty or thirty minutes, or till they are colored a light brown and are firm to the touch. Take them out; dip a knife in boiling water and with it remove the méringues from the paper; scoop out the soft insides with a desertspoon and put them on a sieve in the oven for a few minutes to dry, the moist sides uppermost. When they are dry they are ready, and must be kept in a dry place on a sieve till wanted. They may be filled with jelly or whipped cream (flavored either with vanilla, or strawberry, or raspberry syrup), or with iced cream.

28.—Snow Balls with Custard.

Beat the whites of the eggs to a stiff froth; add one dessertspoonful of sugar; put the milk into a clean stewpan, add the flavouring and the remainder of the sugar; put it over a gentle heat, and when it boils take a tablespoonful of the white of egg and drop it in the form of an egg into the milk; do this till all the egg is used up; let the balls simmer for four

Ingredients.
4 fresh eggs
3 dessertspoonsful of finely powdered loaf sugar
½ pint of new milk
20 drops of vanilla or other flavouring

minutes, then drain on a sieve in a dry place. Beat the yolks of the eggs, add them to the milk, and stir over a slow fire till it thickens and becomes like rich cream; strain it into a glass dish, and when it is quite cold lay in the balls carefully and send to table.

29.—Chocolate Custards.

Ingredients.
2 oz. of chocolate
¼ pint of water
1 ,, ,, new milk
20 drops of vanilla
8 eggs
3 oz. of sugar
½ pint of cream

Dissolve the chocolate in the water beside the fire; then boil till it is perfectly smooth; flavour the milk with vanilla, add it to the chocolate, sweeten with the sugar, and when it boils stir in the yolks of the eggs well beaten and strained. Put this custard into a jar or jug; set it in a pan of boiling water and stir without ceasing till it is thick; stir in the cream carefully. When it is cold pour it into a glass dish or into custard cups and serve with sponge or rice cake.

30.—Currant Custard.

Ingredients.
1 pint of currant-juice
10 oz. of sugar
8 eggs
½ pint of cream
2 tablespoonsful of lemon-juice

Boil the sugar in the currant-juice for three minutes; take off the scum; beat the eggs well; pour the juice, boiling, on to them; put the custard into a jug or jar in a pan of boiling water, and stir carefully till it is thick; pour it out, stir till nearly cold, add the cream and lemon-juice.

Apple, strawberry, and quince custards are made in the same way.

31.—Duke's Custard.

Drain the cherries from their juice and roll them in sifted

SWEET DISHES OR ENTREMETS.

Ingredients of Duke's Custard.
¾ pint of brandied morella cherries
1½ pints of rich cold custard (*see* recipe)
½ pint of thick cream
1 wineglassful of brandy
3 oz. of sugar
The juice of half a large lemon
20 drops of cochineal

sugar; cover the bottom of a glass dish thickly with them; pour the custard over them; garnish the edge with macaroons or Naples biscuits; whip the cream with the lemon-juice, brandy and cochineal, pile it on the custard, and serve.

32.—Buttered Apples.

Pare the apples and core them without piercing them or dividing them; fill their cavities with the butter; put the remainder of the butter, cut small, into a stewpan which will just hold the apples in a single layer; place them in, close together, and stew them as gently as possible, turning them occasionally ill they are almost tender enough to serve; strew the sugar on them, add the cinnamon, shake these well among the fruit, and stew for a few minutes longer. Take out the fruit, arrange it on a hot dish; put into each apple as much apricot jam as it will hold and lay a small quantity on the top; pour the syrup from the pan round but not over the apples, and serve at once with or without whipped cream.

Ingredients.
6 or 8 fine apples
6 oz. of fresh butter
6 to 8 oz. of sugar
1 teaspoonful of cinnamon
Some apricot jam

33.—Stewed Apples or Pears.

Pare them carefully and scoop out the core without breaking them; throw them into a basin of cold water as you do them; take a shallow pan in which they can lie in one layer without touching each other, put

Ingredients.
6 apples
10 drops of cochineal
1 clove
1 inch of cinnamon
The thin rind of half a lemon
The strained juice of half lemon
1 wineglass of whiskey

in enough water to cover them half-way up, with the cochineal, clove, cinnamon, lemon-rind, and juice. Boil them uncovered and watch carefully so as to turn them when the lower side is done. When they are quite tender take them out. Drain the water in which they were boiled through a sieve, add loaf sugar to it in the proportion of one pound to one pint; add the whiskey; simmer gently until in a *very* thick syrup; place the apples in a glass dish, put a morella cherry on the top of each, pour the syrup round (not over), and serve with Devonshire cream in a separate dish.

34.—Rice and Almond Mould.

Ingredients.
2 oz. of sweet almonds
6 bitter almonds
6 oz. of rice
6 ,, ,, sugar
1 quart of milk
¼ pint of thick cream

Blanch the almonds and pound them to a soft paste; wash the rice; put them into a saucepan with the sugar and milk, and simmer till perfectly tender (about 1¼ hours); dip a mould into cold water, press in the rice, and let it stand in a cold place or on ice for four or five hours. Turn out carefully, and serve with stewed prunes or other fruit; pour the cream over it, and serve.

35.—Lemon Rice Mould.

Ingredients.
6 oz. of rice
1 quart of milk
6 oz. of sugar
The grated rind of two lemons
Lemon marmalade
¼ pint of thick cream

Wash the rice and boil it in the milk with the sugar and lemon-rind till tender (about 1¼ hours). Dip a mould in cold water, press in the rice, and let it stand in a cold place for four hours. Serve with lemon marmalade round and the cream poured over.

36.—Shape of Rice.

Ingredients.
¼ lb. of rice
1 quart of milk
2 oz. of loaf sugar
The yolk of one egg
20 drops of vanilla

Simmer the rice in the milk with the vanilla until quite tender; add the sugar, boil gently until the rice is dry; beat the yolk, stir it in; put the rice in a mould and let it stand for three or four hours until well set. Serve with rich custard and stewed fruit.

37.—Shape of Ground Rice.

Ingredients.
2 oz. of rice
1¼ pints of milk
½ oz. of butter
1 egg, well beaten
1½ oz. of sifted sugar
1 dozen of glacé cherries
A little brandy

Mix the rice smoothly into a quarter of a pint of the milk; boil the remainder of the milk; pour it on the rice and stir over the fire for ten minutes. Add the butter, the egg (well beaten), and the sugar; stir over the fire for two or three minutes. Dip a mould in cold water; soak the cherries in the brandy, stir them into the rice, and pour it into the mould. Let it stand three or four hours till set; turn out carefully, pour a little syrup round the base, and serve.

38.—Once a Week.

Ingredients.
4 oz. of rice
1 quart of milk
4 oz. of powdered loaf sugar
2 ,, ,, vanilla sugar
¼ ,, ,, isinglass
½ pint of thick cream
Some rich custard (*see* recipes)
20 drops of vanilla

Wash the rice; let it stand in the milk *beside* the fire for an hour to swell; add the sugar and vanilla and boil till it is tender (about 1½ hours) and all the milk absorbed; stand it aside covered to get cold; put the isinglass in a cup with three tablespoonsful of cold milk; let it stand an hour; put the cup in a small saucepan with boiling water in it (a *bain-marie*) for three minutes; stir it till cool, add it to the rice, and stir it; whip half the cream, stir it into the rice; dip a mould in cold water, press in the rice and let it stand twelve hours, (or on ice till set); when it is ready to serve turn it out carefully, pour the custard over; whip the remainder of the cream with the vanilla and pour over; serve at once.

39.—Sweet Rice.

Ingredients.
3 oz. of rice
1½ pints of new milk
4 oz. of loaf sugar
4 eggs
2 oz. of sweet almonds
½ gill of thick cream

Wash the rice and boil it in the milk with the sugar for one and a half hours. Let the rice stand off the fire for five minutes; beat the eggs well, add them to the rice; stir in the cream; stir over the fire till at boiling heat; take it off, and let it stand, stirring occasionally, till nearly cold. Put it into a glass dish and stand in a cold place for two hours. Blanch and pound the almonds, bake them in a moderate oven till browned through; pound them to dust; strew over the rice, and serve with or without preserve or fruit.

40.—Sweet Macaroni.

Ingredients.
1½ pints of new milk
1 pinch of salt
4 oz. of macaroni
The thin rind of one lemon
3 oz. of sugar
The yolks of 4 eggs
Some crushed macaroons

Boil the milk; drop in the macaroni gently; add the salt and lemon-rind. Simmer gently until the macaroni is tolerably tender; then add the sugar and boil till the macaroni is soft and swollen to its full size; drain and lay it on a hot dish. Beat the yolks, pour the milk on to them, stir quickly and shake it over the fire till it thickens; pour this over the macaroni at once and sift the macaroons over them. Serve with or without apple marmalade or stewed fruit.

Note.—The whites of the eggs may be beaten to a froth, mixed with four tablespoonsful of sifted loaf sugar and baked in the oven so as to form a méringue if desired.

41.—Portuguese Macaroni.

Soak the macaroni in the cold water for one hour, drain on a sieve, put it in a saucepan with one and a half pints of the milk and vanilla, and simmer gently for two hours. Take out the vanilla, add the loaf sugar and a quarter of a pint of the milk; simmer for twenty minutes; stand off the fire for ten minutes; stir in the eggs, well beaten; stir over the fire till at boiling heat; add the brandy and cream. When nearly cold put it in a glass dish, let it stand in a cold place for two hours; strew the macaroon powder over, and serve.

Ingredients.
3 oz. of macaroni
1 quart of water
¾ pints of new milk
1 inch of vanilla
4 oz. of loaf sugar
5 eggs
1 wineglassful of brandy
½   ,,   ,, cream
1 oz. of crushed macaroons

42.—Portuguese Tapioca.

Is prepared precisely as above, only it is not soaked in cold water.

43.—Rice Croquettes.

Wash and drain the rice; put it into a saucepan with the sugar, lemon-rind, cinnamon and milk; stir frequently and boil for three quarters of an hour; rub through a fine wire sieve; beat three of the eggs, yolks and whites separately; add the yolks to the rice; beat for ten

Ingredients.
3 oz. of good rice
3   ,,   ,, sugar
The thin rind of half a lemon
1 inch of cinnamon
Nearly a pint of fresh milk
3 eggs
6 oz. of butter

minutes; add the whites; beat five minutes more; make up into balls the size of walnuts, dip each into the yolks of two beaten eggs, then into sifted loaf sugar, and fry in butter till of a pale brown color. Dry them on a sieve covered with a sheet of blotting paper or a soft white cloth. Pile on a hot dish, and serve with or without stewed fruit or jam, or whipped raspberry cream (which makes this a very delicious dish).

44.—Finer Croquettes of Rice.

Ingredients.
7 oz. of rice
1 quart of milk
25 drops of vanilla
5 oz. of sugar
bitter almonds blanched and pounded
Some fine bread-crumbs
2 yolks of eggs
Some butter

Wipe the rice very clean in a dry cloth; put it into a clean stewpan and pour the milk on it; add the vanilla, and let it swell gently by the side of the fire, stirring that it may not burn for three quarters of an hour; stir in sugar and almond powder and simmer the rice for three quarters of an hour till it is very thick and dry; spread it on a dish to dry, and when it is quite cold roll it into balls; dip these in beaten eggs and then cover carefully with bread-crumbs. When all are ready fry them in plenty of butter, a light brown color, and dry them before the fire on a sieve with a sheet of blotting paper on it. Pile hot on a dish, and serve at once with one pint of cream whipped with some raspberry or strawberry syrup.

45.—Gooseberry Fool.

Ingredients.
1 bottle of gooseberries
The juice of a small lemon

Boil the gooseberries with their own syrup, the lemon-rind, juice, and sugar till it is quite a pulp; pass through a hair sieve;

Ingredients of Gooseberry Fool.
The peel of half the lemon
½ lb. of sugar
1 pint of cream

add the cream, and whip till it thickens. Serve with sponge cakes.

Note.—Apple Fool is made in precisely the same way, substituting a bottle of apples for the gooseberries.

CREAMS, BLANC-MANGER, AND JELLIES.

1.—Vanilla, Coffee, or Fruit Syrup Cream.

Ingredients.
1¼ pints of cream
8 oz. of sugar
5 eggs
½ oz. of isinglass
1 gill of water
25 drops of vanilla, or any kind of fruit syrup, or a cup of strong coffee

Dissolve the isinglass in warm water. Boil half-pint of the cream with the sugar; take the cream off the fire and when it is slightly cooled add the well-beaten yolks of the eggs; mix well; put on the fire again and beat with a whisk until it thickens; lift it off the fire and add the dissolved isinglass warm, whisking all the while; whip the remainder of the cream, stir it to the rest; add the flavoring syrup or coffee; rub a mould with oil of almonds, pour in the cream and stand it in a cool place or on ice until firmly set. When it is ready dip the mould in hot water, wipe it, and turn it out.

2.—Chocolate Cream.

Ingredients.
½ pint and 3 tablespoonsful of cream
½ oz. of isinglass
1 gill of water
¼ lb. of chocolate (finely grated)
½ lb. of sugar (pounded and sifted)
6 yolks of eggs
2 whites
25 drops of vanilla

Boil the half pint of cream; melt the isinglass in the water, add it to the cream; add the chocolate and sugar to the cream; lift the cream off the fire and when it is a little cooled add the yolks and whites of the eggs well beaten; boil the three tablespoonsful of cream, add it to the rest; put the pan on the fire and whip the mixture well till it thickens; add the vanilla. Rub a mould with oil of almonds, pour in the cream and set in a cool place, or on ice. Dip the mould in hot water, wipe it, and turn out the cream.

3.—Chocolate Cream, made without Cream.

Ingredients.
6 oz. of chocolate (grated)
1 pint of new milk
6 oz. of sugar (pounded and sifted)
8 yolks of eggs
2 oz. of gelatine

Dissolve the sugar and gelatine in the milk for ten minutes; stir in the chocolate; lift the pan off the fire; when it is slightly cooled add the yolks of the eggs well beaten; strain it into a basin; put it on the fire again, and whisk well till it thickens; dip a mould in cold water, put in the cream, and place on ice till firmly set. Turn out and serve immediately.

4.—Ratafia Cream.

Ingredients.
4 oz. of ratafias
8 yolks of eggs
1 wineglassful of curaçao
1 stick of cinnamon (bruised)
The thin rind of one orange
1 pint of milk
6 oz. of sugar
2 ,, ,, gelatine
½ pint of cream
2 oz. of preserved ginger, chopped
2 oz. of dried cherries
2 ,, ,, candied peel, chopped

Dissolve the sugar and isinglass in the milk for ten minutes, add the ratafias, cinnamon, and orange rind; take the mixture off the fire; when it is slightly cooled add the well beaten yolks and curaçao; put it on the fire, whisk well, when it thickens pass it through a hair sieve into a basin; whip the cream, add it to the mixture with all the remaining ingredients; mix well; dip a mould in cold water, pour in the cream, imbed it on ice; when ready, dip the mould in hot water, wipe it, turn out the cream, and serve.

5.—Caramel Cream.

Put the sugar, cinnamon, lemon-peel, and half the water

Ingredients of Caramel Cream.
4 oz. of sugar
1 bruised stick of cinnamon
The peel of one lemon
1 gill of water
8 yolks of eggs
1 pint of milk
6 oz. of sugar
½ pint of cream
2 oz. of gelatine (dissolved in a little warm water)

into a stewpan and boil until it is of a light brown; add the remainder of the water, the beaten yolks, milk and sugar; stir over the fire till it thickens; pass it through a hair sieve into a basin; add the cream whipped, and the dissolved gelatine; mix well; dip a mould in cold water, pour in the cream, set in a cold place or on ice.

6.—Italian Cream.

Dissolve the isinglass and sugar in the milk; boil slowly

Ingredients.
¾ oz. of isinglass
5 oz. of loaf sugar
¾ pint of new milk
1 pint of rich cream
35 drops of essence of vanilla or any kind of fruit syrup

for ten minutes; strain into a basin, add the cream and flavoring; turn it rapidly with a whisk over the fire till it begins to thicken; dip a mould in cold water, put in the cream and place it on ice till firmly set. Turn out carefully, and serve at once.

7.—Ginger Cream.

Make a cream as in the preceding recipe (Italian cream)

Ingredients.
4 oz. of preserved ginger
1 dessertspoonful of ginger syrup

omitting the vanilla; cut the ginger into small pieces and add it and the syrup to the cream, stirring continually till it begins to set that the ginger may not sink to the bottom.

8.—Celestine Cream.

Imbed a mould in rough ice; dissolve the isinglass in

Ingredients.
Some Italian cream (*see* recipe)
Some fine ripe strawberries
1 oz. of isinglass
1 gill of water
1 teaspoonful of maraschino

water, add the maraschino; dip each strawberry in the isinglass and line the bottom and sides of the mould with them; when it is completely lined fill it up with the cream, and when it is ready turn out carefully and serve.

9.—Quince, Apple, or Currant Jelly Cream.

Ingredients.
A 1 lb. pot of jelly
1 oz. of isinglass
½ pint of cream

Melt the jelly; dissolve the isinglass in it; whip the cream; pour the boiling jelly into it, stirring briskly; continue stirring till nearly cold; dip a mould in cold water, pour in the cream, and set in a cold place or on ice.

10.—Bavarian Cream.

Ingredients.
1 quart of strawberries
12 oz. of sugar pounded & sifted
2 ,, ,, isinglass
1 pint of new milk
1¼ ,, ,, thick cream
The juice of one lemon

Crush the strawberries with a wooden spoon; strew eight ounces of the sugar over them; let them stand three hours; turn them into a fine hair sieve and rub them through it. Melt the isinglass in the milk over the fire; add the sugar; strain through muslin; add the cream; stir till nearly cold; add the strawberries gradually; whisk briskly together; add the lemon-juice by degrees; dip a mould in cold water, pour in the cream, and set in a cold place for twelve hours.

11.—Strawberry Cream.

Ingredients.
¾ of a pint of fresh strawberries
6 oz. of sifted sugar
10 drops of cochineal
1 pint of whipped cream
2 oz. of isinglass

Dissolve the isinglass, pass it through a piece of muslin; pick the stalks off the strawberries; bruise them with a wooden spoon in a basin, add the sugar and cochineal, mix well; add the cream and isinglass, whisk together; dip a mould in cold water, put in the cream, imbed it in ice. When ready, dip the mould in hot water, wipe it, and turn out the cream carefully.

12.—Raspberry Cream.

Prepare as in the preceding, substituting raspberries for strawberries.

13.—Apricot or Peach Cream.

Ingredients.

1 oz. of isinglass
1 pint of new milk (or cream)
½ pint of cream
3 oz. of sugar
½ lb. of apricot or peach jam*
1 tablespoonful of lemon-juice

* When peach jam is used add seven drops of cochineal

Dissolve the isinglass in the milk and pass it through fine muslin; put it into a saucepan with the sugar, and when it boil; stir in the cream; pass the apricot jam through a sieve; add it, a spoonful at a time, to the cream; mix it very smoothly and continue stirring after you put it into the mould till it is nearly cold that the fruit may not sink to the bottom.

14.—Pineapple Cream.

Ingredients.

1 small ripe pineapple*
½ pint of water
9 oz. of loaf sugar (in powder)
2 tablespoonsful of brandy
¾ of an ounce of isinglass
¾ of a pint of rich cream

* Preserved pine jelly may be used instead of the fresh half pint of the syrup. In this case three ounces of sugar boiled with the isinglass will be sufficient

Pare off the outside of the pineapple; peel it sufficiently thick to take off all the eyes; put the peel into a saucepan with the water, and boil it till the flavour is extracted; strain the liquor and let it get cold. Cut the fruit into half inch squares; strew the sugar over it, add the brandy, let it saturate for two hours; then pour the liquor on to it, put it on the fire and boil fast for ten minutes, skimming constantly; add the isinglass; boil ten minutes more; pour it into a basin; whip the cream, add it to the fruit, whisking constantly; stir briskly till the mixture begins to thicken; dip a mould in cold water (or rub it with oil of sweet almonds,) pour in the cream and place it on ice till firmly set; stir it for ten minutes after placing it on the ice to prevent the fruit from sinking to the bottom.

15.—Milanese Cream.

Ingredients.
1 pint of milk
5 oz. of loaf sugar
¼ ,, ,, isinglass
1 gill of water
The yolks of 8 fresh eggs
1 gill of thick cream
35 drops of vanilla

Dissolve the sugar in the milk over the fire for five minutes; dissolve the isinglass in the water; take the milk off the fire; beat the yolks of the eggs, and when the milk is slightly cooled pour it on to them; stir over a gentle fire till at boiling heat; add the isinglass and cream; stir well; add the vanilla; rub the mould with oil of sweet almonds, and let it stand in a cool place until firmly set.

16.—Lemon Cream.

Ingredients.
½ lb. of loaf sugar
¾ oz. of isinglass
1 gill of water
The strained juice of two lemons
The thin rind of two lemons
¼ of a pint of thick cream

Dissolve the sugar and isinglass in the water; add the lemon-juice and rind; boil and skim till in a thick syrup, then strain; whisk the cream into it; continue whisking till it begins to thicken; pour it into a mould, and place on ice till firmly set.

17.—Lemon Sponge.

Ingredients.
1 pint of cream
The rinds of two medium sized lemons
¾ of an ounce of isinglass
7 oz. of sugar
The juice of 1½ lemons

Infuse the lemon-rind in half the cream by the side of the fire; add the isinglass, and when it is dissolved put in the sugar; do not let it boil, but simmer until the sugar is dissolved and the milk well flavored with lemon; then stir in the remainder of the cream and strain immediately into a large bowl or pan. When it is quite cold add the lemon-juice, whisking well all the time; when the cream begins to get thick, whisk it lightly to a sponge, and pour it into an oiled mould; when it is to be served, dip the mould into hot water, wipe it and turn the sponge out carefully.

18.—Swiss Cream.

Ingredients.
6 oz. of loaf sugar
The thin rind of half a lemon
½ pint of new milk
1 tablespoonful of Oswego flour
1 pint of good cream
The strained juice of one large lemon
1 oz. of ratafias
3 ,, ,, macaroons
1 lb. of any kind of jam

Boil the sugar and lemon-rind in the milk; let it get cold; stir in the flour and cream; put it into an enamelled saucepan (or a basin inside a saucepan with boiling water) and stir over a gentle fire till boiling; strain into a basin, and when nearly cold add the lemon-juice strained. Lay the ratafias and macaroons in a glass dish; spread the jam over them and pour the cream over; let it stand in a cool place for three hours before serving.

19.—Velvet Cream.

Ingredients.
¾ pint of new milk
4 oz. of loaf sugar
The thin rind of half a lemon
1 inch of cinnamon
4 fresh eggs
2 dessertspoonsful of Oswego flour
30 drops of essence of vanilla
Half a bottle of preserved greengages
3 oz. of moist sugar
4 sponge cakes
3 wineglassfuls of ginger wine

Boil the sugar, lemon-peel and cinnamon in the milk; beat the eggs and add the flour, stirring till quite smooth; let the milk stand off the fire for ten minutes; strain the eggs into it, stirring all the time. Put the mixture into a saucepan and stir it over a slow fire till it thickens; pour it into a basin, and when nearly cold add the vanilla. Boil the juice of the greengages with the sugar for ten minutes, add it to the fruit; cut the spongecakes across the centre, lay them on a glass dish, pour the ginger wine over them; lay the greengages round, pour the cream over, and let it remain in a cool place for three hours.

20.—Stone Cream.

Ingredients.
1 pint of rich cream
½ oz. of isinglass
Any kind of jam or preserved fruit
A little angelica
Some dried cherries

Dissolve the isinglass in the least possible quantity of warm water; stir it into the cream. Put the fruit or preserve into a glass dish, pour the cream over and let it stand in a cool place for three hours. Cut the angelica into small pieces and decorate the top of the cream with it and a few cherries.

21.—Crême au Thé.

Ingredients.
½ pint of cream
1 ,, ,, milk
¾ of an ounce of isinglass
1 pinch of salt
4 oz. of sugar
2 spoonsful of good orange Pekoe
The yolks of five eggs

Put the tea into a teapot and pour the milk, boiling, on to it; let it stand till cold; pour it off and strain it if necessary; put it into a stewpan with the insinglass and sugar; simmer gently till both are dissolved; beat the eggs, add the milk to them hot, but not boiling; strain; stir in the cream; stir over the fire till it thickens; dip a mould in cold water, pour in the cream, and put in a cool place or on ice to set.

22.—Millefruit Cream.

Ingredients.
1 teaspoonful each of preserved strawberries, apricots, raspberries, currants, greengages, ginger, pineapple, & plums
1 ounce of isinglass
1 pint of water
3 oz. of sugar
1 pint of rich cream

Boil the isinglass and sugar in the water for half an hour; put in the fruit; whisk till nearly cold; whip the cream, add it to the fruit, mix well; put it in a mould, imbed it in ice, leave it to set; turn out carefully and serve.

23.—Franchipane Cream.

Ingredients.
The yolks of 5 fresh eggs
1 tablespoonful of Oswego flour
3 oz. of sifted loaf sugar
The grated rind of one lemon
½ teaspoonful of orange flowers, (candied or fresh and chopped fine)
½ pint of new milk
1 oz. of sweet almonds ⎫ Blanched
7 bitter almonds ⎬ and pounded
½ gill of thick cream

Put the yolks, flour, sugar, lemon-rind, and orange flowers into a saucepan; beat with a wooden spoon till well mixed; add the milk; stir over a gentle fire for ten minutes after it boils; take it off, and when it is nearly cold add the almonds and cream; stir rapidly till quite cold. Serve in a glass dish with any kind of preserved fruit or jam.

24.—Rheinish Cream.

Ingredients.
2 oz. of sweet almonds
12 bitter almonds
1½ pints of cold water
7 oz. of loaf sugar
1 ,, ,, isinglass
The grated rind of one orange
The ,, ,, ,, ,, lemon
The strained juice of both
The yolks of 7 fresh eggs

Blanch the almonds and pound them to a paste; add half a pint of the water while pounding; let it stand for an hour. Dissolve the sugar and isinglass in one pint of the water; add the orange and lemon-rind, the strained juice and almonds. Simmer ten minutes, strain into a basin. Beat the yolks, add them to the rest, and stir over the fire till a boiling heat. Strain the mixture into a mould and place in a cool place or on ice till firmly set.

25.—A good Common Blanc-Manger.

Ingredients.
1½ pints of new milk
The rind of one small lemon
8 bitter almonds
3 oz. of sugar
1½ ,, ,, isinglass
½ pint of cream
1 sherryglass of brandy

Blanch and bruise the almonds; put them and the lemon-rind into the milk to infuse; add the sugar and isinglass; boil gently over a clear fire until the isinglass is quite dissolved; take off the scum, stir in the cream, strain the blanc-manger into a mould; add the brandy by degrees; stir it gently with a spoon to keep the cream from setting on the surface. Leave it in a cool place, or on ice till set.

26.—A Rich Blanc-Manger.

Blanch the almonds; pound them to a paste; add the water while pounding; let it stand for two hours; pour off the liquid; put the milk, half pint of the cream, the sugar, cinnamon and vanilla into a saucepan, and boil slowly till dissolved; add the isinglass; when it is dissolved strain into a basin; stir in the almonds and the remainder of the cream; when cool pour the mixture into a mould, and let it remain in a cool place till firmly set, or on ice for an hour.

Ingredients.
1 oz. of isinglass
5 ,, ,, loaf sugar
2 inches of stick vanilla
2 ,, ,, cinnamon
½ pint of milk
¾ ,, ,, cream
2 oz. of sweet almonds
10 bitter almonds
½ pint of cold water

27.—American Blanc-Manger.

Peel the nuts and pound them to a paste; add the water while pounding; let it stand two hours to extract the flavour. Beat the eggs, mix them with the flour; dissolve the sugar in the milk, add the nuts, simmer five minutes; stand off the fire five minutes; strain on to the eggs, stirring quickly at the same time; stir over a gentle fire till it thickness. Pour the mixture into a mould, and put it in a cool place or on ice till firmly set. Turn out carefully and garnish with preserve or jelly.

Ingredients.
8 or 10 Brazil nuts
1 gill of water
4 fresh eggs
5 tablespoonsful of Oswego flour
4 oz. of loaf sugar
1 pint of new milk
Some preserved mango, ginger or guava jelly

28.—Quince or Currant Juice Blanc-Manger.

Ingredients.
¾ of a pint of quince or currant-juice.*
1½ oz. of isinglass
9 " " sugar
¾ of a pint of cream

* These can be procured in bottles. If *syrup* is used then omit the sugar.

Boil the juice and dissolve the isinglass in it; add the sugar, boil up and strain; add the cream by degrees; stir well; when it is lukewarm pour it into the mould.

29.—Jaune-Manger or Dutch Flummery.

Ingredients.
The rind of one lemon
8 oz. of sugar
1 pint of water
2 oz. of isinglass
The juice of four lemons
The yolks of eight eggs
1 pint of sherry

Put the lemon-rind, sugar and water in a saucepan, stir them over a gentle fire for three or four minutes; leave by the side of the fire for ten minutes to infuse. Add the isinglass, stir till it is dissolved, add the strained lemon-juice and sherry (or other wine); beat the eggs, pour the mixture on to them, whisk briskly, and pass through a very clean hair sieve. Put it into a jar, stand this in boiling water, and stir till it thickens; turn it out into a bowl; when it cools dip a mould in water and pour the mixture into it. Stand in a cool place, or on ice to set.

30.—Rice Blanc-Manger.

Ingredients.
2 oz. of sweet almonds
10 bitter almonds
½ a pint of cold water
3 oz. of rice
6 oz. of loaf sugar
The thin rind of half lemon
2 inches of cinnamon
1 inch of stick vanilla
1½ pints of new milk
¾ of an oz. of isinglass

Blanch the almonds and pound them to a paste, adding the water while pounding; let this stand for two hours. Boil the rice, sugar, lemon-rind, cinnamon and vanilla in the milk. When the rice is in a pulp put in the almonds with the liquid; simmer gently for ten minutes; add the isinglass, and when it is dissolved, rub the whole through a fine hair sieve. Put into a mould and let it remain in a cool place till firm. Serve with or without cream poured over it.

31.—Calves' Feet Jelly.

Wash the feet well and split them; put them in a stewpan with the water; boil up quickly; skim, and simmer very gently, skimming frequently for six hours; strain into an earthen uncovered pan and let it remain in a cool place until the next day.

Ingredients.
2 large calves' feet
5 pints of cold water
The strained juice of four large lemons
The thin rind of two large lemons
2 inches of cinnamon
14 oz. of loaf sugar
The whites of six eggs
½ gill of cold water
1 gill of Madeira

Take off the fat carefully and wipe the surface of the jelly with a soft warm cloth to absorb any fat that remains. Put the jelly into a bright stewpan, with lemon-rind and juice, the cinnamon and sugar; boil up; beat the whites of the eggs with the water; throw them into the jelly and stir rapidly with a wire whisk for twenty minutes, boiling as fast as possible all the time. Draw it aside and let it simmer uncovered, for twenty minutes more; strain through a jelly bag; add the wine. If not quite bright strain a second time. Put the jelly in a mould, aud let it stand on ice for an hour.

32.—Another Recipe for Calves' Feet Jelly.

Wash the feet well and split them; put them in a stewpan with the water, and boil until the liquor is reduced to two quarts; strain into an uncovered earthen pan. When it is quite firm and cold take off the fat

Ingredients.
4 calves' feet
1 gallon of water
1 bottle of sherry
3 lbs. of sugar
The juice of 6 lemons
The rind of 3 ,,
The whites and shells of 8 eggs
¾ of an ounce of isinglass

and sediment; put the jelly into a stewpan with the sherry, sugar, lemon-juice, the six whites of the eggs and their shells finely crushed.

Let this remain a few minutes to dissolve the sugar; then put the pan on the fire and let the jelly be brought to boil gradually, but do not stir it after it begins to heat; when it begins to boil drop in the isinglass. Boil it for ten minutes, and let it stand for a few moments before it is poured into the jelly bag. Put the thin lemon-rind into the bag, strain the jelly through it into a bowl underneath, and repeat this process twice if the jelly be not clear. Dip the mould (which should be earthenware) into the cold water; when the jelly is cool and clear put it in and leave it to set.

33.—Orange Calves' Feet Jelly.

Ingredients.
2 calves' feet
5 pints of water
1 pint of strained orange-juice
The strained juice of two lemons
The very thin rind of 1 orange
The ,,   ,,   ,, 1 lemon
6 oz. of sugar (broken small)
1 pinch of isinglass

Prepare the calves' feet stock as above, boiling it till it is reduced to one and a half pints; then add the orange and lemon juice, the rind, and sugar. Stir gently over the fire till the scum begins to form but not at all afterwards; add the isinglass; boil up; simmer gently for ten minutes, take it off the fire, let it stand a little and pour it through a jelly bag till perfectly clear. Pour into a mould, and stand on ice.

34.—Lemon Calves' Feet Jelly.

Follow the recipes for Calves' Feet Jelly, adding half a pint of clear lemon-juice, and the rinds of three large lemons.

35.—To clarify Isinglass for Jelly.

Ingredients.
2½ oz. of isinglass
1 pint of filtered water
1 teaspoonful of beaten white of egg

Beat the white of egg with the water and put it with the isinglass into a delicately clean stewpan; stir well together and heat very gradually by the side of a gentle fire, taking care that the isinglass does not stick to the pan. In two or three miuutes the scum will rise; skim it off, boil it up, strain it through muslin, and set it by for use. It should be perfectly transparent, and when lukewarm may be mixed with fruit syrups, or melted currant, apple, or quince jellies, and moulded at once.

36.—To clarify Syrup for Jellies.

Ingredients.
3 lbs. of loaf-sugar
1 quart of water
The white of an egg

Put the ingredients into a delicately clean stewpan; whisk well; boil gently for five minutes, adding a few drops of cold water occasionally; strain through a napkin into a basin. The juice of fruit and clarified isinglass added to the above and flavored with liqueur makes most delicious jellies.

37.—Fine Orange Jelly.

Ingredients.
Clarified isinglass (*see* recipe)
Clarified syrup (*see* recipe and use half the quantities)
The very thin rind of four oranges
The very thin rind of two lemons
The juice of seven oranges
The „   „ three lemons

When the syrup is nearly cold, put in the orange and lemon-rind, and the orange and lemon-juice; when it is cold stir in the isinglass and strain through a piece of muslin folded in four. Lay a china mould in cold water for some time; take it out, pour in the jelly; when it is wanted for table, wrap it in a cloth which has been dipped in boiling water and loosen the edges with a knife.

38.—Strawberry Jelly.

Ingredients.
Clarified isinglass (*see* recipe)
Clarified sugar (*see* recipe and use half the quantities)
1 pint of strawberry juice, or syrup, or two quarts of ripe strawberries
3 tablespoonsful of clear currant juice
The clear juice of two small lemons

Bruise the fruit slightly, powder it with sugar, and let the juice flow from it for an hour or two; pour a little water over it, and when the clarified sugar is nearly cold add the strawberry syrup to it; stir in the currant and lemon-juice, and the isinglass (nearly cold.) Mix and put into moulds.

Note.—All jellies are better set on ice, as only half the quantity of isinglass is required and the flavour is much finer.

39.—Raspberry Jelly.

Prepare exactly as above. A few fine Raspberries may be put into the top of the mould.

40.—Rhubarb Jelly.

Ingredients.
2½ lbs. of young pink Rhubarb stems
1 quart of water
8½ oz. of lump sugar (in large lumps)
1½ oz. of isinglass

Wash and wipe the stems; slice, but do not pare them; take out any coarse or discolored parts. Put the rhubarb into a stewpan with the water and two and a half ounces of the sugar (in lumps); boil it *very* gently for twenty minutes; strain it through a piece of muslin folded in four; take one and a half pints of it; heat it afresh in a clean pan, add the isinglass and the remainder of the sugar; stir it continuously until the isinglass is quite dissolved; then boil up quickly for a few minutes to throw up the scum; clear this off carefully, and strain the jelly through muslin; repeat this process if the jelly is not clear, and when it is cool pour it into moulds and set it in a cool place or on ice.

41.—Pineapple Jelly.

Ingredients.
1 pineapple (1 lb. in weight)
12 oz. of clarified sugar, } *See*
2 „ „ isinglass, } recipes

Prepare some clarified syrup and isinglass; peel the pineapple; pick out the specks cut it up in slices; put these in a basin. Strain the clarified syrup over the fruit and boil them together for ten minutes. Strain the pineapple syrup through a napkin into a basin; add the clarified insinglass. Dip a mould in cold water; set it on ice; pour three tablespoonsful of jelly into the mould; when it is firm arrange some thin pieces of pineapple on it; pour on some more jelly; when this is set lay on some more pieces of the fruit and repeat the process till the mould is filled up. When set quite firm, dip the mould in hot water for a second, turn out the jelly, and serve at once.

42.—Punch Jelly.

Ingredients.
10 oz. of loaf sugar
5 large lemons
4 oranges
1 slice of pineapple
1 wineglassfnl of Madeira (or good brown sherry)
3 wineglassesful of rum
½ wineglassful of brandy
1 tablespoonful of noyeau
1¾ oz. of isinglass
1 tablespoonful of fine green tea
1 pint of water

Pour the water, boiling, on the tea and let it infuse for twenty minutes; strain it through a muslin; rub the sugar on the rinds of the oranges and lemons to extract the essence; bruise the pineapple and press out the juice; squeeze all the juice out of the oranges and lemons and strain it; put the sugar and juice into the tea; boil up; skim carefully and stir rapidly till it is quite dissolved; strain through a jelly-bag; add the spirits and wine; pour the mixture rapidly out of one basin into another, three or four times; put it into a mould, and set for an hour on ice.

43.—Grape Jelly.

Ingredients.
½ lb. of loaf sugar
1¼ oz. of isinglass
½ pint of water
¾ of a pint of strained grape juice
1 wineglassful of brandy

Dissolve the sugar and isinglass in the water; add the grape-juice and brandy. Strain the jelly till it is bright; put a mould in ice; pour in a little jelly; when it is set lay in some good grapes; pour over some more jelly, and repeat this process till the mould is full. Leave in the ice till set.

44.—Maraschino Jelly.

Ingredients.
1 pint of clarified syrup (*see* recipe)
2 oz of clarified isinglass (*see* recipe)
The strained juice of one lemon
1 wineglassful of maraschino

Mix the ingredients in the order in which they are given; set in a mould on ice, and turn out when firm.

45.—Noyeau Jelly.

This and all other Liqueur Jellies are prepared as above.

46.—Oranges filled with Jelly.

Take some fine oranges, and with the point of a knife cut out a piece about the size of an 8 anna piece from the top of each orange; with the small end of a tea or egg spoon scoop out all the pulp, taking great care not to break the rind; throw the empty orange rinds into cold water. Press the juice from the pulp, make it into jelly (*see* recipe); have ready some cream or blanc-manger; lay the empty orange skins on ice and fill them into alternate layers of jelly and cream, or else color half the orange jelly with a few drops of cochineal, and fill the oranges with alternate layers of pink and yellow jelly. When firmly set wipe the oranges and cut them in halves with a sharp knife; build them up with green leaves in between. This makes a very pretty dish.

47.—Orange and Cream Jelly.

Prepare some orange jelly and about half a pint of Italian cream. Put the cream in a breakfast cup on ice to set. Take a plain round mould about one inch deeper than the breakfast cup, and about nine inches in diameter; set it on ice, pour in about one inch depth of jelly, and leave it to set. Divide some oranges into quarters; take off all the fibre. When the cream in the cup is set, and the layer of jelly in the mould firm, dip the cup for a second into hot water; turn out the cream on a plate; lay the mould over it so as to cover it; then turn the plate quickly over so that the cream stands upright on the jelly in the centre of the mould; set the mould on ice; lay in two rows of orange quarters, the one on the top of the other close round the cream on the first layer of jelly, with the thin edge of the quarter next to the cream; pour in some more jelly. When this is set put in two more rows of orange quarters; set these in jelly, and continue the process until the shape is full. When it is all set turn it out and serve at once. This is one of the prettiest dishes we have ever seen.

48.—Macedoine of whole Fruits in Jelly.

Make some very bright clear jelly; have ready any kinds of fruits, grapes, peaches, apricots, cherries, raspberries, strawberries. Place a mould on ice; pour in some jelly an inch thick and leave it to set, pile up the fruit in the centre, pour in some jelly; leave it to set, add more fruit, and fill up with jelly. When set firm turn out carefully.

PRESERVES, COMPOTES, &c.

The greatest care must be taken to have everything scrupulously clean for making preserves. The hair sieve, the muslin, and strainer should *never* be used for any other purpose, such as straining soup, vegetables, &c.

Only *wooden* spoons should be used for skimming and stirring preserves, as metal ones impair the color and even sometimes impart an unpleasant flavour to the preserve.

The pots or bottles in which the preserves are kept must be perfectly clean and dry. Pots should be filled to within a quarter of an inch of the tops, and bottles just above the shoulder, and if a piece of paper dipped in brandy is placed on the top of the preserve it will ensure its keeping. The day after the jams are made the jars or bottles should be closely covered with strong paper (the whitey brown kind known as "cap" paper is the most suitable) and brushed with white of eggs; or else with bladders, soaked, and tied closely over.

The preserving pan should not be placed flat on the fire, but it should either rest on an iron trivet, or three logs of wood should be placed in a triangle over the fire and the pan rest on this.

All fruit should be preserved the same day it is picked.

1.—Strawberry Jam.

The fruit must be fresh gathered; pick off the stalks; weigh them; boil them for thirty-five minutes, stirring constantly; take the pan off the fire; add one pound of pounded loaf sugar for each pound of fruit, mix well; then boil the preserve for twenty minutes, stirring and skimming constantly. No scum must remain on the jam. Pour it into pots, leave it till the following day; then tie it down.

2.—Strawberry Jam.
(Another way).

Strain the red currant juice (or syrup) into a preserving pan; take the stalks off the fruit,

6 lbs. of strawberries
1 pint of red currant juice, (or syrup)
6 lbs. of pounded loaf sugar

weigh it and add it to juice; boil up; skim; add the sugar, stirring constantly and boil moderately fast, and skim carefully for thirty-five minutes. Put the jam into pots. Tie it down the next day.

3.—Strawberry Jelly.

The fruit should be freshly gathered. Pick off the stalks; put the fruit into an enamelled stewpan, if you have one, and stand it very high above a clean fire; turn the fruit over occasionally with a wooden spoon; after about half an hour, when the juice has flowed from it abundantly, put the pan nearer to the fire and let it simmer *very* gently to shrink the fruit for about twenty minutes. Put a delicately clean sieve over a clean pan, pour the fruit into it and leave it there till all the juice has run through. Strain the juice through a muslin strainer into a basin; weigh it and boil it in a clean preserving pan for fifteen or twenty minutes, stirring often,

Take it off the fire and throw in by degrees fourteen ounces of coarsely pounded sugar for each pound of juice, stirring each portion till it is dissolved before you add the next. Place the pan over the fire and boil the jelly quickly for about a quarter of an hour, or until the juice jellies on the skimmer.

This is a delicious jelly and very brilliant in color. It becomes quite firm, and can be turned out in glass dishes for dessert by dipping the pot for a second in hot water.

4.—Raspberry Jam.

This is made in exactly the same way as strawberry jam. (*See* recipes.)

5.—Rhubarb Jam.

Wipe some fresh young rhubarb very clean; pare it, cut it into half inch lengths; weigh it, and for every pound of fruit take one pound of loaf sugar in fine powder; mix the fruit and sugar well and let it remain for a quarter of an hour to extract the juice; put it on the fire and let it heat slowly; as soon as the stalks become tender, let the preserve boil rapidly for about half an hour, stirring constantly and skimming.

6.—Rhubarb Jam.

(Another way.)

Wipe the rhubarb clean; pare it and cut it into half an inch pieces. Put it into a preserving pan with an equal weight of finely pounded sugar, the juice of two lemons, and twelve bitter almonds blanched and chopped; boil up slowly, stirring constantly; skim; boil fast for three quarters of an hour, skimming as long as the scum rises. Put the jam into pots and tie down the following day.

7.—Gooseberry Jam.

(This can be made of the Cape Gooseberries—Tiparri.)

Rub the fruit with a clean coarse cloth; weigh it and take one pound of pounded loaf sugar and the juice of a lemon to each pound of fruit. Boil the fruit and lemon-juice gently for seven minutes, stirring it well; add the sugar *very gradually*, and boil quickly for three quarters of an hour, stirring and skimming constantly. Put into pots and tie over next day.

It is to our thinking an improvement to pass the fruit through a sieve before the sugar is added, and if this is well reduced by boiling, it will make a very nice *gateau* or cheese, and will turn in perfect form out of the jars.

8.—Cape Gooseberry Jelly.

Wash the fruit very clean; pick off the stalks; put it into a preserving pan with three quarters of a pint of filtered water to each pound of fruit and simmer until the gooseberries are well broken. Turn the contents of the pan into a jelly bag, or fine cloth, and let all the juice drain through; weigh the juice; boil it rapidly for fifteen minutes, and skim it. Take as many pounds of sugar as you have pounds of juice; draw the pan from the fire; stir the sugar into it by degrees and until it is entirely dissolved; boil and skim it fifteen or twenty minutes longer, until it jellies on the spoon; clear it perfectly from scum and pour it into jars or bottles. Tie down the following day.

9.—Red Currant Jelly.

Strip the currants from their stalks; put them into a preserving pan, and stir them gently over a clear fire until the juice flows freely from them; turn the contents of the pan on to a fine hair sieve, and leave them to drain, but do not press them through. Pass the juice through a jelly bag, or folded muslin; weigh it; boil it *fast* for a quarter of an hour and clear off all the scum. For each pound of juice take eight ounces of coarsely pounded sugar; stir it into the juice (off the fire) until it is well dissolved; boil the juice fast for eight minutes, clearing off all the scum as it rises; pour it into jars or bottles, and tie it down the following day.

10.—Greengage Jam.

The fruit should be freshly picked and quite ripe. Take off the skins; stone and weigh it. Put it in a preserving pan and boil quickly for fifty minutes, keeping it well stirred. Add an equal weight of sugar finely pounded; boil the preserve ten minutes longer, clearing off all the scum as it rises; put it into jars and tie down the following day. Plum and Damson Jam are made in the same way.

Note.—When the flesh of the fruit does not separate easily from the stones which is the case with most Indian plums, weigh the fruit and throw it whole into the pan; boil it to a pulp, pass it through a sieve, and deduct the weight of the stones when apportioning the sugar to the jam.

11.—Apricot Jam.

Peel, stone, and quarter ripe apricots, break the stones, blanch the kernels and wipe them dry. Put the fruit into a preserving pan with the same weight of loaf sugar; place the pan over a gentle heat until the sugar is dissolved; then boil up and skim; boil moderately fast, skimming constantly for three quarters of an hour; five minutes before it is done put in the kernels. Put the jam into pots and tie it down the next day.

Note.—When the apricots are very small, as in the case of those grown in the hills, it would be well to use only half the kernels.

12.—Apricot Marmalade.

Wipe the fruit, cut it in half, and boil it for twenty minutes; blanch the kernels; take the pan off the fire; add an equal weight of sugar to the fruit very gradually until it is all dissolved; boil fast for ten minutes, skimming very carefully; three minutes before it is done add the kernels. Put the jam into pots and tie down the next day.

13.—Peach Jam.

Follow the recipe for Apricot Jam.

14.—Peach Marmalade.

The fruit must be ripe but perfectly sound. Peel, stone, and weigh it. Boil the fruit quickly for three quarters of an hour; stir and skim it often; blanch the kernels; take the fruit off the fire and stir in very gradually an equal weight of finely pounded sugar; boil it briskly for ten minutes, clearing off the scum carefully; add the strained juice of two lemons and the blanched kernels; boil for three minutes; put it into pots and tie it down the next day.

15.—Nectarine Jam or Marmalade.

Follow the preceding recipes.

16.—Peach, Apricot, or Plum Jelly.

Wipe the fruit, put it in a pan on the fire and boil it quickly for forty minutes. Tie it into a muslin bag, hang it over a basin, and leave it for twelve hours to drain. Take one cup of finely pounded sugar for each cup of juice, boil it for eight minutes, skimming carefully; strain again through muslin; then boil gently until it jellies in dropping from a spoon; pour into jars or bottles and tie down the next day.

17.—Apple Jam.

Peel, core, and quarter some apples, weigh them quickly so that they may not discolor, and boil them for thirty minutes; to each pound add the strained juice of a lemon and three quarters of a pound of powdered loaf sugar; stir and simmer for fifteen minutes. Put the jam into pots and tie down the next day.

18.—Apple Jelly.

Peel, core, quarter, and weigh the apples; put them into a large jar with the thin rind of one lemon, four cloves, two inches of cinnamon, and a pint of water to each pound of fruit; tie the jar closely over and bake it in a moderate oven for one and a half hours; strain off the juice without pressing the apples; take one pound of loaf sugar and one tablespoonful of lemon juice for each pint of juice; put it into a pan and boil *fast* for forty-five minutes, skimming constantly. Pour it into pots and tie down the next day. The apples will make jam as in the preceding recipe.

19.—Quince Marmalade.

Pare the quinces; cut them in halves, scoop out the cores, and put them into cold water as you do them to preserve the color. Put the parings and cores into a stewpan with sufficient cold water to cover them well; boil till in a soft pulp; strain through a sieve without bruising the pulp. Weigh the quinces and the juice, and allow three quarters of a pound of loaf sugar for every pound. Put the quinces, juice, and sugar into a stewpan, and simmer gently, skimming carefully and breaking up the fruit with the juice till it becomes a marmalade. Then boil fast to lessen the juice, and when the whole forms a firm marmalade, put it into jars and tie down the following day.

20.—Quince Jelly.

Prepare the fruit as above, and put the parings and cores into a stewpan with enough water to cover them well; boil till in a soft pulp; strain the juice through a sieve. Weigh the quinces; for every four pounds of fruit, take two quarts of the juice and put them into a stewpan and stew gently until they are well broken but not reduced to pulp. Turn them into a jelly bag or tie them up in a fine cloth, and let all the juice strain into a deep pan.

If the juice is not clear, strain it again. Weigh the juice, put it into a delicately clean preserving pan, and boil it quickly for twenty minutes. Take it off the fire and stir into it until it is entirely dissolved twelve ounces of sugar for each pound of juice. Put it on the fire, stir and skim it for ten or twenty minutes, or until the syrup jellies strongly in falling from the skimmer. Put it into jars and tie it down the following day.

21.—Damson Cheese.

(This may be made from small Red Plums.)

Take the stalks off the fruit; reject any which are not perfectly sound; give each plum a gash with a knife; put them into large stone jars; tie them over with bladders and put them into large pans or degchees with water reaching two-thirds their height. Boil them for two or three hours, or until the fruit is quite soft and has yielded all its juice. Drain off the juice; skin and stone the fruit; weigh it and put it into a stewpan with half the juice, and boil briskly over a clear fire until it forms a dry-paste; add nine ounces of pounded sugar for each pound of fruit, stirring it in off the fire until it is quite dissolved; boil it again, stirring constantly until it leaves the pan quite dry and adheres in a mass to the spoon. Press it quickly into jars or moulds; when it is quite cold lay on it a paper steeped in spirit; tie it closely over with another paper or bladder.

22.—Damson or Red Plum Jelly.

Steam the fruit in jars as above; when it is done pour off the juice, strain and weigh it. Boil it quickly for twenty-five minutes; take it off the fire and stir in ten ounces of pounded sugar for each pound of fruit. Boil it quickly for ten minutes longer, stirring constantly, and carefully clearing off the scum. Put it into jars or moulds and tie them down the next day.

23.—Guava Jelly.

Follow the recipe for Quince Jelly.

24.—Guava Cheese.

Keep back one-third of the juice when you make the jelly, and put it into a preserving pan with the guavas from which the jelly was strained, adding six ounces of sugar for each pound of fruit; boil it over a clear fire until it forms a thick paste; pass it through a hair sieve; press it into jars, and tie down the next day.

25.—Mixed Fruit Jelly.

Take one pound of orange-juice, the same quantities of grape-juice, half a pound of lemon-juice and eighteen ounces of loaf sugar. Put all this into a preserving pan and stir with a wooden spoon until the sugar is dissolved; then boil fast for one hour. Pour the jelly into moulds or pots, and the next day tie them down.

26.—Orange Marmalade.

For seven dozen oranges take one dozen fine lemons; wipe all the fruit with a clean cloth. Peel the oranges with a very sharp knife, only taking off the yellow part; put the rind into cold water and boil it till it is tender. Grate the peel of the lemons; take the white peel and pith off all the fruit; cut it into quarters and take out the pips and white fibre; strain out the juice; strain the peel and cut it into shreds; put the pulp from which the juice was extracted into the water in which the peel was boiled, and boil it till it is quite soft; rub it through a sieve. Mix the shreded and grated peel, the pulp and juice; weigh it, and take an equal weight of loaf sugar. Put the whole into a preserving pan, stir it with a wooden spoon till the sugar is dissolved, then skim and boil it till it becomes a rich marmalade (about an hour). Put it into pots and tie it down the following day.

27.—Orange or Lemon Marmalade.
(*Another way.*)

Rasp the rinds of the oranges very lightly on a fine grater; cut them into quarters and separate the flesh from the rinds; with the small end of an egg or saltspoon clear them from the pips and inner skin and film. Put the rinds in plenty of cold water; boil them for twenty minutes and then change the water and boil them again. When they are quite tender, take them out and drain them on a sieve. Slice them thin, and take eight ounces of the rind for each pound of the pulp and juice, and one and half pounds of powdered loaf sugar. Put the rind, pulp, juice and sugar into a preserving pan and boil fast for half an hour, skimming well. Put into jars and tie down the next day.

28.—Scotch Marmalade.

Cut the rind of three pounds of bitter oranges into quarters, peel it off and pare off the white film inside. Cut the rind into chips as thin as possible and about half an inch long; divide the pulp into small bits, take out the pips; put the chips and pulp into a deep earthen dish; pour three quarts of boiling water on them; let them stand twelve or fourteen hours; turn the contents of the dish into a preserving pan and boil it until the peel is quite tender; add six pounds of pounded sugar and boil until the preserve jellies; then put it into pots and tie down the next day.

29.—Clear Orange Marmalade.

Cut the rind of some oranges in quarters, strip it off, free it from fibre. Divide the oranges in quarters, free them from pips, thin skin and fibre. Throw the skins into plenty of boiling water; when they are tender drain them on a sieve and scrape off the white skin entirely while they are still warm. Pound them to a paste, add the pulp and juice by degrees, taking care that no lumps are formed. Immerse the seeds in a quarter of a pint of water, add it to the paste, pass it through a coarse bobbin-net strainer, pour it into a preserving pan; take it off the fire, stir in by degrees some pounded sugar in the proportion of one and half pounds of sugar for each pound of fruit; when the sugar is all dissolved, put the preserve on the fire and boil it quickly for twenty minutes, or until it jellies. Put it into pots, and tie it down the following day.

30.—Fine Orange Jelly.

Choose eighteen ripe oranges; take off the rind of ten of them in quarters, free them entirely from their tough white skin, and cut them into rather thick slices with a sharp knife; put them with all their pips into one and a half pint of water. Halve the remainder of the fruit without paring it, and squeeze out the juice and pips on to the sliced oranges. Put the fruit into a stewpan (which it must not more than two-thirds fill); heat it gently and boil for twenty or thirty minutes; strain the juice from the fruit through a large square of muslin folded in four. Weigh the juice, boil it quickly for five minutes; for each pound of juice take fourteen ounces of roughly powdered loaf-sugar; stir it into the juice off the fire; when it is entirely dissolved boil it for a few minutes till it jellies. It will be firm and clear and beautifully transparent.

31.—Pineapple Marmalade.

Cut some ripe pineapples into slices; pare off the rind and take out every speck and grate it on a delicately clean grater; weigh it; beat it gently and boil it for ten minutes; take it off the fire and stir in gradually fourteen ounces of dry powdered sugar for each pound of fruit; boil it until it thickens and becomes transparent, which will be in about fifteen minutes if the quantity is not large.

32.—Preserved Pineapple.

The pieces must be ripe and perfectly sound; cut them into slices half an inch thick. Pare off the outer rind, and take out all the eyes and specks; weigh them, and for each pound of fruit allow fourteen ounces of loaf sugar and half a gill of cold water. Put the sugar and water into a preserving pan and stir over a slow heat until it boils and the sugar is dissolved; boil it up quickly and skim; put in the fruit and boil gently for twenty minutes, skimming constantly. Lay the fruit in a deep dish or basin, pour the syrup over and let it stand for two days. Put it again into a preserving pan and boil slowly for a quarter of an hour, skimming if necessary. The next day put it into pots and tie it down.

Note.—It is a good plan to cut off the yellow outside skin as thin as possible and then pare the slices thickly enough to take out all the eyes. When this is done, the thick inside parings should be put into coarse muslin and the juice expressed and added to the sugar and water.

33.—Preserved Melon.
(For Dessert.)

The melons must be perfectly sound and not over-ripe. Pare and quarter them, take out the pulp, place it on a sieve with a basin underneath to receive the juice from it. Weigh the fruit and put it in an earthen pan; cover it with cold water with salt and vinegar in it (in the proportion of one teaspoonful of salt and one dessertspoonful of French vinegar to three pints of water); let it remain in this pickle for 26 hours; then wash and drain it. Take the same weight of loaf sugar as of fruit; put it into a stewpan with the juice from the pulp and boil it, skimming carefully till it becomes a clear syrup. When the syrup is cold, put in the melon; boil it up slowly, skim, and simmer gently for a quarter of an hour. Put the melon carefully into a basin; pour the syrup over it and let it stand for three days; each day drain off the syrup, boil it fast for three minutes, pour it over the melon. The last time it is boiled add one ounce of ginger lightly bruised to the syrup. Put the melon in a jar, pour the syrup over, and place the ginger on the top; the next day tie it closely down.

34.—Preserved Peaches, whole.
(For Dessert.)

The peaches must be sound and not over-ripe. Wipe off the bloom and throw them into a preserving-pan more than half filled with boiling water. Cover it with a cloth and let it stand where it will keep hot, but not boil, for an hour. Then take them out and put them into cold water. When they are cold, take off the peel, open the ends sufficiently to take out the stones, break the stones and blanch the kernels. Weigh the peaches and take an equal weight of loaf sugar. Put the sugar into a preserving pan with enough water to moisten it and boil it till it is a syrup. Put in the peaches and kernels and let them boil for five minutes; then put them into a dish and pour the syrup over them. Cover the dish with a sheet of paper, and let it remain until next day. Drain off the syrup, boil it for three minutes; pour it over the peaches. Do this every day for a week; the last time put in the peaches and boil fast for ten minutes. Put them carefully into pots, pour the syrup over, put a portion of the kernels into each pot, and the next day tie them down.

35.—Preserved Nectarines.

Follow the preceding recipe, but leave the peel on.

36.—Preserved Quinces.

Pare the quinces, cut them in halves, scoop out the cores, and put them in cold water to preserve the color. Put the parings and cores into a stewpan with three times their weight of apples cut in slices, and sufficient cold water to cover them well and boil till in a soft pulp; then strain through a sieve without bruising the pulp. Weigh the quinces and the juice and allow three quarters of a pound of loaf sugar to every pound. Put the quinces, juice and sugar into a stewpan and simmer gently, skimming often, till they are tender and the juice is clear. Put the quinces carefully into jars and fill up with juice. When cold, tie them down and keep them in a dry place.

37.—Pumpkin Ginger.
(For Dessert.)

The pumpkin must not be ripe. Peel it and remove the seeds and cut it into pieces like the West Indian Ginger in form and size. Make a pickle with two quarts of cold water a teaspoonful of salt, and a teacupful of white vinegar. Put the pieces of pumkin into this and let them remain for twenty, four hours. Make a syrup as follows: To every pound add the strained juice of one lemon, half an ounce of ground ginger, and a quarter of a pint of cold water; boil and stir till it becomes a syrup; take out the pieces of pumpkin and wash them in cold water; put them into the syrup and simmer gently until tender but not *soft;* turn the whole into a basin; the next day pour off the syrup, boil it up and pour it back on to the pumpkin; do this for three days; taste the syrup, and if it is not sufficiently strongly flavored with ginger, add a saltspoonful more ginger each day; the third day when the preserve is cold, put it into jars, let the syrup well cover the pumpkin; tie the jars over with bladder and keep them in a dry place for six months before using.

38.—Oranges in Syrup.

Peel the oranges; then with a small sharpe knife remove every particle of white skin and fibre, taking care not to prick the inner skin or the juice will escape. For eight oranges boil one pound of loaf sugar in half a gill of water; when the syrup is quite bright add a wineglassful of rum. Put the oranges into a pie-dish which will just hold them; pour the syrup over and let it remain till cold; turn the oranges; pour off the syrup, boil it up, pour it over again, and let them stand till the following day.

39.—Orange Salad.
(For Dessert.)

Peel the oranges; free them from skin and fibre; cut them into slices one-sixth of an inch thick. For nine oranges take one pound of finely powdered loaf sugar, one wineglassful of Madeira, one wineglassful of brandy, and one wineglassful of whisky or rum. Lay the oranges and sugar in layers, pour the wine and syrup over, and let it stand six hours before serving. Baste the oranges frequently with the syrup, using a silver spoon.

Note.—Powdered sugar-candy may be substituted for the loaf sugar, and a little curaçao may be added to the brandy.

40.—Whisky Apples.
(For Dessert.)

Take some sweet sound apples; peel them neatly and scoop out the core with a narrow pointed knife (or better still a long narrow cutter, three inches deep and half an inch in diameter). Take three quarters of a pound of loaf sugar for each pound of apples, the thin rind and strained juice of a lemon, two inches of cinnamon, two cloves, half an inch of bruised ginger, half a gill of whisky, and half an inch of stick vanilla. Put the whole into a stewpan, place it over a slow heat and simmer gently for one and a half hour; turn the apples frequently with a wooden spoon and skim constantly. If carefully done the apples become quite transparent and will keep for a year. Put them in large glazed jars; boil the syrup for five minutes, strain it over the apples, and when cold tie them down. Serve with a preserved cherry on the top of each.

41.—Stewed Pears.
(For Dessert.)

Put the pears into a tin stewpan with sufficient cold water to cover them, and boil them slowly till they begin to feel soft. Take them out; put them into cold water for a few minutes, the skin will come off quite easily; scoop out the core. To each pound of pears allow nine ounces of loaf sugar, two cloves, one inch of cinnamon, the thin rind of a lemon, one tablespoonful of curaçao, or one sherryglass of port wine, and fifteen drops of cochineal. Put all the ingredients into a tin stewpan and simmer very gently until the pears are quite tender, stirring frequently and skimming with a wooden spoon. Take out the pears, boil the syrup quickly for ten minutes; strain it over the pears, and serve when quite cold.

42.—Stewed Pippins.

For each pound of pippins take one quart of water and six ounces of sugar. Put all these into a stewpan with some cloves and strips of lemon-peel and simmer very gently for three hours, or until perfectly tender. Take out the pippins, boil the syrup quickly for ten minutes, pour it over the fruit, and serve when cold with whipped cream or rich custard.

43.—Stewed Prunes.

For each pound of prunes take one pound of brown sugar and one pint of water. Boil the water and sugar together for ten minutes, put in the fruit and simmer gently for two hours, or until it is perfectly tender so that it breaks if touched with the finger. Drain the syrup from the prunes and boil it till it is very thick. Put the prunes back into it and let them stand till next day.

44.—Compôte of Peaches.

Pare six ripe peaches; boil six ounces of sugar in half a pint of water for ten minutes; put in the peaches; stew them very gently for twenty minutes, turning them constantly. Take out the fruit; add one large teaspoonful of lemon-juice to the syrup, boil it quickly for ten minutes, pour it over the peaches, and serve cold for dessert.

Note.—Nectarines, apricots, and greengages may be prepared in the same way.

45.—Compôte of Cherries.

Put six ounces of loaf sugar and half pint of water with a teaspoonful of white of egg in a stewpan; whisk well over the fire, boil gently for five minutes; if it gets too thick add a few drops of cold water; strain through a napkin into a basin. Take some fine cherries; cut off the stalks half-way and all the same length, put them into the syrup, simmer for three minutes, add a dessertspoonful of noyeau, and serve cold for dessert.

46.—Compôte of Strawberries.

Prepare exactly as above, only substitute one small wineglassful of maraschino for the noyeau.

47.—Bottled Strawberries.

Prepare some syrup as directed for compôte of cherries; have some freshly picked strawberries ripe and perfectly sound, taking care not to bruise them. Put them into a glass bottle; fill this up with the syrup; cork them tightly down and tie the corks over with string. Put the bottles in a deep pot or pan, and put in cold water which must reach up to the necks of the bottles. Put the lid on the pot, stand it on the fire, and as soon as it boils lift it off the fire and let it stand till the water is nearly cold. Then tie the corks over with bladders, or cover them well with sealing-wax or bottle-wax melted in the proportion of one pound of bottle-wax to one ounce of bees-wax.

48.—Bottled Apricots.

The apricots must not be over-ripe; split them in halves; peel them carefully; lay them in layers in dry bottles; fill them up with syrup, and proceed as directed for bottled strawberries.

49.—Bottled Peaches.

Split the peaches in halves; scald them in their syrup to remove the skins; arrange the halves in dry clean bottles, and proceed as for bottled strawberries.

CAKES.

General Directions and Remarks.

The ingredients of cakes should be perfectly fresh and good, and well dried, especially during the rainy season. The ordinary bazaar flour is often adulterated, and its inferior quality spoils the cakes and makes them heavy; great care must therefore be taken to procure it pure and of a good quality, and where this cannot be done it is well to use corn-flour which insures the cakes being light and good.

All light cakes require a brisk oven to make them rise, large rich ones a sustained heat to bake them through.

To ascertain whether a cake is done thrust a larding needle or bright skewer into the centre, and if it comes out clean take out the cake instantly; if the paste adheres to the needle continue the baking.

Cakes should not be moved or shaken in the oven before they are done. When they are sufficiently baked loosen them gently, turn them out of the mould, set them on a sieve at the mouth of the oven to dry the surface, then put them aside on the sieve until cold.

1.—Rich Plum Cake.

Ingredients.
¾ lb. of good butter
½ ,, ,, rich moist sugar
¾ ,, ,, currants (washed and dried)

Beat the butter to a cream and put it into a basin with the other ingredients, except the whites of eggs, in the order in which they are given. Beat the

Ingredients of Plum Cake.
¾ lb. of raisins (carefully stoned)
6 oz. of mixed candied peel (finely chopped)
1 ,, ,, bitter almonds (blanched and pounded)
6 bitter almonds (blanched and pounded)
The grated rind of one lemon
The strained juice of ,, ,,
1 grain of powdered cloves
2 grains of powdered cinnamon
⅙ part of a nutmeg, grated
14 oz. of flour (sifted and dried)
½ gill of new milk
The yolks of 6 eggs beaten with a wineglassful of brandy
The whites of 6 eggs beaten to a froth

whole together until it is well mixed, add the whites of eggs, and continue to beat rapidly for twenty minutes. Line a large cake tin with buttered paper, and bake in a moderate oven for two-and-a-half hours. Turn out the cake carefully, dry it at the mouth of the oven; put it on a sieve to cool, and serve either plain or with almond paste and icing. (*See* recipes.)

2.—To blanch and pound Almonds.

Put the almonds in a saucepan with plenty of cold water and heat slowly; when it is just scalding turn the almonds into a basin, peel them and throw them into cold water as they are done; dry them well in a soft cloth before they are used. If the water be too hot it will make them yellow. They should be *very* slightly warmed before they are pounded; while beating sprinkle in a few drops of water or lemon-juice and pound them to a smooth paste in a mortar.

3.—Almond Paste for Cakes.

Blanch and pound the almonds as directed; add the

Ingredients.
12 bitter almonds
7 oz. of sweet almonds
10 ,, ,, sifted loaf sugar
1 tablespoonful of orange flower water
The whites of ten eggs

sugar, orange flower water, and the whites of eggs beaten to a stiff froth; stir the mixture till it becomes a smooth paste. Spread it over the cake one-sixth of an inch thick and let it stand in an airy place while the icing is being prepared.

4.—Sugar Icing for Cakes.

Ingredients.
The whites of six eggs
1 lb. of loaf sugar (pounded and sifted)
The strained juice of half a lemon

Break the eggs one by one and separate the yolks from the whites; with a small fork take the specks out of each egg as it is broken. Whisk the eggs to a perfectly solid froth; stir in the sugar with a wooden spoon; work it in well; add the lemon-juice; spread the icing over the cake, and dry it very gently in a quite cool oven or in a meat screen placed before the fire.

5.—Plum Cake.

(Another way.)

Ingredients.
1½ lbs. of flour (sifted & dried)
1 lb. of fine sugar
1 ,, ,, dried cherries (slightly chopped)
1½ lbs. of currants (washed and dried)
½ lb. of candied orange peel
¼ ,, ,, ,, citron,
½ ,, ,, ,, lemon, } Cut into fine shreds
8 oz. of pounded almonds
8 whole eggs (beaten)
The rind of two oranges (rubbed off on two lumps of sugar)
½ oz. of ground spicies (cinnamon, cloves, and nutmeg in equal proportions)
½ pint of Cognac brandy
1 teaspoonful of salt

Place the butter in a large white earthen pan or wash-hand basin and work it with a wooden spoon to cream; add the flour, sugar and eggs, carefully working the butter the whole time; when these are thoroughly mixed, add the cherries, candied peel and almonds; then very gradually the brandy, spices and salt. When these are well incorporated, line a large tin with double bands of buttered paper; pour in the mixture; put two sheets of buttered paper on a stout baking sheet; stand the cake on that, and put it in a moderate oven for about two and a half hours. When it is ready proceed as in the preceding recipe and ice as directed.

6.—A good Sponge Cake.

Ingredients.
3 or 4 lumps of sugar
The rasp rind of 1 large lemon
10 eggs
The weight of the eggs in dry sifted sugar
Half their weight in good flour*
1 oz. of butter

* Unless very good fine flour can be procured always use cornflour for sponge cakes

Rasp the rind of a good sound lemon on the lumps of sugar; crush the lumps to powder. Break the eggs one by one, separate the yolks from the whites and take out any specks with a fork. Beat the yolks in a large bowl for ten minutes; stew in the sugar by degrees and beat them well together. In the meantime let the whites be mixed to a stiff froth, whisk in the yolks, and when they are well mixed stir in the flour gently, but do not beat the mixture any more. Put one ounce of butter into a tin, melt it in the oven for a few seconds, turn the mould round and round till it is well covered; sift in some fine powdered sugar, shake it well all over the butter; turn out the loose sugar, pour in the cake, and bake it for one and a quarter hours in a moderate oven. Serve plain or with chocolate icing, (*see* recipe). Sponge cakes may be flavoured with twenty drops of vanilla.

7.—Chocolate Icing.

Ingredients.
6 oz. of finely grated chocolate
2 lbs. ,, ,, powdered sugar
¼ pint of good filtered water

Boil the sugar in the water until it throws up peal-like bubbles; take it off the fire. Dissolve the chocolate in a wineglassful of water, and after the sugar has stood off the fire ten minutes stir in the chocolate; work well together, and while still hot spread it over the cakes and leave it to dry. This is a great improvement to Rice, Madeira, and Oswego cakes.

8.—Tea or Coffee Icing for Cakes.

Proceed as above, substituting a small teacupful of *very* strong tea or coffee for the chocolate.

9.—A good Madeira Cake.

Ingredients.
5 fresh eggs
9 oz. of sugar (dried, pounded and sifted)
6 ,, ,, flour (dried and sifted)
4 ,, ,, butter (dissolved but not heated)
The rind of one lemon
½ of a teaspoonful of carbonate of soda

Whisk the eggs until they are as light as possible; add the ingredients very gradually in the order in which they are given, whisking well all the time. Special care must be taken in mixing the butter which must be put in by degrees, each portion being well incorporated before the next is added. Butter a tin, lay two or three thin pieces of candied peel in the bottom, pour in the mixture at once, and bake instantly for one hour in a moderate oven.

Note.—The candied peel may be omitted, and the cake iced with chocolate, tea or coffee. (*See* recipes.)

10.—Rice Cake.

Ingredients.
1 lb. of fresh butter
1 lb. of loaf-sugar (dried, pounded and sifted)
1 lb. of finely ground rice (dried and sifted)
The grated rind of one small lemon
The yolks of twelve eggs
The whites of eight ,,

Beat the butter to a cream; stir in the ingredients gently and by degrees, beating the yolks and whites separately; melt a lump of butter in a cake mould by putting it in the oven; turn the mould round and round till it is covered in every part shake in some sugar, cover the butter well with it; shake out all that does not adhere. Pour in the cake, and bake in a moderate oven for one-and-three-quarter hours.

Note.—This cake may be flavored with vanilla or iced with chocolate, tea, or coffee iceing. (*See* reipes.)

11.—Another Rice Cake.

Ingredients.
6 eggs
Their weight in sugar
½ ,, ,, ,, rice-flour
½ ,, ,, ,, wheaten or cornflour
20 drops of vanilla
⅓ teaspoonful of carbonate of soda

Whisk the eggs until they are as light as possible; stir in the sugar, flour and rice-flour; add the vanilla, and at the last moment the soda. Butter a mould, pour in the mixture, and bake in a moderate oven for one hour and ten minutes.

12.—Oswego Cake.

Ingredients.
6 oz. of Oswego flour
7 ,, ,, sifted loaf sugar
5 ,, ,, fresh butter
4 fresh eggs
1 tablespoonful of new milk

Beat the butter to a cream and the eggs to froth. Mix all the ingredients together in the order in which they are given and beat for ten minutes. Butter a tin mould, pour in the mixture, and bake in a quick oven. Currants (chopped), candied peel, or caraway seeds may be added.

13.—Pound Cake.

Ingredients.
1 lb. of fresh butter
1 ,, ,, loaf sugar in powder
1 ,, ,, dried and sifted flour
8 fresh eggs
The grated rind of a small lemon
The strained juice ,, ,, ,, lemon
One tablespoonful of brandy

Beat the eggs; beat the butter to a cream with a wooden spoon, and add all the other ingredients in the order in which they are given; beat the mixture for fifteen minutes; line a tin with buttered paper, pour in the mixture, and bake in a moderate oven for one-and-three quarter hours.

14.—A Plain Seed Cake.

Ingredients.
6 oz. of butter
6 ,, ,, moist sugar

Beat the butter to a cream; add the sugar, flour and caraway seeds; beat the eggs with the milk; add them to the mixture

Ingredients of a Plain Seed Cake.
1 saltspoonful of caraway seeds
¾ lb. of dried and sifted flour
3 eggs
1 gill of milk

butter a tin mould, pour in the cake, and bake in a moderate oven for fifty minutes.

15.—Soda Cake.

Ingredients.
½ lb. of butter
1 ,, ,, dried and sifted flour
½ saltspoonful of salt
½ lb. of currants (washed and dried)
3 oz. of candied peel, chopped
⅙th part of a nutmeg, grated
2 beaten eggs
⅛ of a pint of new milk (tepid)
1 small teaspoonful of carbonate of soda

Rub the butter into the flour; add the salt and the other ingredients, the milk (with the soda in it) last. Beat for five minutes; butter a tin, put in the mixture, and bake in a moderate oven for about 1⅓ hours.

16.—Almond Cake.

Ingredients.
½ lb. of Jordan almonds
1 oz. of bitter ,,
12 eggs
1 lb. of sugar, dried and sifted
3 lbs. of flour ,, ,, ,,
The rinds of two lemons grated

Blanch and dry the almonds and pound them to the finest possible paste (*see* recipe); whisk the eggs till they are *exceedingly* light, and add them *very* gradually to the almonds; throw in the sugar by degrees and keep the mixture light by beating it constantly with a large wooden spoon as the other ingredients are added. Mix in the flour very gradually; just melt the butter but do not let it get very hot, and beat it very gradually into the cake, taking care that each portion is entirely absorbed and incorporated before the next is added: put in the lemon-rind; fill a thickly buttered mould with the mixture, and bake in a well-heated oven for an hour-and-a half to two hours. When the top is sufficiently colored lay a piece of paper over it to prevent its being burned.

17.—Cream Cake.

This is made with cream which, in sultry weather, has

CAKES. 371

Ingredients of Cream Cakes.
5 oz. of good butter
1 lb. of fine flour (dried and sifted)
½ ,, of pounded, dried, and sifted sugar
A pinch of salt
2 oz. of candied citron (sliced thin)
½ pint of thick cream
2 eggs
1 teaspoonful of carbonate of soda
½ pint of thick sour cream

become acid; if it is the least *putrid* it must be thrown away. Take two teaspoonsful each of the flour and sugar; mix these with the soda, pound them in a mortar, and put them aside for use. Crumble the butter down in the flour; add the sugar and salt; mix well; add the citron; whisk the eggs; beat them with the cream; butter a mould; add the cream to the mixture which should be converted by it to the consistency of *thick* batter; beat it up lightly with a wooden spoon; put in the carbonate of soda (prepared as directed) and pour the mixture instantly into the mould. Bake for about three quarters of an hour in a moderate oven; it should be firm on the surface so as not to sink and be heavy when it is drawn out. Put it on its side on a sieve reversed to cool.

18.—Sweet Rusks.

Prepare the mixture as above, (only put it in a buttered baking sheet instead of in a mould) and after it has been slightly baked pull the mixture apart with a couple of forks and then re-set it in the oven to get crisped.

19.—A French Galette.

Work the butter lightly into the flour, add the salt; beat

Ingredients.
1 lb. of fine flour
¾ ,, ,, butter
1 saltspoonful of salt
The yolks of three eggs
1 small cupful of cream

two of the eggs with the cream, and work the flour into a paste with it. Roll it into a round shape three quarters of an inch thick; mark it into small diamonds with a knife, brush some yolk of eggs over the top, and bake the galette in a tolerably quick oven for about half an hour. It is generally eaten hot.

20.—Savoy Cake.

Ingredients.
1 lb. of loaf sugar, pounded and sifted
14 eggs
4½ oz. of the finest flour
4½ „ „ cornflour
1 saltspoonful of salt
25 drops of vanilla or other essence

Divide the yolks from the whites carefully; put the latter in a china bowl in a cool place till required. Add the sugar, salt, and essence to the yolk; work these together with a wooden spoon till they look like creamy batter. Whisk the whites to a stiff froth, mix the flour and cornflour gradually with the batter; when they are well incorporated stir the white in by degrees gently until the whole is thoroughly mixed. Put some butter in a plain mould, stand it in the oven until it is dissolved, cover the mould well with it in every part, sift in some finely powdered loaf sugar, and when the whole surface of the batter is covered with it, shake out the remainder; pour in the batter, tie a broad band of paper round the mould, put a few wood-ashes on the baking sheet, place the mould on that, and bake till done in a *gentle* oven.

21.—Chantilly Cake.

Ingredients.
10 eggs
12 oz. of finely powdered sugar
Some essence of vanilla
6 oz. of well dried and sifted flour
¾ of a pint of thick cream

Separate the yolks and whites carefully; whip the yolks with eight ounces of the sugar and thirty drops of vanilla till in a firm froth; beat the whites to a stiff froth and add them to the yolks; stir in the flour gently and by degrees; beat the mixture for ten minutes; while this is being done take a mould with a hollow centre, rub it with butter, fill it half full with the mixture, and bake it in a moderate oven for one hour. Turn it out on a sieve on its side to cool, and when it is quite cold, whip the cream with the remainder of the sugar and twenty drops of vanilla to a firm froth and fill the centre of the cake with it.

22.—Genoa Cake.

Ingredients.

1 lb. of fine flour, dried and sifted
¾ lb. of loaf sugar, pounded
½ ,, ,, currants (washed and dried)
½ lb. of Sultana raisins (picked and rubbed in a cloth)
6 oz. of mixed candied peel (chopped)
¼ of a nutmeg, grated
The grated peel of a lemon.
The strained juice of a lemon
Two tablespoonsful of rum
8 fresh eggs, beaten
1 lb. of fresh butter

Ingredients of Glaze.

3 oz. of sweet almonds
The white of one egg
2 dessertspoonsful of powdered loaf sugar
20 drops of orange-flower water

Mix all the ingredients except the butter; melt the butter, but do not oil it; add it to the mixture and beat for a quarter of an hour. Have ready a tin nine inches square and two inches deep, pour in the mixture, and bake in a moderate oven for one-and-a-quarter hours.

Blanch and chop the almonds; beat the white of egg with the sugar and orange-flower water; brush the cake over with this, strew it with the almonds, and bake for about a quarter of an hour longer.

23.—Guernsey Cake.

Ingredients.

¾ lb. of fresh butter
½ ,, ,, dried flour
¼ ,, ,, finely ground rice
¾ ,, ,, loaf sugar, powdered
¼ ,, ,, dried cherries, slightly chopped
2 oz. of sweet almonds. (blanched and pounded)
2 oz. of candied orange-peel, (chopped)
2 oz. of angelica, (chopped)
The yolks of eight eggs
The whites of three eggs
2 tablespoonsful of brandy

Beat the butter to a cream and mix in the ingredients in the order in which they are given; beat the mixture for ten minutes; line a tin with buttered paper, pour in the mixture, and bake in a well heated oven for an hour and twenty minutes. Turn out the cake on its side on a sieve to get cold.

24.—Thick light Gingerbread.

Ingredients.
8 oz. of butter
2 lbs. of flour
½ lb. of blown sugar
2 lbs. of powdered ginger
⅓ oz. of ground caraway seeds
2 lbs. of treacle
4 eggs
⅜ of an ounce of carbonate of soda

Crumble the butter into the flour and add the sugar, ginger, and caraway seeds; mix well and then beat in the treacle gradually: when that is well incorporated whisk the eggs well and add them; dissolve the soda in half a teacupful of warm water; add it to mixture, stir briskly; pour it into a shallow well buttered tin, and bake in a moderate oven for one-and-half hours.

Note.—This is a light good gingerbread, and for children less butter and caraway seeds may be used.

25.—Rich Gingerbread.

Ingredients.
4 eggs
1¼ lbs. of treacle
6 oz. of pale brown sugar
1 lb. of sifted flour
6 oz. of fresh butter
1 ,, ,, Jamaica ginger, pounded
1 large teaspoonful of finely pounded ginger
The grated rinds of two fresh large lemons

Whisk the eggs to the lightest possible froth and pour the treacle gently and by degrees on to them, beating lightly with a wooden spoon; continue to beat while you add gradually the sugar and flour. Warm the butter *just* enough to liquify it; add it in small portions to the mixture which must be well beaten till each is incorporated. The success of the cake depends on this process, and when it is all mixed, no butter should be visible on the surface, and large bubbles will appear in it to the last. Now add the ginger, cloves and lemon-rind. Butter a shallow square tin, pour in the gingerbread, and bake it for about an hour in a gentle oven. Let it cool a little before it is turned out and set it on its edge, supporting it against a jar, till it is cold.

26.—Good common Gingerbread.

Ingredients.
1 lb. of flour
6 oz. of butter
¼ lb. of brown sugar
1 oz. of ginger powdered
½ teaspoonful of pounded cloves and mace
The grated rind of one lemon
¾ lb. of treacle

Work the butter into the flour and mix the ginger, cloves and mace thoroughly with them; moisten this mixture with the treacle (adding a little more if needed); add the lemon-rind; pour it into a buttered tin and bake in a moderate oven; or it may be rolled out; cut into cakes with a tin cutter and laid on a floured or buttered tin.

27.—Short Bread.

Ingredients.
1 lb. of flour
2 oz. of sugar, pounded and sifted
1 oz. of candied orange or citron
8 oz. of butter

Chop the candied peel small and mix it and the flour and sugar well together; warm the butter enough to make it just liquid, and with it make the other ingredients into a paste, press this paste together with the hands; cut it with a large tin cutter about six inches in diameter into round cakes about an inch thick, pinch the edges with the fore-finger and thumb, lay it on large tins, and bake it in a moderate oven for twenty minutes or longer if it is not quite crisp.

28.—A Richer Short Bread.

Ingredients.
½ lb. of dry sifted flour
¼ ,, ,, rice-flour
¼ ,, ,, sifted loaf sugar
1 oz. of sweet almonds, blanched and pounded
¾ lb. of fresh butter
2 oz. of candied orange peel, chopped small
The yolks of two fresh eggs
Some caraway comfits

Put the flour, rice-flour, sugar, almonds and butter into a basin; rub the ingredients together until the butter is well mixed in; add the orange peel and yolks of eggs; knead to a firm smooth paste; roll it out three quarters of an inch thick; cut it into four square cakes; notch round the edges with a knife, prick them over with a skewer, strew the confits over the top, and bake upon paper in a moderate oven till crisp and of a pale brown color all over, about three quarters of an hour.

29.—Excellent Scotch Short Bread.

Ingredients.
1 lb. of flour
1 ,, ,, sugar, pounded and sifted
1 lb. of butter
10 eggs
½ lb. of candied lemon, orange and citron peel in equal proportions } Cut into shreds
1 gill of Cognac brandy
The rind of two lemons rubbed off on lumps of sugar
1 pinch of salt
4 oz. of white comfits

Put the butter in a basin and beat it to a thick cream with a wooden spoon; add the flour and sugar *gradually;* beat the eggs; add them very gradually to the rest; when the whole is thoroughly mixed, add the brandy; pound the lumps of sugar and add them; spread some circular tins about two inches deep with butter, pour in the paste, strew the comfits over them, sprinkle some fine sugar over the top, place them on baking sheets in a moderate oven, and bake until crisp and very lightly colored.

30—Orange Flower Macaroons.

Ingredients.
2 lbs. of dry sifted white sugar
2 oz. of the petals of freshly gathered orange blossoms
The whites of eight fresh eggs

Put the sugar (which must be *very* dry) into a basin. The moment the orange-flowers come in, pick the petals off the stems, weigh them and chop them *at once* with a pair of scissors *into* the sugar; if there is any delay they will be discolored. Add the whites of the eggs and whisk the whole well together until it looks like snow; drop the mixture at once on to a sheet of paper in little cakes, the size of a walnut, and bake in a very cool oven for about twenty minutes or more. When they are ready they will be delicately colored a pale fawn color and dried through.

31.—Almond Macaroons.

Ingredients.
1 lb. of sweet almonds
1½ lbs. of fine sugar, pounded
The whites of eight fresh eggs
Some wafer-paper

Blanch and pound the almonds; wipe them and set them in a very cool oven to dry; pound them to a very smooth paste, adding while pounding the white of an egg; whisk the remaining whites to a stiff froth; stir in the sugar; add the almonds by degrees, whisk the whole well together, drop the mixture upon wafer-paper, and bake in a moderate oven till quite crisp and of a pale brown.

32.—Macaroon Cakes.

Ingredients.
4 oz. of sweet almonds
¼ ,, ,, bitter almonds
1 teaspoonful of brandy
10 oz of loaf sugar
The whites of six eggs
The rind of a lemon

Before you pound the sugar take two lumps and grate the rind off the lemon on them. Pound and sift the remainder of the sugar. Blanch all the almonds; pound two ounces of the sweet and all the bitter, and add while pounding the brandy and the whites of two eggs; beat till in a stiff froth. Chop the remaining almonds into small pieces; add them to the mixture; now add the sugar; pound the lumps with the lemon-rind on them; add them; beat the whites of the remaining eggs to a stiff froth; add them, and beat the mixture till it becomes a firm paste; drop it on sheets of writing paper in little lumps the size of walnuts, and bake in a moderate oven till dry and of a pale fawn color, about eighteen minutes.

33.—Queen's Cakes.

Mix all the ingredients in a basin in the order in which

Ingredients of Queen's Cakes.
½ lb. of dried fine flour
½ ,, ,, sifted loaf sugar
6 oz. of currants, well washed and dried
6 fresh eggs, well beaten
½ lb. of fresh butter, dissolved but not oiled
The grated rind of half a lemon
Two tablespoonsful of brandy

they are given and beat the mixture for about ten minutes; butter some little tin moulds of various shapes, pour in the mixture, and bake in a quick oven for about fifteen minutes.

34.—Banbury Cakes.

Ingredients.
1 lb of currants (well washed and dried)
4½ oz. of beef suet (finely minced)
3 oz. of candied orange peel (shredded small)
3 oz. of candied lemon-peel
1 small pinch of salt
¼ oz. of mixed spices (pounded)
4 ,, ,, macaroons or ratafias (rolled to powder)
14 oz. of butter
1 lb. of flour

Mix all the ingredients except the butter and flour well together; make a light paste with the butter and flour; roll it out once or twice to prevent its rising too much; roll out half of it in a very thin square and spread the mixed fruit and spice equally upon it. Moisten the edges, lay on the remaining half of the paste rolled equally thin; press the edges securely together; mark it over with the back of a knife in regular divisions two inches wide and three long; bake it in a well-heated oven for from twenty-five to thirty minutes, and divide it into cakes while still warm.

35.—Tea Cakes.

Ingredients.
1 lb. of good flour, dried and sifted
1 saltspoonful of salt
¼ oz. of German yeast
¼ lb. of sifted loaf sugar
⅙ of a nutmeg, grated
6 oz. of butter, beaten to a cream
4 fresh eggs well beaten

Put aside a teacupful of the flour; put the rest into a large basin with the salt; mix the yeast with rather more than a gill of tepid water and stir it into the flour till it forms a soft paste; cover the basin with a clean cloth and let it stand on the hearth not too close to the fire for an hour to rise; then add the other ingredients in the order in which they are given. Divide the dough into eight cakes; use the reserved flour for making them up; place them on a tin and bake in a quick oven until nicely browned, about twenty minutes. Cut through the centre, spread with fresh butter, and serve very hot.

36.—Plain Buns without Butter.

Dilute the yeast with the milk till it is quite smooth; put as much of the flour to it as will make a smooth thick batter; throw a thick cloth over the pan in which you have mixed it and stand it where the fire will warm but not heat it. When it is well risen (which will take two hours or more) and bubbles appear on the top, add the salt and sugar and as much more of the flour as will form a light dough. Leave it to rise again, and if it is too firm to mould with the fingers, beat it with a strong wooden spoon and put it into tin pans, slightly buttered, to bake. Strew a few currants on the surface; put the tins into a quick oven and bake until the entire surface is browned.

Ingredients.
1 oz. of sweet German yeast
1 pint of warm new milk
2 lbs. of flour
½ lb. of sugar
1 saltspoonful of salt
A few currants washed and dried

Note.—To make these richer use less milk, crumble up two or three ounces of butter very finely in the flour which is added to the batter after it has risen. When the dough is ready, roll it into balls, put them on the tin some inches apart, wash the tops with milk, sift sugar over the top, and bake as directed.

37.—Soda Buns.

Work the butter into the flour with the fingers until it is quite in crumbs; mix in the sugar, salt, and rind; boil the cream and add it to the rest; mix

Ingredients.
½ lb. of flour
3 oz. of butter
4 ,, ,, sugar
A pinch of salt

Ingredients of Soda Buns.
1 oz. of candied orange peel (chopped fine)
1 *small* teacupful of cream
2 yolks of eggs
1 white „ „
⅓ of a teaspoonful of carbonate of soda

and add at once the yolks and whites of the eggs; when the whole is well mixed, dust over the soda and beat it well into the mixture. Rub an oven tin with butter, drop the buns on it with a spoon, and bake in a moderate oven. When they are firm to the touch all over and well colored underneath, they are done.

38.—Oat Cakes.

Crumble the butter into the oatmeal; add the salt; work the meal into a dough with as little warm water as possible; roll them out *very* thin, and bake on a girdle or in a *very* thick frying pan till quite crisp. They may also be made without butter.

Ingredients.
2 lbs. of coarse Scotch oatmeal
¼ lb. of butter
1 pinch of salt

39.—Soda Scone.

Rub the lard carefully into the flour in a basin until there are no lumps; add the salt; make it into a dough with the butter milk; sift the soda carefully through your fingers over the dough; mix it well in. Lay the dough on a pastry board with plenty of flour; knead it, roll it out to about half an inch thick. Put a girdle or *very* thick frying pan on the fire to warm; when it is well warmed cut the paste into triangles, lay it on the girdle, and bake. When it is done on one side, *slightly* browned, and with small bubbles on it, turn it over and bake in the same way on the other side. If you have not used up all the dough repeat the process

Ingredients.
5 oz. of fresh lard
10 „ „ dry fine flour
½ saltspoonful of salt
Some sour buttermilk
½ saltspoonful of carbonate of soda

When the cakes are ready put a sieve near the fire, cover it with a cloth, and lay the scones on this as they are done. Eat at once with butter.

Note—The lard may be omitted.

40.—Gingerbread Nuts.

Ingredients.
1 lb. of sifted flour
¾ of an oz. of finely powdered ginger
The grated rind of a lemon
The strained juice ,, ,,
5 oz. of good butter
2 ,, ,, honey
½ lb. of good treacle (slightly warmed)

Rub the butter into the flour, add the ginger and lemon-rind; add the lemon-juice, honey and treacle; knead to a firm paste and let it stand in a cool place for an hour or longer. Roll it out a quarter of an inch thick, cut it into small round cakes with a tin cutter, and bake in a quick oven till quite crisp, about fifteen minutes.

41.—Plain Dessert or Wine Biscuits.

Ingredients.
1 lb. of flour
2 oz. of fresh butter
About half a pint of new milk

Rub the butter into the flour in fine crumbs and make it into a stiff paste with the milk. Roll the paste out about half an inch thick, and cut it with a tin cutter into round pieces the size of a rupee. Pile them one on the other till all are done; then roll them out very thin, prick them and lay them on lightly floured tins, the pricked side downwards; put them in a moderate oven for a few minutes. They should be very crisp and *slightly* browned.

42.—Sweet Biscuits.

Ingredients.
2 lbs. of very good flour
3 oz. of good butter
4 ,, ,, fine dry sifted sugar
Some new milk

Mix the butter into the smallest possible crumbs in the flour; add the sugar and make this into a firm paste with the milk; beat this mixture well with a rolling pin, and when it is extremely smooth roll the paste out one-third of an inch thick, cut it into squares with a small cutter, and bake the biscuits in a very slow oven until they are quite crisp all over.

43.—Arrowroot Biscuits.

Ingredients
6 oz. of butter
3 ,, ,, sugar
3 eggs
1 breakfastcupful of arrowroot
1 ,, ,, fine flour
25 drops of vanilla

Beat the butter to a cream; add the sugar; beat the eggs with the vanilla, add them to the butter; beat in the arrowroot and flour very gradually; when the whole is well mixed, let it stand two hours. Roll it out, cut into circles with a tin cutter, and bake in a moderate oven until quite crisp.

44.—Brown Bread Biscuits.

The almonds are to be pounded without being blanched.

Ingredients.
1 lb. of pounded sugar
8 oz. of brown flour
6 ,, ,, Jordan almonds
6 drops of essence of bitter almonds
12 eggs

Break the eggs, the yolks into a basin, the whites into a bowl; add the sugar, flour and almonds to the yolks, and beat them well together for twenty minutes with a wooden spoon; whisk the whites to a firm froth, add them to the rest. Have ready some small paper cases; fill them with the mixture, powder them with sugar, and bake in a moderate oven until crisp.

45.—Naples or Finger Biscuits.

Prepare some batter as for Savoy Cake (*see* recipe); have ready a sheet of foolscap paper; cut it in two, fold each piece lengthwise in order to mark a straight line down the centre. Fill a biscuit forcer* with some of the batter; fold down the open end; hold the forcer in the right hand, press the batter out with the thumb, and guide the pointed end with the left hand. By this means the biscuits must be spread in straight lines like fingers, on each side of the straight line in the middle of the sheet of paper. When the sheet is full, place it on a baking sheet, sift finely pounded sugar over it; shake off the loose sugar, put the sheet in a *very* moderate oven, and bake for about a quarter of an hour.

* When there was none at hand we have made cones of thick cartridge paper which have answered the purpose very well.

46.—Finger Biscuits Glacé.

Prepare some finger biscuits (*see* preceding recipe), or else bake the batter of Savoy or Spongecakes on a baking tin, and afterwards cut them into small cakes any sizes or shapes which may be liked. Prepare some chocolate, tea or coffee icing (*see* recipes), and while it is hot dip the finger biscuits or cakes in the icing and leave to dry. Cakes prepared in this way are delicious, and make a nice dessert dish.

BREAD.

General Remarks.

A brick oven heated with wood is far the best to bake bread in, but we have seen excellent bread made in the ordinary camp ovens; when these are used it is desirable to make it up in very small loaves or rolls, otherwise the surface becomes hardened and browned long before the heat has penetrated to the centre of the dough.

When a brick oven is used it should be well heated with faggot wood and two or three solid logs; when it is cleared the door should be closely shut for quite half an hour before the baking commences. The heat will then be well sustained for a succession of bread, pies, cakes, and pastry.

Bread requires great care to keep it wholesome and fresh. It should, as soon as it is perfectly cold, be laid in a large earthen pan with a cover which should be kept free from crumbs and frequently scalded, and then wiped very dry for use. Loaves which have been cut, should have a smaller pan appropriated to them, and this also should have the loose crumbs wiped from it daily. The pans should stand on two pieces of wood about four inches deep, so as to allow a current of air to pass under them.

1.—To freshen Stale Bread and Pastry.

If loaves be placed in a *gentle* oven and heated quite through they will eat like newly-baked bread. Pastry can be heated in the same way. They must not however be left in it so long as to become hard and dry, but they must be heated through. *Large* loaves may be just dipped in cold water and placed in a quick oven until they are thoroughly dried. As it is very difficult to procure yeast in India we have confined ourselves to recipes for making bread without it. If carefully made, unfermented bread is quite equal to that made with yeast, but the greatest care must be taken to procure really good pure flour.

2.—Unfermented Bread.

Ingredients.
1 lb. of flour
40 grains of the purest carbonate of soda
1 teaspoonful of sugar
50 drops of muriatic acid
½ pint of water (more if needed)

Put the flour into a bowl; mix the soda and sugar with one dessertspoonful of the flour, and rub it through a hair sieve with a wooden spoon on to the flour in the bowl; stir it up well until the whole is *thoroughly* mingled; dilute the acid in the water and with it make the flour into firm dough (using more water if needful); stir it constantly into a smooth mass, divide it into a couple of loaves or small rolls and put it instantly into the oven.

Note.—Brown bread may be made in exactly the same manner, using either half meal and half flour mixed, or meal only. Baron Liebeg considers bread made with wheat only, exactly as it is ground, no part being subtracted, as far the most the nutricious and wholesome, and he directs that if possible the millers should be induced to prepare it *without* damping it first.

3.—Dairy-Bread made without Yeast.

Ingredients.
1 teaspoonful of pounded sugar
50 grains of the purest carbonate of Soda
1 saltspoonful of salt
1 lb. of flour
Some sour buttermilk

Blend the sugar and soda well together; mix the salt with the flour, put it in a basin, and rub the sugar and soda through a fine hair sieve into it. Mix them *thoroughly*, and make them into a firm but not hard dough with the butter-milk. Divide the dough into two or more loaves, and bake *at once* in a thoroughly heated but not *fierce* oven.

Note.—The buttermilk must be quite acid, but if it is the least degree rancid it will spoil the bread. This and all other unfermented bread must be baked the moment it is ready, or it will be heavy.

4.—An Indian Recipe for Bread.

Ingredients.
24 oz. of pure atta (for *brown* bread, or 24 oz. of pure soojee for *white* bread)
1 saltspoonful of salt
Some sour butter-milk
1 teaspoonful of carbonate of soda

Put the flour in a basin, sprinkle the salt over it, knead it with as much butter-milk as will make a soft dough; let it stand for a quarter of an hour; sprinkle the soda over this, mix it lightly, divide it into seven loaves, and bake *instantly* in a common *degchee* or camp oven over a moderate heat. If the dough is allowed to stand after the soda has been added the bread will be heavy.

DESSERT DISHES, DRIED FRUITS, CONFECTIONERY.

Many of the dishes given under the head of Preserves may be served as Dessert, and any kind of fruit-jelly taken out of its own pot and moulded on ice (if it is not stiff enough) makes very pretty Dessert Dishes. As it is not always easy to get good Confectionery in India, and as preserved fruits are very expensive, we give some excellent recipes for preparing certain kinds at home.

1.—Peaches in Brandy.

Pare some ripe peaches and take out the stones; prepare a syrup with seven ounces of sugar and half a pint of filtered water for every six peaches, boiled together, for ten minutes; put the peaches into the syrup and stew them very gently for eighteen or twenty minutes, turning them constantly. Pour off the syrup; boil it quickly to reduce and thicken it for ten minutes; break the stones, blanch the kernels; put the peaches with the syrup into large glass jars (empty preserve bottles do well) which they should only half fill. When they are quite cold pour in very pale French brandy to within half-an-inch of the brim; put in a few of the kernels, six or eight, and cork down the jars.

2.—Brandied Cherries.

Take some fine cherries, cut off half the length of stalks and drop them gently into bottles with wide necks; leave sufficient space in each bottle for four ounces of pounded sugar-candy; fill them up with pale fresh brandy and add a few of the kernels, or of apricot kernels, blanched, if preferred. Tie the bottles down closely.

3.—Salad of mixed Fruits.

Pick the stalks off fine strawberries and raspberries, and put a quantity of them into a bowl. Strew them very plentifully with powdered loaf sugar, and lay thick Devonshire cream (*see* recipe) entirely over the whole.

4.—Chestnuts.

Make a slight incision in the outer skin only of each chestnut, to prevent its bursting, and when all are done throw them into plenty of boiling water, with a teaspoonful of salt to each quart. Boil them for seven or eight minutes; drain them; wipe them on a coarse cloth; while still hot, roast them in a coffee roaster or in a Warren's corrugated frying pan for ten or fifteen minutes, and send them to table in a very hot napkin.

5.—Pearled Fruit.

Any fruits, such as small bunches of grapes, Cabul grapes, gooseberries, cherries, strawberries, raspberries, mulberries, &c., may be used for this dish. Very good fruit must be selected. Whip the white of a *fresh* egg with half a sherry-glass of water on a plate with the blade of a knife until both are well mixed and frothed. Dip the fruit into this mixture for an instant; roll it carefully in hot sifted sugar until it is well covered; shake it gently and lay it in rows on a wire sieve, or on sheets of white paper in bright sunshine to dry.

These fruits dished up on fresh green leaves on a compotier form one of the prettiest dessert dishes imaginable.

6.—Pistachio Shamrocks.
(Very good and very pretty.)

Whisk the white of an egg to a very firm froth; work half a pound of very fine dry sifted sugar into it, or more if needed, to bring it to a consistency in which it can be worked with the fingers. Dry the pistachio nuts at the mouth of an oven, or in the sun; roll each nut in the icing until it is covered and a good shape; lay them on sheets of thick writing paper, placing three together in the shape of a shamrock or trefoil, with a small bit of sugar twisted from the centre nut, to form a stalk; when all are ready set them in a very slow oven (or in the sun) for twenty minutes or longer, until they become quite firm without being colored. Pile up on a dish.

7.—Orange and Lemon Rings.

Cut some fine oranges and lemons into slices one-sixth of an inch thick; cut out the pulp carefully with a sharp pointed knife, leaving a very thin coating of white pith on the peel; soak these rings for twenty-four hours in cold water with a saltspoonful of salt in it; wash them, drain them, and boil them in sufficient water for them to float in till quite tender; drain them, and when they are cold dip them in brandy. Prepare some clarified sugar (*see* recipe), put in the rings, and let them remain until cold; take them out and put them on a wire sieve to dry; boil up the syrup and dip in the rings while it is hot, but not boiling; then dry them on a sieve as before; do this twice every day until they become candied. These rings should be made at the same time as jelly or punch so as to use the fruit.

Orange and lemon-rind may be preserved in the same way without being cut into rings. Merely divide them in half and take out the pulp.

8.—Chestnuts Glacé.

Make a slight incision in the outer skin only of each chestnut, and when all are done throw them into plenty of boiling water with a saltspoonful of salt to each quart. Boil them for half an hour or until tender; free them from their husks. Have ready some liquid barley sugar (*see* recipe), stick each chestnut with a fork and dip them singly in it; lay them on an oiled wire tray or sieve to dry. Serve piled up on lace papers on glass dishes.

Note.—If the barley-sugar gets too hard before the chestnuts are all ready, put the pan in which it is into another half filled with boiling water and melt it again.

9.—Pineapple Glacé.

Cut a pineapple in slices half an inch thick; peel it and cut out all the specks and eyes; prepare some clarified sugar (*see* recipe), using one pound of sugar for each pound of fruit; simmer the pineapple in it for five minutes; take it out; drain it on a wire sieve and place it in the sun or before the fire to dry for about an hour. Boil the syrup till it hangs in a long string from the skimmer, (about ten minutes will bring it to this point); dip each piece of pineapple in this; lay it on a wire sieve or fruit-drainer, and stand it in the sun. In about ten minutes the fruits may be detached without disturbing the sugar, and the fruit will be Glacé. It should be kept in a box lined with paper with strips of paper between the fruit, and stored in a very dry place.

10.—Peaches or Apricots Glacé.

The fruit must be quite ripe and sound. Wipe off the bloom, cut them in half, and take out the stones. Take one pound of sugar for each one pound of fruit and prepare some clarified sugar (*see* recipe). Dip the fruit twice into brandy; put it into the syrup and let it come slowly to the boil (five or six minutes); turn it carefully into a pan or basin, pour the syrup over, and let it stand till next day. Pour off the syrup, boil it quickly for five minutes, and pour it over the fruit boiling hot. Do this every day for a week; the last time boil it ten minutes; then put in the fruit and boil it ten minutes more. When cold take the fruit out, lay it on a sieve, dredge it over with pounded loaf sugar, and place it in the sun or on a slack oven until it is dry. Keep it in a paper box or one lined with paper, with a strip of soft writng paper round each piece of fruit.

11.—Melon Glacé.

Follow the preceding recipe, putting twenty drops of essence of vanilla into the syrup.

12.—Pears Glacé.

Follow the recipe for Peaches and Apricots Glacé.

13.—Strawberries and Cherries Glacé.

Follow the recipe for Peaches and Apricots, but they will only take three days instead of a week, and two minutes boiling on the last day.

14.—To boil Sugar from Syrup to Candy.

Make some clarified sugar (*see* recipe). Boil it quickly for five or ten minutes. It will then form a *thick* syrup, and it may be drawn out in long threads without breaking, and will hang in a long string from the skimmer. After this a few minutes boiling will cause it to whiten and form large bubbles in the pan. Continue to boil it, stir it without ceasing until it rises to the top of the pan, and then *instantly* ladle it out into paper cases or into dishes.

15.—Caramel.

Prepare the sugar as for Candy (*see* recipe), but when it begins to whiten add some lemon-juice or any kind of fruit-juice and stir it with a wooden spoon until it is a clear smooth mass. Oil a baking sheet with oil of almonds. Pour on the caramel. When it becomes set and before it cools, mark it in oblong shapes with the back of a knife. When it is cold the pieces will break off quite easily.

16.—Barley Sugar.

Prepare the sugar as for Candy (*see* recipe), using three pounds of sugar and one-and-a-quarter pints of filtered water. When it begins to whiten and bubble and to get very thick, add a few drops of essence of lemon and a tea-spoonful of citric acid. When it looks clear, pour it on to a marble slab or a shallow dish (slightly oiled), and when it begins to

DESSERT DISHES, DRIED FRUITS, CONFECTIONERY. 393

harden at the edges form it into lozenges, balls, sticks or any form you desire. If it is wanted to form into baskets or to glaçé chestnuts or small cakes, the vessel in which it is placed must be set in a pan of boiling water and liquified. Barley sugar must be put in tin canisters as soon as it is cold.

17.—Ginger Candy.

Ingredients.
1 lb. of sugar
½ of a pint of water
1 teaspoonful of the very best gioger in powder
The rind of one large lemon, freshly grated

Break the sugar into lumps; put it into a preserving pan with the water. When the sugar is nearly dissolved, set the pan on a perfectly clear fire and boil it till it becomes a thin syrup. Put the ginger in a large cup; stir two or three spoonsful of the syrup very gradually and smoothly into it; then stir it into the syrup in the pan. Watch the mixture carefully, keep it stirred with a wooden spoon and drop it often to ascertain the exact point of boiling it has reached. When it begins to fall in *flakes* instead of drops, throw in the grated lemon-rind, working the sugar round quickly as it is added. Now stir the candy constantly till it falls in a mass from the spoon and does not fall when heaped up. Then ladle out *instantly* (or it will fall into powder) and drop in cakes on to sheets of *dry* foolscap paper laid on dishes. Do not touch it until it is quite cold, when it can be moved without difficulty.

18.—Orange Flower Candy.

Ingredients.
¼ of a pint of filtered water
½ the white of an egg
2 lbs. of best loaf sugar in lumps.
3 oz. of the petals of orange blossom

Beat the egg into the water and pour it on the sugar; leave it for ten minutes; place it over a very clear fire and let it boil for a few minutes; set it on one side until the scum has subsided; clear off the scum; boil the sugar until it is very thick; strew in the orange blossoms by degrees; continue to stir the candy till it rises in a white mass in the pan, then lay it *instantly* upon thick dry sheets of paper laid quite flat on the backs of dishes or on stone slabs. Take the candy off before it is quite cold and lay the other side on the dishes. When quite cold shut them up in tin boxes.

19.—Cocoanut Candy.

Grate some cocoanuts; strain the milk; take the same weight of sugar as of cocoanut; put the sugar into an enamelled saucepan with the milk a little *above* the fire; boil and skim; when it gets thick and white, add the cocoanut and stir till it becomes a paste. When it rises in a mass turn it out and proceed as for Orange Flower Candy. *(See preceding recipe.)*

20.—Everton Toffy.

Ingredients.
3 oz. of butter
1 lb. of brown or loaf sugar

Put the butter into a preserving pan, and as it is just dissolved add the sugar; stir these gently over a very clear fire for fifteen minutes; drop a little of it into a basin of cold water, and then if it breaks clean between the teeth it is ready, if not continue to boil till it reaches this point; pour out *instantly* on to some dishes rubbed with butter or oil of almonds and leave it till cold. Some grated lemon-rind or a few drops of essence of lemon may be added to the toffy when it is half done.

21.—Almond Toffy.

Blanch the almonds, divide them and dry them in a slow

Ingredients of Almond Toffy.
1 ℔. of brown or loaf sugar
5 oz. of butter
2 ,, ,, almonds

oven or before the fire. Boil the sugar and butter together for twenty minutes; stir in the almonds, and boil together until the toffy crackles when dropped into cold water or snaps between the teeth without sticking.

22.—Chocolate Drops.

Heat a metal mortar; throw in some cake chocolate broken small, and pound it with a heated pestle till it is in a smooth paste; add the same weight of finely powdered sugar and beat them till they are thoroughly blended. Roll the mixture into small balls, lay them on sheets of writing paper, and take them off when they are nearly cold.

23.—Chocolate Bon-Bons.

Dissolve the chocolate in the water; add the sugar when it is dissolved, put the stewpan on the fire and stir till it is hot, but not boiling. Place on sheets of white paper in drops the size of a 4-anna piece.

Ingredients.
½ ℔. of coarsely sifted sugar
2 oz. of fine French chocolate
1 wineglassful of water

24.—Coffee Bon-Bons.

Put the coffee and sugar on the fire, and boil till it whitens and bubbles; then add a *very* little more coffee and work the mixture with a wooden spoon at the sides of the pan for about five minutes. When it thickens pour it out on an oiled baking sheet about one-sixth of an inch thick. When it sets, and before it cools, make it into oblong forms one inch by one-and-a-half inch; when it is quite cold the cakes can easily be snapped asunder.

Ingredients.
¼ ℔. of loaf sugar
1 small cup of very strong coffee

25.—Burnt Almonds or Pralines.

Ingredients.
½ lb of almonds
¾ of a lb. of loaf sugar
1 spoonful of vanilla sugar
Some cochineal

Rub the almonds in a cloth to clear them from dust, and put them in a slack oven or in front of the fire to dry. Prepare the sugar as for Clarified Sugar (*see* recipe), and boil it till it is white and bubbles; add the vanilla, sugar and some cochineal. Take it off the fire instantly; throw in the almonds and stir well with a wooden spoon; so soon as the almonds are well covered, turn them out on a wooden spoon and cover with paper; leave them for five minutes. Pick the almonds from the sugar and put it back into the stewpan; add enough water to dissolve it, boil it till it bubbles as before, throw in the almonds again, stir carefully, and when they are well covered with sugar turn them out again on a wire sieve. Again pick the almonds from the sugar; put it back in the saucepan with a few drops of cochineal; boil it again till it whitens and bubbles; stir in the almonds again, and when they are well covered drain them on the wire sieve as before. They should now be about three times their original size and should be served piled up on a glass compotier.

26.— Pistachio Pralines.

Prepare according to the preceding recipe.

ICES.

DIRECTIONS FOR FREEZING.

To make ices, it is necessary to have a vessel called a freezing pot, an ice-pail, and an ice-spoon. When the composition to be frozen is ready, the ice must be beaten quite small with a mallet and mixed quickly with two or three handsful of saltpetre, or double as much salt. Place the freezing-pot firmly in the centre of the ice and press the ice closely round it up to the top. Take off the cover of the ice-pot and pour in the preparation to be frozen. Work it round or backwards and forwards by means of the handle at the top, for eight or ten minutes; then scrape away the portion which has frozen to the inside of the pot with the ice-spoon and mix it with the rest, otherwise the mixture will be full of lumps, and continue the process until the whole mass is uniformly frozen.

1.—Strawberry Water Ice.

Ingredients.
2 lbs. of strawberries
Some cold clarified syrup (*see recipe*).
The strained juice of two small lemons

Strip the stalks off the strawberries; rub them through a fine sieve; mix them with enough of the syrup to make them agreeably sweet; add the lemon-juice, pour the mixture into the freezing pot, and proceed as directed above.

Note.—All water ices are made in the same way by extracting the juice from the fruit, according to the preceding recipe. Where there is no fruit, fruit syrups of any kind may be used instead. These ices are much more refreshing and wholesome than cream ices.

2.—Ginger Cream Ice.

Ingredients.
1 pint of milk
6 yolks of eggs
8 oz. of sugar
4 ,, ,, preserved ginger chopped small
2 spoonsful of its syrup
1 teaspoonful of essence of ginger, or of ground ginger

Boil the milk, stir in the beaten yolks, the sugar, and all the other ingredients in the order in which they are given. Stir over the fire until the mixture thickens slightly. Take it off, stir it a little longer, and when cold freeze it according to directions.

3.—Brown Bread Ice.

Ingredients.
8 oz. of bread-crumbs
1 pint of thick cream
6 oz. of sifted sugar
1 wineglassful of any kind of liqueur

Dry the bread-crumbs in a very slack oven; whip the cream, stir in the crumbs, sugar, and liqueur; mix well and freeze.

Note.—This cream is delicious, served with fresh strawberries.

4.—Apricot Cream Ice.

Ingredients.
10 ripe apricots
8 oz. of sugar
1 gill of water
½ pint of milk
6 yolks of eggs

Boil the apricots with six ounces of the sugar and water for ten minutes. Rub them through a hair sieve; make a plain custard with the milk, two ounces of sugar and the yolks; when it is ready stir in the fruit pulp, and when cold, freeze.

Note.—Peaches and plums are prepared in the same way.

5.—Pineapple Cream Ice.

Ingredients.
12 oz. of pineapple
1 gill of water
10 oz. of sugar
½ pint of milk
6 yolks of eggs

Peel and slice the pineapple; boil it till tender (about fifteen minutes) with the water and eight ounces of the sugar. Pound the pine, add it to the syrup, rub this through a hair sieve; make a custard with the milk, eggs, and two ounces of sugar, stir in the fruit, and freeze.

6.—Strawberry Cream Ice.

Ingredients.
1 lb. of strawberries
8 oz. of sifted sugar
1 pint of cream
10 drops of cochineal

Take the stalks off the strawberries; bruise them with the sugar; rub this through a hair sieve; add the pulp to a pint of cream; put in the cochineal, and freeze.

7.—Coffee Cream Ice.

Ingredients.
8 yolks of eggs
1 large cup of *strong* coffee
1 pint of boiled milk
8 oz. of sugar
½ pint of *thick* cream

Beat the yolks; add the coffee, milk and sugar; stir this over the fire, strain it through a hair sieve, add the cream, freeze and mould the ice.

8.—Chocolate Cream Ice.

This is prepared in the same way as the preceding recipe, except that six ounces of chocolate dissolved in a gill of hot water must be substituted for the cup of coffee.

Many of the recipes for creams may be converted into excellent ices by omitting the isinglass, and freezing according to directions.

COFFEE, TEA, CHOCOLATE.

1.—Coffee.

It is even more rare to get a good cup of Coffee than to get a good dinner or pure wine, and yet nothing is easier.

In the first place get the berry good, and if you are not certain that it has been stored for some time, keep it a year. Only as much coffee as is needed should be roasted or ground at one time, as it loses its flavour and aroma if kept. We should recommend every one to procure a coffee-roaster and grinder; they are inexpensive and simple, and it is almost impossible to get a native servant to roast coffee without burning some and leaving some raw, or to pound it without reducing it to powder. When properly roasted the berries are of a fine light brown, equally colored all over. Then grind it, *not* to powder, and use at once.

The best kind of coffee pot is Adam's percolator, or the French coffee percolator which can be procured almost anywhere and is very inexpensive. The proportions to use are *one ounce of coffee to a large breakfast cup of filtered water.* Heat the coffee pot; put the coffee into the well; place the presser on it, stand it near the fire; pour in a little boiling water, two minutes later add a little more, and so on till you have put in the requisite quantity. By attention to the foregoing, excellent coffee will invariably be produced. When coffee is served after dinner it should be handed round with lump sugar and sugar-candy and small glasses of liqueur.

2.—Tea.

There is no great difficulty in making tea, and yet how rare it is to get it really good. Filtered water should always be used, and if possible a small kettle should be kept solely for this purpose. First heat the tea-pot by pouring in scalding water; pour this out; put in the tea-leaves instantly and leave them there for two minutes; add a little water (less than a quarter of a pint); let it stand three or four minutes; fill up the tea-pot, and pour out a well made cup of tea. Serve with good fresh milk or cream, and lump sugar.

3.—Russian Tea.

A most delicious beverage for hot weather is procured by making tea as above directed (the tea should be of the very *finest* quality), and pouring it off at once into tumblers containing two lumps of sugar and one slice of lemon.

4.—Chocolate.

Rasp one ounce of good chocolate and boil it from five to ten minutes with four tablespoonsful of water. When it is quite smooth add a pint of new milk, boil it again, and stir it quickly to froth it.*

For water-chocolate, use three quarters of a pint of water instead of the milk and send rich cream to table with it.

5.—A Spanish Recipe for serving Chocolate.

Take one ounce of chocolate and half a pint of cold water for each person; rasp it in a small mortar, put it over a slow fire, and stir it quickly till it is as smooth as custard; pour it at once into cups and serve it with a glass of sugar and water, iced water or water 'ice, and with very delicate toast cut in narrow strips, or finger biscuits. Milk may be used instead of water if preferred.

DRINKING CUPS, SYRUPS, LIQUEURS, &c.

1.—Claret Cup.

Ingredients.
1 bottle of claret
2 bottles of soda water
1 sprig of mint (or burrage)
A few slices of cucumber or lemon
4 grates of nutmeg
1 liqueur glass of curaçao
1 oz. of bruised sugar-candy.

Put the mint in a wineglass of claret to infuse. Put all the ingredients into a jug; imbed it in ice; leave it for half an hour. Take it out, strain off the ingredients, add the claret in which the mint was steeped. Serve at once.

2.—Badminton Cup.

Ingredients.
1 bottle of red Burgundy
2 bottles of soda water
The rind of one orange
The juice of two oranges
1 wineglass of curaçao
1 sprig of burrage (or mint)
1 sprig of Verbena
1 oz. of bruised sugar-candy
A few slices of cucumber

Place these ingredients in a covered jug imbedded in rough ice for about one hour before it is wanted. Strain it off into another jug.

3.—Champagne Cup.

Ingredients.
1 bottle of champagne
2 bottles of soda water
1 bunch of mint or burrage
1 orange sliced, or 1 slice of a large lemon
1 oz. of pounded sugar-candy
4 grates of nutmeg

Place all these ingredients in a covered jug enbedded in rough ice for an hour, then decanter it free from the herbs, &c.

4.—Sauterne Cup.

Use the same ingredients as for Champagne Cup, substituting Sauterne for Champagne.

5.—Moselle Cup.

Use the same ingredients as for Champagne Cup, substituting Moselle for Champagne.

6.—Chablis Cup.

Use the same ingredients as for Champagne Cup, substituting Chablis for Champagne.

7.—Cider Cup.

Use the same ingredients as for Champagne Cup, substituting Cider for Champagne and adding one small glass of Cognac.

8.—Beer Cup.

Ingredients.
1 quart of stout or pale ale
½ oz. of moist sugar
A small slice of bread, toasted brown
4 grates of nutmeg
4 ,, ,, ginger

Mix the ingredients in a jug, and leave them to steep for half an hour before they are required.

9.—Oxford Punch.

Ingredients.
10 lemons
4 oranges
6 glasses of calf's-foot jelly
2 quarts of water
1 bottle of capillaire
½ ,, ,, white wine
1 pint of French brandy
1 ,, ,, Jamaica rum
1 bottle of orange shrub

Rub the rind of three lemons with lump sugar; put this sugar into a large jug with the peel of two oranges and two of the lemons cut very thin, the juice of all the oranges and lemons and the jelly, liquid. Stir these well together; pour two quarts of boiling water on them; cover the jug closely and set it near the fire for a quarter of an hour. Strain the mixture through a sieve into a punch bowl; sweeten it with the capillaire, and add the remainder of the ingredients, stirring the mixture all the while. If not sweet enough add some sugar.

10.—The Regent's Punch.

Ingredients.
3 oranges
1 lemons
½ pint of cold thin syrup
1 pint of strong green tea
Some sugar
1 glassful of old Jamaica rum
1 ,, ,, arrack
1 ,, ,, French brandy
1 ,, ,, pineapple syrup
2 bottles of champagne

Pare the oranges and lemon as thin as possible; infuse them for an hour in the syrup; add the juice of the oranges and lemons. Sweeten the tea; when it is quite cold, add it to the syrup; put in all the other ingredients, pass it through a fine muslin sieve into a jug, and put it in ice till required.

11.—Milk Punch.

Ingredients.
8 lbs. of loaf sugar
16 fine lemons
4 oranges
3 bottles of old rum
1 bottle of French brandy
1 ,, ,, old Madeira
3 quarts of boiling water
½ drachm of grated nutmeg
4 inches of cinnamon
3 pints of new milk

Rub the sugar on the lemons and oranges to extract the essence from the peel; squeeze the fruit and strain the juice. Put the sugar and juice into an earthen pan and pour the water *boiling* on to it. Take a quart jug in each hand; dip them in the liquid, lift them up and pour the liquid back rapidly from as great a height as possible; do this for twenty minutes. Then add the spirit and wine, a bottle at a time, and continue the mixing process until the punch has a smooth soft flavour; this will take about three quarters of an hour. Boil the spice in the milk; pour it into the punch; stir it *once*, quickly; then cover the pan with an earthen lid, lay a thick cloth over that, and let it remain undisturbed for eight hours. Strain it twice through flannel or three times if it is not bright; put it into bottles and cork it securely. It improves by keeping.

12.—Milk Punch.

(Another way.)

Ingredients.
10 bottles of rum
5   ,,   ,, water
2   ,,   ,, lime-juice
7 lbs. of loaf sugar
3 quarts of milk
2 nutmegs (grated)
The peel of 25 limes

Two or three days before making the Punch, steep the lime-peel in the liquor of one of the bottles of rum. Mix all the ingredients together; strain the rum in which the lime-peel has been steeped over the rest; bottle the mixture and seal the corks down.

13.—Turtle Punch.

Follow the directions for milk-punch and substitute a quart of green tea made as follows, for the milk and spice:—Put two ounces of fine gunpowder tea into a jug, pour a quart of boiling water over it, and let it stand ten minutes; then strain.

14.—Pineapple Punch.

Follow the recipe for milk-punch, substituting one pound of ripe pineapple (cut into very thin slices) for the oranges, and a quart of rice water (made as follows) for the milk:—Boil half pound of the best rice in two quarts of water till it is soft and pulpy; then strain the water through a fine sieve.

15.—Cambridge Milk Punch.

Ingredients.
2 quarts of new milk
The rind of one large lemon
½ lb. of good lump sugar
The yolks of 4 fresh eggs
⅓ of a pint of cold milk
1 pint of rum
½ ,,   ,, brandy

Put the milk, the thinly-pared lemon-rind, and sugar into a saucepan; bring it *slowly* to boil, take out the lemon-rind; take the saucepan off the fire; beat the yolks with the cold milk; strain this through a sieve; stir it into

16.—Hot Punch.

Ingredients.
1 pint of rum
1 wineglassful of brandy
1 tablespoonful of noyeau
6 oz. of loaf sugar
3 lemons
1½ pints of boiling water

Rub the sugar on the lemons to extract the essence of the peel; squeeze out the juice and strain it; put the sugar and juice in a bowl; pour the water, *boiling*, into it; stir rapidly till the sugar is dissolved; then add the spirit, and stir till it is well mixed.

17.—Whisky Punch.

Follow the preceding recipe, using a pint of Whisky instead of the three kinds of spirits mentioned.

18.—Bishop.

Ingredients.
2 bottles of either claret or port
3 oranges
3 tangerine oranges
10 oz. of loaf sugar
6 cloves
¼ of a nutmeg
2 inches of cinnamon
4 allspice

Stick the oranges with the cloves; put them into a quick oven till the skin is dry and crisp. Put the other ingredients with the wine into a saucepan and make them boiling hot. Put the oranges into a large china bowl, pour the wine over, and serve at once.

19.—Mulled Claret or Port.

Ingredients.
1 bottle of wine
5 oz. of loaf suger
3 cloves
⅙ of a nutmeg, grated

Put these ingredients into a bright tin pot with a lid; place it over a gentle heat till nearly boiling; turn it into a hot silver jug with a lid and send it to table.

20.—A French Recipe for Mulled Wine.

Ingredients.
1½ wineglassful of water
2¼ cloves
⅛ of an ounce of ginger and cinnamon pounded
2 oz. of sugar
1 pint of claret or port wine
The rind of an orange

Boil the spice in the water with the sugar and orange-rind until they form a thick syrup, which must on no account be allowed to burn. Pour in the wine, stir it till it is on the *point* of boiling; serve at once.

21.—Negus.

Ingredients
1 pint of red or white wine
1 ,, ,, boiling water
3 oz. of loaf sugar
1 lemon
½ of a nutmeg, grated

Rub the sugar on the lemon peel to extract the flavour; squeeze out and strain the juice; mix all the ingredients together and serve either hot or cold.

22.—Sherry Cobbler.

Ingredients.
1 tumblerful of clear ice, pounded
1 tumblerful of fresh strawberries
1 large wineglassful of curaçao
6 oz. of finely powdered loaf sugar
1 pint of fine old sherry

Put all the ingredients into a glass jug; stir for eight minutes; imbibe through straws or glass tubes.

23.—Gin Sling.

Ingredients.
2 slices of lemon
3 lumps of loaf sugar
1 wineglassful of old gin

Put the lemon and sugar into a large tumbler; fill up nearly to the brim with pounded clear ice; add the gin; stir and suck through a straw.

24.—Brandy Smash.

Ingredients.
3 slices of lemon
2 ,, ,, pineapple
1 dessertspoonful of sifted loaf sugar
1 wineglassful of brandy

Put the lemon, pineapple, and sugar into a large tumbler; fill up with pounded ice; add the brandy. mix well and drink.

25.—Institution Cup.

Ingredients.

1 pint of champagne
1 gill of pineapple syrup
1 ,, ,, strawberry
1 orange, sliced
1 glass of brandy
1 tumblerful of pounded ice

Shake all these well together; strain into tumblers.

26.—Pineapple Jelly.

Ingredients.

1 ripe pineapple
The juice of 2 oranges
1 gill of raspberry syrup
1 ,, ,, maraschino
1 ,, ,, old gin
1 bottle of sparkling moselle
1 lb. of clear ice, pounded

Peel and slice and cut up the pineapple into a large bowl; add the remainder of ingredients; mix well, and serve.

27.—Knickerbocker.

Ingredients.

2 tablespoonsful of lemon-water, iced
½ pint of Madeira
1 bottle of iced soda water

Mix these together and drink at once.

28.—Froster.

Ingredients.

1 gill of pale sherry
½ ,, ,, noyeau
6 peach leaves
3 slices of lemon
1 oz. of sugar
1 bottle of iced soda water
1 lump of ice

Mix all these ingredients well, and drink at once.

29.—Ching-Ching.

Ingredients.

1 gill of old rum
1 sliced orange
A few drops of essence of cloves
A ,, ,, ,, peppermint
4 lumps of sugar
1 tumblerful of pounded ice

Mix and drink at once.

30.—St. Charles.

Ingredients.

2 tablespoonsful of cherry or raspberry water, iced
1 small glass of kirsch-water
1 bottle of iced soda water

Mix and drink at once.

31.—Cocktail.

Ingredients.
3 lumps of sugar
1 dessertspoonful of Savory and Moore's essence of Jamaica-ginger
1 wineglassful of hot water

Put these into a tumbler and fill up with hot water.

32.—Mint Julep.

Put the orange-rind and juice, the sugar and mint, into a large tumbler; fill up nearly with ice, mix well; add the gin and sherry, pour rapidly from one tumbler to another, and serve at once.

Ingredients.
The thin rind of half an orange
The juice of one orange, strained
1 sprig of young mint
1 spoonful of sugar
1 glass of gin
1 " " sherry
1 tumblerful of pounded ice

33.—Ginger Beer.

Boil the ginger, sugar, and lemon-peel in the water till the sugar is dissolved; pour it into an earthen pan; put in the cream of tartar and lemon juice, and let it stand 24 hours; add the yeast; let it stand 24 hours; strain; bottle and cork securely. It will be ready for use in a week.

Ingredients.
3½ lbs. of loaf sugar
6 oz. of bruised ginger
2 " " cream of tartar
The thin rind of four lemons
The strained juice of four lemons
2 gallons of water
1 tablespoonful of good yeast

34.—Lemonade.

Mix all the ingredients in a jug imbedded in ice; let it stand for two hours. Strain through a jelly bag or very fine muslin. Serve in a large glass jug.

Ingredients.
1¼ pints of clarified syrup (*see recipe*)
2½ " " spring water
The juice of 6 lemons
The rind of 2 "

Note—A cheaper kind of lemonade is made by slicing two lemons in a jug, adding four ounces of sugar, and pouring one quart of boiling water on them.

35.—Milk Lemonade.

Ingredients.
6 oz. of loaf sugar
1 pint of boiling water
¼ of a pint of lemon juice
¼ ,, ,, ,, ,, sherry
¾ ,, ,, ,, ,, cold milk

Dissolve the sugar in the water; add the lemon juice and sherry; stir in the milk, mix well, and pass through a jelly bag till clear.

36.—Orangeade.

Ingredients.
12 oranges
4 pints of filtered water
12 oz. of sugar

Make a syrup with one pint of water and the sugar; steep the rind of three oranges in it for half an hour; extract the orange-juice from all the oranges; pass it through a clear hair sieve or muslin into a jug; add the syrup and the rest of the water; mix well and stand in ice for an hour.

37.—Strawberry Water.

Ingredients.
1 lb. of ripe strawberries
½ ,, ,, finely sifted sugar
3 pints of filtered water
The juice of one lemon

Pick off the stalks; add half a pint of the water; bruise with a wooden spoon; add the sugar; let it stand for two hours; pass it through a hair sieve and repeat the process if it is not clear. Add the remainder of the water and lemon-juice, put it into a jug, and stand in ice for an hour.

38.—Pineapple Water.

Ingredients.
A small pineapple
1 pint of boiling syrup made with one pint of water and 12 oz. of sugar
The juice of 1 lemon
1 quart of filtered water

Peel, slice, and pound the pineapple to pulp; put this into a basin; add the boiling syrup, then the lemon-juice; stir together; cover with a plate and let it stand for two hours; filter through a silk sieve or fine muslin folded in four; add the water, stand it in ice for an hour, and serve in a jug.

39.—Pomegranate Water.

Take the red pulp and put it into a basin with the sugar;
Ingredients.
6 pomegranates
12 oz. of sugar
1½ pint of water
The juice of two lemons
A few drops of cochineal

bruise well with a wooden spoon, add the water, lemon-juice and cochineal; mix and filter through a jelly-bag; stand in ice for an hour.

40.—Mango Water.

Take out all the pulp and put it in a basin with the
Ingredients.
4 mangoes
12 oz. of sugar
1½ pints of water

sugar; bruise well with a wooden spoon; add the water; mix well and stand in ice for an hour.

41.—Syllabub.

Put the sugar into a large bowl and pour the strained
Ingredients.
½ lb. of sugar, broken small
The juice of 2 lemons, strained
1 pint of port-wine
1 ,, ,, sherry
½ ,, ,, brandy
1 nutmeg
2 quarts of milk

lemon-juice on to it; stir these well together; add the port-wine, sherry, and brandy; grate in the nutmeg; hold the bowl under the cow and milk it full. In serving, put a portion of the curd into each glass, fill it up with whey and pour a little rich cream on the top.

42.—Strawberry Vinegar.

The strawberries must be ripe and freshly gathered;
Ingredients.
4 quarts of strawberries
3 quarts of vinegar
1 lb. of best loaf sugar for each
1 lb. of vinegar

weigh them and put them into large glass jars or wide-necked bottles; and to each pint pour one-and-a-half pints of fine pale white-wine vinegar. Tie a thick paper over them and let them stand two or three days. Pour off the vinegar; empty the strawberries into a jelly bag, or suspend them in a cloth that all liquid may drop from them without pressure; replace them with the same weight of fresh fruit; pour the vinegar upon this, and let it stand three days as before; repeat the process again until the flavour of the strawberries preponderates over that of the vinegar. Drain the liquid off very closely; strain it through a flannel bag, weigh it and mix it with the same weight of sugar, roughly powdered; when it is nearly dissolved, stir it in an enamelled stewpan (or a stone jar set in boiling water) over a very clear fire until it has boiled for five minutes; skim it thoroughly; pour it into a delicately clean stone bottle or china jug, cover it over with a thick folded cloth, and let it stand till next day. Put it into pint or half pint bottles, cork it *lightly*, and five days afterwards cork tightly down and store in a dry cool place.

A spoonful or two of this in a glass of iced water forms a delicious summer drink; and it makes excellent sauces for common custard, batter or rice-pudding.

43.—Cherry Brandy.

Either fresh or preserved cherries may be used. Cut off half the stalks, drop them into clean dry bottles with wide necks; for each pound of cherries add ten ounces of powdered sugar-candy; fill up the bottles with French brandy, cork securely and tie over the top. Keep for nine months before using.

A few cherry or apricot kernels put into each bottle improves the flavour.

44.—Lime Juice.
(To Preserve.)

Extract and strain the juice; bottle it; to each bottle add one teaspoonful of chalk-powder. Let it stand for two days; then strain through muslin. Bottle again and add one teaspoonful of salad oil to keep out the air. The oil will float at the top and can be removed either by pouring off, or by inserting a piece of cotton-wool which will absorb it.

ITEMS FOR INVALIDS.

1.—Beef Tea.

The beef should be very fresh; chop it into small dice, (leaving out every particle of fat), put it into a jar with the salt and water; tie it closely down; place it in a saucepan of water and let it boil gently for five hours. Strain and serve with fresh made thin toast cut in fingers.

Ingredients.
4 lbs. of beef (the upper side of the round)
1 saltspoonful of salt
3 pints of cold water

2.—Beef Tea in Haste.

When beef tea is required at once, chop two pounds of beef as fine as mincemeat, put it into a stewpan with one pint of boiling water, stir it over the fire for ten minutes, and strain it through a napkin.

3.—Extract of Beef.

Cut the beef into pieces half an inch square, free from fat; put them into a jar with one gill of water and stand it in the oven for half an hour; then add a pint of water and put it back into the oven for one-and-a-half hours; strain it through muslin and use.

Ingredients.
1 lb. of lean beef
1 gill of water
1 saltspoonful of salt

4.—Extract of Veal.

Proceed exactly as above, substituting Veal for Beef.

5.—Mutton Tea.

Cut the meat into small pieces without any fat; put it into an enamelled stewpan with the barley and cold water; stir it frequently till it boils; skim it with care. Simmer it for three hours; add the salt. Take out the mutton, strain off the tea, rubbing as much of the pulpy part of the barley through the sieve as will pass through without much pressure. Skim off every particle of fat, and serve.

Ingredients.
3 lbs. of lean mutton
1 oz. of Scotch barley
1 quart of cold water
1 saltspoonful of salt

6.—Mutton Broth.

Put all the ingredients into a stewpan and simmer for three-and-a-half hours, skimming constantly. Then strain it through a sieve into a basin and serve with dry toast cut in fingers.

Ingredients.
3 lbs. of scrag of mutton
1 turnip
1 sprig of parsley
The heart of a white lettuce
1 teaspoonful of salt
3 pints of cold water

If rice or tapioca are added they must be boiled separately till tender, put into the broth after it is strained and boiled ten minutes longer.

7.—Chicken Broth.

Cut up a fowl and break the leg bones; put it in a stewpan with the water, salt, and sugar. Boil gently, skimming constantly for four hours. Strain into a basin; when cold take off the fat and heat a cupful when required.

Ingredients.
1 fowl
1 quart of water
A teaspoonful of salt
A ,, ,, sifted loaf sugar

Note.—Very strong chicken broth may be made by following the recipe for extract of beef, using only half a pint of water.

8.—Calf's-foot Broth.

Ingredients.
1 calf's-foot
1¼ pints of new milk
1½ ,, ,, water
1 saltspoonful of salt
1 ,, ,, sifted sugar

Split the calf's-foot and put it into a fire-proof jar with all the ingredients. Tie down the jar, and bake it in a slow oven for eight hours. Strain through a sieve into a basin, and when cold remove the fat. Heat it when required for use.

9.—Convalescent Soup.

Ingredients.
1 sheep's head
2 lbs. of fresh lean beef
½ turnip
½ of a small lettuce
1 saltspoonful of salt
1 ,, ,, loaf sugar
1 ,, ,, fresh made mustard
3 pints of cold water
2 dessertspoonsful of fine oatmeal
¼ gill of water
2 tablespoonsful of port-wine

Split and wash the head; put it into a stewpan with the vegetables, salt, sugar, mustard, and cold water. Simmer gently, skimming frequently for two hours. Take out the head; cut the meat off the cheeks in neat half-an-inch pieces, free from fat; put the bones and trimmings back into the soup. Moisten the oatmeal with the gill of water and stir it into the soup; simmer two hours longer, then strain. Put the pieces of meat into the soup; simmer for three-quarters of an hour; skim off every particle of fat, add the port-wine, and serve the quantity required immediately. There will be about one-and-a half pints of soup.

10.—Savoury Custard.

Ingredients.
1 tablespoonful of Robinson's patent barley
½ pint of good beef-tea, (*see recipe*)

Stir the barley into the beef-tea; mix well and stir over the fire for five minutes.

B3

11.—Hasty Oswego Pudding.

Ingredients.
¾ pint of new milk
2 tablespoonsful of Oswego flour
1 new-laid egg

Boil the milk; stir in the flour; boil five minutes; add the egg, well-beaten; boil one minute more. Turn the pudding on a hot plate and serve with cream or honey, if permitted.

12.—Crumb Pudding with Arrowroot Sauce.

Ingredients.
1 oz. of bread, without crust
1 ,, ,, loaf sugar
¼ of a pint of new milk
1 fresh egg

Ingredients of Sauce.
1 saltspoonful of arrowroot
1 teaspoonful of cold water
½ gill of boiling water
2 teaspoonsful of sifted sugar
The yolk of a new-laid egg

Put the bread into a cool oven until it is perfectly dry but not colored; pound it to fine dust; mix the sugar, milk, and egg (well beaten) with it; beat for twenty minutes. Butter a basin, pour in the pudding, tie it over and boil rapidly for half-an-hour. Make a sauce as follows:—Mix the arrowroot with the cold water, pour the boiling water on it, stir in the sugar; beat the yolk, add it to the sauce, and beat it over the fire for one minute after it is at boiling heat.

13.—Sago.

Ingredients.
½ oz. of sago
¾ of a pint of cold water
1 dessertspoonful of sifted loaf sugar

Put the sago and water into a saucepan and boil gently for one-and-a-quarter hours. Skim it when it comes to the boil, and stir frequently. Sweeten with the sugar. If wine is ordered add two dessertspoonsful; if brandy one dessertspoonful.

14.—Tapioca Milk.

Ingredients.
½ oz. of the best tapioca
1¼ pints of new milk
1 dessertspoonful of sifted sugar

Put the tapioca and milk into a saucepan; simmer gently for two-and-a-quarter hours, stirring frequently. Sweeten with the sugar.

15.—Arrowroot.

Ingredients.
2 teaspoonsful of the best arrowroot
½ wineglassful of cold water
½ pint of boiling water
3 teaspoonsful of sifted loaf sugar

Mix the arrowroot with the cold water; add the boiling water; put it into an enamelled saucepan and stir over the fire for three minutes. Add the sugar. If wine or brandy are ordered, put in one wineglassful of white-wine, or a tablespoonful of brandy.

16.—Arrowroot Milk.

Ingredients.
2 teaspoonsful of arrowroot
1 wineglassful of new cold milk
½ pint of new boiling milk
1 dessertspoonful of loaf sugar

Mix the arrowroot with the cold milk; add the boiling milk; stir over the fire for three minutes; add the sugar.

17.—Isinglass and Eggs.

Ingredients.
⅓ oz. of best isinglass
⅓ pint of water
1 dessertspoonful of loaf sugar
3 drops of orange-flower water
The yolks of two fresh eggs

Boil the isinglass and sugar in the water; add the orange-flour water and the yolks (well beaten.) Boil up for one minute. Strain through muslin into a small mould, and serve when cold.

18.—Isinglass Jelly.

Put the isinglass in a delicately clean stewpan with the

Ingredients of Isinglass Jelly.
1 oz. of isinglass
3 " " sugar
½ pint of water
A little white wine, or some orange-juice

sugar and water; stir this over the fire until it boils, and set it on one side to simmer for twenty minutes; add a few drops of cold water from time to time to facilitate throwing up the scum; remove this as it rises; strain the jelly through a napkin into a basin; add the wine or orange-juice, pour the jelly into glasses, and stand it on ice or in a very cold place.

19.—Gruel.

Mix the groats with the cold water; when quite smooth

Ingredients.
1 dessertspoonful of Robinson's Patent Groats
½ wineglassful of cold water
¾ of a pint of boiling water

pour over the boiling water; put it in an enamelled saucepan and stir it till it boils; let it boil ten minutes. Rum, brandy, wine, or sugar may be added according to taste.

20.—Barley Water.

Put the barley with the cold water into an enamelled

Ingredients.
1 oz. of pearl-barley
Some sugar-candy crust
Some strained lemon-juice (if permitted)

saucepan and boil for two-and-a-half hours. Stir it occasionally and skim frequently. Strain it through muslin into a jug and sweeten to taste.

21.—Barley Water.
(Another way.)

Wipe the barley very clean by rolling it in a cloth; put

Ingredients.
2 tablespoonsful of pearl-barley
2 lumps of sugar
1 pinch of salt
1 strip of thin lemon-peel
2 oz. of rice
1 quart of water

it into a quart jug with the other ingredients and fill up the jug with boiling water, keeping it gently stirred for some minutes. Cover it over and let it stand for twelve or fourteen hours.

A glass of calf's-foot jelly melted may be added. The invalid should be consulted before the lemon-peel is put in, as its flavour is unpalatable to some people, and orange-juice is often preferred.

Note.—After the barley water has been poured off the jug may be filled up again with boiling water.

22.—Rice Water.

Ingredients.
2 oz. of rice
1 quart of water

Wash the rice in several waters; put it into a very clean saucepan (enamelled if you have it) with the water; boil for two-and-a-half hours, stirring and skimming frequently. Strain it into a jug through a *fine* wire sieve; rub through the part that is glutinous and goes through without pressure.

23.—Toast Water.

Toast a piece of bread slowly before a clear fire until it is browned through but not the least burnt; put it into a jug and pour a quart of boiling *filtered* water over it. Cover till cold.

24.—White Wine Whey.

Ingredients.
½ pint of new milk
1 dessertspoonful of sifted sugar
1 wineglassful of sherry or Madeira

Boil the milk and sugar; pour in the sherry; drink hot.

25.—White Wine Whey with Eggs.

Ingredients.
The yolks of two new-laid eggs
1 dessertspoonful of sifted sugar
¼ of a pint of boiling white wine

Beat the eggs with the sugar, and stir them into the wine. Drink hot.

MENU.

(For a Party of Four.)

Celery Soup.
Salmon fried with Tartar Sauce.*
Chicken with Green Peas.
Fillet of Beef, larded.
Asparagus and Eggs.
Vol-au-vent of Greengages.
Coffee Cream Ice.
Cheese Biscuits, Anchovy Butter.
Dessert.

MENU.

(For a Party of Four.)

Golden Quenelle Soup.
Turbot with Cream Sauce.*
Stewed Patridges with Soubise Sauce.
Leg of Mutton with Anchovy Sauce.
Stuffed Tomatoes.
Charlotte Russe.
Delicate Trifles and Cheese, etc.
Dessert.

---

* Any fish in season is to be substituted for these, and whenever tinned fish are mentioned, the fish of the locality, when it can be procured, is to be dressed in the same way.

MENU.

(For a Party of Eight.)

Partridge Soup.

Soles fried in Oil.

Aspic of Fillets of Chicken and Game.

Lamb Cutlets with Cucumbers.

Stewed Beef with Macaroni and Tomato Sauce.

Teal with Christopher North's Own Sauce.

Spinach Puree with Cream.

Grilled Mushrooms.

Charlotte of Apples.

Orange and Cream Jelly.

Cream Cheese, Devilled Biscuits, Maitre d'hotel Butter.

Dessert.

MENU.

(For a Party of Eight.)

Italian Soup.

Fish Cutlets with Indian Sauce.

Small fricandeau of Veal.

Mutton Cutlets with Portuguese Sauce.

Fowls braised with Beef and Chestnuts.

Snipe Pudding a l'Epicurean.

Peas a la Française.

Eggs and Mushrooms.

Nesselrode Pudding.

Oranges in Syrup.

Cream Cheese, Oat Cakes, etc.

Dessert.

MENU.

(For a Party of Six.)

———

Julien Soup.
Fish with Cream Sauce.
Sweetbreads with Green Peas.
Pigeons a la Tartare.
Saddle of Mutton with Haricot Beans.
Pheasant with Truffles.
Puree of Spinach with poached Eggs.
Pancakes with Raspberry Cream.
Noyeau Jelly.
Epicurean Butter, Cheese Straws, Cheese, etc.
Dessert.

———◆———

MENU.

(For a Party of Six.)

———

Almond Soup.
Fillets of Fish with Caper Sauce.
Mutton Cutlets, braised.
Rabbit fried in butter.
Pheasant braised, with Beef and Chestnuts.
Cheese Fondu.
Truffles a l' Italienne.
Cream Cheese, Olives, etc.,
Dessert.

MENU.

(For a Party of Four.)

Clear Soup with Poached Eggs.
Fish, buttered.
Chicken Legs in papillottes.
Shoulder of Lamb stewed with Green Peas.
Sardine Toast,
Canapees.
Iced Milanese Cream.
Cheese, etc.
Dessert.

MENU.

(For a party of Four.)

Asparagus Soup.
Vol-au-vent of Oysters.
Sheep's Kidneys stewed in Port Wine.
Fowl, braised with Tomatoes.
French Beans a la Francaise.
Dresden Patties.
Meringue of Pears.
Cheese Straws, Parsley Butter, etc.
Dessert.

MENU.

(For a Party of Six.)

Macaroni Soup.
Mayonnaise of Fish.
Chicken Croquettes with Green Peas.
Lamb Cutlets with Milanese Sauce.
Shoulder of Mutton boiled.
Gateau de riz with Strawberry Cream.
Artichokes.
Curried Toasts with Anchovies.
Buttered Cheese Biscuits, Cream Cheese.
Dessert.

MENU.

(For a Party of Ten.)

Ravinoli Soup.
Fillets of Fish with Tartar Sauce.
Timbale of Fowl and Macaroni.
Braised Mutton Cutlets.
Turkey with Chestnut stuffing.
Brisket of Beef stewed with French Beans.
Roast Partridges.
Russian Salad.
Celery with Brown Sauce.
Macedoine of whole fruits in Jelly.
Caramel Cream, iced.
Cheese Truffles, Cheese Biscuits devilled.
Dessert.

MENU.

(For a Party of Eight.)

Pea Soup.
Fillets of Fish, with Milanese Sauce.
Sweetbreads with Truffles.
Mutton Cutlets with white Mushroom Sauce.
Two Chickens for Eight persons.
Asparagus Salad.
Tomato Toast.
Russian Pudding.
Oranges filled with Jelly.
Cheese, Herrings a la Sardine, etc.

MENU.

(For a Party of Ten.)

Celery Soup.
Fried Fillets of Fish with Tartar Sauce.
Mutton Cutlets, braised.
Vol-au-vent of Sweetbreads.
Fillet of Beef, larded.
Ducks braised with Green Peas.
Russian Salad, Eggs and Mushrooms.
Souffle Pudding, Meringues a la Vanille, iced.
Pate de foie-gras, Devilled Biscuits, Cheese.
Dessert.

INDEX.

ALMOND cakes,
,, cheesecake mixture, 243.
,, paste for cakes,
,, ,, sandwiches,
,, and rice mould,
,, soup,
Almonds, to blanch and pound, 365.
,, burnt, or pralines,
,, nougat of,
American drinks, (see Drinking Cups.)
d'Anchois, roties,
Anchovies,
Anchovy butter,
,, toast,
,, ,, with poached eggs,
,, toasts, curried,
Apple cream,
,, dumplings and rice,
,, fritters,
,, hedgehog,
,, jam,
,, jelly, 350.
,, ,, cream,
,, marmalade,
,, mould,
,, sauce,
,, snow, with sponge cakes,
,, tart,
Apples, buttered,
,, charlotte of,
,, méringue of,

Apples, stewed,
,, whiskey, (for dessert,)
Apricot cream,
,, ,, ice,
,, jam,
,, jelly,
,, marmalade,
Apricots, bottled,
,, glacés,
Arrowroot,
,, biscuits,
,, milk,
Artichokes,
,, Jerusalem,
,, ,, fried,
Asparagus,
,, and eggs,
,, salad, cold,
,, soup,
,, toast,
Aspic of fillets of chicken or game,
,, jelly, 43.
,, ,, savoury,

BACON and eggs,
,, and marcaroni,
Baked flour,
Barley broth and sheep's head with mashed potatoes,
,, sugar,
,, water,
Bath chap,
Batter, French,
,, frying,
Beans, broad, à la Française,

INDEX

Beans, broad, with parsley sauce, 173.
,, French, à la Française,
,, ,, fried,
,, ,, plain,
,, ,, stewed,
,, Haricot,
Bechamel sauce,
Beef, brisket, stewed with French beans, 57.
,, extract of, *(for invalids,)*
,, fillet, larded,
,, ribs or sirloin, roast,
,, round, boiled,
,, rump steak, *see page*
,, spiced and pressed,
,, steak, with anchovy butter,
,, ,, epicurean,
,, ,, à la Française,
,, ,, and oyster pie,
,, stewed, with macaroni and tomato sauce,
,, tea,
,, ,, in haste,
,, 2nd dressing of :—
,, ,, with acid sauce,
,, ,, cutlets in paper,
,, ,, pie with potato crust,
,, ,, with sauce appetissante,
,, ,, with savoury rice,
,, ,, vinagaret of,
Beetroot, baked,
,, boiled,
,, cold, with French sauce,
,, and onions, with sauce piquante,
,, stewed,
Biscuit pudding,
Biscuits :—
 Arrowroot,
 Brown bread,
 Finger,
 ,, glacés,
 Naples,

Biscuits :—*(Continued.)*
 Plain dessert or wine,
 Sweet,
Biscuits, cheese,
,, devilled,
,, ,, dry,
,, ,, buttered,
Black onions for soup,
Blanc-manger, American,
,, currant,
,, good, common,
,, quince
,, rich,
,, rice,
Bloaters, Yarmouth,
Bottled apricots,
,, peaches,
,, strawberries,
Brains, calf's, with brown sauce,
,, ,, with white sauce,
,, ,, fried,
,, sheep's, with white sauce,
Brandy, cherry,
,, peaches in,
,, sauce,
Brawn, 111.
,, calf's head,
,, mock,
,, sauce, Oxford,
Bread :—
 an Indian recipe for, 386.
 brown,
 stale, to freshen,
 unfermented,
 without yeast,
Bread, brown, pudding,
,, ,, biscuits,
,, ,, ice,
,, and butter pastry,
,, ,, ,, pudding, plain,
,, ,, ,, pudding, rich, 289.
,, and cheese pudding,
,, crumbs, dried or prepared,
,, pudding, baked,
,, ,, ,, with marmalade,

Bread, pudding plain,
  ,,   ,,   rich,
  ,, pulled,
  ,, sauce,
Broad beans, à la Française,
  ,,   ,, with parsley sauce,
Brocoli,
Broth, calf's foot,
  ,, chicken,
  ,, mutton,
  ,,   ,, *(for invalids,)*
Brown bread,
  ,,   ,, biscuits,
  ,,   ,, ice,
  ,,   ,, pudding,
  ,,   ,, soufflé,
Brussel sprouts,
  ,,   ,, French way,
Buns, plain, without butter,
  ,, soda,
Burnt sugar, for colouring,
Butter, anchovy,
  ,, epicurean,
  ,, maitre d'hotel,
  ,, melted, 11.
  ,,   ,, for vegetables,
  ,, sauce,

CABBAGE,
  ,,   stewed,
  ,,   stuffed,
Cabinet pudding,
  ,,   ,, very rich,
Cakes :—
  Almonds,
  Banbury,
  Chantilly,
  Cream,
  Genoa,
  Guernsey,
  Macaroon,
  Madeira,
  Oat,
  Oswego,
  Plum,
  ,, rich,
  Pound,
  Queen's,

Cakes :—*(Continued.)*
  Rice,
  ,, *(another)*,
  Savoy,
  Seed,
  Soda,
  Spong,
  Tea,
Cakes, almond paste for,
  ,, almonds to blanch and pound for,
  ,, chocolate icing for,
  ,, sugar icing for,
  ,, tea or coffee, icing for,
Calf's brains with brown sauce,
  ,,   ,, with white sauce,
  ,,   ,, fried,
  ,, feet with sharp sauce,
  ,, foot broth,
  ,,   ,, stock,
  ,, head, boiled, with white sauce,
  ,, head brawn,
Calves' feet jelly,
  ,,   ,,   ,, lemon,
  ,,   ,,   ,, orange,
Canapees,
  ,, cheese,
Candy, cocoanut,
  ,, ginger,
  ,, orange flower,
  ,, sugar,
Caramel,
Carrot soup,
Carrots,
  ,, with butter,
  ,, à la Française,
  ,, purée of,
Casserole of rice,
  ,,   ,,   ,, sweet,
Cauliflower, plain,
  ,,   with Parmesan cheese,
  ,,   stewed,
Celery sauce,
  ,, soup,
  ,, stewed with brown sauce,

Celery stewed with white sauce,
Chantilly basket with whipped cream and strawberries,
Charlotte pudding,
,, of apples,
,, jam or marmalade,
,, à la Parisienne,
,, Russe,
Chartreuse of vegetables,
Cheese biscuits,
,, and bread pudding,
,, boiled,
,, canapees,
,, cream, and
,, damson,
,, guava,
,, ramakins,
,, soufflé or fondu,
,, stewed,
,, straws,
,, toast,
Cheesecake,
,, almond,
,, lemon,
,, orange,
Cherries, compôte of,
,, brandied,
,, glacés,
Cherry brandy,
,, sauce,
Chestnut pudding,
,, baked,
,, ,, iced,
Chestnuts,
,, glacés,
Chicken, aspic of fillets of,
,, broth,
,, with green peas,
,, legs en papillotes,
,, and onions,
,, à la Tartare,
,, sandwiches,
Chickens, two for eight persons,
Chocolate,
,, a Spanish recipe for,
,, bon-bons,
,, cream,

Chocolate, cream without cream, 327.
,, ,, ice, 403.
,, custards, and
,, drops,
,, icing for cakes,
Christopher North's own sauce,
Chutney, ne-plus-ultra,
,, sauce,
Clarified syrup of jellies,
,, isinglass,
Compôte of cherries,
,, ,, peaches, &c.,
,, ,, strawberries,
Cocoanut candy,
,, cream,
,, pudding,
Coffee, and
,, bon-bons,
,, cream, 326.
,, cream ice,
,, icing for cakes,
,, soufflé,
Confectionery, (see Dessert Dishes)
Convalescent soup,
Cornflour, Indian, pudding,
Cream, apple, (for puddings,)
,, brandy,
,, cake,
,, cheese, and
,, curds,
,, ,, (without rennet),
,, Devonshire,
,, ices,
,, pastry,
,, raspberry, (for puddings,)
,, soufflé,
,, sauce.
,, strawberry, (for puddings,)

Creams :—
Apple,
Apricot,
Bavarian,
Caramel,
Celestine,
Chocolate,

INDEX. 433

Creams :—*(Continued.)*
    Chocolate without cream, 237.
    Cocoanut,
    Coffee,
    Currant jelly,
    Fruit syrup,
    Franchipane,
    Ginger,
    Italian,
    Lemon,
    Milanese,
    Millefruit,
    Orange,
    Peach,
    Pineapple,
    Quince,
    Raspberry,
    Ratafia,
    Rhenish,
    Stone,
    Strawberry,
    Swiss,
    Vanilla,
    Velvet,
Crême, gertrude à la,
  ,, au thé,
  ,, gateau à la,
Croquettes of fowl,
  ,, ,, potato,
  ,, ,, rice,
  ,, ,, ,, finer,
Crôustade of sweetbreads, mushrooms and potato balls,
Crumb pudding,
  ,, ,, *(for invalids,)*
  ,, dried or prepared,
Crust, cream,
  ,, French, for meat pies,
  ,, suet, common,
  ,, ,, excellent,
  ,, for tarts,
Cucumber,
  ,, stewed, brown,
  ,, ,, white,
Cups, *(See Drinking Cups.)*
Curaçao sauce,
Curds, rennet, for making,

Curds, cream,
  ,, ,, without rennet,
  ,, and whey,
Curded milk,
Currant custard,
  ,, jelly cream,
  ,, ,, red,
  ,, juice blanc-manger,
  ,, pudding,
Currants, to clean,
Curried eggs,
  ,, fish,
  ,, fowl,
  ,, rabbit,
  ,, toasts with anchovies,
  ,, vegetables,
Curries :—
    Egg,
    Fish,
    Fowl,
    Kid,
    Kid and egg,
    Meat, egg, and vegetable,
    Mutton, egg and vegetable, 155.
    ,, ,, and pistachio Nut,
    ,, and mangoe,
    Partridge,
    Rice, to boil for,
Curry powders,
  ,, rice,
Custard,
  ,, currant,
  ,, Duke's,
  ,, fritters,
  ,, pudding, baked,
  ,, pudding, boiled,
  ,, ,, Oswego,
  ,, Queen's,
  ,, savoury,
  ,, with snow balls,
  ,, whip,
Custards, chocolate, and

DAMSON cheese,
  ,, jelly,
Delicate trifles,

Dessert dishes:—
   Almond toffee,
   Apples, whiskey,
   Apricots glacés,
   Barley sugar,
   Brandied cherries,
   Burnt almonds,
   Caramel,
   Cherries, glacés,
   Chestnuts,
      ,, glacés,
   Chocolate bon-bons,
      ,, drops,
   Cocoanut candy,
   Coffee bon-bons,
   Everton toffee,
   Ginger candy,
   Lemon rings,
   Melon glacés,
      ,, preserved,
   Orange rings,
   Orange flower candy,
   Peaches glacés,
      ,, in brandy
      ,, preserved,
   Pearled fruit,
   Pears glacés,
      ,, stewed,
   Pineapple glacés,
   Pistachio pralines,
      ,, shamrocks,
   Pumpkin ginger,
   Strawberries glacés,
   Salad of mixed fruits,
Devil mixture,
Devilled biscuits,
   ,, ,, buttered,
   ,, ,, dry,
   ,, salmon, sardines, &c.,
Devonshire cream,
   ,, junket,
Dresden Patties,
Drinking Cups:—
   Badminton Cup,
   Beer Cup,
   Bishop,
   Brandy Smash,
   Chablis Cup,

Drinking Cups:—*(Continued.)*
   Champagne Cup,
   Ching-Ching,
   Cherry Brandy,
   Cider Cup,
   Claret Cup,
   Cock Tail,
   Froster,
   Ginger Beer,
   Gin Sling,
   Institution Cup,
   Knickerbocker,
   Lemonade,
   Lime juice, *(to preserve)*
   Mango water,
   Milk Lemonade,
   Mint Julep,
   Moselle Cup,
   Mulled Claret,
      ,, Port,
      ,, wine,
   Negus,
   Orangeade,
   Pineapple jelly,
      ,, water,
   Pomegranate water,
   Punch, Cambridge milk,
      ,, Hot,
      ,, Milk,
      ,, Oxford,
      ,, Regent's,
      ,, Turtle,
      ,, Pineapple,
      ,, Whisky,
   Sauterne Cup,
   Sherry Cobbler,
   St. Charles,
   Strawberry water,
      ,, vinegar,
   Syllabub,
Dried Fruits *(see Dessert Dishes.)*
Ducks, braised,
   ,, or ducklings, roast,
   ,, wild,
Dumplings, apple and rice,
   ,, apple, baked,
   ,, apple and plum,
   ,, currant, light,

INDEX. 435

Dumplings, lemon,
Dutch sauce,
" flummery,

EGGS and asparagus,
" bacon,
" boiled,
" á la bonne femme,
" buttered,
" " with truffles,
" with cheese,
" curried,
" aux fins herbes,
" grated,
" au gratin,
" and mushrooms,
" with nut brown butter,
" au plat,
" in paper cases,
" poached,
" " with anchovy toast,
" sandwiches,
" à la tripe,
" turkey, forced,
Endive, stewed,
Entrées:—
  Aspic of fillets of chicken or game,
  Beef, fillet, larded,
  " steak, epicurean,
  " " à la Française,
  " stewed with macaroni & tomato sauce,
  " 2nd. dressings of:—
  " with acid sauce,
  " cutlets in paper,
  " with sauce appetissante, 97.
  " with savoury rice,
  Calf's brains with brown sauce,
  " " with white sauce,
  " " fried,
  " feet with sharp sauce,
  Casserole of rice,

Entrées:—(Continued.)
  Chicken fillets, aspic of,
  " with green peas,
  " legs, en papillottes,
  Chickens, for persons,
  " à la Tartare,
  Croustade of sweetbreads, mushrooms and potato balls,
  Fowl. croquettes of,
  " fricasseed,
  " minced with savoury rice,
  " timbale of, with macaroni,
  Game, salmi of,
  Hare, jugged,
  Lamb, chops,
  " cutlets,
  " " with cucumbers,
  " pelau,
  " sweetbreads, roasted with green peas,
  Mutton cutlets, braised,
  " " bread crumbed,
  " " with Portuguese sauce,
  " " with white mushroom sauce,
  " fillets of,
  Mutton, 2d dressings of:—
  " cutlets, minced with tomato sauce,
  " cutlets, pounded, with Tartar sauce,
  " hashed, venison fashion,
  " minced, with macaroni,
  " with mushrooms,
  Ox-palates, stewed,

Entrées :—(Continued.)
  Ox-tail, broiled,
  Partridges, braised,
    ,,   with cabbages,
    ,,   stewed with celery, and soubise sauce,
  Patties, Dresden,
    ,,   veal,
  Pheasant, pulled,
    ,,   salmi of,
  Pigeons, boiled,
    ,,   roast,
    ,,   stewed,
    ,,   à la Tartare, 135.
  Rabbit, brown fricassee of,
    ,,   fried in butter,
    ,,   à la Tartare,
  Rump steak with fried potatoes,
    ,,   ,, stewed with oysters,
  Sausages and chestnuts, 113.
  Sheep's brains with white sauce,
    ,,   kidneys stewed in port wine,
  Sweetbreads, Croûstade of, 98.
    ,,   with green peas,
    ,,   veal, with truffles,
  Timbale of macaroni with fowl,

Entremets, Savoury :—
  Anchovy toast,
    ,,   ,, with poached eggs,
    ,,   ,, curried,
  Asparagus and eggs,
    ,,   salad, cold,
    ,,   toast,
  Beans, French, à la Française,

Entremets :—(Continued.)
  Brussels sprouts, French way,
  Canapees,
  Celery stewed with brown sauce,
    ,,   ,, with white sauce,
  Cheese and bread pudding, 213.
    ,,   boiled,
    ,,   ramakins,
    ,,   soufflé or fondu,
    ,,   stewed,
  Delicate trifles,
  Eggs and asparagus,
    ,, with cheese,
    ,, and mushrooms,
    ,, in paper cases,
    ,, with anchovy toast,
    ,, turkey's, forced,
  Macaroni, savoury,
    ,,   ,, with cheese,
  Macedoine of vegetables,
  Mushrooms, baked,
    ,, fried,
    ,, grilled,
    ,, toast,
  Oysters, scolloped,
    ,, vol-au-vent of,
  Onions and beet-root with sauce piquante,
  Peas à la crême,
  Portugal onions, stuffed,
  Rice, Florentine fashion,
    ,, Piedmontese fashion,
    ,, Polish fashion,
  Rizzoletti,
  Rôties d'anchois,
  Russian salad,
  Salsifis, fried,

INDEX. 437

Entremets:—(Continued.)
   Sardine toast,
   Scotch woodcock,
   Sea kale,
   Spinach and poached, eggs,
   ,, purée with cream,
   Toast, kidney,
   ,, tomato,
   Toasts, savoury,
   Tomatoes à la Provençale,
   ,, stuffed,
   Truffles à Italienne,
   ,, à la Piedmontaise,
   ,, à la Serviette,
   Turkey's eggs, forced,
   Turnips glacés with sugar,

   Vegetable marrow, stuffed,

   Welch Rabbit,
Epicurean butter,

FIG pudding,
Fish,
   ,, curried,
   ,, scolloped,
   ,, sauce for cold,
   ,, sandwiches,
Flavourings, 23.
Flour, baked,
Flummery, Dutch,
Fondu, cheese,
Forcemeat of veal,
Fowl, boiled,
   ,, braised with tomatoes,
   ,, ,, with braised beef and chestnuts,
   ,, croquettes of,
   ,, curried,
   ,, devilled,
   ,, fricasseed, white,
   ,, ,, in oil,
   ,, Guinea, larded,
   ,, mayonnaise of,
   ,, minced with savoury rice,

Fowl pie,
   ,, pulled,
   ,, quenelles of,
   ,, roast, with gravy and bread sauce,
   ,, with savoury macaroni,
   ,, timbale of, with macaroni,

Freezing, directions for,
French beans à la Française,
   ,, ,, fried,
   ,, ,, plain,
   ,, ,, stewed,
Fritters, apple,
   ,, cake and pudding,
   ,, custard,
   ,, lemon,
   ,, peach,
   ,, plain,
   ,, potato,
   ,, orange,
   ,, rice,
Fruit salad,
   ,, syrup cream,
   ,, vol-au-vent,
Fruits, dried, for dessert,

GALETTE, a French,
Game,
   ,, aspic of fillets,
   ,, sandwiches with Tartar sauce,
Garlic,
Gâteau à la crême,
   ,, de riz, and
German sauce,
   ,, ,, *(for puddings,)*
Giblets, stewed,
   ,, soup,
Ginger beer,
Gingerbread, good common,
   ,, nuts,
   ,, rich,
   ,, thick light,
Ginger cream,
   ,, ,, ice,
   ,, pudding,
   ,, pumpkin,

438   INDEX.

Glaze,
Goose, roast,
  ,,   ,, with tomatoes and chestnuts,
Gooseberries, méringue of,
Gooseberry fool,
  ,, jam,
  ,, sauce,
Greengage mould,
  ,, jam,
Green sauce,
Grilled kippered salmon,
Gruel,
Guava cheese,
  ,, jelly,
Guinea fowl, larded and roasted,

HADDOCKS, dried,
    am, baked, 110.
  ,, boiled,
  ,,   ,, French way, and 110.
Hare, braised,
  ,, jugged,
  ,, roast,
Haricot beans,
Herb seasoning, Francatelli's, 24.
Horse-radish sauce,
Hotch potch,

CES :—
    Apricot cream,
    Brown bread,
    Chocolate cream,
    Coffee cream,
    Ginger cream,
    Pineapple cream,
    Strawberry cream,
      ,, water,
Icing, tea or coffee,
  ,, chocolate,
  ,, sugar,
Irish stew,
Italian soup,
  ,, sweetmeat,
Items for Invalids :—
    Arrowroot,

Items for Invalids :—*(Continued.)*
    Arrowroot milk,
    Barley water,
    Beef, extract of,
    ,, tea,
    ,,   ,, in haste,
    Calf's foot broth,
    Chicken broth,
    Convalescent soup,
    Crumb pudding, 418.
    Custard, savoury,
    Gruel,
    Isinglass and eggs,
    ,, jelly,
    Mutton broth,
    ,, tea,
    Oswego pudding,
    Rice water,
    Sago,
    Tapioca milk,
    Toast water,
    Veal, extract of,
    White wine whey,
    ,,   ,,   ,, with eggs, 421.
Isinglass, to clarify,
  ,, and eggs,
  ,, jelly,

JAM Charlotte,
  ,, pudding,
  ,,   ,, boiled,
  ,, rolls, baked,
Jams :—
    Apple,
    Apricot,
    Gooseberry,
    Nectarine,
    Greengage,
    Peach,
    Raspberry,
    Rhubarb,
    Strawberry,
Jaune-manger,
Jellies :—
    Apple,
    Apricot,
    Aspic,

INDEX.

Jellies:—*(Continued.)*
  Aspic, savoury,
  Calves' feet,
    ,, ,, lemon,
    ,, ,, orange,
  Damson,
  Gooseberry, Cape,
  Grape,
  Guava,
  Isinglass, *(for invalids,)*
  Macedoine of whole fruits in, 343.
  Maraschino,
  Mixed fruit,
  Noyeau,
  Orange and cream,
  Orange,
    ,, *(to keep,)*
  Peach,
  Pineapple,
  Punch,
  Plum,
  Quince,
  Raspberry,
  Red currant,
  Red plum,
  Rhubarb,
  Stockmeat,
  Strawberry,
    ,,
Jugged hare,
Junket, Devonshire,

KABOBES and Kedcheree,
Kanapees,
Kale cannon,
Kedcheree,
Ketchup, mushroom,
  ,, sauce,
Kidneys, ox, grilled,
  ,, ,, stewed,
  ,, sheep's broiled,
  ,, ,, stewed in port wine,
  ,, on toast,
  ,, omelet,
Kitchen utensils,

LAMB chops,
  ,, cutlets,
  ,, ,, with cucumbers,
  ,, forequarter,
  ,, haunch,
  ,, head,
  ,, leg, boiled,
  ,, ,, roast,
  ,, pelau,
  ,, ribs or target,
  ,, saddle,
  ,, shoulder,
  ,, stewed with peas,
  ,, sweetbreads roasted with green peas,
Leeks, boiled,
  ,, stewed,
Lemonade,
  ,, milk,
Lemon calves' feet jelly,
  ,, cream.
  ,, juice, 23.
  ,, cheese cakes,
  ,, fritters,
  ,, rings,
  ,, marmalade,
  ,, sandwiches,
  ,, sauce,
  ,, sponge,
  ,, suet pudding,
  ,, tartlets, common,
Lettuces, stewed,
Leveret, braised,
Lime juice, *(to preserve,)*
Ling pie,
Liqueurs, *(see Drinking Cups.)*
Liver and bacon,
Lobster salad,
  ,, sauce,

MACARONI with bacon,
  ,, ,, bread-crumbs,
Macaroni Portuguese,
  ,, pudding,
  ,, ,, savoury,
  ,, à la reine,

Macaroni, savoury,
,, ,, with cheese,
,, soup,
,, sweet,
,, timbale of, with fowl,
Macaroon cakes,
Macaroons, almond,
,, orange flower,
Macedoine of whole fruits in jelly, 343.
,, of vegetables,
Mahaseer, boiled,
,, cold,
,, ,, sauce for,
Maître d'hotel butter,
,, ,, sauce,
Maraschino syrup,
,, jelly
Marmalade, apple,
,, apricot,
,, charlotte,
,, lemon,
,, nectarine,
,, orange,
,, ,, clear,
,, ,, fine,
,, peach,
,, pineapple,
,, pudding,
,, quince,
,, Scotch,
Marrow pudding,
Mayonnaise of fowl,
,, ,, salmon,
,, sauce,
Melon, glacés,
,, preserved,
Melted butter,
,, ,, for vegetables,
Ménus, to
Méringue of apples,
,, ,, pears,
,, ,, rhubarb,
,, ,, tart,
Méringues,
Mince-meat,

Mince-meat, pudding,
Mince pies,
,, ,, with egg icing,
Milk, curded,
,, lemonade,
,, punch, and
Mint sauce,
Mock turtle soup,
Mould, almond and rice,
,, apple,
,, greengage,
,, lemon rice,
,, rhubarb,
Moulds,
Mulled claret,
,, port,
,, wine, a French recipe,

Mulligatawny soup,
Mushroom ketchup,
,, toast,
Mushrooms baked, and
,, and eggs,
,, fried,
,, grilled,
,, stewed,
Mutton chops, plain,
,, cutlets, braised,
,, ,, bread crumbed, 83.
,, ,, with Portuguese sauce, 84.
,, ,, ,, white mushroom sauce, 84.
,, broth,
,, ,, (for invalids,)
,, fillets,
,, leg, boiled,
,, ,, roast,
,, ,, with anchovy sauce.
,, loin, roasted,
,, ,, stuffed,
,, saddle of,
,, shoulder, boiled,
,, ,, roast,
,, steak and fried potatoes,
,, tea (for invalids,)
,, 2nd dressings of :—

INDEX.

Mutton cutlets, minced, with tomato sauce,
,, ,, pounded with Tartar sauce,
,, fillet,
,, hashed, venison fashion,
,, minced, with macaroni,
,, with mushrooms,
,, saddle, à la Polonnaise,

NECTARINE jam,
,, marmalade,
Nectarines preserved,
Nesselrode pudding,
Nougat of almonds,
,, Parisian,

OAT CAKES,
Omelets, with cheese,
,, common,
,, good,
,, ham, tongue or hung beef,
,, kidney,
,, light,
,, oyster,
,, savoury, 208.
,, soufflé,
,, sweet,
,, ,, potato,
,, with preserve,
Once a week (rice mould,)
Onion sauce,
,, soup, brown,
,, ,, white,
Onions, black, for soup,
,, and beetroot with sauce piquante,
,, Portugal, boiled,
,, ,, fried,
,, ,, roasted,
,, ,, stewed,
,, ,, stuffed,
Orangeade,
Orange calves' feet jelly,
,, and cream jelly,
,, fritters,
,, flower candy,

Orange flower macaroons,
,, jelly, fine, and
,, marmalade,
,, ,, clear,
,, rings,
,, salad,
Oranges filled with jelly,
,, in syrup,
Oswego cake,
,, custard pudding,
,, ,, ,, hasty,
Ox-kidney, grilled,
,, stewed,
Oxford brawn sauce,
Ox-palates, stewed,
Ox-tail broiled,
Oyster patties,
,, omelet
,, sauce,
,, soup,
,, vol-au-vent,
Oysters,
,, fried,
,, scolloped,

PALESTINE soup,
Pancakes,
,, French,
,, rice,
,, rich,
Parsley sauce,
Parsnips, boiled,
,, fried in batter,
,, ,, plain,
Partridge, braised,
,, ,, with cabbages,
,, roast,
,, soup,
,, stewed with celery or soubise sauce,
,, with tomato sauce,
Paste, very good, light,
Pastry,
,, or almond paste sandwiches,
,, bread and butter,
,, cream,
,, stale, to freshen,

INDEX.

Patties, Dresden,
„ veal,
Pea soup,
„ „ green,
Peach cream,
„ fritters,
„ jam,
„ jelly, 349.
„ marmalade,
Peaches, in brandy,
„ bottled,
„ compôte of,
„ glacés,
„ preserved whole,
Pearled fruit,
Pears glacés,
„ méringue of,
„ stewed,
„ „ (for dessert,)
Peas green, à la Française,
„ „ à la crême,
„ „ plain,
„ „ purée of, for garnish,

Pelaus :—
Pelau, lamb,
Fish,
Fowl and Egg,
Meat and Egg,
„ and Plantain,
Pheasant, cold, with Balbirnie sauce,
„ boiled, with celery sauce,
„ braised, with beef and chestnuts,
„ pulled,
„ roast,
„ salmi of,
„ sauce for cold,
„ with truffles,
Pickled walnuts,
Pig, sucking, roast, 108.
„ „ „ with chestnuts,

Pigeons, boiled,
„ broiled,
„ pie,
Pigeons, roast,
„ stewed,
„ à la Tartare,
Pineapple cream,
„ glacé,
„ ice, 398.
„ jelly,
„ jelly cup,
„ marmalade, 355.
„ preserved,
„ punch,
„ water,
Pippins, stewed,
Pistachio pralines,
„ shamrocks,
Plaits,
Plum jelly, red,
Poached eggs with anchovy toast,
Pork cutlets, with mushroom sauce,
„ fillets, with apple sauce,
„ loin, French fashion,
„ „ roast,
Potato croquetts,
„ fritters,
„ flour soufflé, 248.
„ hash,
„ omelet,
„ pudding,
„ puffs,
„ salad,
„ soup,
„ snow,
Potatoes, baked,
„ boiled,
„ fried,
„ à l'Italienne,
„ mashed,
„ à la maître d'hotel,
„ new,
„ „ in butter,
„ „ à la crême,
„ „ à la Provençale,
Potted veal and tongue,
Poultry,
Preserved melons,
„ nectarines, 358.

INDEX. 443

Preserved peaches, whole,
,, pineapple,
,, quinces,
,, vegetables,
Preserves,
,, stewed,
Puddings :—
  Almond and potato,
  Apple,
  ,, baked,
  Baked jam roll,
  Bakewell,
  Batter, baked,
  ,, common,
  ,, Derbyshire,
  ,, fruit,
  Biscuit,
  Bread, baked,
  ,, brown,
  ,, and cheese,
  ,, with marmalade,
  ,, plain,
  ,, rich,
  ,, and butter, plain,
  ,, ,, ,, rich,
  Cabinet,
  ,, a very rich,
  Charlotte,
  Chestnut,
  ,, baked,
  ,, iced,
  Clarence,
  Cocoanut,
  College,
  Cornflour, Indian,
  Crumb,
  ,, (for invalids)
  Cup,
  Currant, 278.
  Custard, baked,
  ,, finer,
  ,, boiled,
  Diplomatic,
  Fig,
  Gâteau de riz, &
  Ginger,

Puddings :—(Continued.)
  In haste,
  Jam,
  ,, boiled,
  Jersey,
  Lemon,
  ,, suet,
  Macaroni,
  ,, Savoury,
  Marmalade,
  Marrow,
  Mincemeat,
  Nesselrode,
  Oatmeal,
  Oswego custard,
  ,, (for invalids)
  Paradise,
  Parisian,
  Pineapple,
  Plum, a Christmas,
  ,, an excellent,
  Plum, small,
  ,, vegetable,
  Potato,
  ,, and almond,
  ,, a rich,
  for a Prince,
  Prince Albert, No.
  ,, No.
  Publisher's,
  Raisin,
  Rice, baked,
  ,, ,, without eggs,
  ,, boiled, good,
  ,, ,, with raisins,
  ,, plain,
  ,, ground,
  ,, ,, cup,
  ,, ,, plain,
  ,, méringue,
  ,, rich,
  ,, savoury,
  Rump steak and oyster,
  Rusk,
  Russian,
  Sago,
  Semolina, &

444 INDEX.

Puddings :—*(Continued.)*
  Semolina, French,
  Soojee,
    ,, another,
  Sponge cake,
  Soufflé,
  to steam in a common saucepan,
  Tapioca, baked,
    ,, boiled,
  Vermicelli,
  Yorkshire,
    ,, family,
  Young wife's,
  Zandima,
Puff paste, English,
,, ,, French,
,, ,, Patties,
Puffs, hasty,
,, German,
,, Polish,
,, potato
Pulled bread,
Pumpkin ginger,
Punch, *(see Drinking Cups.)*
,, jelly,

QUAIL, roast,
  Quenelle forcemeat of veal,
Quince juice blanc-manger,
,, jelly,
,, jelly cream,
,, marmalade,

RABBIT, boiled,
  ,, brown fricasse of,
  ,, curry,
  ,, fried in batter,
  ,, pudding,
  ,, à la Tartare,
  ,, Welsh,
Raisin pudding,
Raspberry cream,
,, ,, *(for puddings,)*
  ,, jelly, 340.
Ratafia cream,

Raviuoli Soup,
Rennet *(for making curds,)*
,, jam,
Rhubarb, jelly,
,, méringue of,
,, mould,
Rice and almond mould,
,, apple dumplings,
,, blanc-manger,
,, cake,
,, casserole of,
,, ,, ,, sweet,
,, croquettes,
,, ,, finer,
,, for curry,
,, Florentine fashion,
,, flour soufflé,
,, fritters,
,, gâteau, and
,, and haddock,
,, kedgeree,
,, lemon mould,
,, pancakes,
,, Piedmontese fashion,
,, Polish fashion,
,, shape of,
,, shape of ground,
,, savoury, and
,, ,, pudding,
,, Spanish fashion,
,, sweet,
,, Rizzoletti,
,, water, *(for invalids,)*
Rosengrötze,
Rôties d'anchois,
Rump steak, broiled,
,, ,, with fried potatoes,
,, ,, kidney and oyster pudding,
,, ,, pie,
,, ,, stewed with oysters,
Rusk pudding,
Rusks, sweet,
Russian pudding,

SAGO pudding,
  ,, *(for invalids,)* 418.

INDEX.

Salads :—195.
    Asparagus, cold,
    Cold meat,
    Flemish,
    French,
    Fruit,
    English, and
    Lobster,
    Orange *(for Dessert,)*
    Potato,
    Russian,
    Tomato,
    Vegetable, hot,
Salmi of snipe or other game,
  ,, ,, wild fowl,
Salmon, boiled,
  ,, cutlets with Milanese sauce, 45.
  ,, ,, ,, Indian sauce,
  ,, fried, with Tartar sauce,
  ,, kippered, grilled,
  ,, mayonnaise,
  ,, 2nd dressing of,
Salsifis,
  ,, fried,
Sandwiches, chicken or game,
  ,, egg and cress,
  ,, fish,
  ,, game and Tartar sauce,
  ,, lemon,
  ,, minced,
  ,, pastry or almond paste,
Sardine toast,
Sardines,
Sauces, *for Fish, Meats and Vegetables:*—
    Anchovy butter,
    Appetissante,
    Apple,
    Bechamel,
    Brawn, Oxford,
    Bread,
    Butter,
    Caper,
    Celery, 13.

Sauces :—*(Continued.)*
    Christopher North's,
    Chutney,
    for cold pheasant,
    ,, ,, fish, and
    Cream,
    Dutch,
    Epicurean butter,
    German, and
    Green,
    Gooseberry,
    Horse-radish,
    Indian,
    Lobster,
    Ketchup,
    Mahaseer, for cold,
    Maître d'hotel,
    ,, ,, butter,
    Mayonnaise,
    Melted butter, 11.
    Milanese,
    Mint,
    Onion,
    Oxford brawn,
    Oyster,
    Parsley,
    Shrimp,
    Soubise,
    Spinach,
    Tapp,
    Tartar,
    Tomato,
    ,, *(to keep,)*
    White,
Sauces, *for Puddings and Sweet Dishes:*—
    Apple cream,
    Brandy,
    ,, cream,
    Curaçoa,
    Cherry,
    Cocoanut cream,
    Custard whip,
    German,
    Lemon,
    Maraschino syrup,
    Orange cream,
    Pineapple,

INDEX.

Sauces :—(*Continued*).
    Punch,
    Raspberry,
    Sweet,
    Strawberry,
    Very rich,
    Victoria,
    Vanilla,
    Wine,
Sausages and chestnuts,
Scones, soda,
Scotch short bread, and
    ,, woodcock,
Sea-kale,
Semolina pudding,
    ,, ,, French,
Sheep's brains with white sauce,
    ,, kidneys, broiled,
    ,, ,, stewed in port wine,
    ,, head,
    ,, ,, with barley broth and mashed potatoes,
    ,, liver and bacon, &
Shortbread,
    ,, excellent Scotch,
Shrimp sauce,
Snipe and woodcock,
    ,, pudding à ' epicurien,
    ,, potted,
    ,, salmi,
Snow balls, with custard,
Soda cake,
    ,, buns,
    ,, scones,
Soles, buttered,
    ,, fillets of,
    ,, fried in oil,
Sorrel,
    ,, stewed,
Soubise sauce,
Soufflé, brown bread,
    ,, cheese,
    ,, coffee,
    ,, cream,
    ,, fruit,
    ,, omelet,
    ,, potato flour, 248.

Soufflé pudding,
    ,, rice flour,
Soups :—2.
    Almond,
    Asparagus,
    Carrot,
    Celery,
    Convalescent (*for Invalids,*) 417.
    Economical, Nos. &
    Giblet,
    Gravy, clear,
    ,, thick,
    Green Pea,
    Hotch-potch, Scotch,
    Italian,
    Julien,
    Macaroni,
    Mock turtle,
    Mulligatawney,
    ,, pea-fowl,
    Mutton broth,
    Onion, brown,
    ,, white,
    Oyster,
    Palestine,
    Partridge,
    Pea,
    Pea-fowl,
    Potato,
    Quenelle, golden,
    Raviuoli,
    Scotch hotch-potch,
    Veal and rice,
    Vermicelli,
Spiced and pressed beef,
Spinach, greening, for sauces,
    ,, plain,
    ,, and poached eggs,
    ,, purée,
    ,, ,, with cream,
    ,, sauce,
Soojee pudding,
Sponge cake pudding,
    ,, ,, with apple snow,
Stewed apples,
    ,, peaches,
    ,, pears,

Stewed pippins,
,, prunes,
Stock for soup, Nos. and
,, calf's foot,
,, fat,
,, meat,
,, jelly,
,, economical,
Stores, list of, and.
Strawberry cream,
,, ,, ice, 399.
,, sauce,
,, jelly, and
,, jam,
,, vinegar,
,, water,
,, ,, ice,
Strawberries, bottled,
,, compôte of,
,, glacés,
Sucking pig, roast,
,, ,, with chestnuts,
Suet crust, common, for pies,
,, ,, excellent,
Sugar, barley,
,, burnt, for soups,
,, candy,
,, vanilla,
Sweetbreads, lamb, roasted, with green peas,
,, veal, will truffles,
,, croûstade of, with mushrooms, and potato balls,
Sweet dishes,
,, sauce, and
Sweetmeat, Italian,
Syrup, to clarify,
,, maraschino,
Syrups, (see Drinking Cups.)

TAPIOCA, Portuguese,
,, pudding, baked,
Tapioca, pudding, boiled,
,, milk,
Tapp sauce,
Tart apple,
,, méringue,
Tartar sauce,

Tartlets, jelly, or custard,
,, lemon, common,
,, strawberry,
Tea, and
,, cakes,
,, cream, (crême au thé,)
,, icing for cakes,
,, Russian,
Teal and widgeon,
Timbale of macaroni, with fowl,

Tipsy cake,
,, ,, or trifle,
Toast, anchovy,
,, asparagus,
,, kidney,
,, mushroom,
,, sardine,
,, tomato,
,, water (for Invalids,)
Toasts curried with anchovies,
,, savoury,
Toffee almond,
,, Everton,
Tomato sauce,
,, ,, (to keep,)
,, salad,
,, toast,
Tomatoes à la Provençale,
,, purée of,
,, roast,
Tomatoes, stewed,
,, stuffed,
Trifle or tipsy cake,
,, Swiss,
Truffles à Italienne,
,, à la Piedmontaise,
,, à la Serviette,
Turbot,
,, fried in butter,
,, with cream sauce,
Turkey, boiled, with celery sauce,
,, boned with tongue and forcemeat,
,, eggs, forced,
,, legs, broiled,
,, pulled,

Turkey roast, with chestnut stuffing,
,, ,, with pâte de foie gras stuffing,
,, stuffed and roasted,
Turnips, glaçes, with sugar, 178.
,, mashed,
,, plain,
,, stewed in butter,

VANILLA, cream,
,, sauce,
,, sugar,
Veal, breast, stewed with oysters,
,, ,, ,, with white sauce, 93.
,, cutlets,
,, ,, à la maintenon,
,, ,, braised with fresh tomatoes,
,, extract of,
,, forcemeat,
,, fricandeau, small,
,, galantine,
,, and ham pie,
,, loin, à la créme, 91.
,, ,, stuffed and roasted,
,, patties,
,, sweetbreads, with truffles, 97.
Veal, and tongue, potted,
Vegetable marrow,

Vegetable marrow, fried,
,, ,, stuffed, 182.
,, salad, hot,
Vegetables,
,, chartreuse of,
,, curried,
,, macedoine,
,, to preserve,
Vermicelli pudding,
,, soup,
Vol-au-vent, and
,, ,, ,, of fruit,
,, ,, ,, of oysters,

WALNUTS, pickled,
Weights and measures,
Welsh rabbit,
Whiskey apples,
Whitebait fried,
White bechamel sauce,
,, sauce,
Wild duck,
,, fowl, salmi of,
Widgeons and teal,
White wine whey,
,, ,, ,, with eggs,
Woodcock, Scotch,
,, and snipe,

YARMOUTH bloaters,
Yorkshire, pudding,
,, ,, family,

ADVERTISEMENT.

T. E. THOMSON & Co.,
9, ESPLANADE ROW, CALCUTTA.

For Camping, Boating, Picnic Parties, Domestic Use, &c., &c.
PATENT PORTABLE MINERAL OIL COOKING STOVES,
New and Improved Patterns.

Particulars, with prices, on application.
T. E. THOMSON & CO., CALCUTTA.

CASH & CO.

IMPORTERS OF WINES, BEER,

AND TABLE SUPPLIES OF EVERY DESCRIPTION,

FROM

Crosse & Blackwell, John Moir & Son, and other first class Manufacturers.

FRUIT SYRUPS.

FLAVOURING ESSENCES.

JAMS.   **JELLIES.**

TART FRUITS.

CHUTNEYS.   **PICKLES.**

INDIAN CONDIMENTS.

MUSTARD.   **VINEGAR**

SAUCES.

Detailed price lists are supplied post free on application.

CASH & CO.,

11, Dalhousie Square, Calcutta.

G. F. KELLNER & CO.

TRUFFES PURES.

				Rs.	A.
Large	... per tin Rs. 5 0	Small	... per tin	3	0

PATES.

				Rs.	A.
Pâté de Faisan Truffés	...Patty of Truffled Pheasant	... per tin	3	2
,, Lievre do. ... ,,	,, Hare ... ,,	3	10
,, Perdreaux do. ... ,,	,, Partridge ... ,,	3	12
,, Becasses do. ... ,,	,, Woodcock ... ,,	3	12
,, Foie Gras do. ... ,,	,, Fat Liver ... ,, 3 & 4	0
,, Cailles do. ... ,,	,, Quails ... ,,	3	12
,, Grives do. ... ,,	,, Thrush ... ,,	3	8
,, Bécassines do. ... ,,	,, Snipe ... ,,	3	12
,, Chevreuil do. ... ,,	,, Venison, large ,,	2	4
,, ,, do. ... ,,	,, ,, small ,,	1	8

FLAVORING ESSENCES.

Lemon, Sage, Ratafia, Thyme, Parsley, Cloves,
Mint, Orange, Celery, Vanille, Nutmeg, Almond.

In 1 oz. bottles, Rs. 7-8 per doz.

Essence of Rennet for making curds and whey, Rs. 9 per doz.

CANDIED PEELS.
In stoppered bottles.

Peels—Orange, Lemon, Citron, and Candied Mixed Peels, per bottle ... ... R. 1

DRIED HERBS.

Thyme, Sweet Marjoram, Sage, Taragon, Savory, Parsley, Mint, Lemon and Celery ... ... large ... 0 14
Ditto Ditto ... ... small ... 0 8

MARSALA.

Marsala choice full-bodied ... ... per doz. qts. ... 18 8

LIQUEURS (DUTCH.)

	Rs. A.		Rs. A.	
Curaçoa, finest, red, per doz.	53 0	Cherry Brandy ℔ doz.	21 0	
Do. do. white ,,	53 0	Chartreuse green ,,	50 0	Ge-
Crême de Noyeau ,,	53 0	Yellow Char-		nuine
Maraschino ,,	53 0	treuse ... ,,	42 0	*"pints"*

We invite comparison of our supplies against those of any ohter House at similar Prices.

[*All articles supplied under a guarantee.*]

Detailed List of Wines, Stores and Cheroots on application.

G. F. KELLNER & CO.,
WINE MERCHANTS,
BY APPOINTMENT TO, AND UNDER THE PATRONAGE OF,

H. E. the Viceroy, H. R. H. the Prince of Wales, and H. R. H. the Duke of Edinburgh.

4, Esplanade East, Calcutta.

W. NEWMAN & CO.,
3, DALHOUSIE SQUARE, CALCUTTA

MENU CARDS.

(In all Cases the prices quoted are per 100.)

No.		Size.	Rs.	A.
39.	Plain white, with embossed border	3¾ × 2½	2	4
30.	,, ,, ,, ,,	4½ × 3	2	8
49.	Plain white, with embossed border, and gold line	3¾ × 2½	3	6
302.	Parian Enamel Surface Card, with gilt and tinted border	6 × 4	5	8
303.	,, ,, ,,	7 × 4½	6	12
304.	,, ,, ,,	8 × 5	8	0
114.	Plain White Card with embossed border	6½ × 5¼	4	0
19.	White Card, plain gold border	6 × 4¼	5	4
E.	White and Tinted Cards, border (in variety) in gold and tint	4¾ × 3⅛	5	4
20.	,, ,, ,, Cards, Plain double line border, gold or silver	4¾ × 3⅛	3	0
11.	Tinted Card, Grecian gilt line border	5 × 3½	5	10
240.	,, fancy gold border and colored edge	4½ × 2¾	5	0
244.	,, ,, ,, ,,	8 × 5	9	0
231.	,, border in gold and color	5 × 3½	5	10
232.	,, ,, ,,	6 × 3¾	6	12
42½.	,, ochre tint, with gilt "frame" border	5½ × 3½	8	0
211a.	,, gold border and Menu printed in gold, French	5 × 3½	5	10
611.	,, broad border in gold and colors	6¾ × 4½	9	0
2461.	White Card, Holly border in gold and tint	5¼ × 3½	6	12
2575.	Tinted Card, broad border in gold and color	5¼ × 3	6	12
2576.	,, ,, ,,	5½ × 3⅜	6	12
101.	Floral Cards of six designs with "Menu" at top	6½ × 4¼	5	0
2587.	Tinted Card, fancy figures and ribbon border, in gold	,,	6	12
2582.	Very handsome Cards, with border of figures of Bacchus, fruits, game, &c., on gold ground, and "Menu" at top	,,	18	0
2580.	Ditto ditto on silver ground	,,	18	0
333K	Very thick "slab" Cards, plain, gilt edged, rose tint	5¼ × 3¾	13	0
340K	,, ,, silver grey tint	,,	13	0

ADVERTISEMENT.

No.				Size folded.	Rs.	A.
	Two-fold Card, plain parian enamel surface, five tints ...			$6\frac{1}{2} \times 4\frac{1}{2}$ ...	9	0
	,, ,, with masonic border		...	$5 \times 3\frac{3}{8}$ ...	9	0
128.	,, ,, white, with narrow line border of gold and colour ...			,, ...	13	8
124.	Three-fold Card, white with gold and black line border and "Menu" ...		...	6×4 ...	12	0
2473.	Three-fold Card, tinted, Japanese pattern, very handsome design in gold and colours out-side, and design in gold and tint inside, with "Menu"			$5\frac{5}{8} \times 4$ ...	25	0

"STEEL PLATE" MENU CARDS.

Very handsome Cards, printed in black from steel plates, in a variety of choice designs, Japanesque, Landscape, Æsthetic, &c.

Series.					Size.	Rs.	A.
39-45.	Two-fold Card, Japanesque designs, on front page				$7 \times 4\frac{1}{2}$ ...	14	8
35A-43A.	,,	,,	Landscape and Marine designs		$7 \times 4\frac{1}{2}$ ...	14	8
62-66.	,,	,,	Landscapes on front page, and flowers on the back	...	$6\frac{1}{2} \times 3\frac{1}{2}$ ...	15	12
1-11.	,,	,,	Japanesque and Æsthetic designs on front and back pages		$5 \times 3\frac{1}{2}$ ...	10	0
100.	,,	,,	Landscapes on front and back		$4\frac{1}{2} \times 3$ ...	10	0
1015.	,,	,,	Superb Japanesque designs on front and back, with space for printing the date of dinner, &c. ...	...	$7\frac{1}{2} \times 5\frac{1}{4}$ ...	26	0
1015S.	,,	,,	Ditto, with silver border	...	,, ...	29	0
10.	Single Card, one-half of the above			...	$7\frac{1}{2} \times 5\frac{1}{4}$ ...	13	0
15.	,, the other half of the above			...	$7\frac{1}{2} \times 5\frac{1}{4}$ ...	13	0
503.	,, Japanesque design of Birds, to fold in half with space for guest's name			...	$5\frac{1}{4} \times 3\frac{3}{4}$ ...	12	0
250.	Single Card, Landscape, Birds, and Japanesque designs to fold in three with space for guest's name			...	$6\frac{1}{2} \times 4\frac{1}{4}$ ...	11	4

GUEST'S NAME CARDS.

A variety of neat designs, many of them being designed to match the Menu Cards mentioned above ... ...As. 4 to R. 1 per dozen.
Amusing Pictorial Cards with spaces for guest names, in
   · very great variety ... ... per dozen As. 12-0
"Sporting" Name Cards ... a packet of 2 ,, Rs. 2-8
"Classical" Name Cards ... ,, 1 ,, ,, 1-4

BALL PROGRAMME CARDS.

A large assortment of Standard and Novel Patterns to select from.

ND - #0023 - 260224 - C0 - 229/152/25 [27] - CB - 9780365377504 - Gloss Lamination